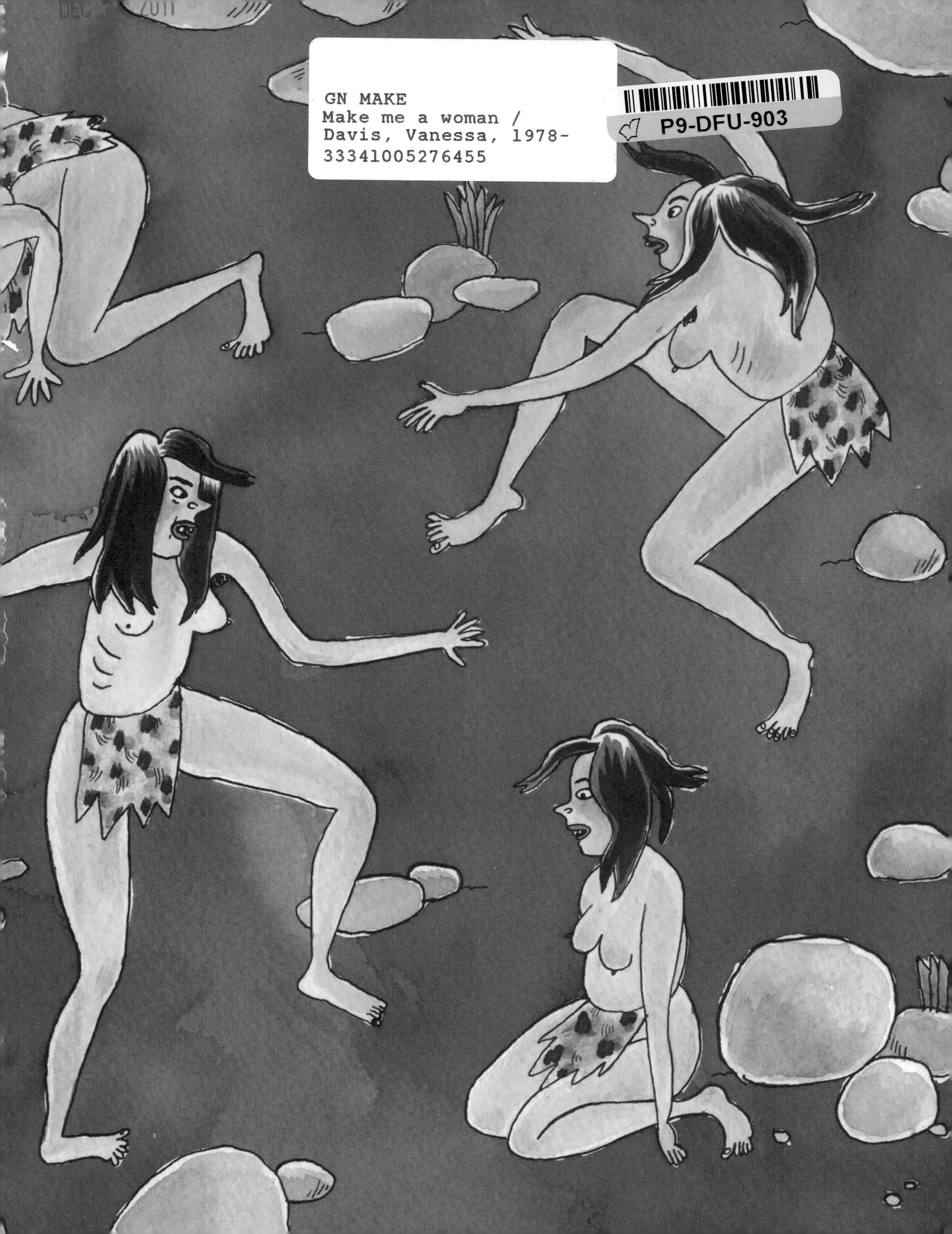

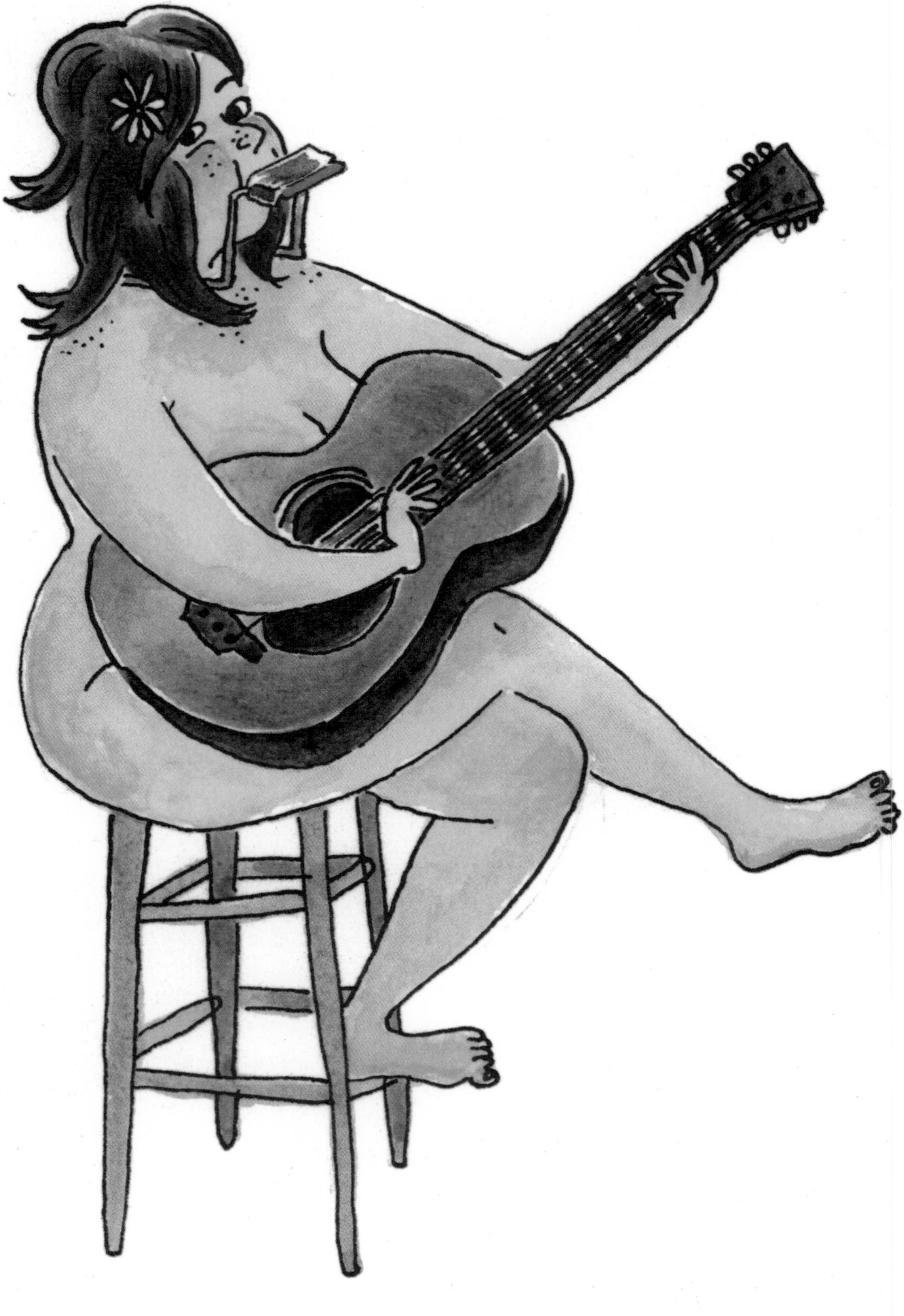

Make Me a Woman

Vanessa Davis

DRAWN & QUARTERLY, MONTREAL

Production assistance by Sarah Moses-Winyard and Denise Kwan.

Drawn & Quarterly
Post office Box 48056
Montreal, Quebec
Canada H2V 4S8
www.drawnandquarterly.com

First Hardcover Edition: September 2010.
10 9 8 7 6 5 4 3 2 1
Printed in China.

Library and Archives Canada Cataloguing in Publication

Davis, Vanessa, 1978 —
    Make me a Woman / Vanessa Davis

ISBN 978-1-77046-021-8

    1. Title

PN6727. D365 M35 2010   741.5'973 C2010-901611-4

Distributed in the United States by:
Farrar, Straus & Giroux
18 West 18th Street
New York, NY 10011
Call Toll-free: 888.330.8477 ext 6540
Fax Toll-free: 800.672.2054
www.fsgbooks.com

Distributed in Canada by:
Raincoast Books
9050 Shaughnessy Street
Vancouver, BC V6P 6E5
Call Toll-free: 800.663.5714
Fax Toll-free: 800.565.3776
www.raincoast.com customerservice@raincoast.com

Distributed in the UK by:
Publishers Group UK
8 The Arena
Mollison Avenue
Enfield
EN3 7NL
Tel: 020 8804 0400
Fax: 020 8804 0044
Web: www.pguk.co.uk

This book collects comics and drawings that I made between 2004 and 2010. Some are as yet unpublished strips and sketchbook pages. I moved: Diary entries take place in New York, where I used to live; California, where I moved in 2005; and Florida, where I grew up and where my mom still lives. A lot of the stories were printed in zines and anthologies. And a bunch of them appeared on-line as part of a monthly column I did for Tablet magazine.

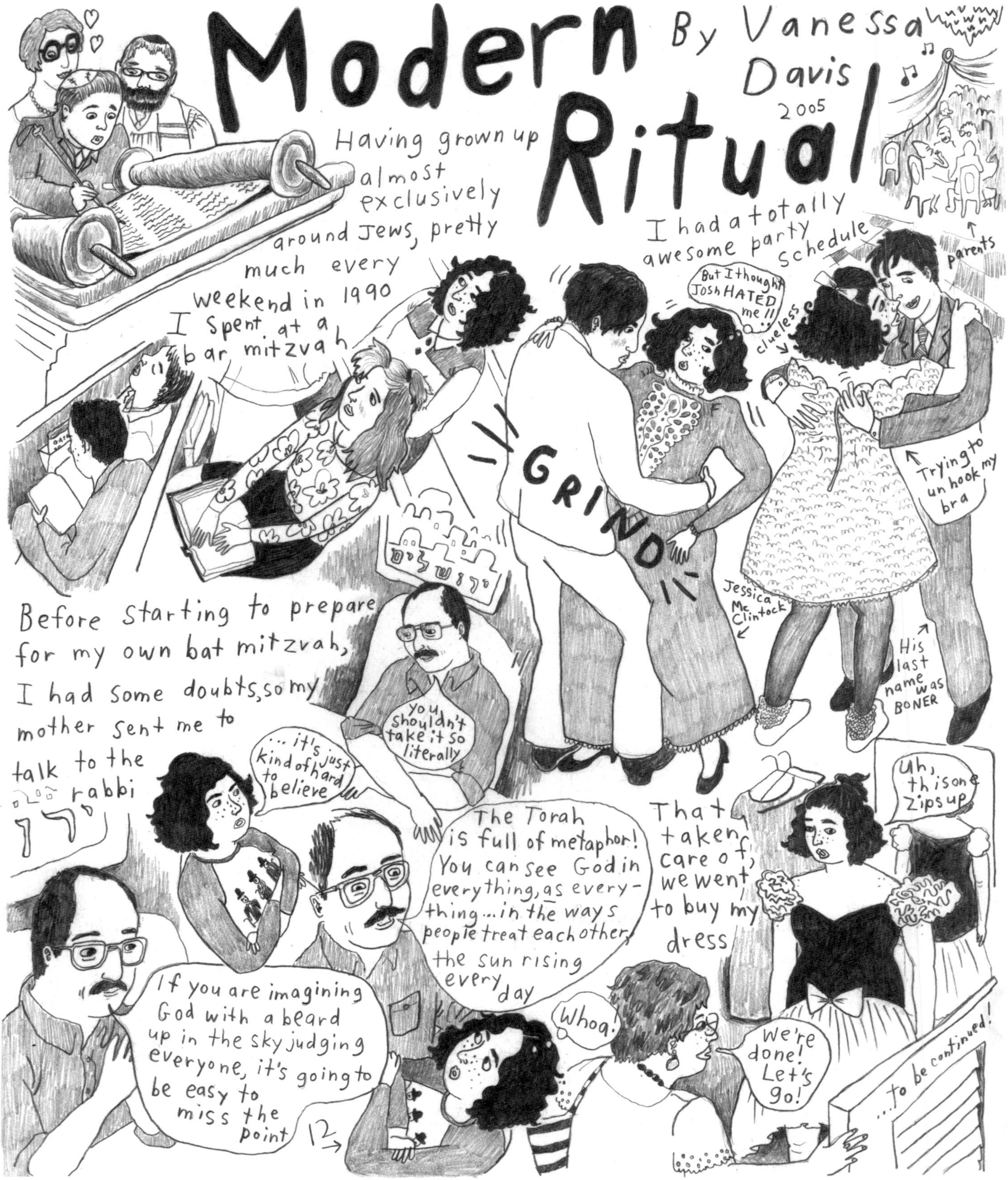

Modern Ritual
By Vanessa Davis
2005
Having grown up almost exclusively around Jews, pretty much every weekend in 1990 I spent at a bar mitzvah
I had a totally awesome party schedule
parents
But I thought JOSH HATED me!!
clueless
GRIND
Trying to unhook my bra
Jessica Mc Clintock
His last name was BONER
Before starting to prepare for my own bat mitzvah, I had some doubts, so my mother sent me to talk to the rabbi
you shouldn't take it so literally
... it's just kind of hard to believe
The Torah is full of metaphor! You can see God in everything, as everything ... in the ways people treat each other, the sun rising every day
If you are imagining God with a beard up in the sky judging everyone, it's going to be easy to miss the point
That taken care of, we went to buy my dress
Uh, this one zips up
Whoa!
We're done! Let's go!
... to be continued!

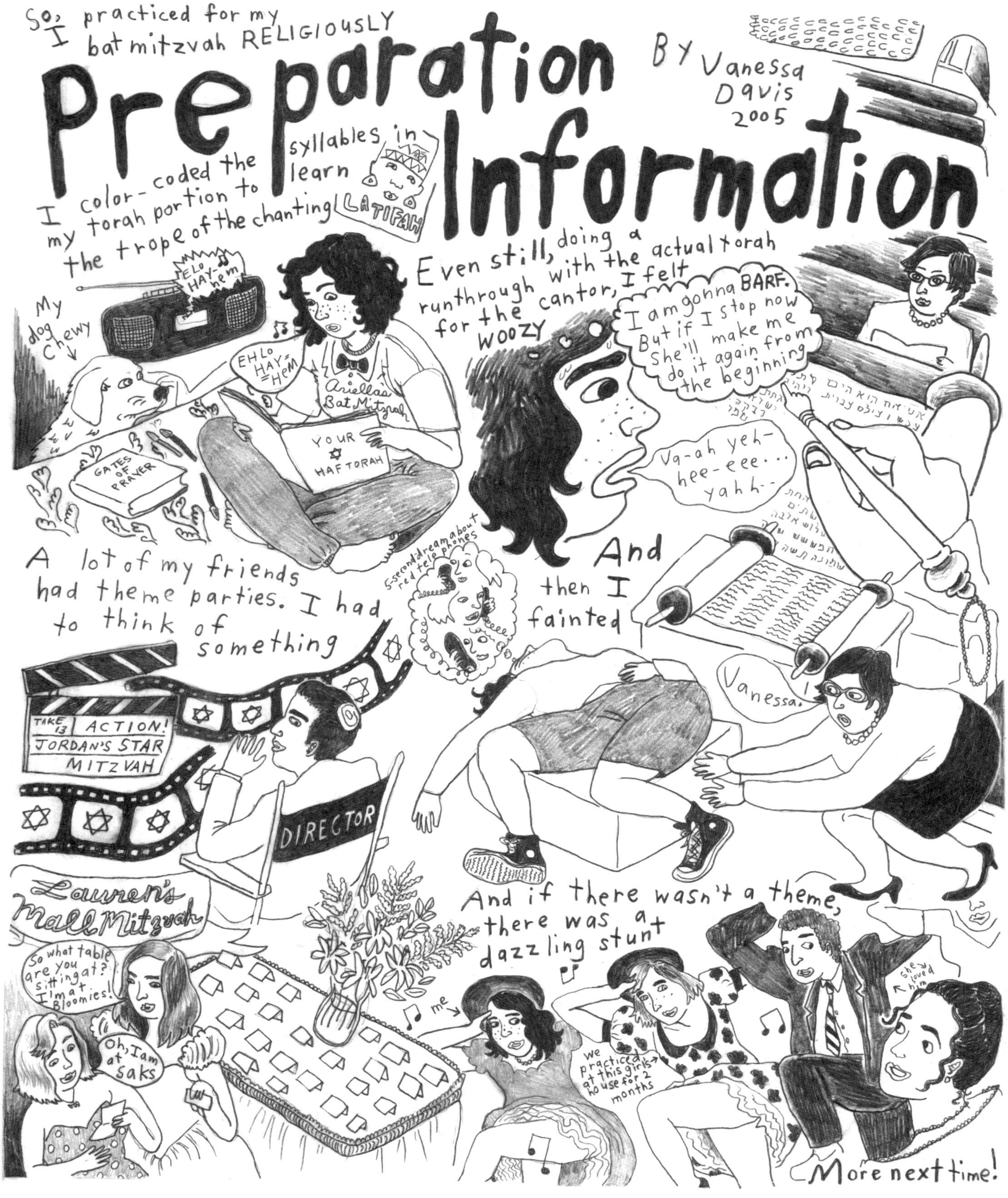
So, I practiced for my bat mitzvah RELIGIOUSLY
Preparation Information
BY Vanessa Davis 2005
I color-coded the my torah portion to learn syllables in the trope of the chanting
LATIFAH
ELO HAY-hem
My dog Chewy
EHLo HAY=HeM
Ariella's Bat Mitzvah
YOUR HAFTORAH
GATES OF PRAYER
Even still, doing a runthrough with the actual torah for the cantor, I felt WOOZY
I am gonna BARF. I stop now But if I make me She'll do it again from the beginning
Va-ah yeh-hee-eee... yahh...
A lot of my friends had theme parties. I had to think of something
5-second-dream about red tele phones
And then I fainted
Vanessa!
TAKE 13 ACTION! JORDAN'S STAR MITZVAH
DIRECTOR
Lauren's Mall Mitzvah
So what table are you sitting at? I'm at Bloomies!
Oh, I am at saks
And if there wasn't a theme, there was a dazzling stunt
me
we practiced at this girl's house for 2 months
she loved him
More next time!

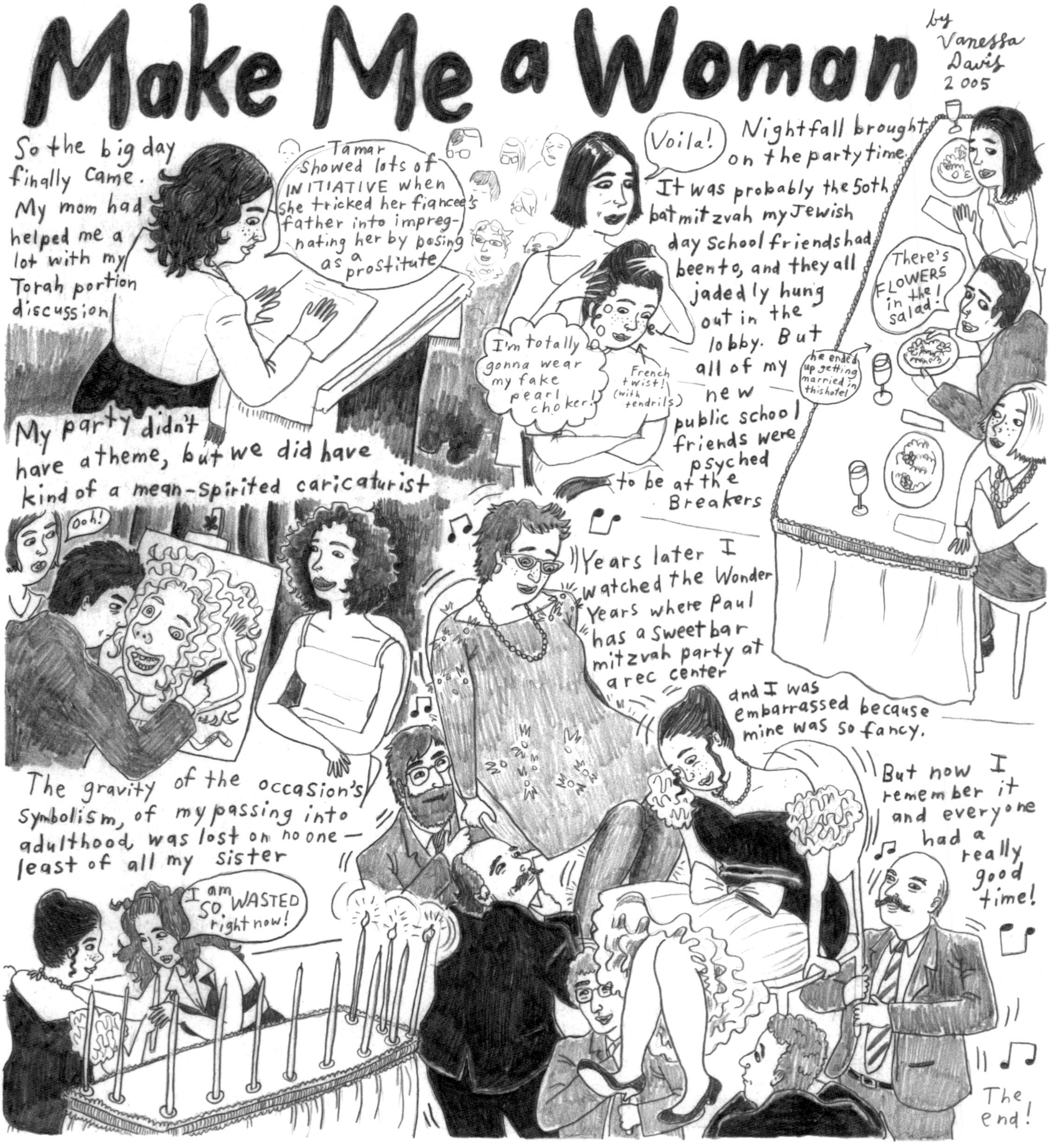
Make Me a Woman
by Vanessa Davis 2005
So the big day finally came. My mom had helped me a lot with my Torah portion discussion
Tamar showed lots of INITIATIVE when she tricked her fiancee's father into impregnating her by posing as a prostitute
Voila!
I'm totally gonna wear my fake pearl choker!
French twist! (with tendrils)
Nightfall brought on the party time.
It was probably the 50th bat mitzvah my Jewish day school friends had been to, and they all jadedly hung out in the lobby. But all of my new public school friends were psyched to be at the Breakers
There's FLOWERS in the salad!
he ended up getting married in this hotel
My party didn't have a theme, but we did have kind of a mean-spirited caricaturist
Ooh!
Years later I watched the Wonder Years where Paul has a sweet bar mitzvah party at a rec center
and I was embarrassed because mine was so fancy.
But now I remember it and everyone had a really good time!
The gravity of the occasion's symbolism, of my passing into adulthood, was lost on no one — least of all my sister
I am SO WASTED right now!
The end!

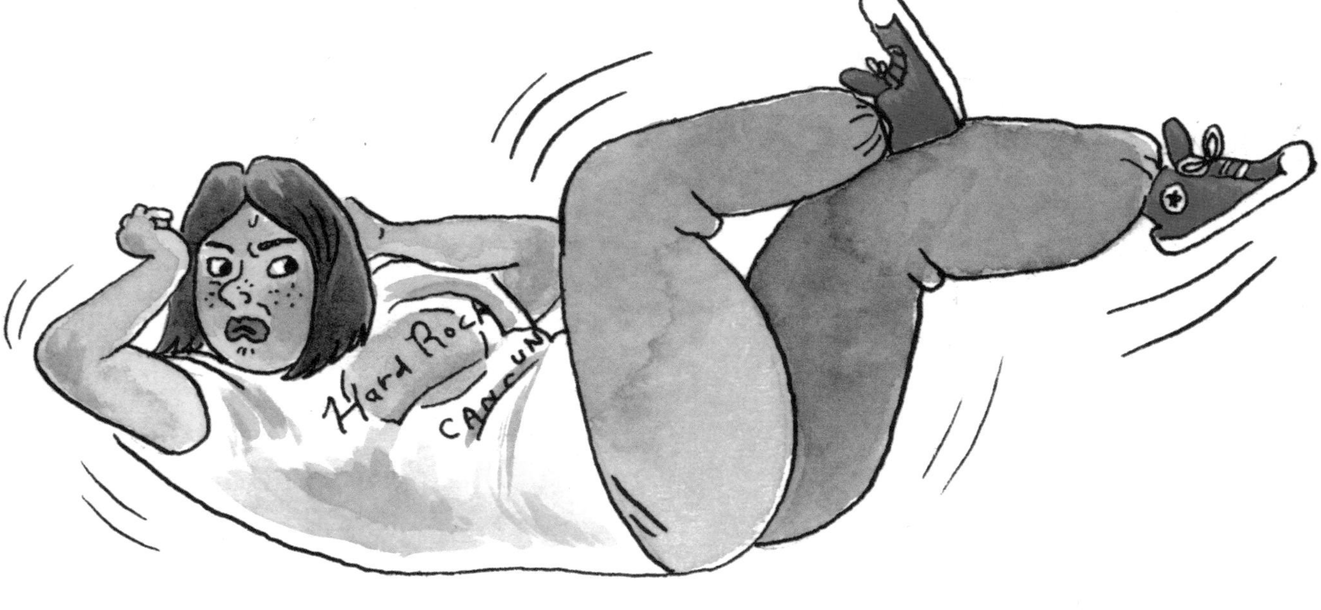
Hard Rock
CANCUN

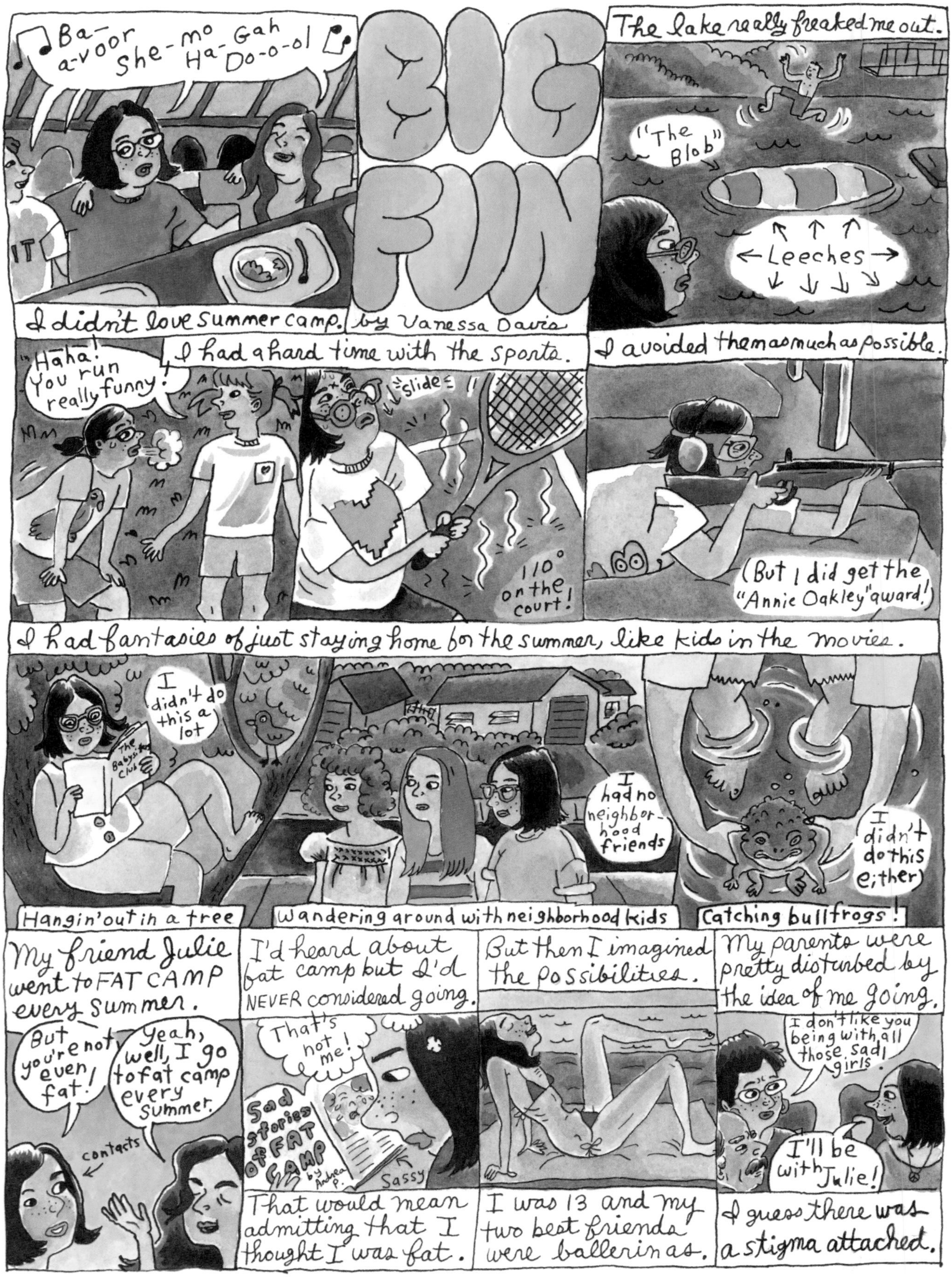

Ba-a-voor She-mo Gah Ha-Do-o-ol
I didn't love summer camp.
BIG FUN
by Vanessa Davis
The lake really freaked me out.
"The Blob"
Leeches
I avoided them as much as possible.
I had a hard time with the sports.
"Haha! You run really funny!"
slide
110° on the court!
(But I did get the "Annie Oakley" award!)
I had fantasies of just staying home for the summer, like kids in the movies.
I didn't do this a lot
The Babysitters Club
Hangin' out in a tree
I had no neighborhood friends
Wandering around with neighborhood kids
I didn't do this either)
Catching bullfrogs!
My friend Julie went to FAT CAMP every summer.
But you're not even fat!
Yeah, well, I go to fat camp every summer.
contacts
I'd heard about fat camp but I'd NEVER considered going.
That's not me!
Sad stories of FAT CAMP by Andrea P.
Sassy
That would mean admitting that I thought I was fat.
But then I imagined the possibilities.
I was 13 and my two best friends were ballerinas.
My parents were pretty disturbed by the idea of me going.
I don't like you being with all those sad girls!
I'll be with Julie!
I guess there was a stigma attached.

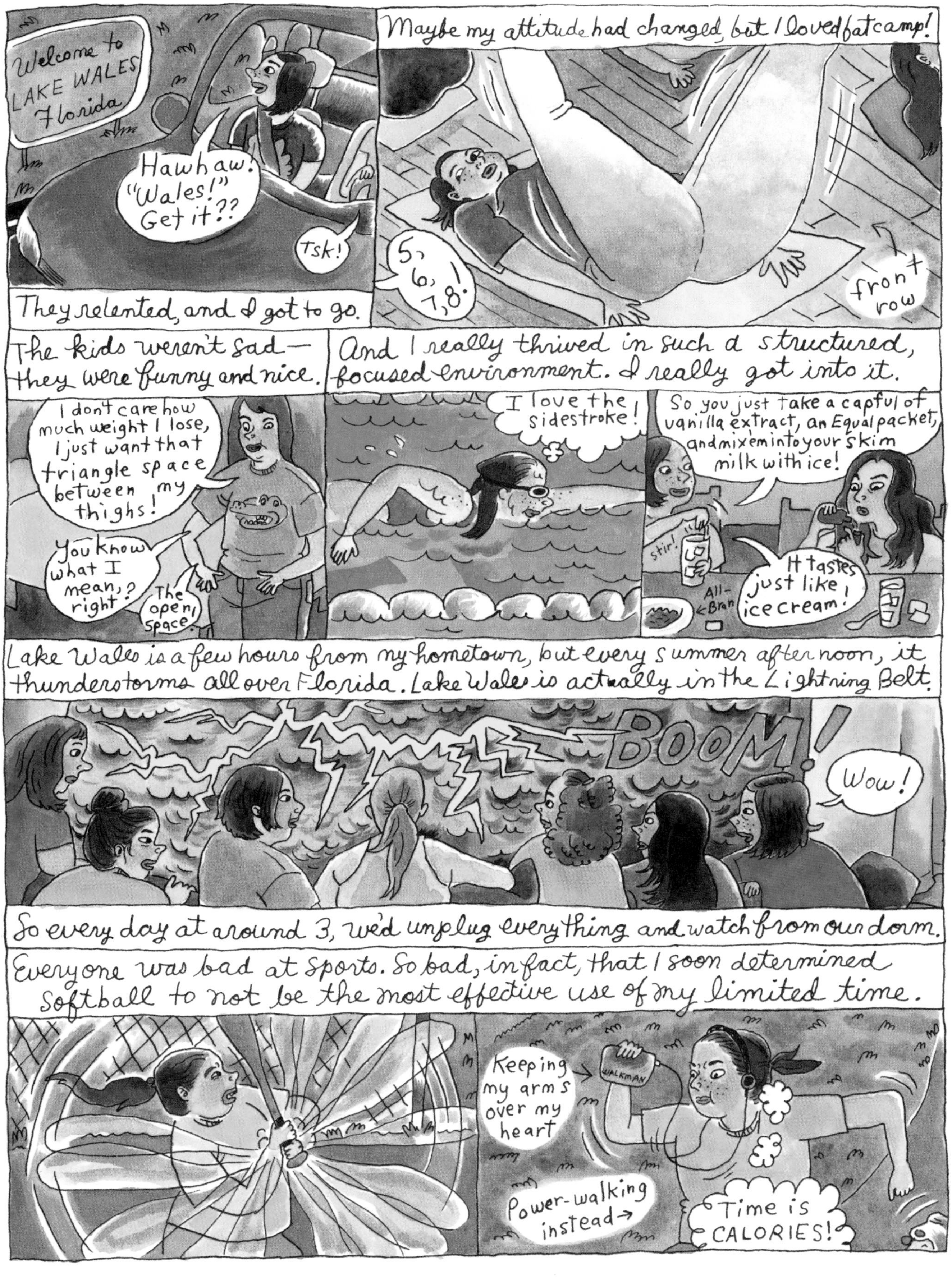
Welcome to LAKE WALES Florida
Hawhaw! "Wales!" Get it??
Tsk!
They relented, and I got to go.
Maybe my attitude had changed, but I loved fat camp!
5, 6, 7, 8!
front row
The kids weren't sad— they were funny and nice.
And I really thrived in such a structured, focused environment. I really got into it.
I don't care how much weight I lose, I just want that triangle space between my thighs!
You know what I mean, right?
The open space.
I love the sidestroke!
So you just take a capful of vanilla extract, an Equal packet, and mix 'em into your skim milk with ice!
Stir!
All-Bran
It tastes just like ice cream!
Lake Wales is a few hours from my hometown, but every summer afternoon, it thunderstorms all over Florida. Lake Wales is actually in the Lightning Belt.
BOOM!
Wow!
So every day at around 3, we'd unplug everything and watch from our dorm.
Everyone was bad at sports. So bad, in fact, that I soon determined softball to not be the most effective use of my limited time.
Keeping my arms over my heart
WALKMAN
Power-walking instead
Time is CALORIES!

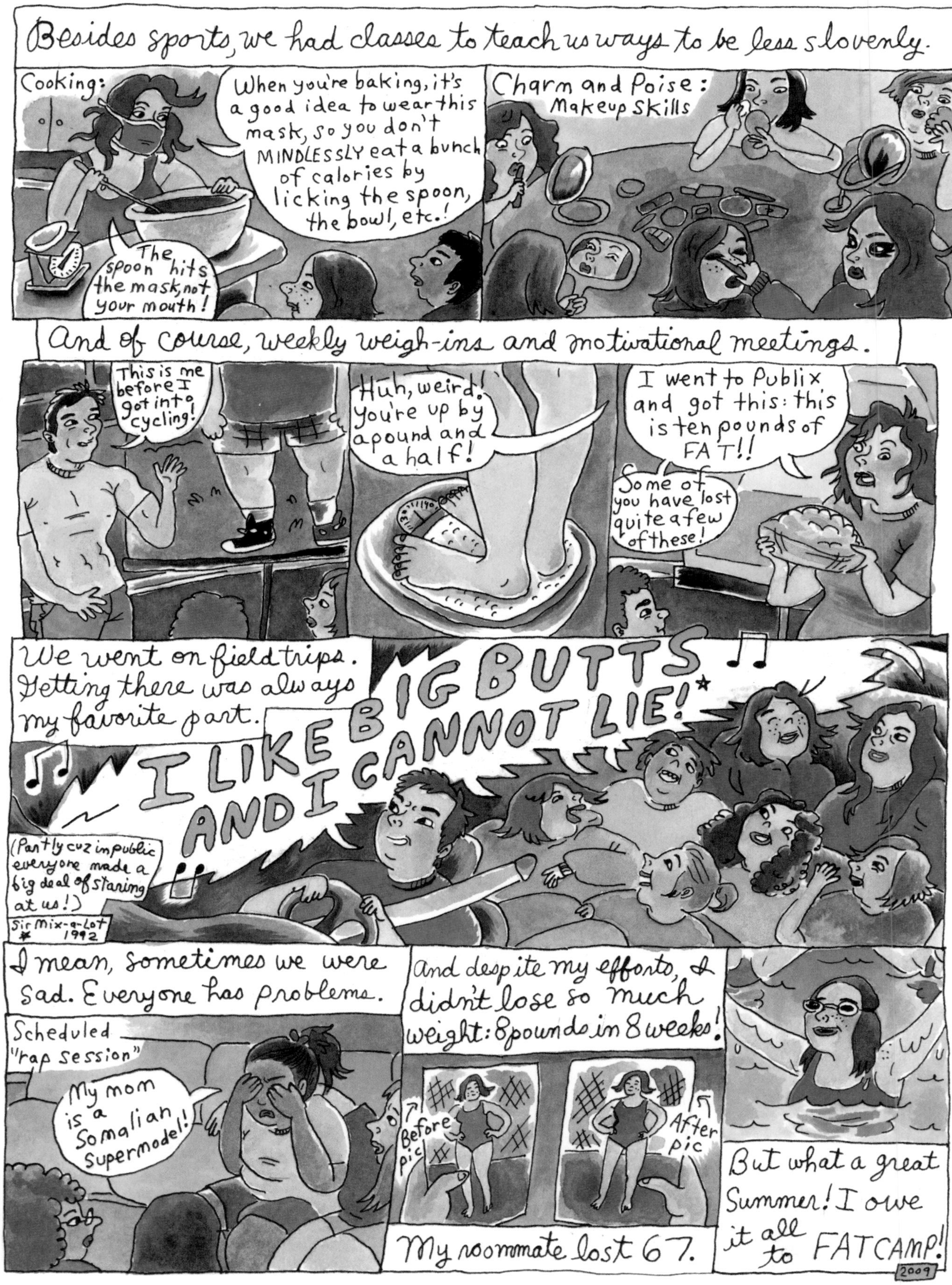

Besides sports, we had classes to teach us ways to be less slovenly.
Cooking:
When you're baking, it's a good idea to wear this mask, so you don't MINDLESSLY eat a bunch of calories by licking the spoon, the bowl, etc.!
The spoon hits the mask, not your mouth!
Charm and Poise: Makeup Skills
And of course, weekly weigh-ins and motivational meetings.
This is me before I got into cycling!
Huh, weird! You're up by a pound and a half!
I went to Publix and got this: this is ten pounds of FAT!!
Some of you have lost quite a few of these!
We went on field trips. Getting there was always my favorite part.
I LIKE BIG BUTTS AND I CANNOT LIE!*
(Partly cuz in public everyone made a big deal of staring at us!)
* Sir Mix-a-Lot 1992
I mean, sometimes we were sad. Everyone has problems.
Scheduled "rap session"
My mom is a Somalian supermodel!
And despite my efforts, I didn't lose so much weight: 8 pounds in 8 weeks!
Before pic
After pic
My roommate lost 67.
But what a great Summer! I owe it all to FATCAMP!
2009

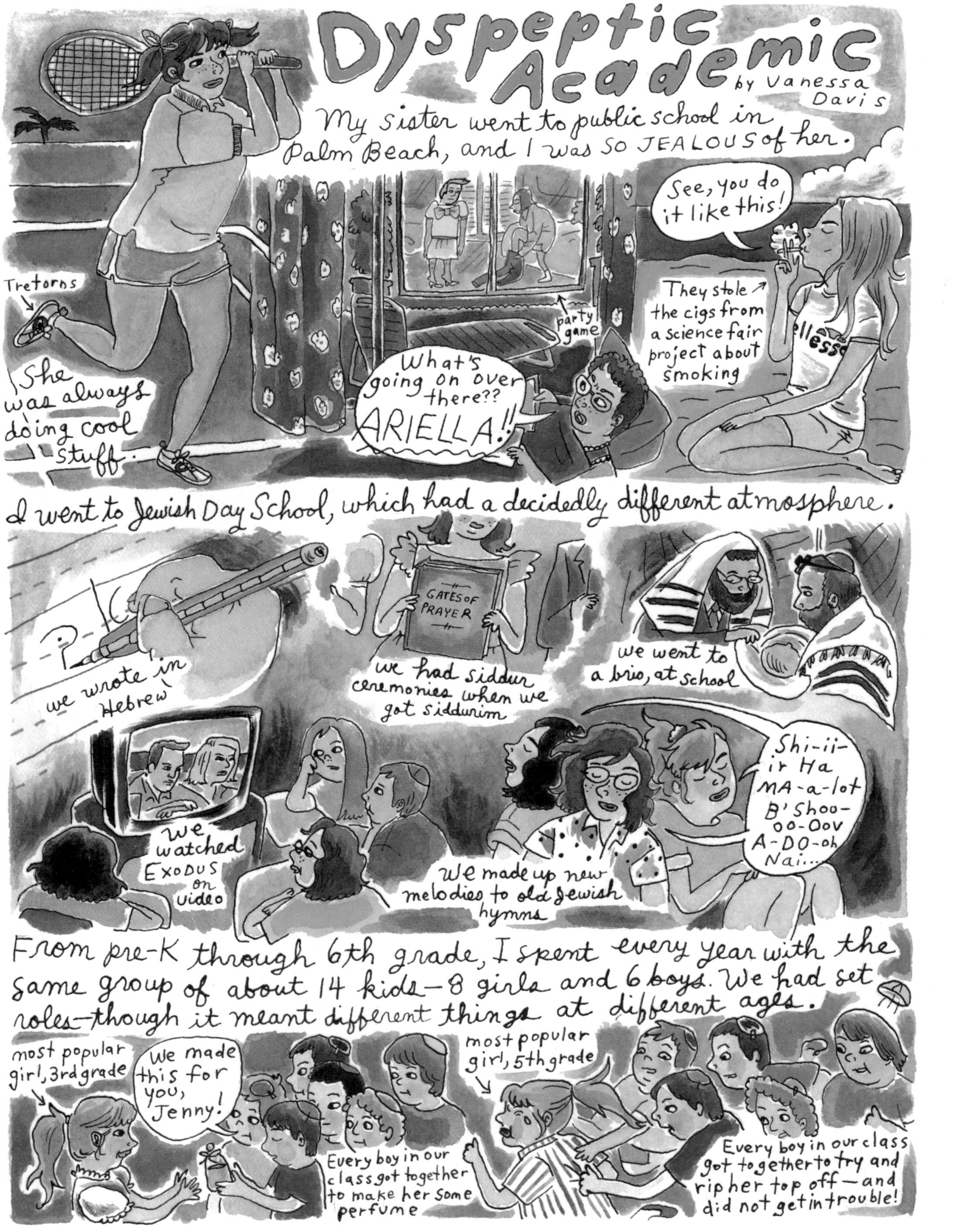

Dyspeptic Academic
by Vanessa Davis
My sister went to public school in Palm Beach, and I was SO JEALOUS of her.
Tretorns
She was always doing cool stuff.
party game
What's going on over there?? ARIELLA!!
See, you do it like this!
They stole the cigs from a science fair project about smoking
ellesse
I went to Jewish Day School, which had a decidedly different atmosphere.
we wrote in Hebrew
GATES OF PRAYER
we had siddur ceremonies when we got siddurim
we went to a bris, at school
we watched EXODUS on video
We made up new melodies to old Jewish hymns
Shi-ii-ir Ha MA-a-lot B'Shoo-oo-Oov A-DO-oh Nai...
From pre-K through 6th grade, I spent every year with the same group of about 14 kids—8 girls and 6 boys. We had set roles—though it meant different things at different ages.
most popular girl, 3rd grade
We made this for you, Jenny!
Every boy in our class got together to make her some perfume
most popular girl, 5th grade
Every boy in our class got together to try and rip her top off—and did not get in trouble!

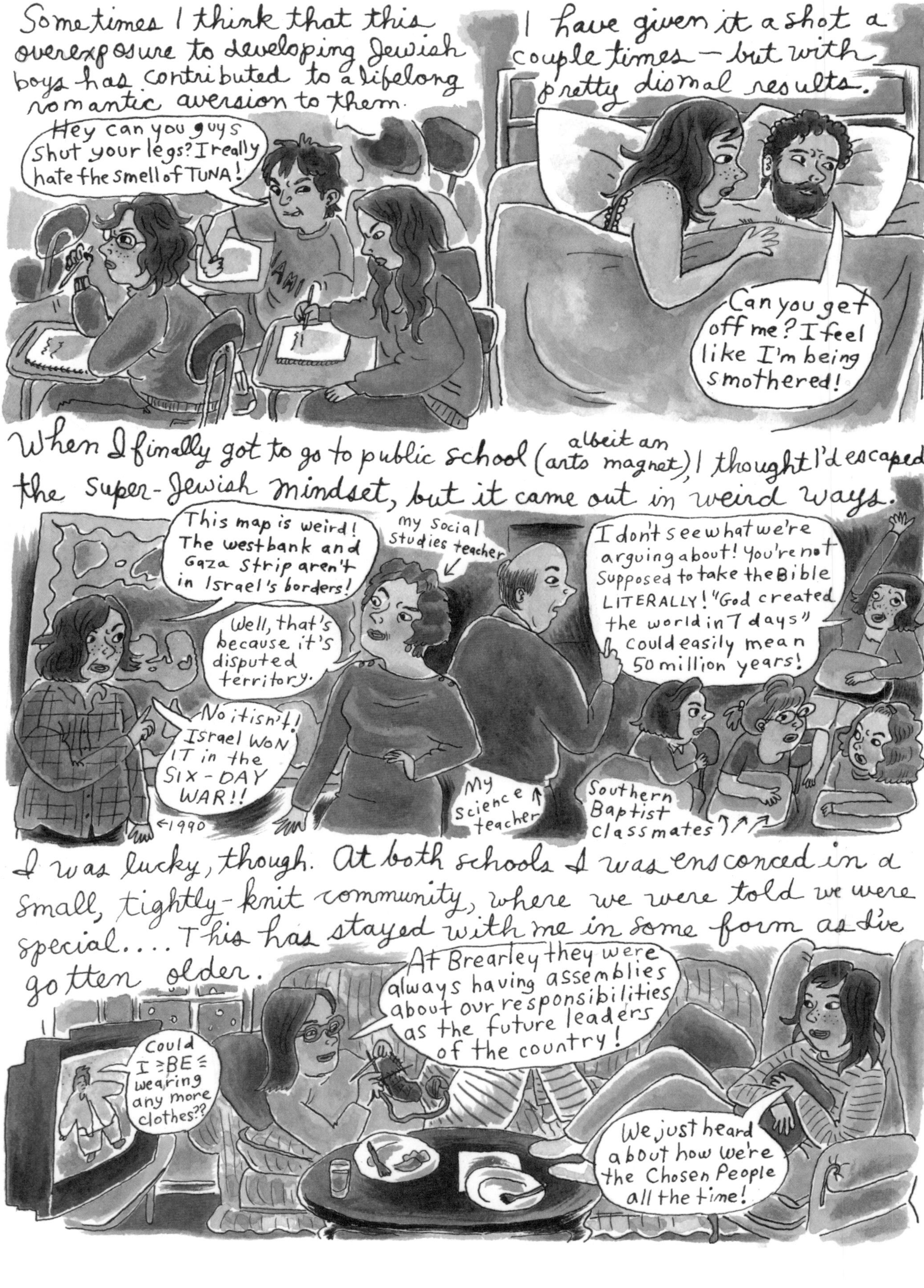
Sometimes I think that this overexposure to developing Jewish boys has contributed to a lifelong romantic aversion to them.
Hey can you guys shut your legs? I really hate the smell of TUNA!
I have given it a shot a couple times — but with pretty dismal results.
Can you get off me? I feel like I'm being smothered!
When I finally got to go to public school (albeit an arts magnet), I thought I'd escaped the super-Jewish mindset, but it came out in weird ways.
This map is weird! The westbank and Gaza strip aren't in Israel's borders!
my social studies teacher
Well, that's because it's disputed territory.
No it isn't! Israel WON IT in the SIX-DAY WAR!!
←1990
I don't see what we're arguing about! You're not supposed to take the BIBLE LITERALLY! "God created the world in 7 days" could easily mean 50 million years!
My science teacher
Southern Baptist classmates
I was lucky, though. At both schools I was ensconced in a small, tightly-knit community, where we were told we were special.... This has stayed with me in some form as I've gotten older.
At Brearley they were always having assemblies about our responsibilities as the future leaders of the country!
Could I BE wearing any more clothes??
We just heard about how we're the Chosen People all the time!

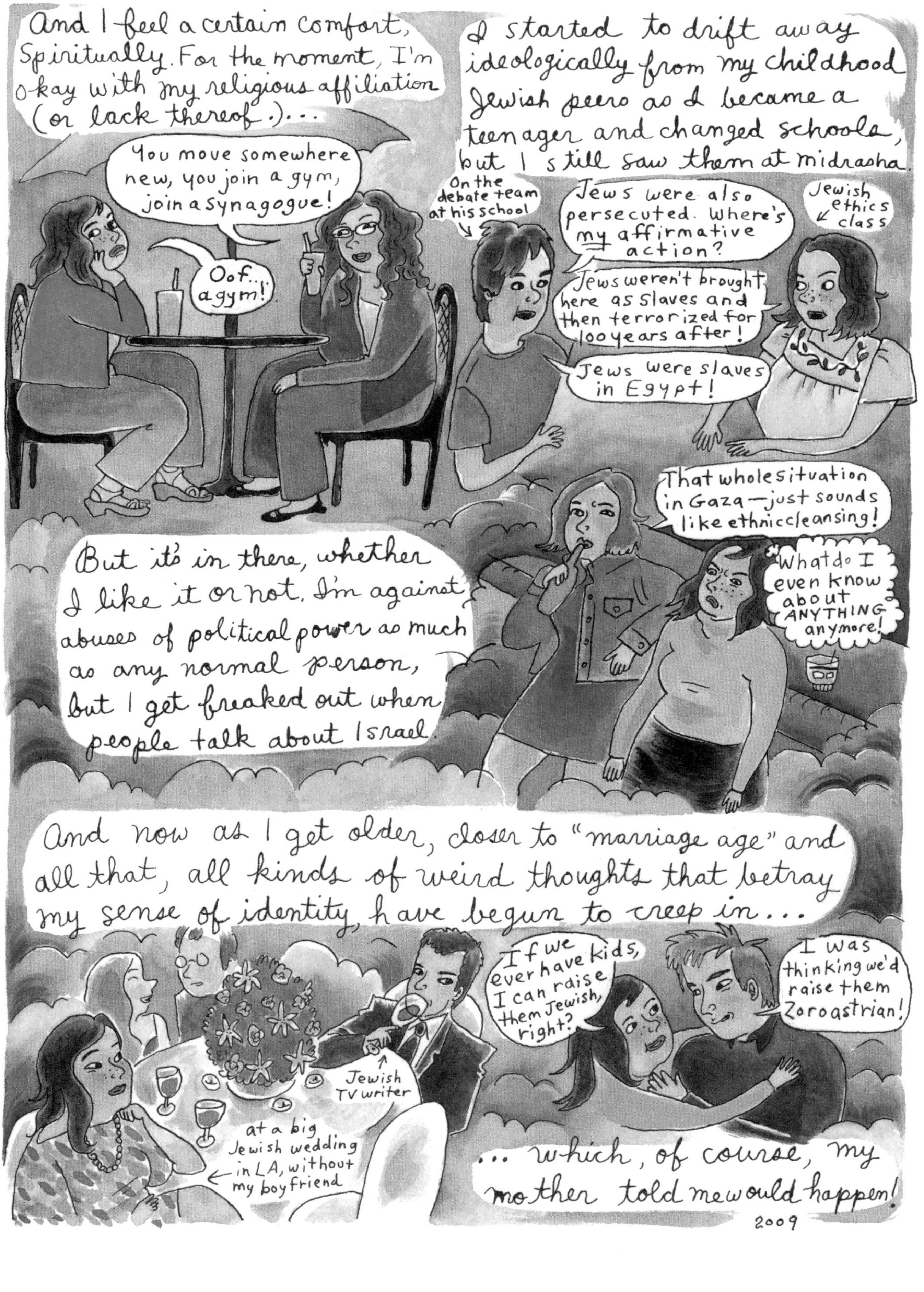
And I feel a certain comfort, Spiritually. For the moment, I'm o-kay with my religious affiliation (or lack thereof.)...
You move somewhere new, you join a gym, join a synagogue!
Oof... a gym!
I started to drift away ideologically from my childhood Jewish peers as I became a teenager and changed schools, but I still saw them at midrasha.
On the debate team at his school
Jews were also persecuted. Where's my affirmative action?
Jewish ethics class
Jews weren't brought here as slaves and then terrorized for 100 years after!
Jews were slaves in Egypt!
But it's in there, whether I like it or not. I'm against abuses of political power as much as any normal person, but I get freaked out when people talk about Israel.
That whole situation in Gaza—just sounds like ethnic cleansing!
What do I even know about ANYTHING anymore!
And now as I get older, closer to "marriage age" and all that, all kinds of weird thoughts that betray my sense of identity, have begun to creep in...
Jewish TV writer
at a big Jewish wedding in LA, without my boyfriend
If we ever have kids, I can raise them Jewish, right?
I was thinking we'd raise them Zoroastrian!
... which, of course, my mother told me would happen!
2009

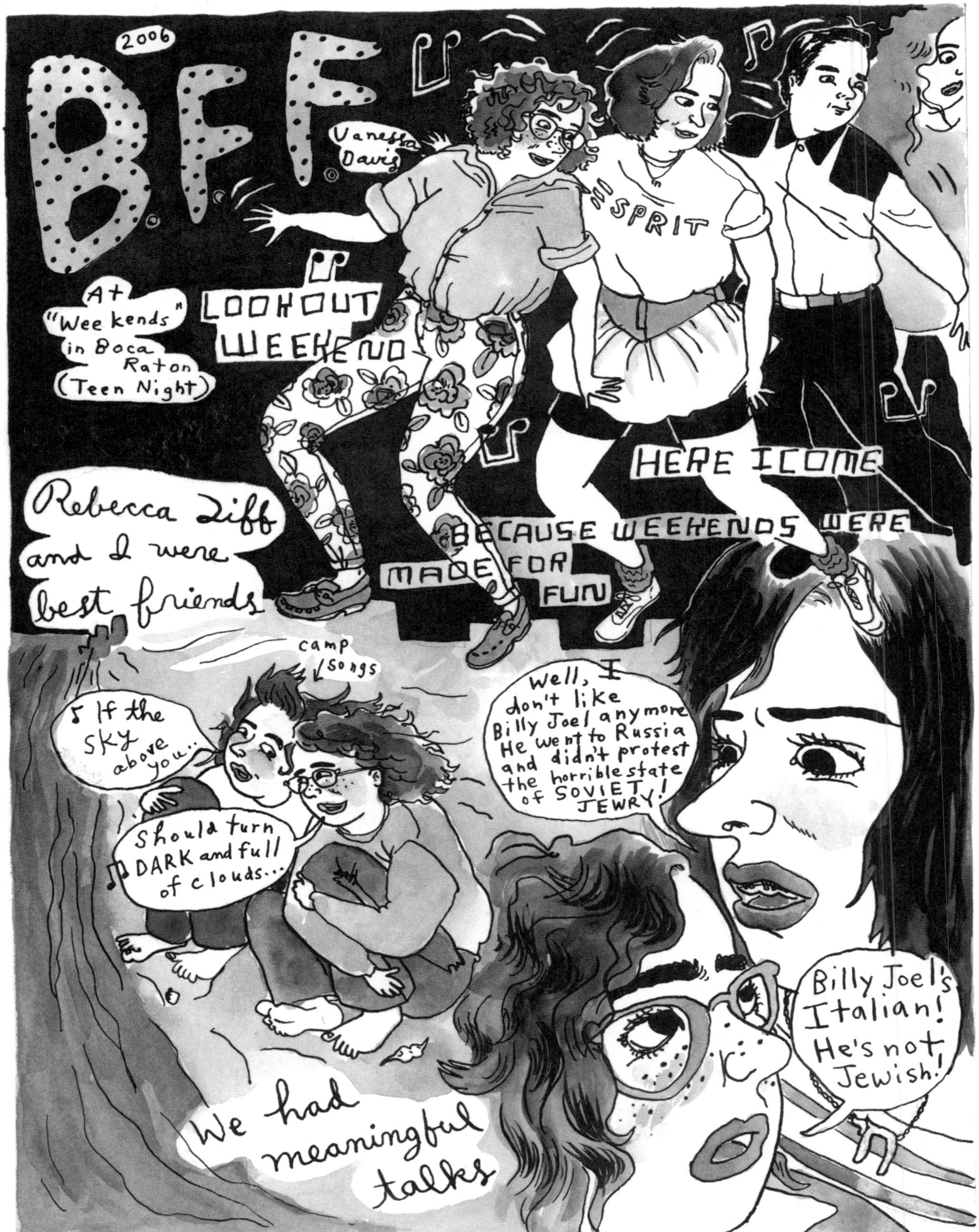
2006
B.F.F.
Vanessa Davis
At "Weekends" in Boca Raton (Teen Night)
LOOKOUT WEEKEND
ESPRIT
HERE I COME
BECAUSE WEEKENDS WERE MADE FOR FUN
Rebecca Ziff and I were best friends
camp songs
If the sky above you...
Should turn DARK and full of clouds...
Well, I don't like Billy Joel anymore. He went to Russia and didn't protest the horrible state of SOVIET JEWRY!
Billy Joel's Italian! He's not Jewish!
We had meaningful talks

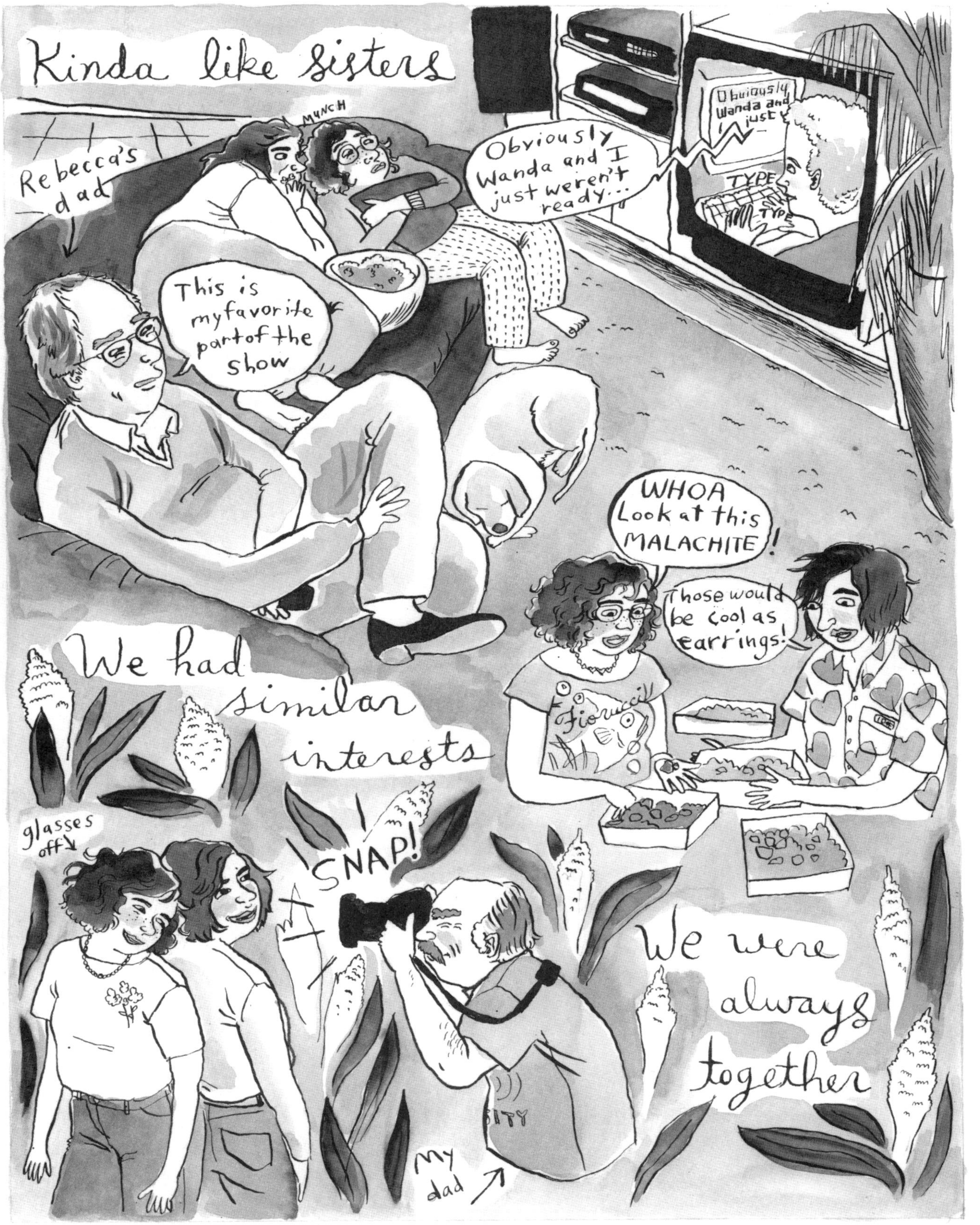
Kinda like sisters
MUNCH
Rebecca's dad
Obviously Wanda and I just weren't ready...
Obviously Wanda and just
TYPE
TYPE
This is my favorite part of the show
WHOA Look at this MALACHITE!
Those would be cool as earrings!
We had similar interests
Fiorucci
glasses off
SNAP!
We were always together
My dad

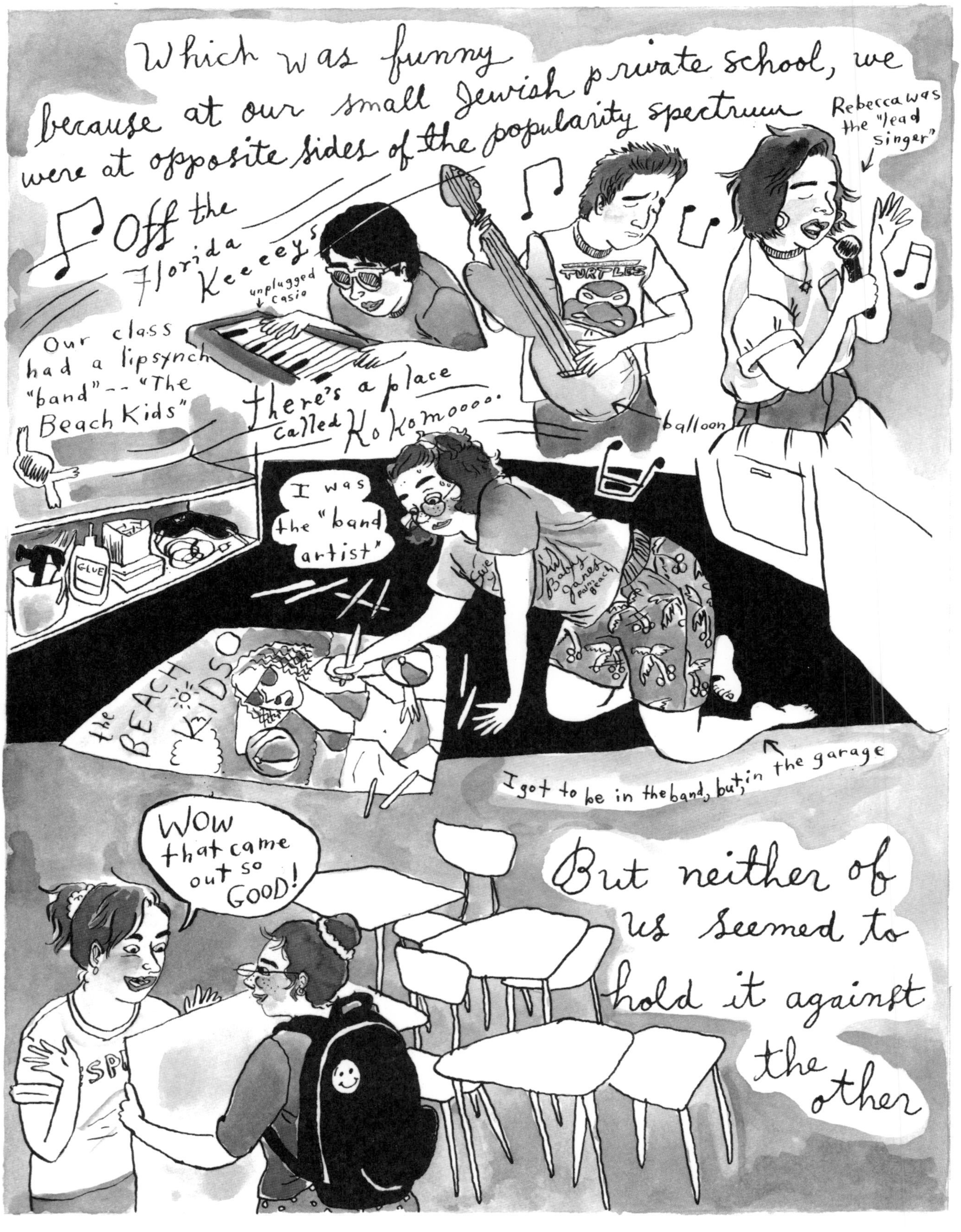

Which was funny because at our small Jewish private school, we were at opposite sides of the popularity spectrum
Rebecca was the "lead singer"
Off the Florida Keeeeys
unplugged casio
TURTLES
Our class had a lipsynch "band"-- "The Beach Kids"
There's a place called Kokomoooo..
balloon
I was the "band artist"
GLUE
the BEACH KIDS
I got to be in the band, but, in the garage
WOW that came out so GOOD!
But neither of us seemed to hold it against the other

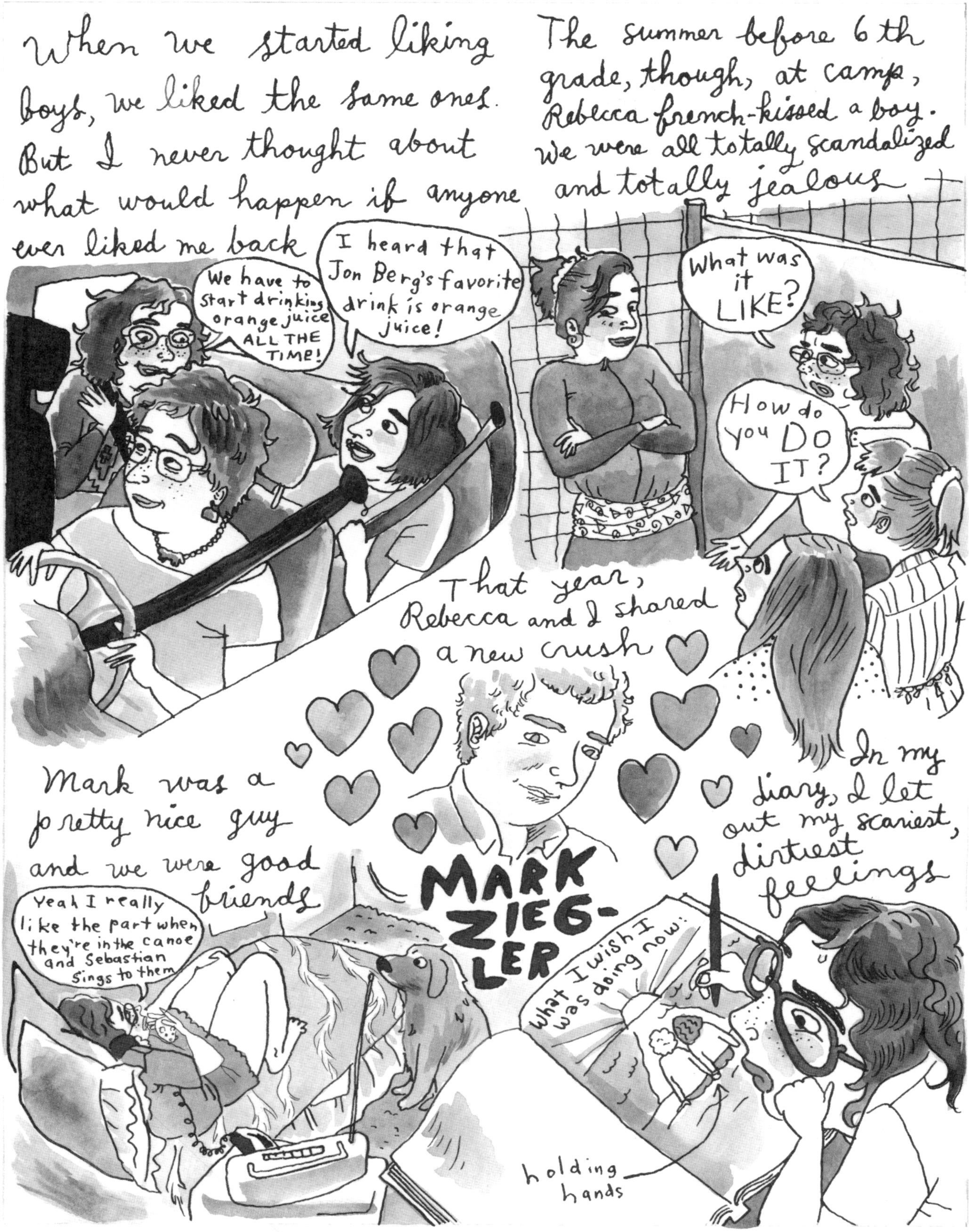

When we started liking boys, we liked the same ones. But I never thought about what would happen if anyone ever liked me back
We have to start drinking orange juice ALL THE TIME!
I heard that Jon Berg's favorite drink is orange juice!
The summer before 6th grade, though, at camp, Rebecca french-kissed a boy. We were all totally scandalized and totally jealous
What was it LIKE?
How do you DO IT?
That year, Rebecca and I shared a new crush
MARK ZIEG-LER
Mark was a pretty nice guy and we were good friends
Yeah I really like the part when they're in the canoe and Sebastian sings to them
In my diary, I let out my scariest, dirtiest feelings
What I wish I was doing now:
holding hands

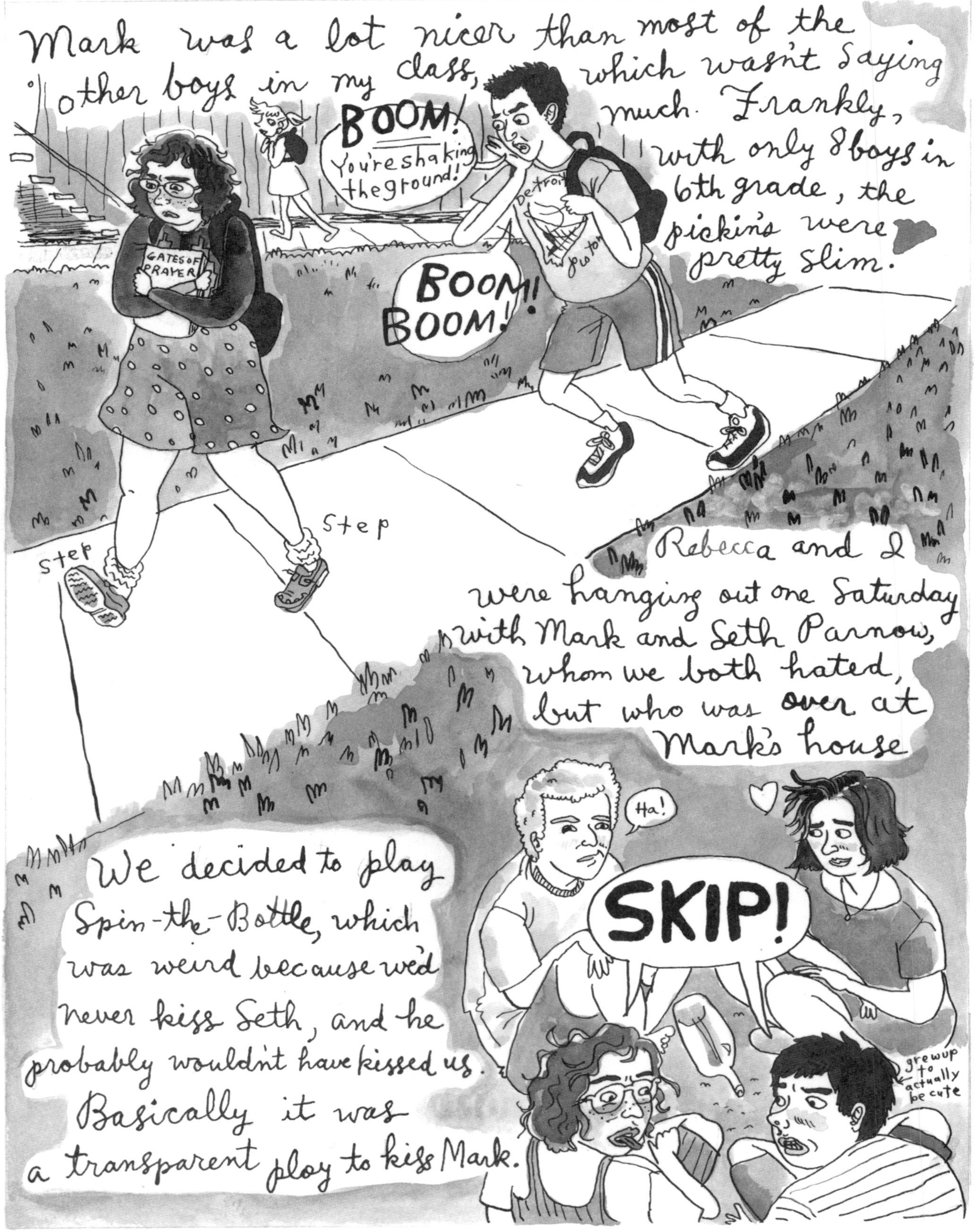
Mark was a lot nicer than most of the other boys in my class, which wasn't saying much. Frankly, with only 8 boys in 6th grade, the pickin's were pretty slim.
BOOM! You're shaking the ground!
BOOM! BOOM!!
GATES OF PRAYER
Detroit Pistons
step
step
Rebecca and I were hanging out one Saturday with Mark and Seth Parnow, whom we both hated, but who was over at Mark's house
Ha!
SKIP!
We decided to play Spin-the-Bottle, which was weird because we'd never kiss Seth, and he probably wouldn't have kissed us. Basically it was a transparent ploy to kiss Mark.
grew up to actually be cute

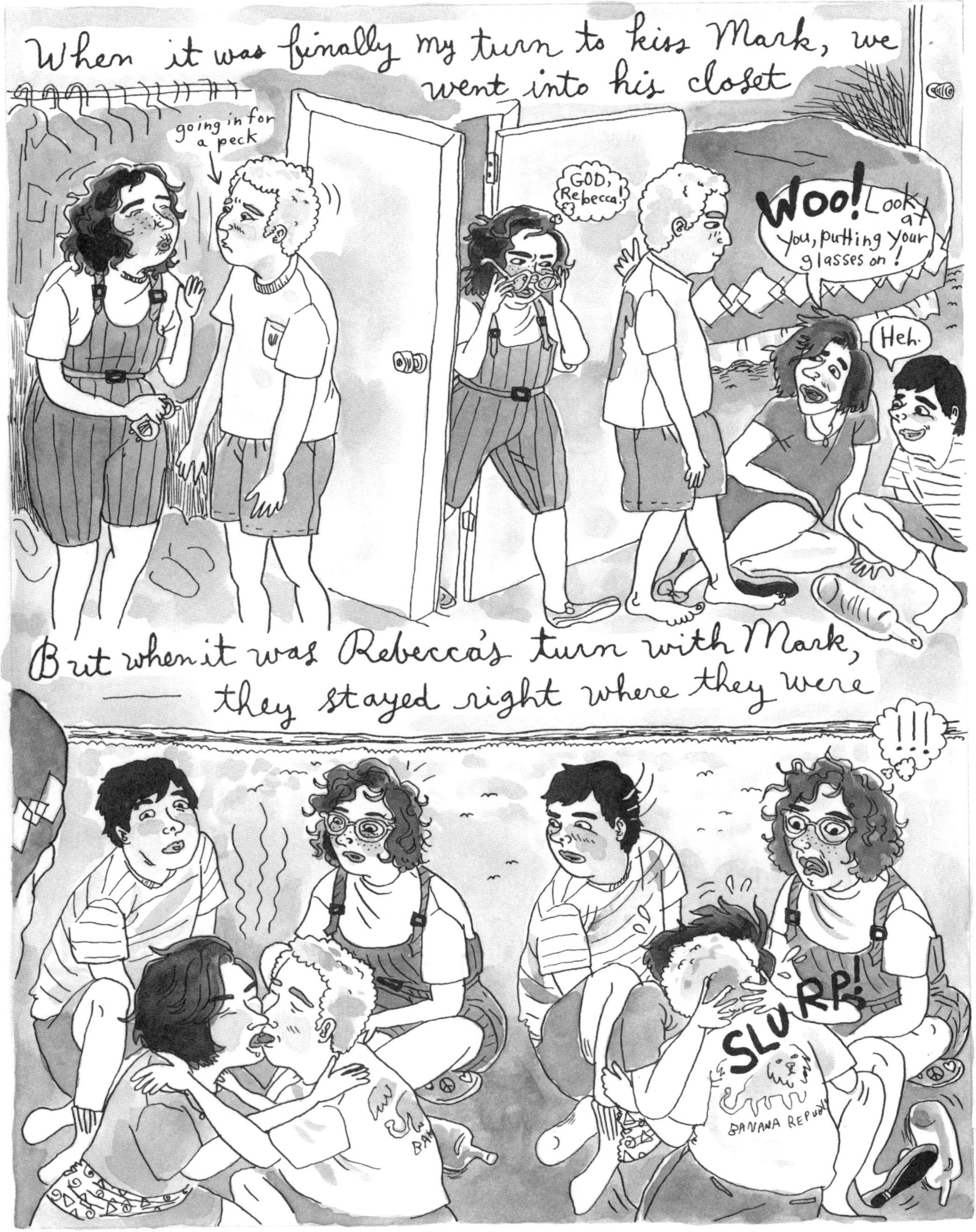
When it was finally my turn to kiss Mark, we went into his closet
going in for a peck
GOD, Rebecca!
WOO! Look at you, putting your glasses on!
Heh.
But when it was Rebecca's turn with Mark, — they stayed right where they were
!!!
SLURP!

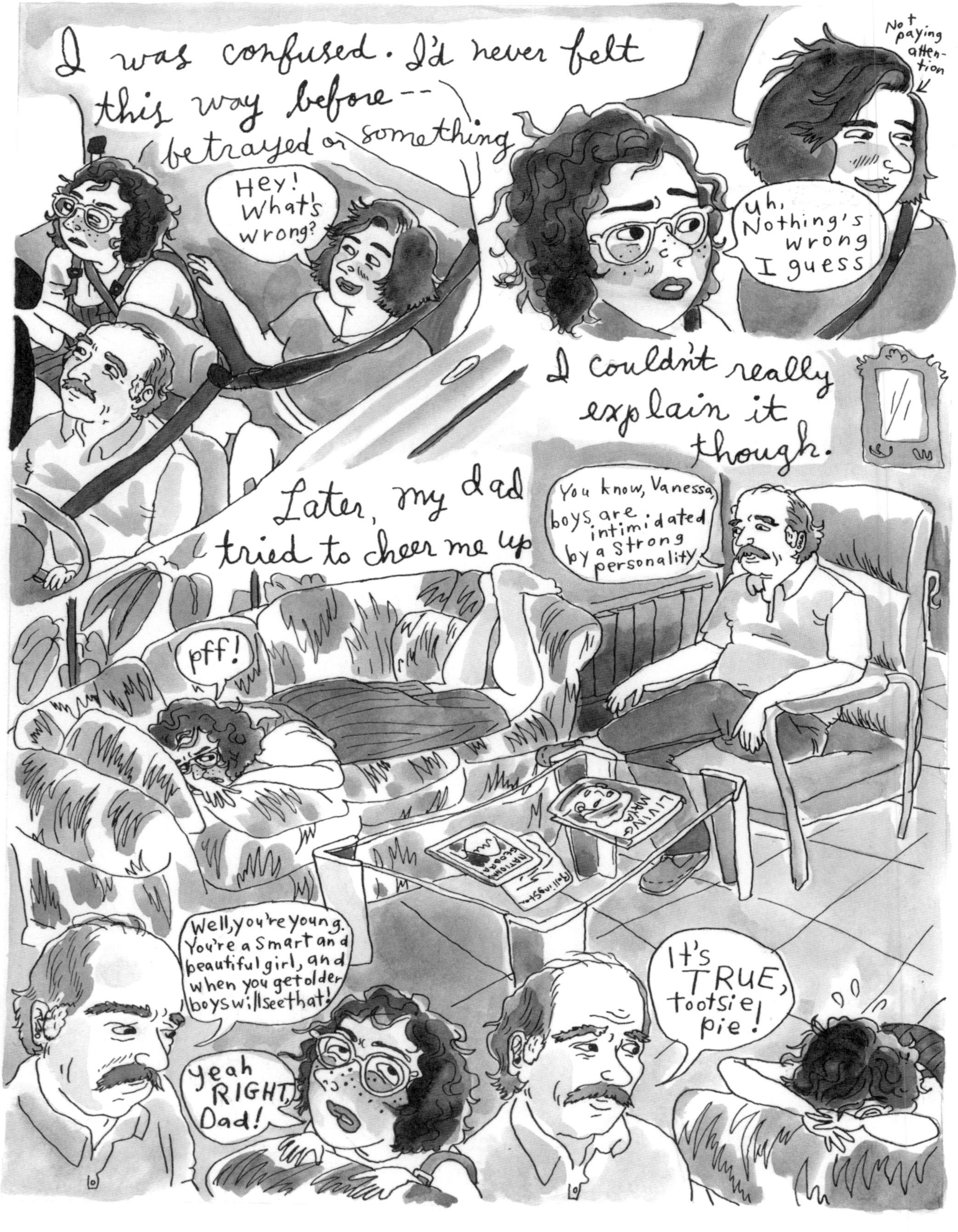

I was confused. I'd never felt this way before--
betrayed or something
Not paying attention
Hey! What's wrong?
Uh, Nothing's wrong I guess
I couldn't really explain it though.
Later, my dad tried to cheer me up
You know, Vanessa, boys are intimidated by a strong personality
pff!
LIVING
Well, you're young. You're a smart and beautiful girl, and when you get older boys will see that!
Yeah RIGHT, Dad!
It's TRUE, tootsie pie!

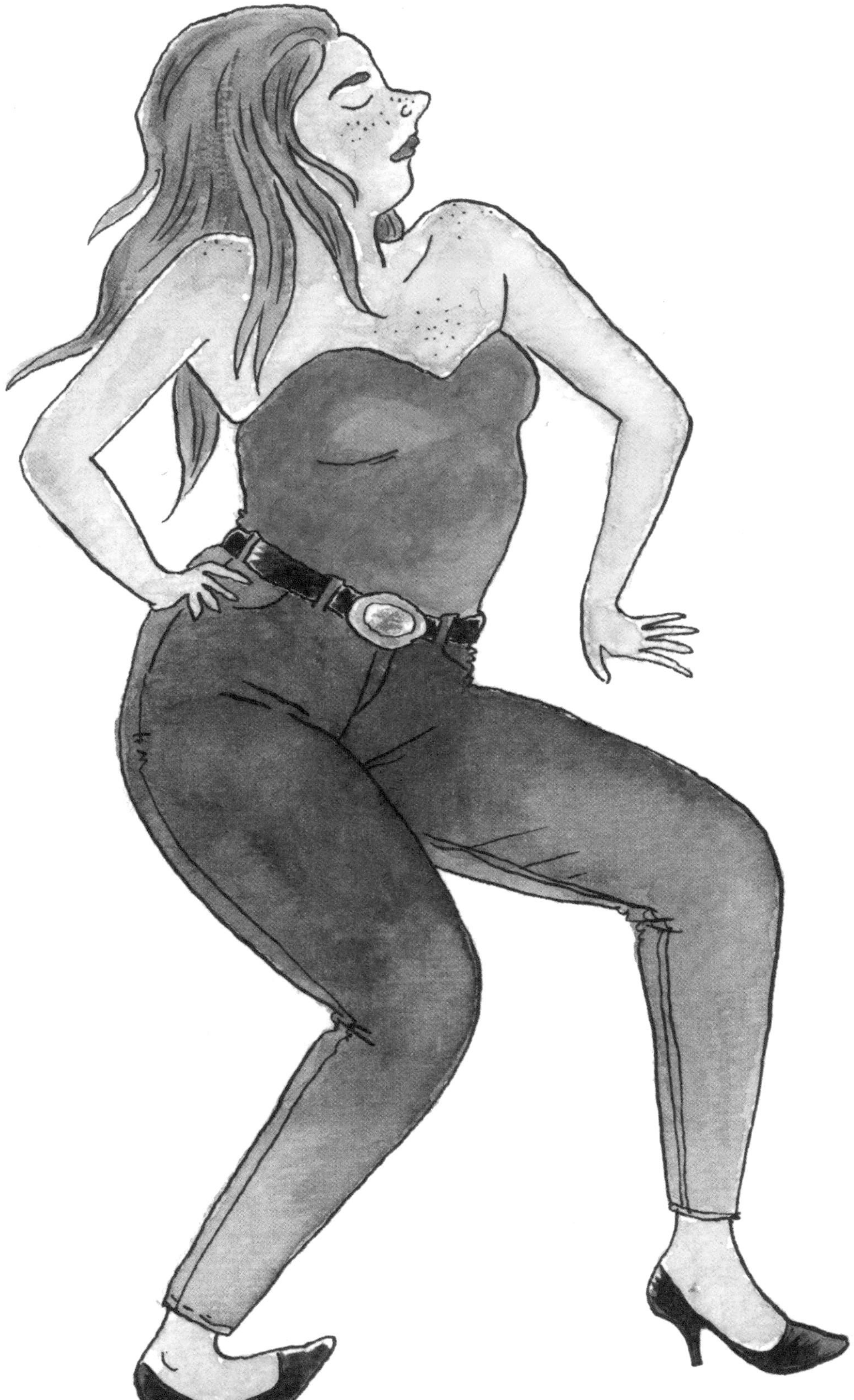

ORIGAMI WEEKEND

One spring day, in N.Y. Central Art Supply's Paper Department:

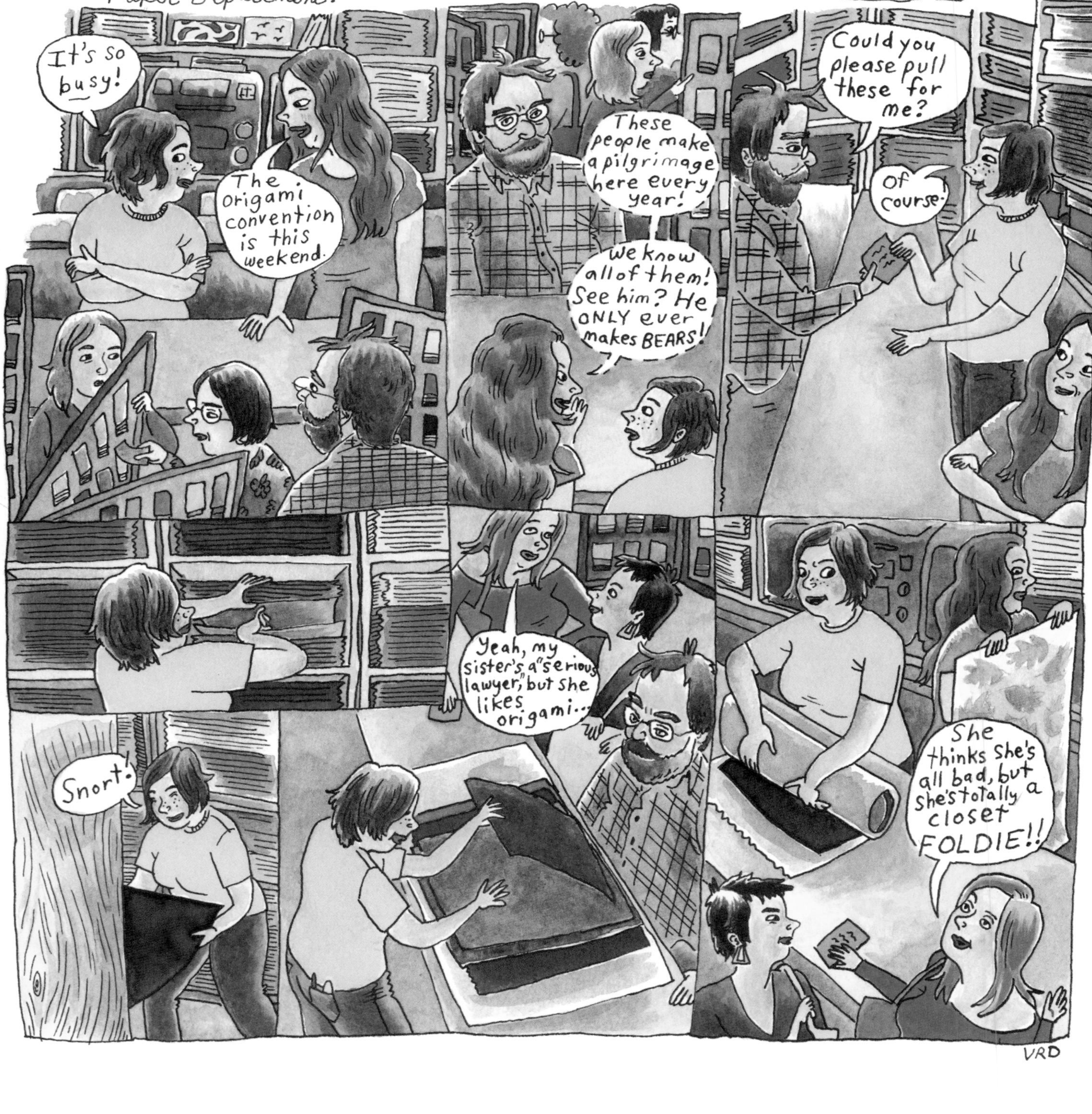

It's so busy!
The origami convention is this weekend.
These people make a pilgrimage here every year!
We know all of them! See him? He ONLY ever makes BEARS!
Could you please pull these for me?
Of course.
Yeah, my sister's a "serious lawyer," but she likes origami...
Snort!
She thinks she's all bad, but she's totally a closet FOLDIE!!

VRD

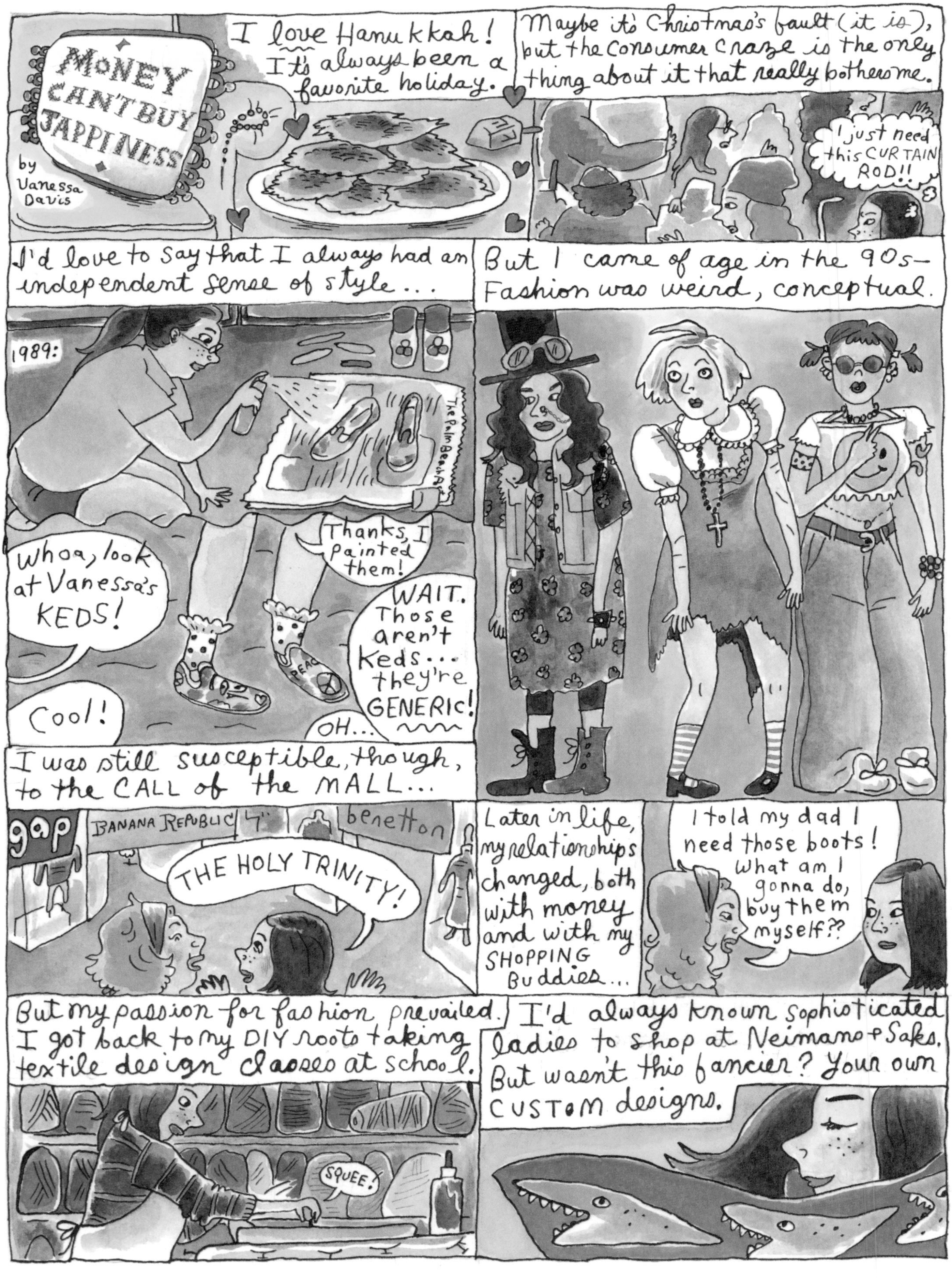

MONEY CAN'T BUY JAPPINESS
by Vanessa Davis
I love Hanukkah! It's always been a favorite holiday.
Maybe it's Christmas's fault (it is), but the consumer craze is the only thing about it that really bothers me.
I just need this CURTAIN ROD!!
I'd love to say that I always had an independent sense of style...
1989:
The Palm Beach Post
Whoa, look at Vanessa's KEDS!
Thanks, I painted them!
WAIT. Those aren't Keds... they're GENERIC!
Cool!
OH...
But I came of age in the 90s— Fashion was weird, conceptual.
I was still susceptible, though, to the CALL of the MALL...
gap
BANANA REPUBLIC
benetton
THE HOLY TRINITY!
Later in life, my relationships changed, both with money and with my SHOPPING BUDDIES...
I told my dad I need those boots! What am I gonna do, buy them myself??
But my passion for fashion prevailed. I got back to my DIY roots taking textile design classes at school.
SQUEE!
I'd always known sophisticated ladies to shop at Neimans & Saks. But wasn't this fancier? Your own CUSTOM designs.

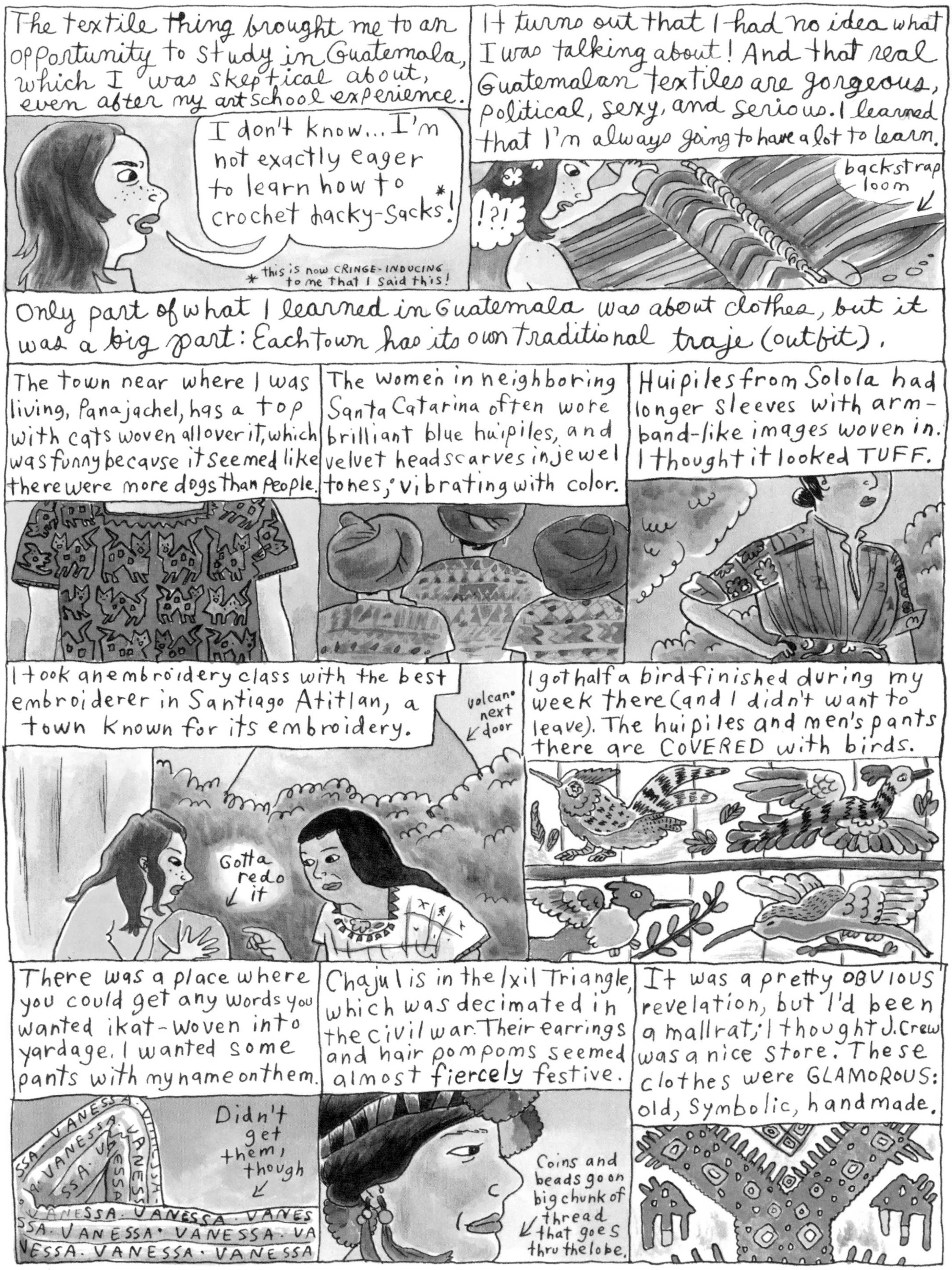
The textile thing brought me to an opportunity to study in Guatemala, which I was skeptical about, even after my art school experience.
I don't know... I'm not exactly eager to learn how to crochet hacky-sacks!*
* this is now CRINGE-INDUCING to me that I said this!
It turns out that I had no idea what I was talking about! And that real Guatemalan textiles are gorgeous, political, sexy, and serious. I learned that I'm always going to have a lot to learn.
!?!
backstrap loom
Only part of what I learned in Guatemala was about clothes, but it was a big part: Each town has its own traditional traje (outfit).
The town near where I was living, Panajachel, has a top with cats woven all over it, which was funny because it seemed like there were more dogs than people.
The women in neighboring Santa Catarina often wore brilliant blue huipiles, and velvet headscarves in jewel tones, vibrating with color.
Huipiles from Solola had longer sleeves with arm-band-like images woven in. I thought it looked TUFF.
I took an embroidery class with the best embroiderer in Santiago Atitlan, a town known for its embroidery.
volcano next door
Gotta redo it
I got half a bird finished during my week there (and I didn't want to leave). The huipiles and men's pants there are COVERED with birds.
There was a place where you could get any words you wanted ikat-woven into yardage. I wanted some pants with my name on them.
Didn't get them, though
VANESSA · VANESSA · VANESSA · VANESSA
Chajul is in the Ixil Triangle, which was decimated in the civil war. Their earrings and hair pompoms seemed almost fiercely festive.
Coins and beads go on big chunk of thread that goes thru the lobe.
It was a pretty OBVIOUS revelation, but I'd been a mallrat; I thought J.Crew was a nice store. These clothes were GLAMOROUS: old, symbolic, handmade.

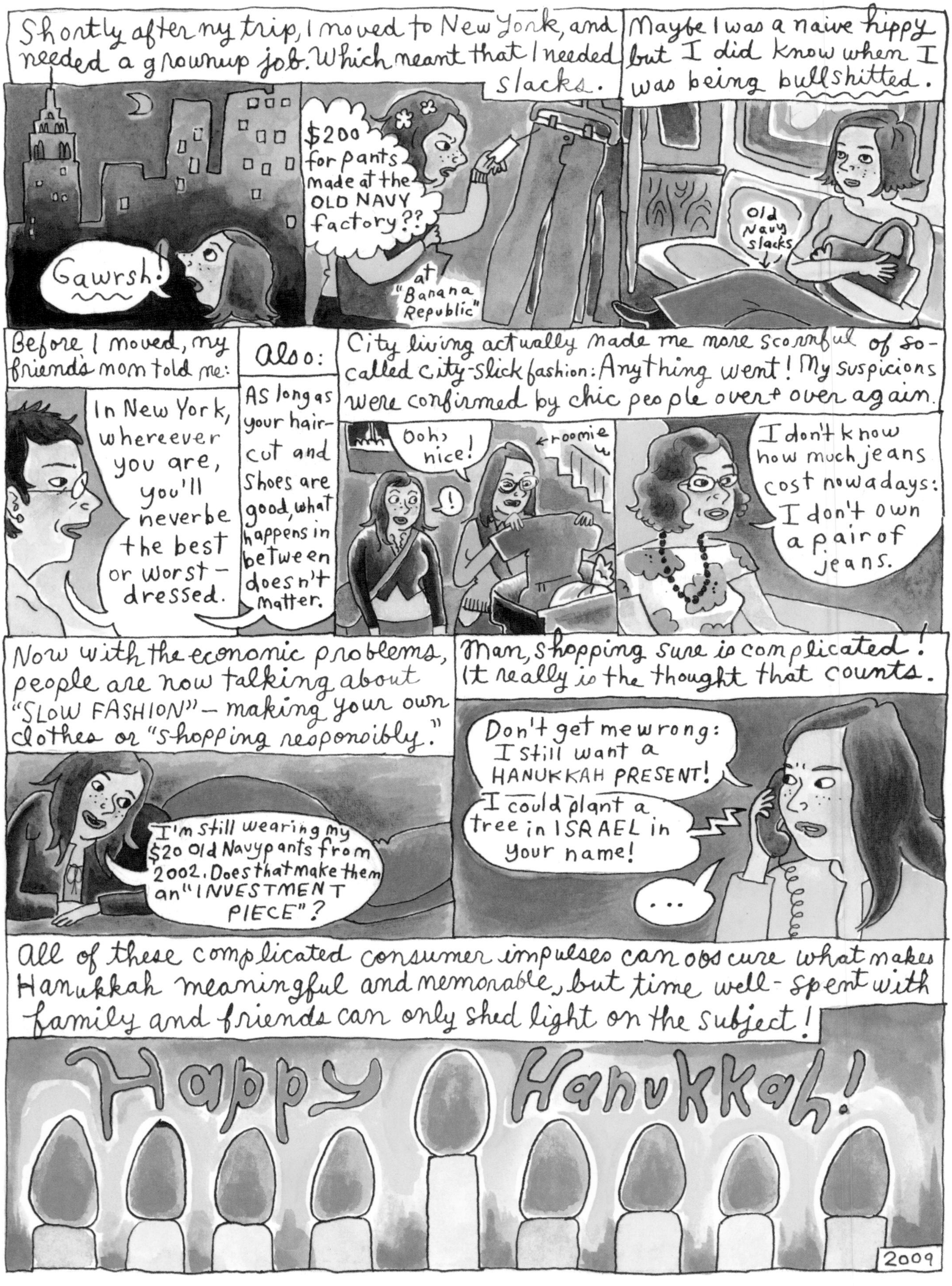
Shortly after my trip, I moved to New York, and needed a grownup job. Which meant that I needed slacks.
Gawrsh!
$200 for pants made at the OLD NAVY factory??
at "Banana Republic"
Maybe I was a naive hippy but I did know when I was being bullshitted.
Old Navy slacks
Before I moved, my friend's mom told me:
In New York, whereever you are, you'll never be the best or worst-dressed.
Also:
As long as your haircut and shoes are good, what happens in between doesn't matter.
City living actually made me more scornful of so-called city-slick fashion: Anything went! My suspicions were confirmed by chic people over + over again.
Ooh, nice!
!
← roomie
I don't know how much jeans cost nowadays: I don't own a pair of jeans.
Now with the economic problems, people are now talking about "SLOW FASHION" – making your own clothes or "shopping responsibly."
I'm still wearing my $20 Old Navy pants from 2002. Does that make them an "INVESTMENT PIECE"?
Man, shopping sure is complicated! It really is the thought that counts.
Don't get me wrong: I still want a HANUKKAH PRESENT!
I could plant a tree in ISRAEL in your name!
...
All of these complicated consumer impulses can obscure what makes Hanukkah meaningful and memorable, but time well-spent with family and friends can only shed light on the subject!
Happy Hanukkah!
2009

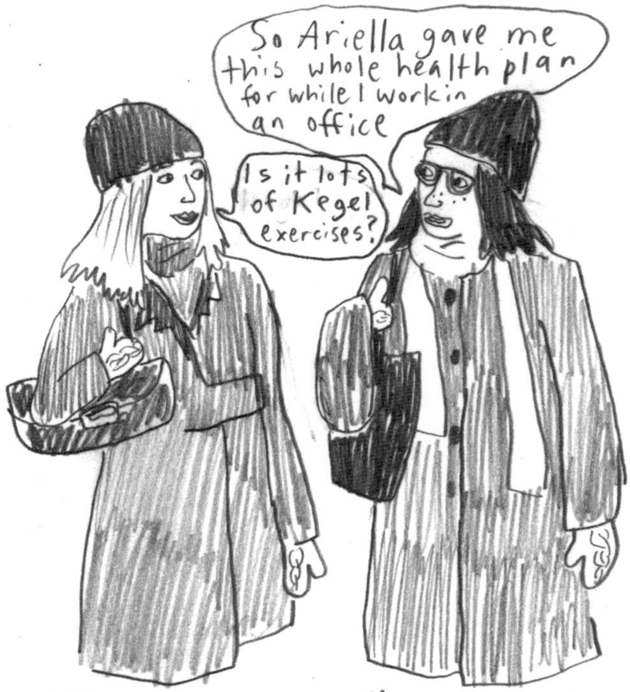
So Ariella gave me this whole health plan for while I work in an office
Is it lots of Kegel exercises?

January 8, 2004

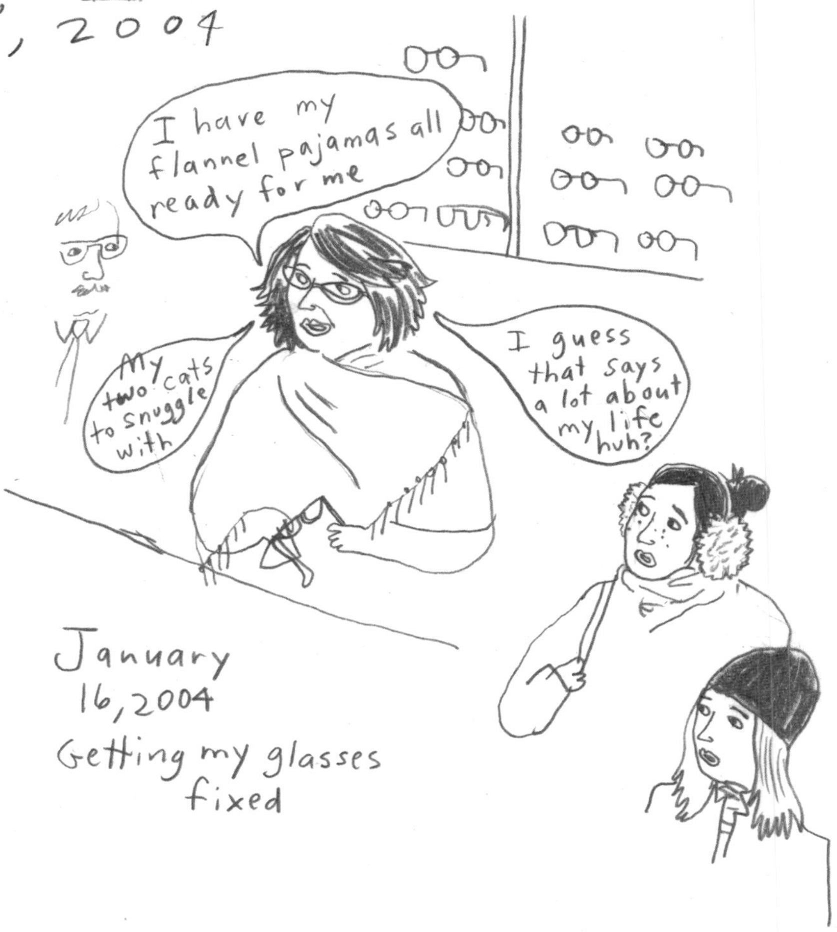
I have my flannel pajamas all ready for me
My two cats to snuggle with
I guess that says a lot about my life huh?

January 16, 2004
Getting my glasses fixed

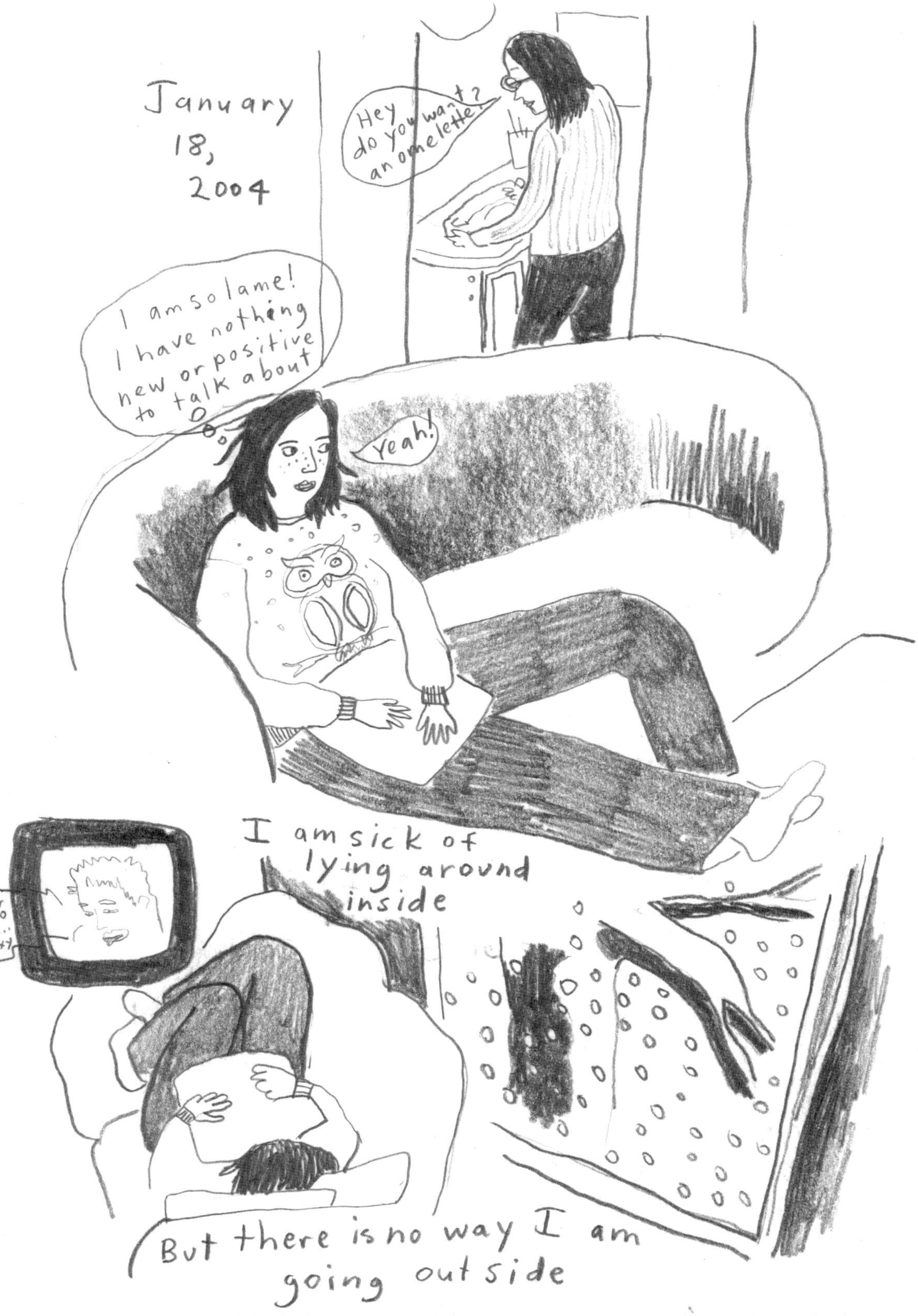
January 18, 2004
Hey do you want an omelette?
I am so lame! I have nothing new or positive to talk about
Yeah!
I am sick of lying around inside
Your tattoo is... sexy
But there is no way I am going outside

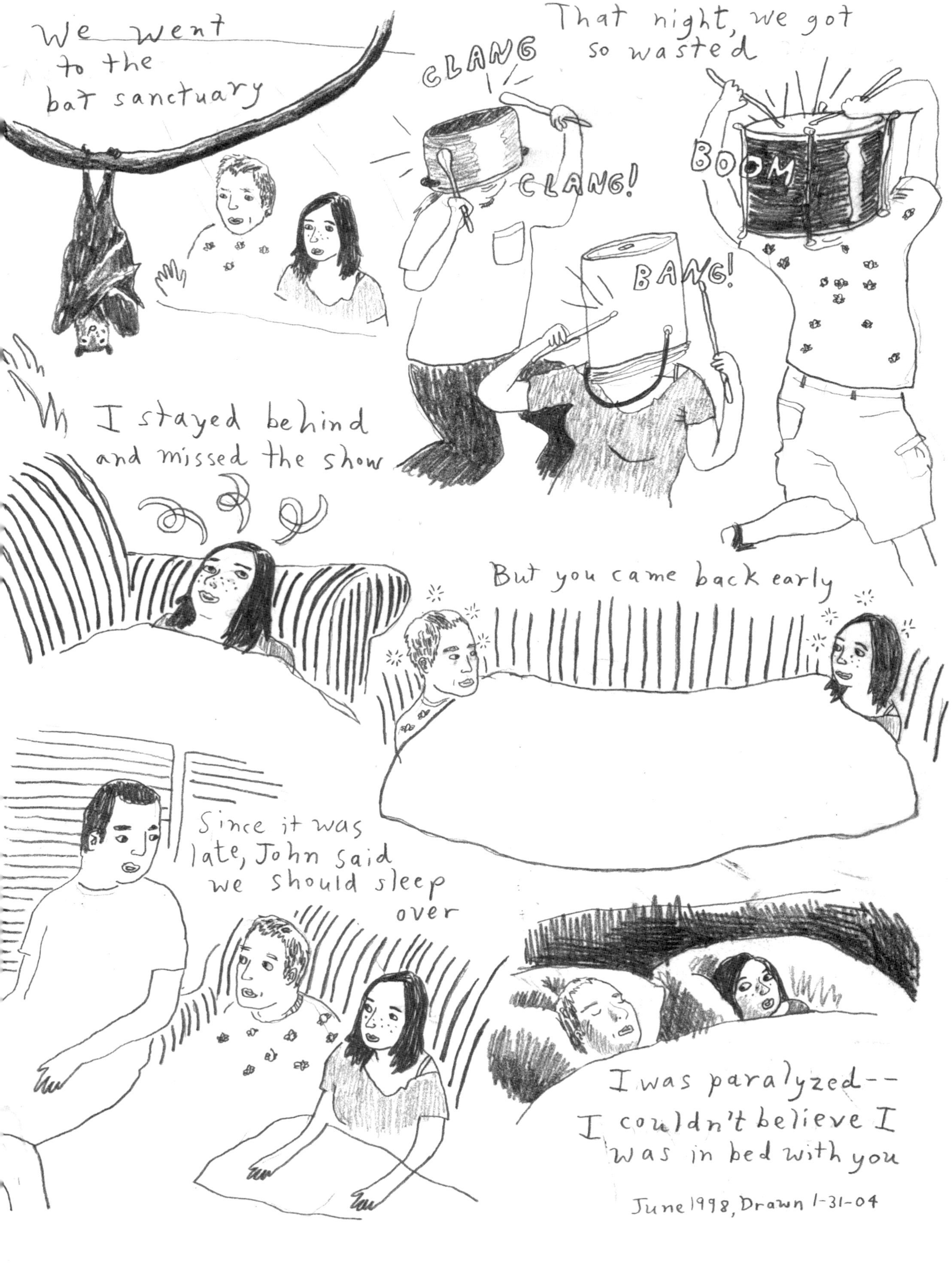
We went to the bat sanctuary
That night, we got so wasted
CLANG
CLANG!
BOOM
BANG!
I stayed behind and missed the show
But you came back early
Since it was late, John said we should sleep over
I was paralyzed-- I couldn't believe I was in bed with you
June 1998, Drawn 1-31-04

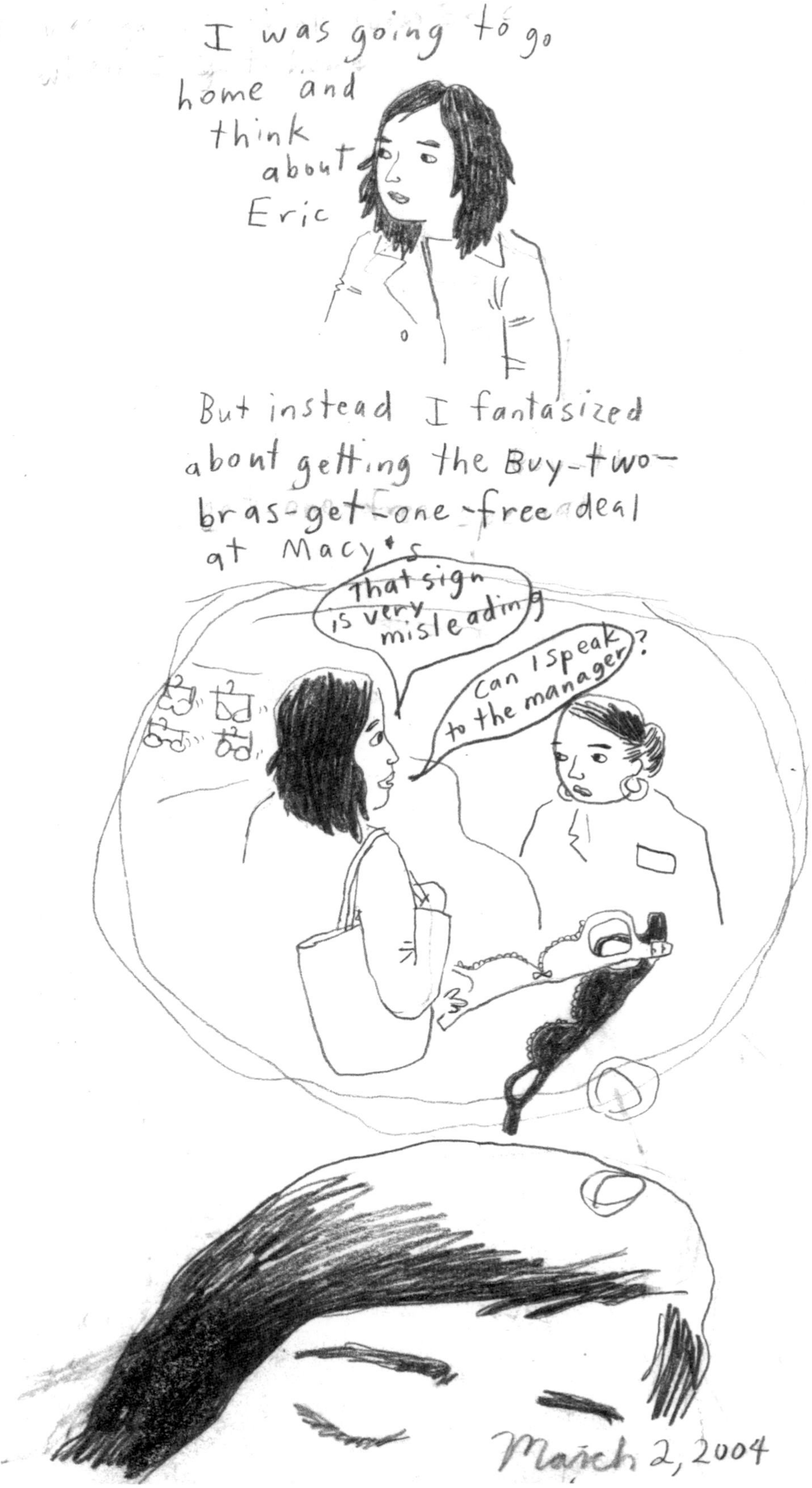

I was going to go home and think about Eric
But instead I fantasized about getting the Buy-two-bras-get-one-free deal at Macy's
That sign is very misleading
Can I speak to the manager?
March 2, 2004

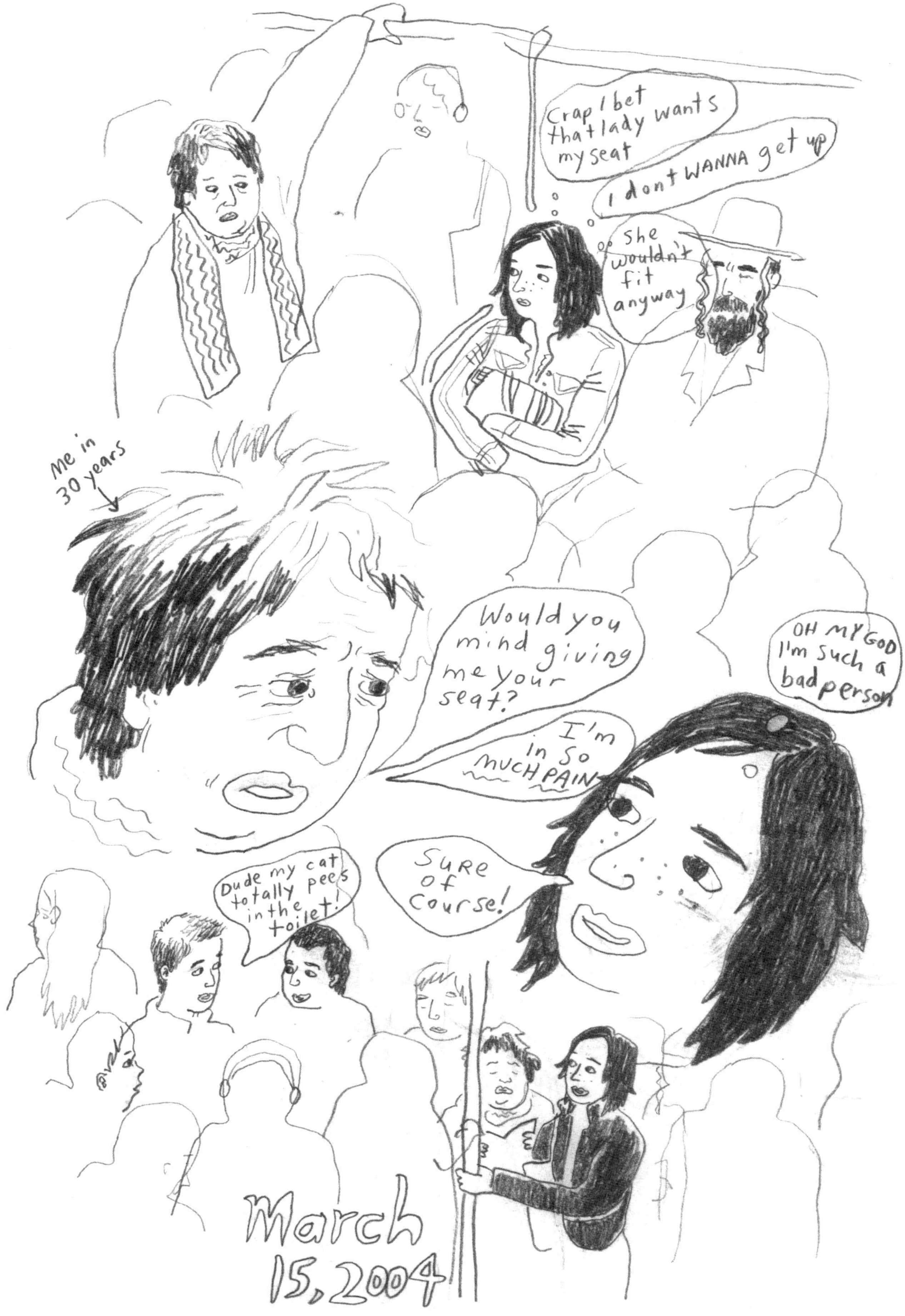

Crap I bet that lady wants my seat
I dont WANNA get up
She wouldn't fit anyway
Me in 30 years
Would you mind giving me your seat?
I'm in so MUCH PAIN
OH MY GOD I'm such a bad person
Sure of course!
Dude my cat totally pees in the toilet!
March 15, 2004

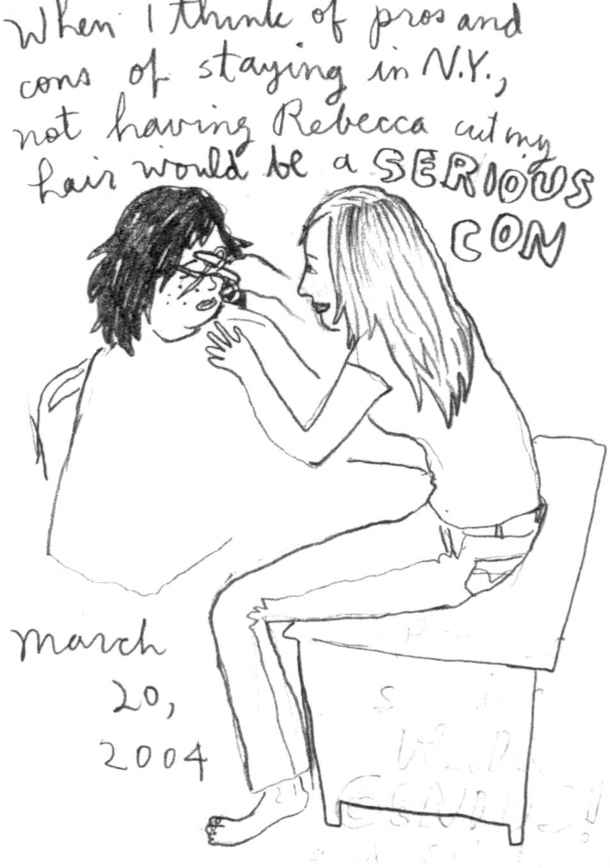
When I think of pros and cons of staying in N.Y., not having Rebecca cut my hair would be a SERIOUS CON
March 20, 2004

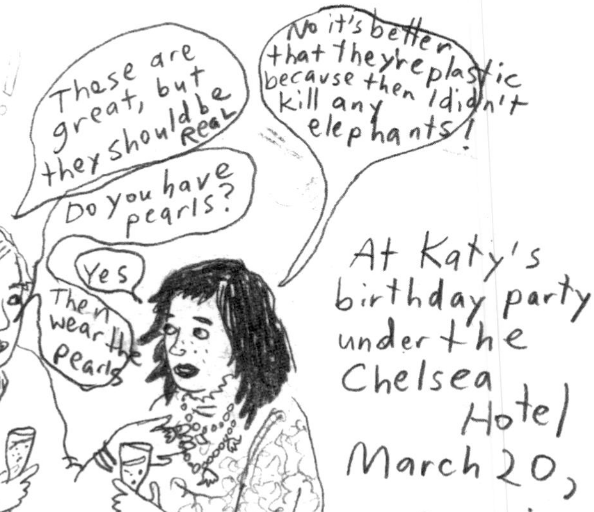
These are great, but they should be REAL
No it's better that they're plastic because then I didn't kill any elephants!
Do you have pearls?
Yes
Then wear the pearls
At Katy's birthday party under the Chelsea Hotel March 20, 2004

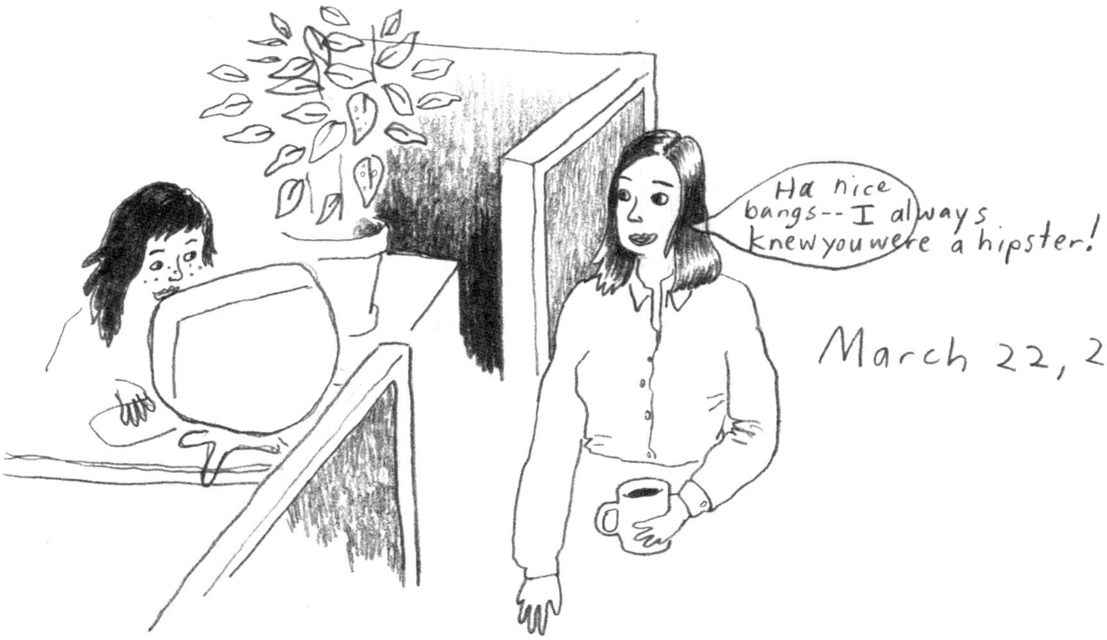
Ha nice bangs-- I always knew you were a hipster!

March 22, 2004

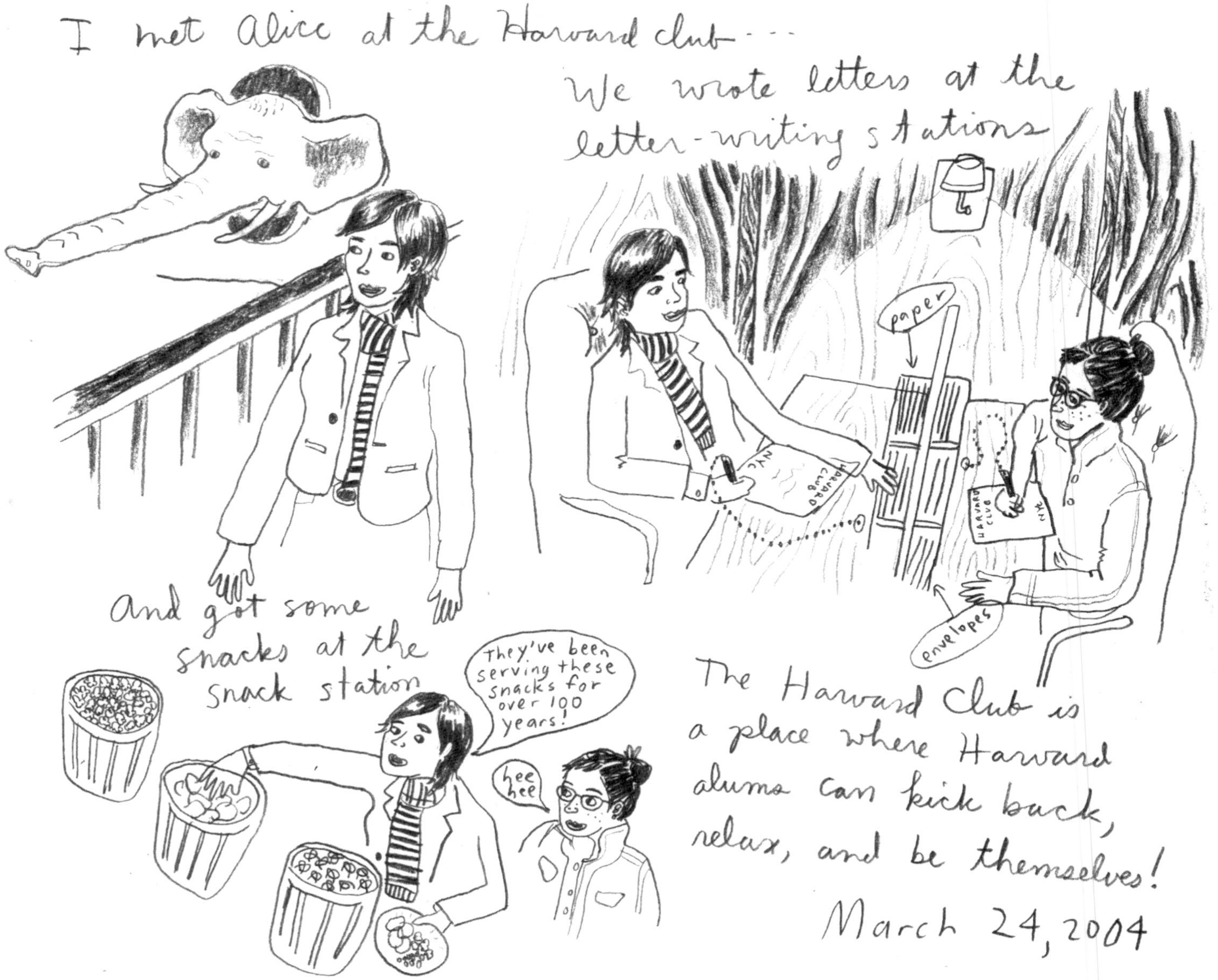
I met Alice at the Harvard club...
We wrote letters at the letter-writing stations
paper
NYC
Harvard Club
envelopes
and got some snacks at the snack station
They've been serving these snacks for over 100 years!
hee hee
The Harvard Club is a place where Harvard alums can kick back, relax, and be themselves!
March 24, 2004

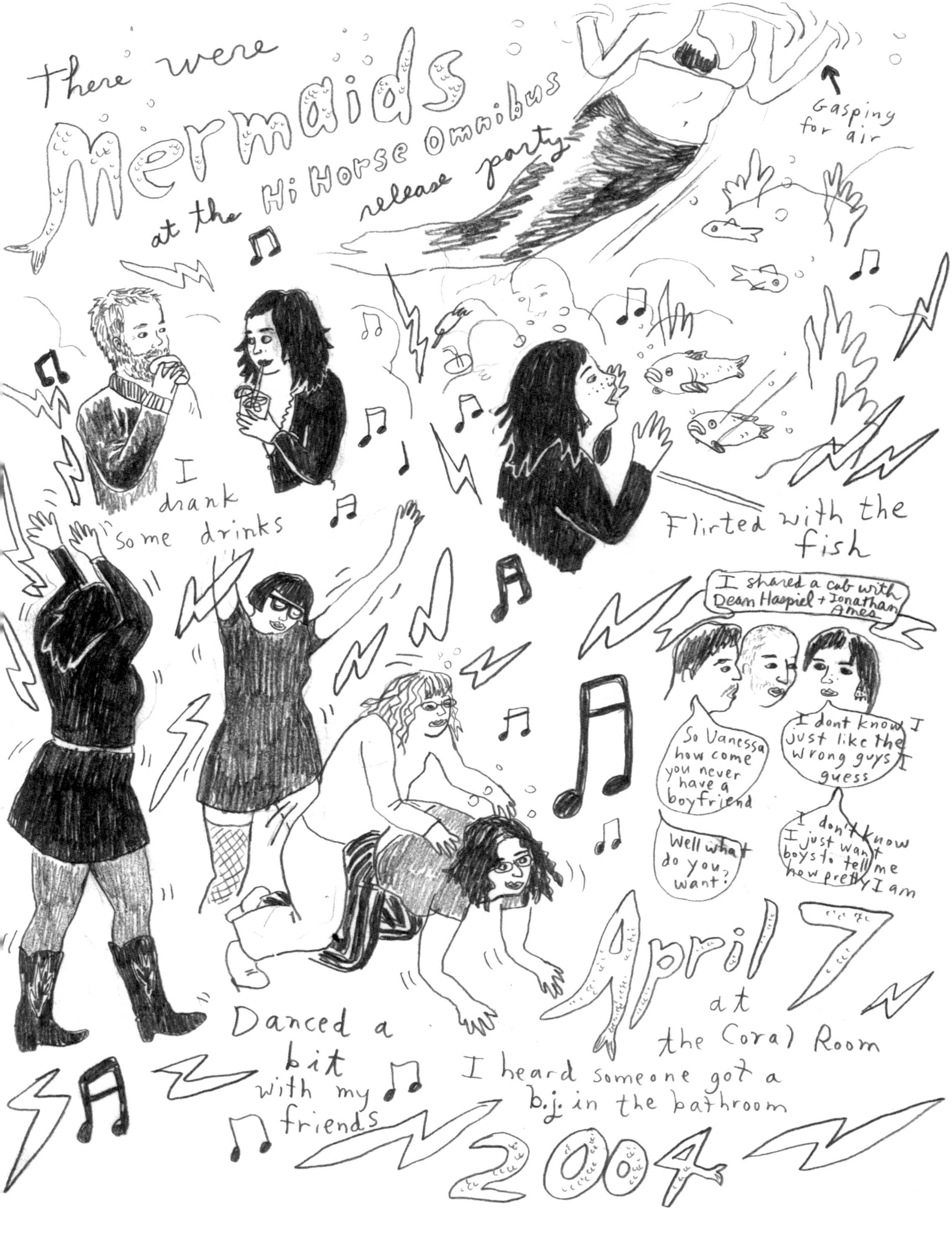

There were
Mermaids
at the Hi Horse Omnibus release party
Gasping for air
I drank some drinks
Flirted with the fish
I shared a cab with Dean Haspiel + Jonathan Ames
So Vanessa how come you never have a boyfriend
I dont know I just like the wrong guys I guess
Well what do you want?
I don't know I just want boys to tell me how pretty I am
Danced a bit with my friends
April 7
at the Coral Room
I heard someone got a b.j. in the bathroom
2004

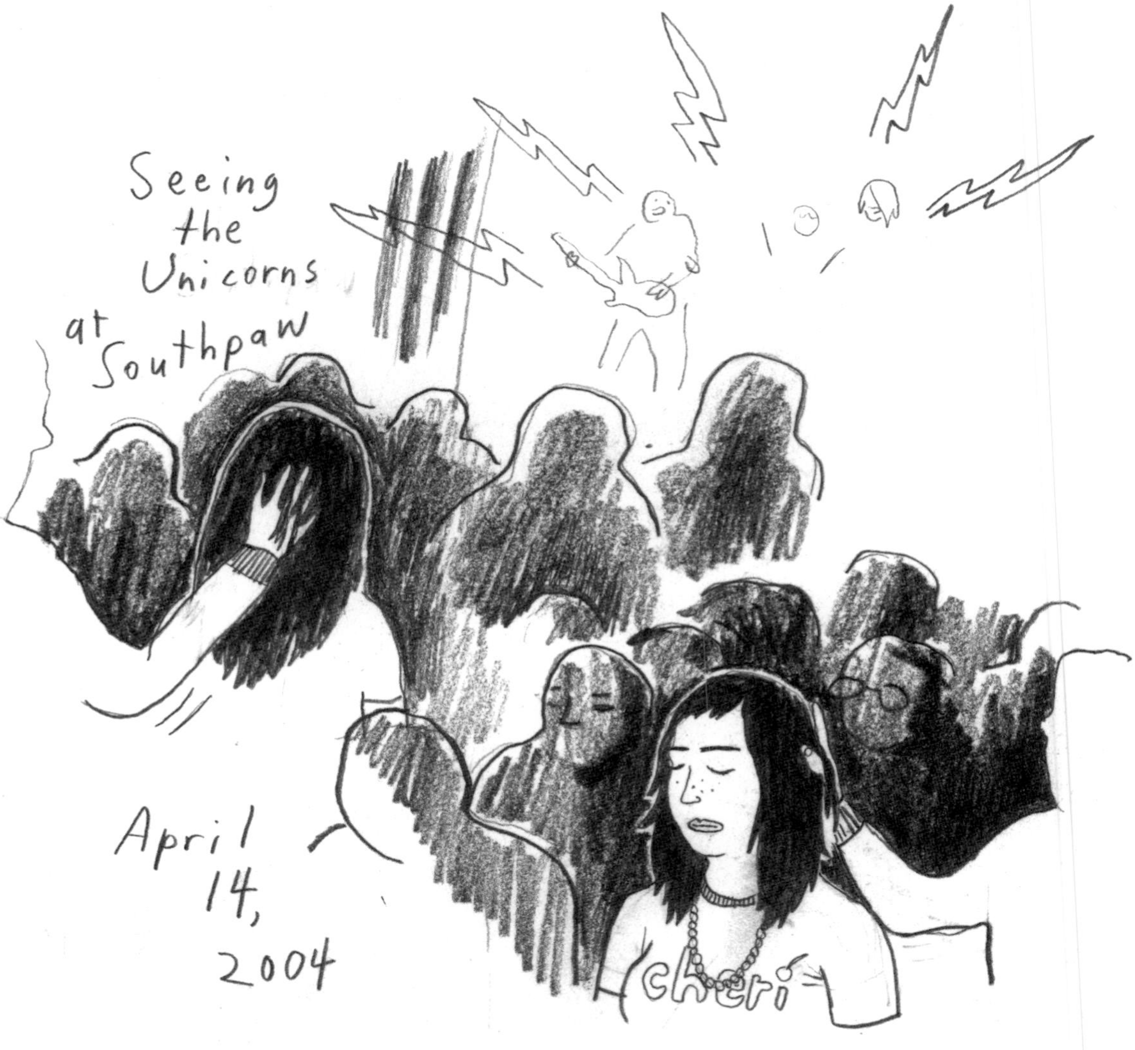
Seeing the Unicorns at Southpaw
April 14, 2004
cheri

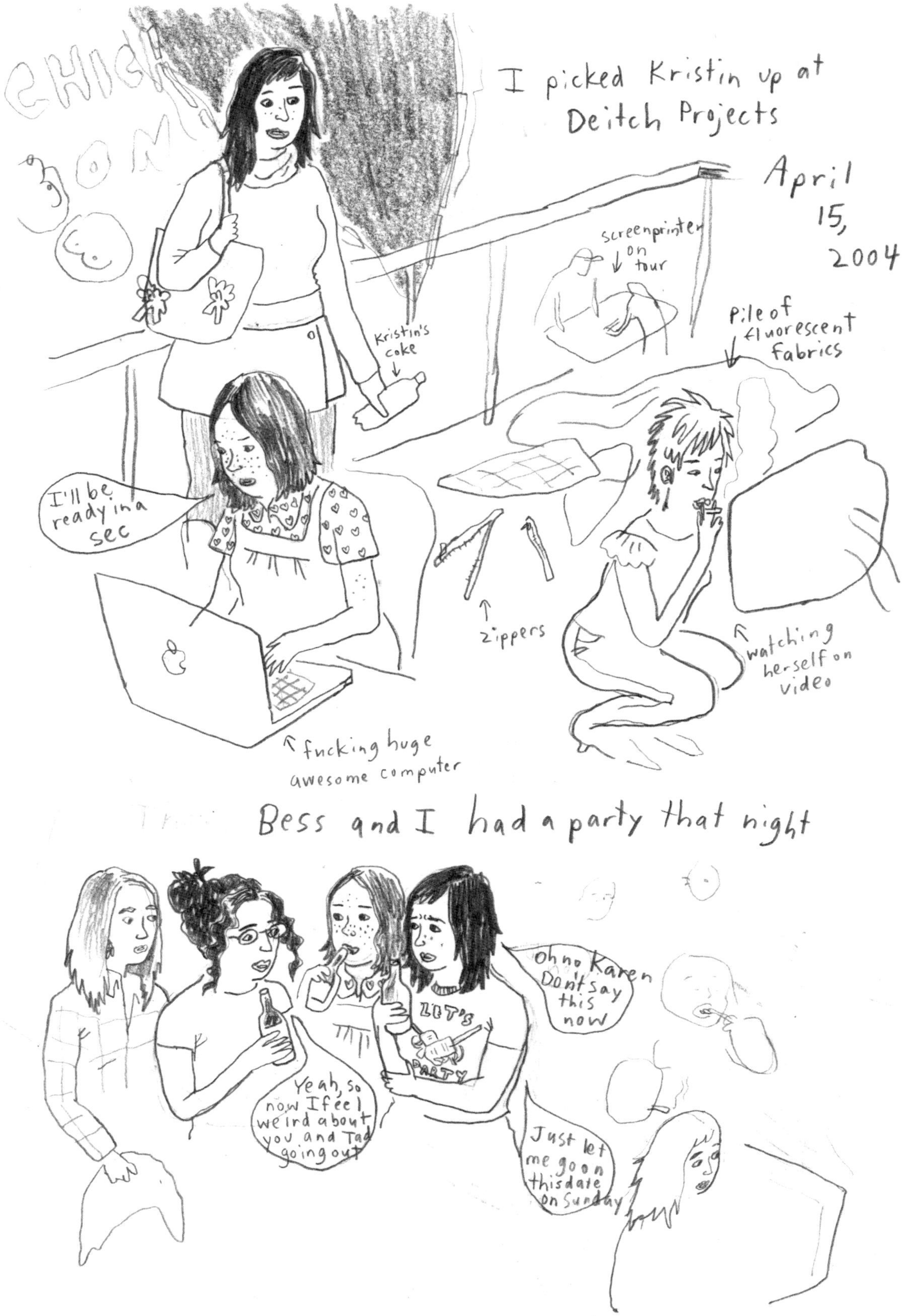
I picked Kristin up at Deitch Projects
April 15, 2004
screenprinter on tour
Pile of fluorescent fabrics
Kristin's coke
I'll be ready in a sec
zippers
watching herself on video
fucking huge awesome computer
Bess and I had a party that night
Oh no Karen Don't say this now
LET'S PARTY
Yeah, so now I feel weird about you and Tad going out
Just let me go on this date on Sunday

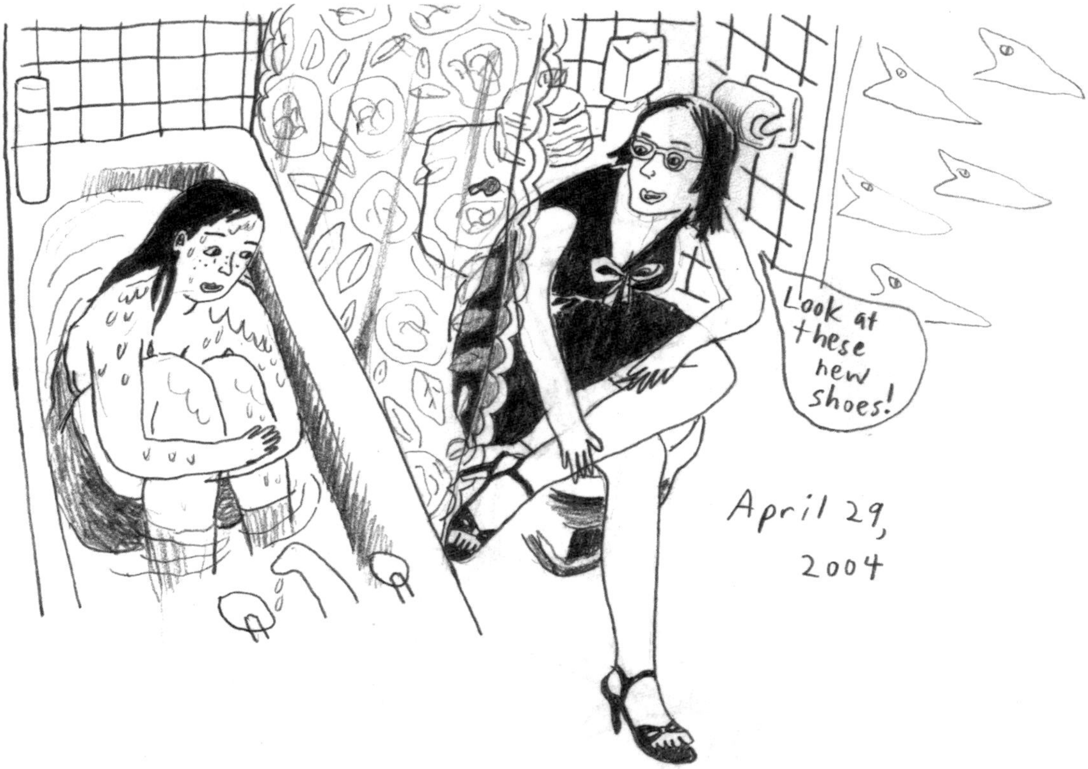
Look at these new shoes!
April 29, 2004

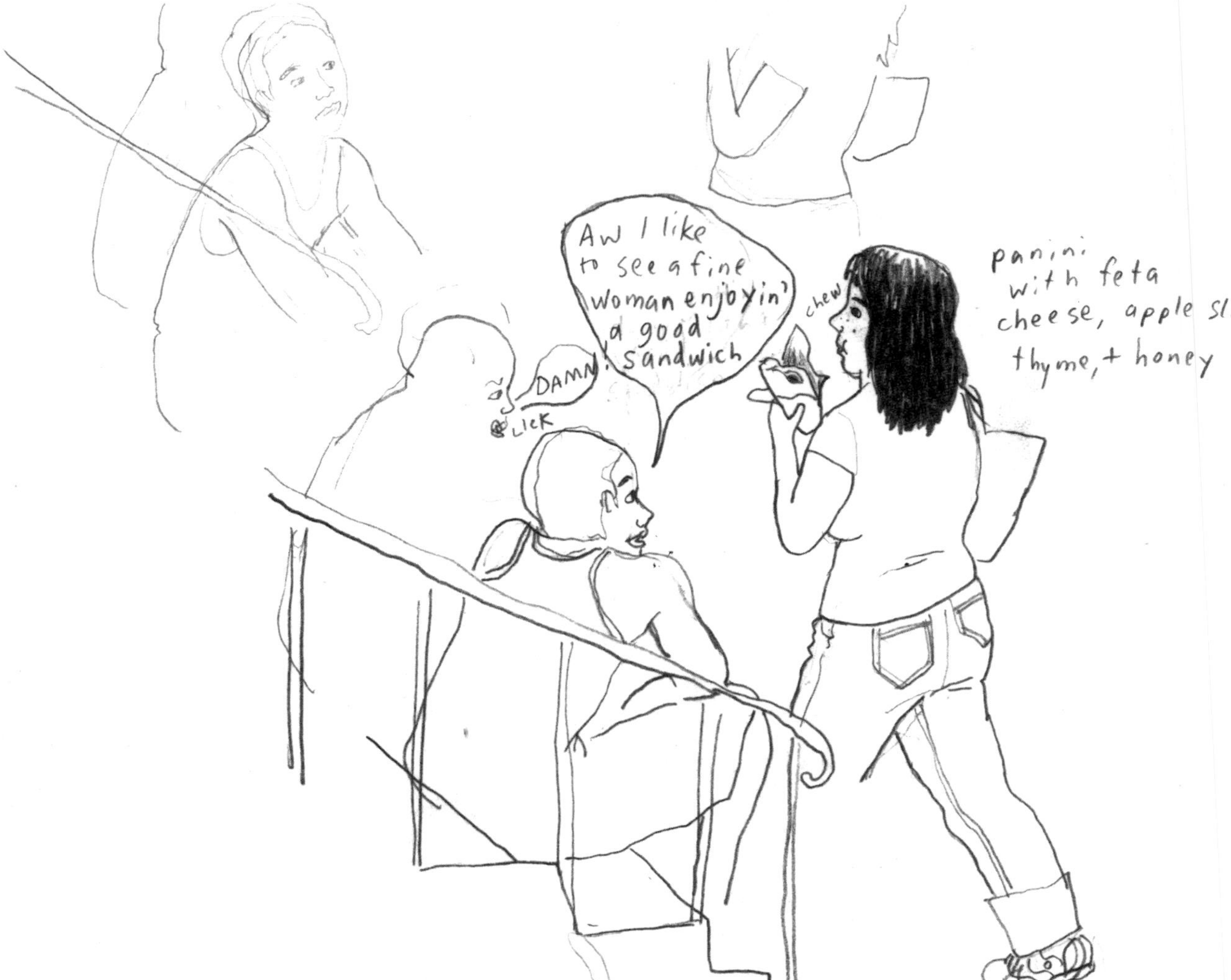
Aw I like to see a fine woman enjoyin' a good sandwich
DAMN!
LICK
chew
panini with feta cheese, apple slices, thyme, + honey

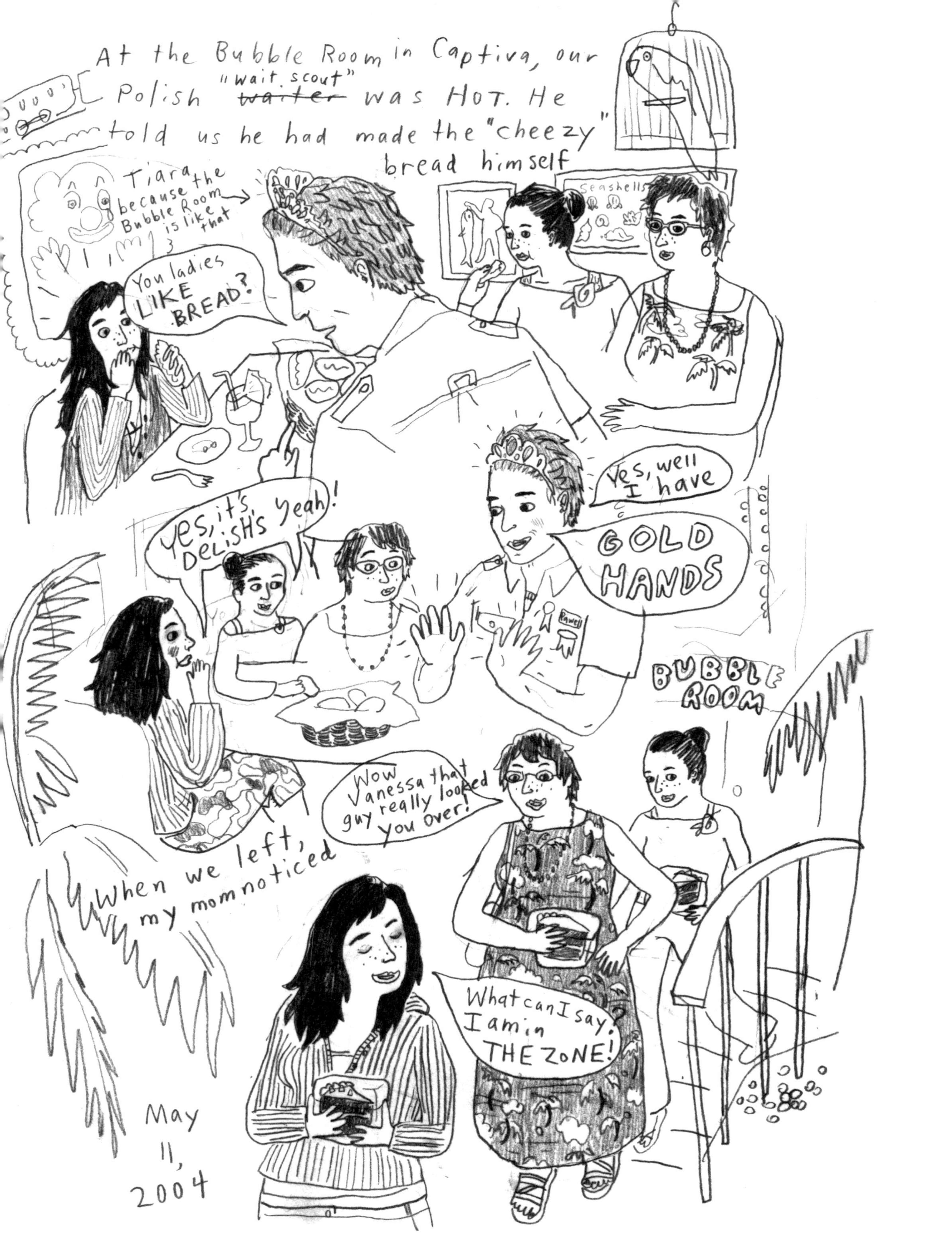

At the Bubble Room in Captiva, our Polish "wait scout" waiter was HOT. He told us he had made the "cheezy" bread himself
Tiara because the Bubble Room is like that
Seashells
You ladies LIKE BREAD?
Yes, it's DELISH's yeah!
Yes, well I have
GOLD HANDS
Rawell
BUBBLE ROOM
When we left, my mom noticed
Wow Vanessa that guy really looked you over!
What can I say, I am in THE ZONE!
May 11, 2004

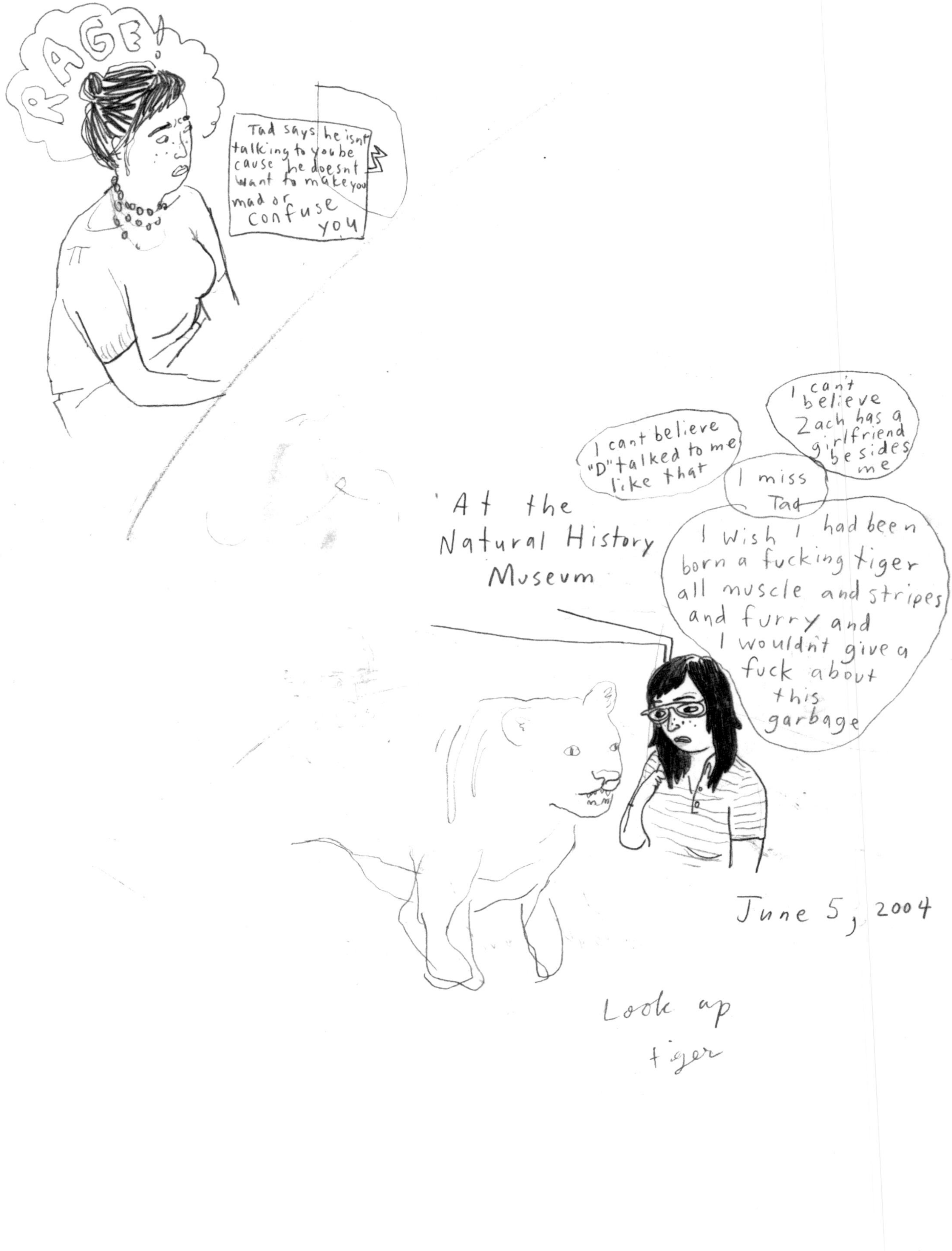
RAGE!
Tad says he isnt talking to you because he doesnt want to make you mad or confuse you
I cant believe "D" talked to me like that
I can't believe Zach has a girlfriend besides me
I miss Tad
At the Natural History Museum
I wish I had been born a fucking tiger all muscle and stripes and furry and I wouldn't give a fuck about this garbage
June 5, 2004
Look up tiger

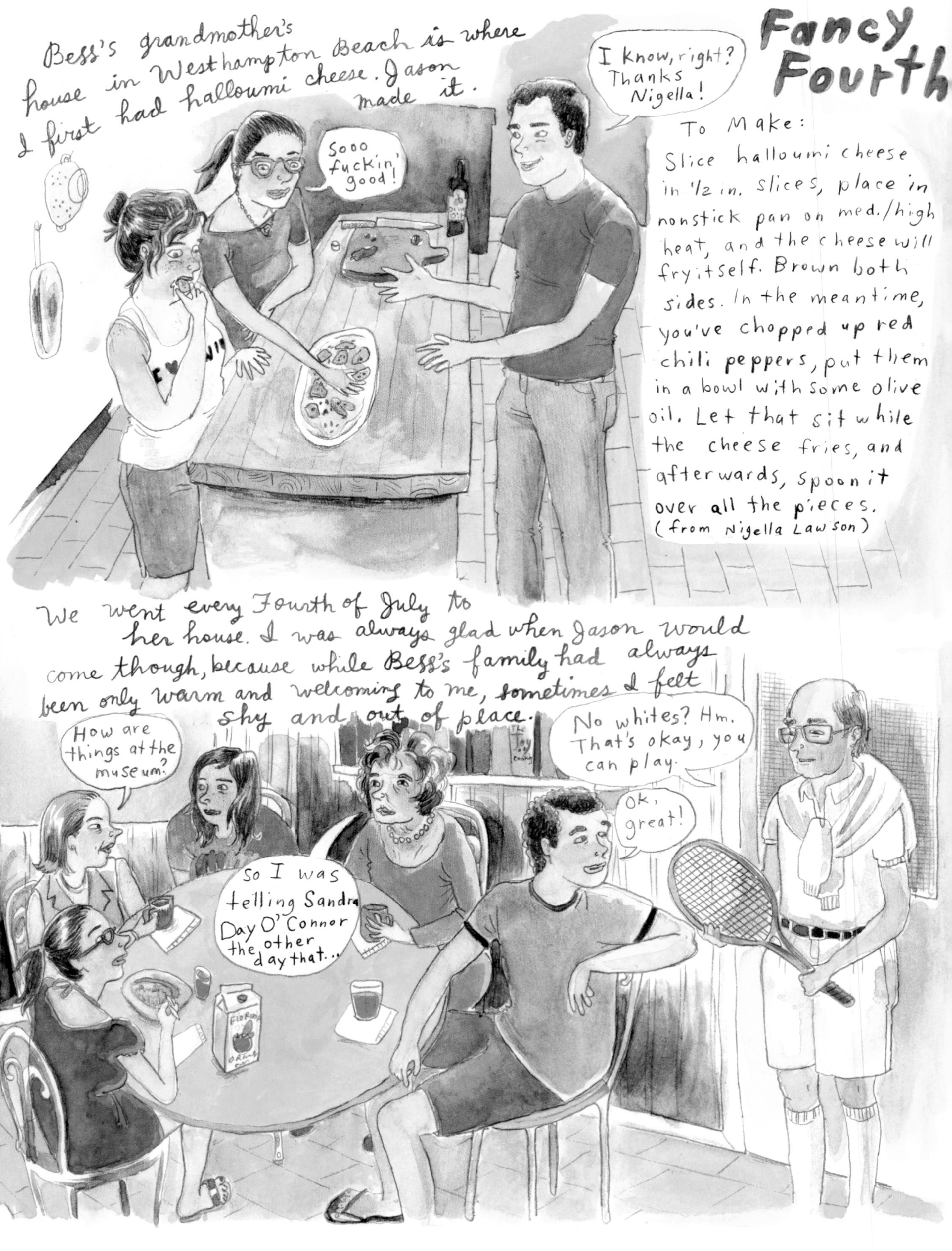
Fancy Fourth
Bess's grandmother's house in Westhampton Beach is where I first had halloumi cheese. Jason made it.
Sooo fuckin' good!
I know, right? Thanks Nigella!
To Make:
Slice halloumi cheese in 1/2 in. slices, place in nonstick pan on med./high heat, and the cheese will fry itself. Brown both sides. In the meantime, you've chopped up red chili peppers, put them in a bowl with some olive oil. Let that sit while the cheese fries, and afterwards, spoon it over all the pieces.
(from Nigella Lawson)
We went every Fourth of July to her house. I was always glad when Jason would come though, because while Bess's family had always been only warm and welcoming to me, sometimes I felt shy and out of place.
How are things at the museum?
So I was telling Sandra Day O'Connor the other day that...
No whites? Hm. That's okay, you can play.
Ok, great!

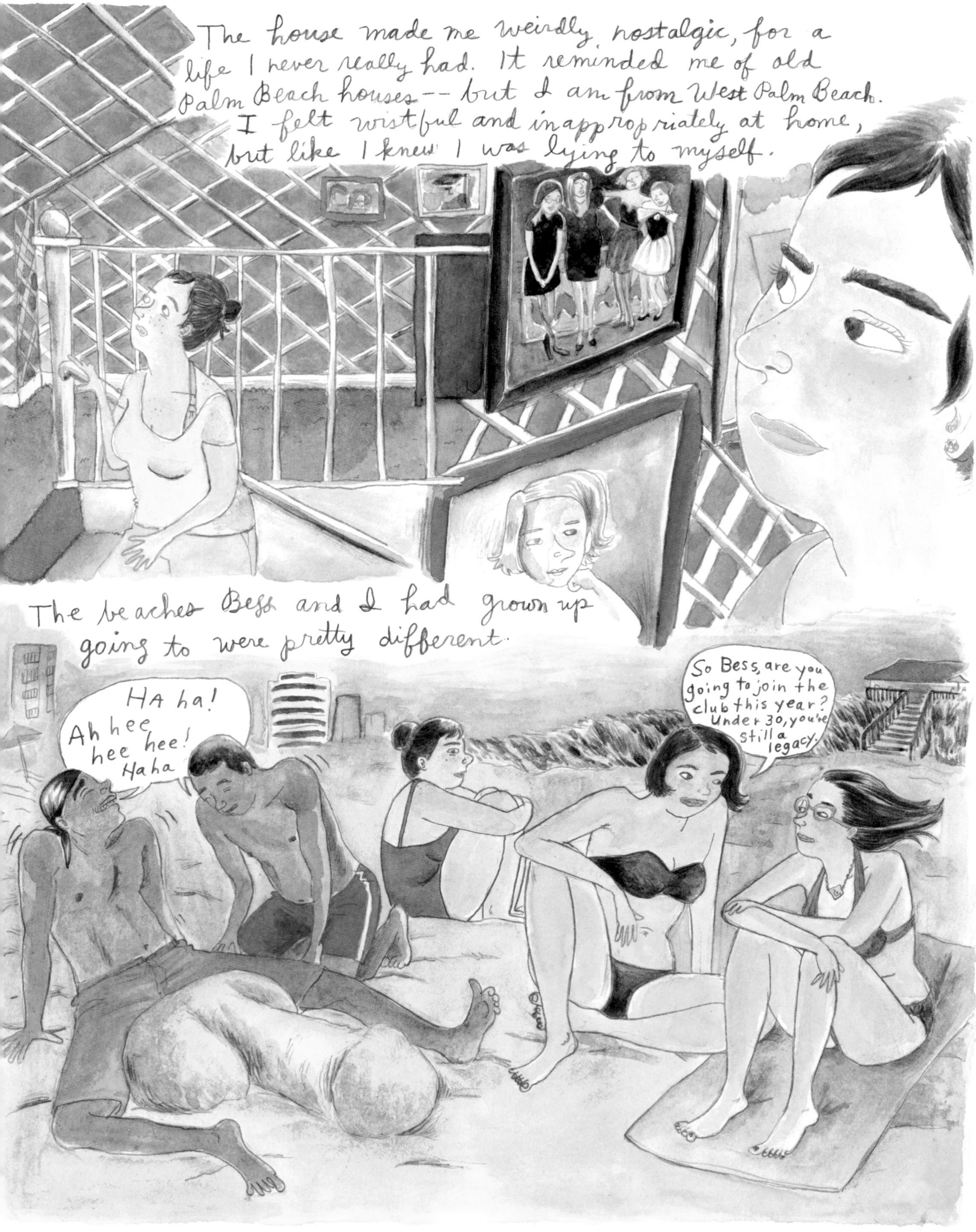
The house made me weirdly nostalgic, for a life I never really had. It reminded me of old Palm Beach houses -- but I am from West Palm Beach. I felt wistful and inappropriately at home, but like I knew I was lying to myself.
The beaches Bess and I had grown up going to were pretty different.
HA ha! Ah hee hee hee! Haha
So Bess, are you going to join the club this year? Under 30, you're still a legacy.

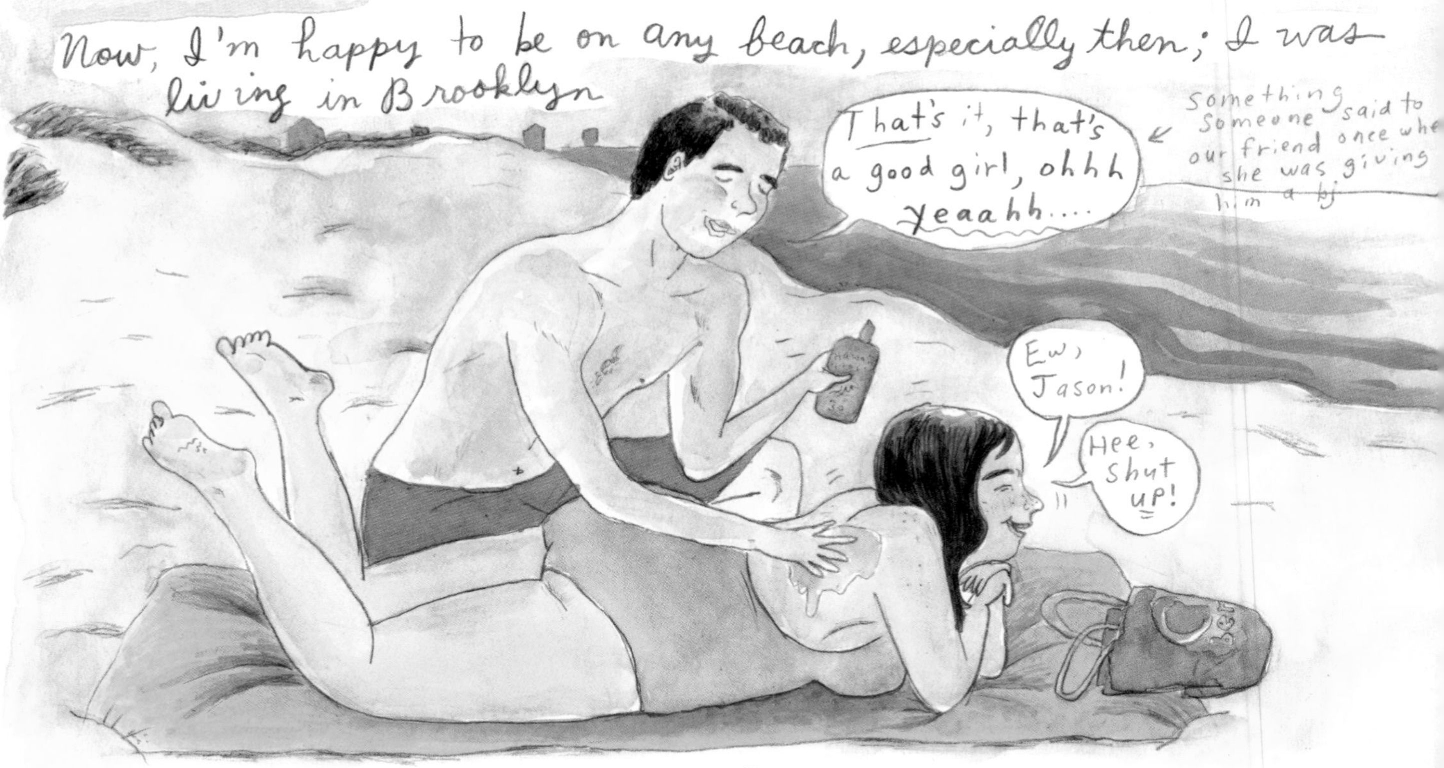
Now, I'm happy to be on any beach, especially then; I was living in Brooklyn
That's it, that's a good girl, ohhh yeaahh....
something someone said to our friend once whe she was giving him a bj
Ew, Jason!
Hee, shut up!

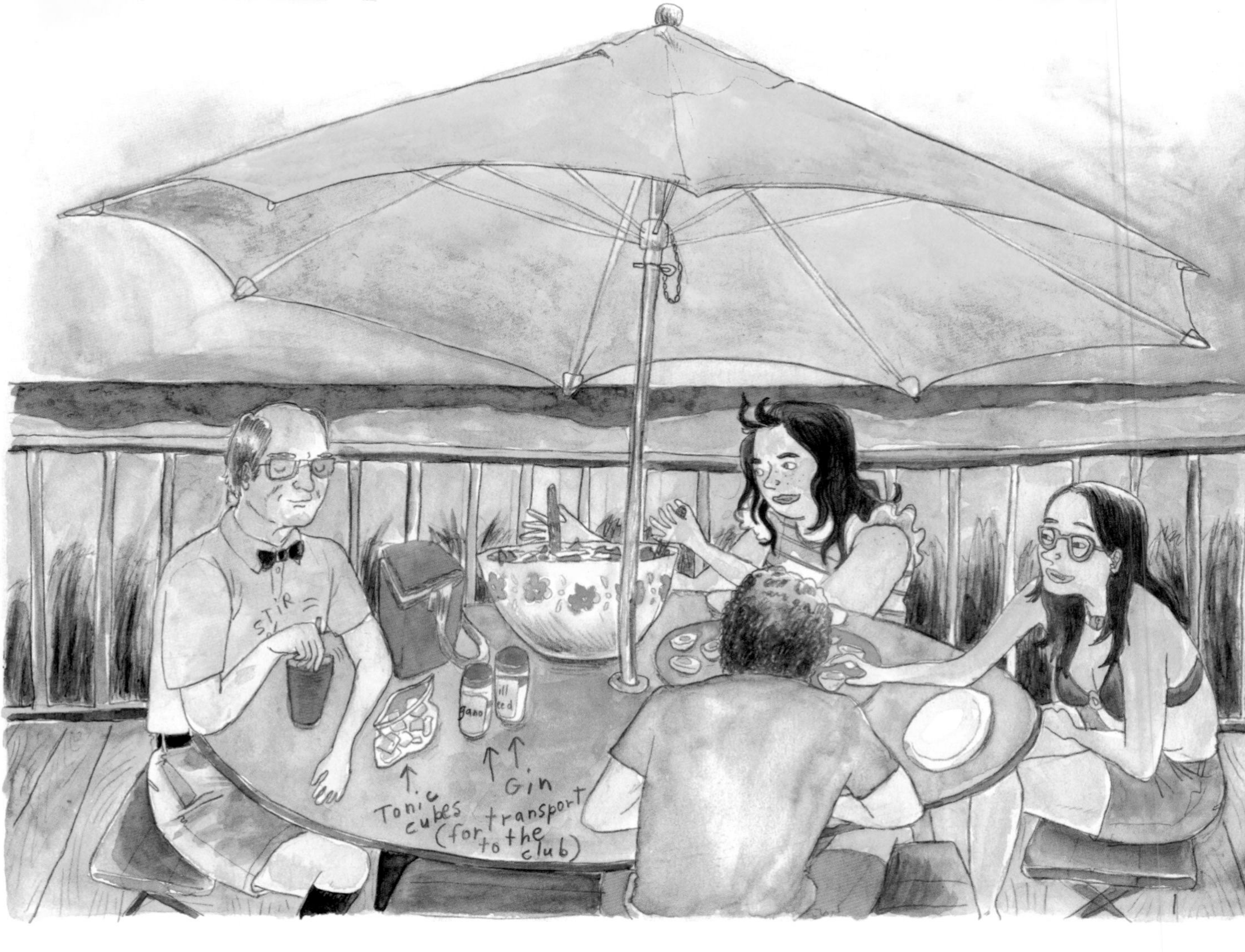
STIR
Tonic cubes
Gin transport (for to the club)

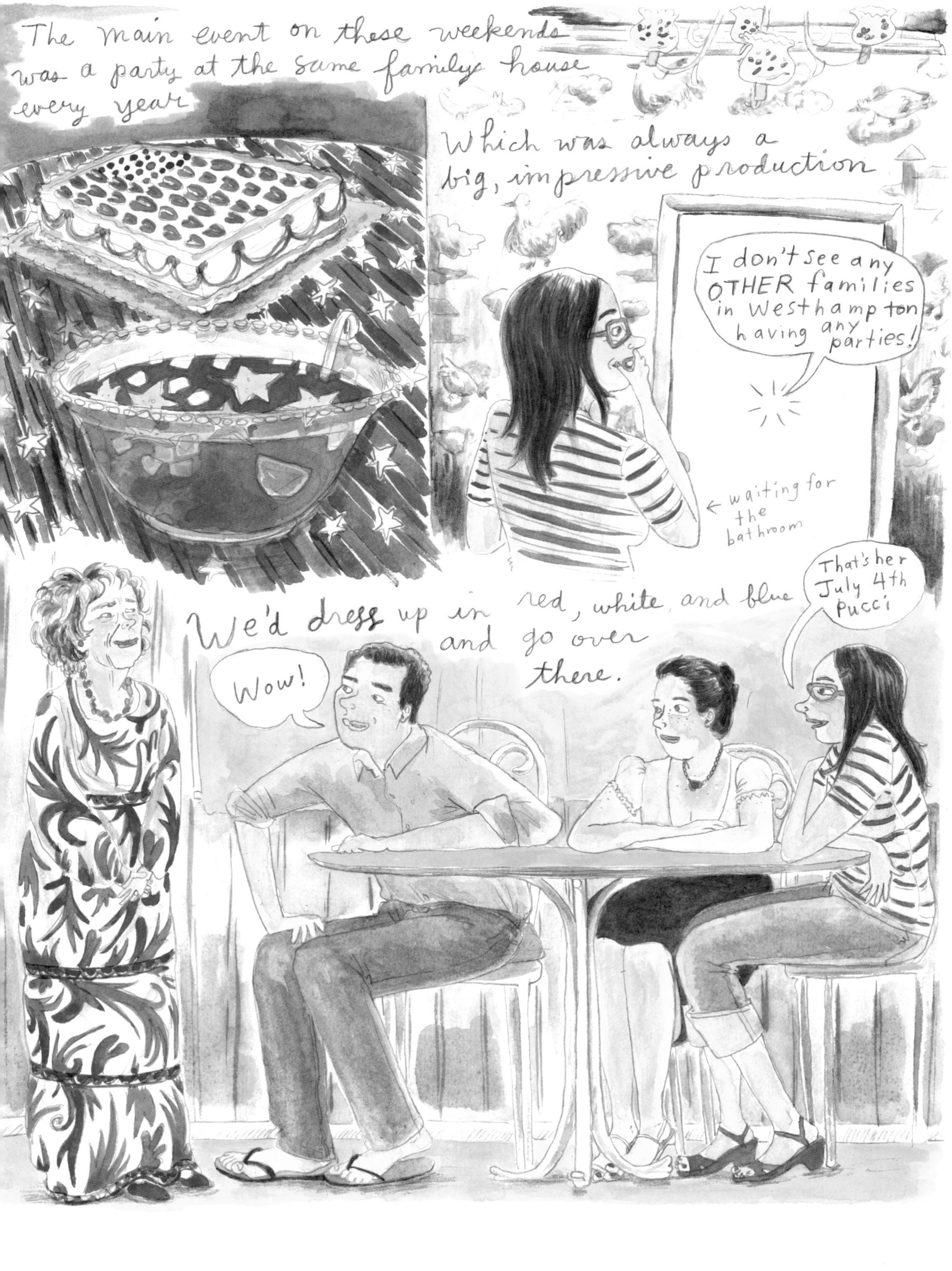
The main event on these weekends was a party at the same family's house every year
Which was always a big, impressive production
I don't see any OTHER families in Westhampton having any parties!
← waiting for the bathroom
We'd dress up in red, white, and blue and go over there.
Wow!
That's her July 4th Pucci

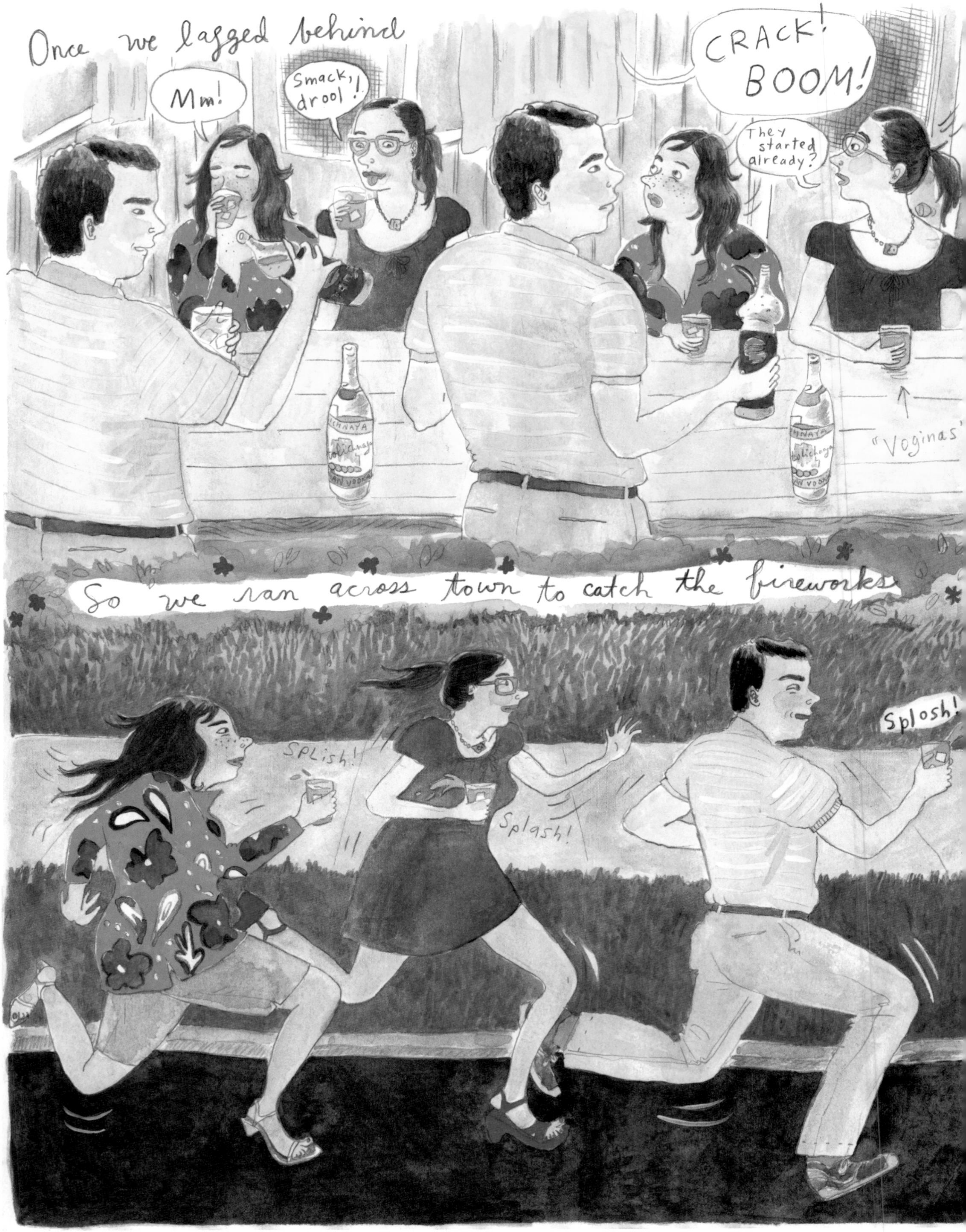

Once we lagged behind
Mm!
Smack, drool!
CRACK! BOOM!
They started already?
"Voginas"
So we ran across town to catch the fireworks
SPLish!
Splash!
Splosh!

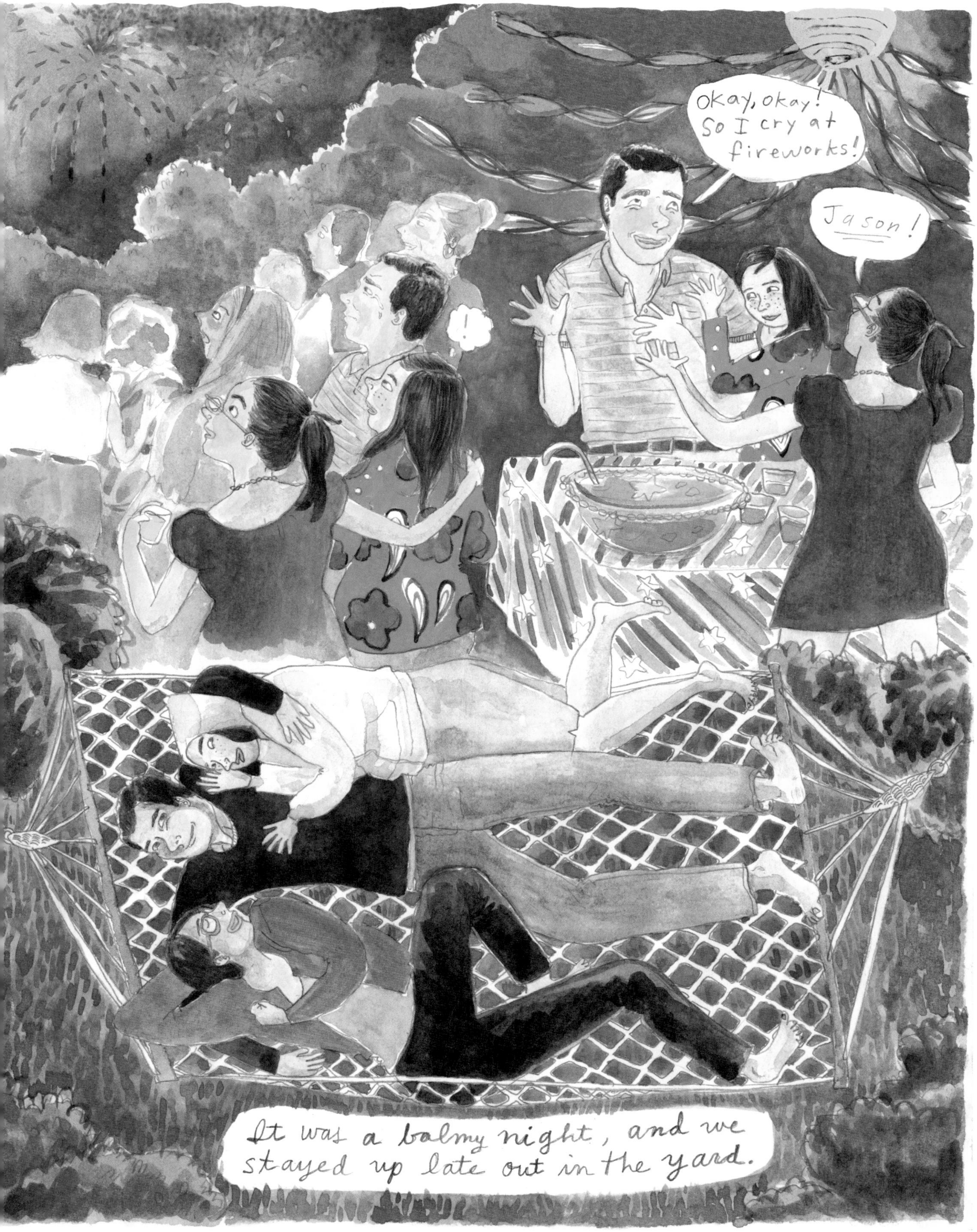
Okay, okay! So I cry at fireworks!
Jason!
!
It was a balmy night, and we stayed up late out in the yard.

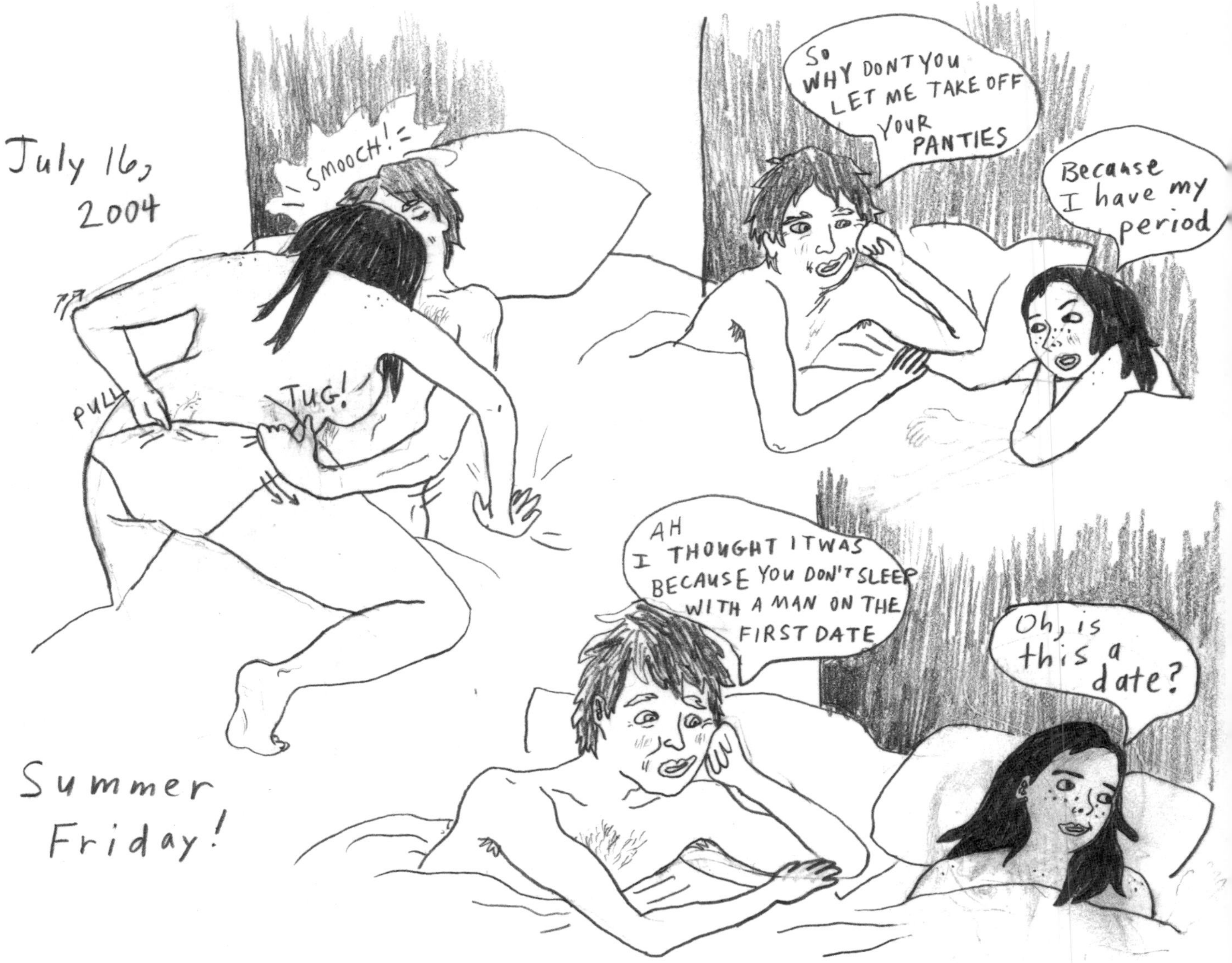
July 16, 2004
SMOOCH!
PULL
TUG!
Summer Friday!
SO WHY DONT YOU LET ME TAKE OFF YOUR PANTIES
Because I have my period
AH I THOUGHT IT WAS BECAUSE YOU DON'T SLEEP WITH A MAN ON THE FIRST DATE
Oh, is this a date?

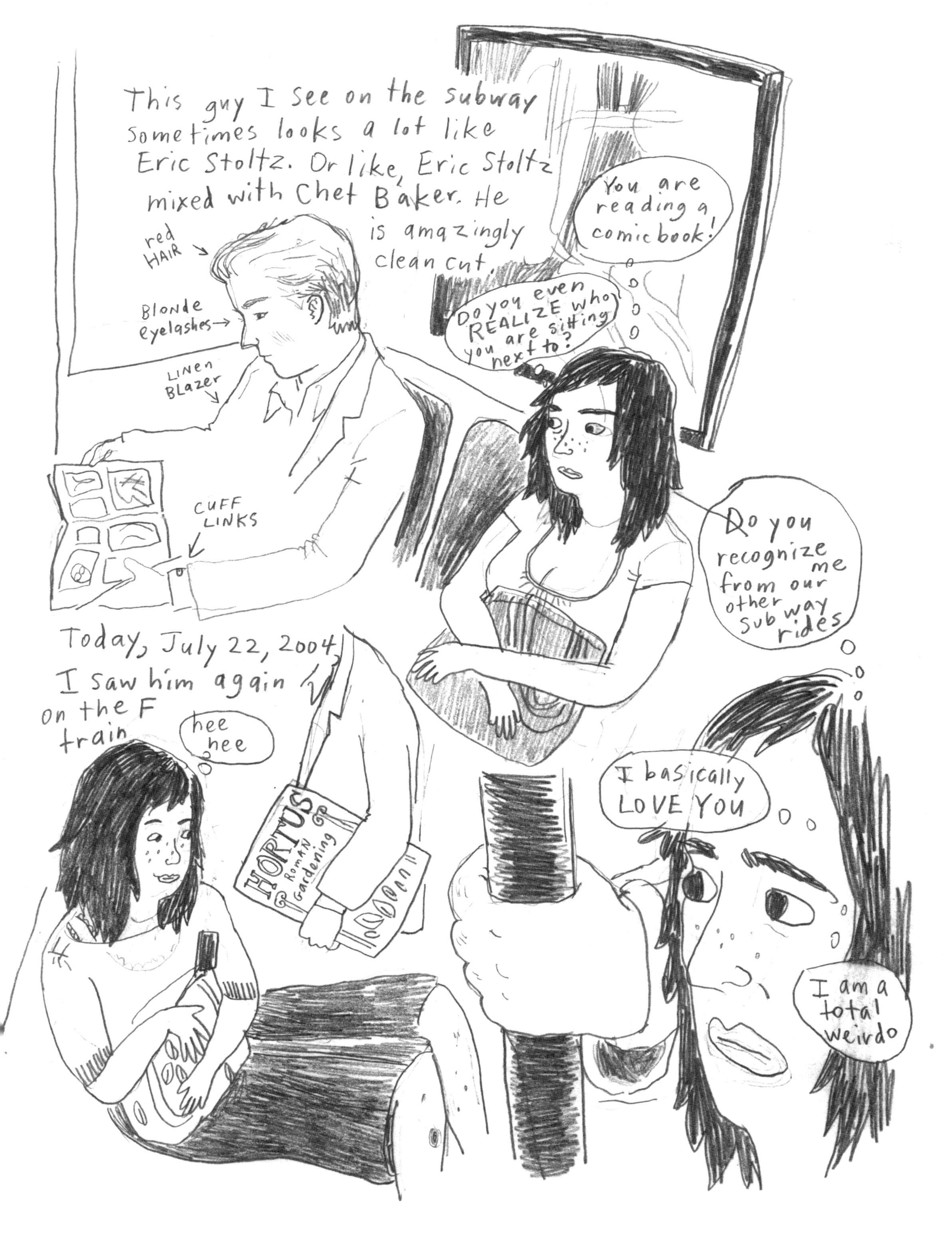
This guy I see on the subway sometimes looks a lot like Eric Stoltz. Or like, Eric Stoltz mixed with Chet Baker. He is amazingly clean cut.
red HAIR
Blonde eyelashes
LINEN BLAZER
CUFF LINKS
You are reading a comic book!
Do you even REALIZE who you are sitting next to?
Do you recognize me from our other subway rides
Today, July 22, 2004, I saw him again on the F train
hee hee
HORTUS
ROMAN Gardening
I basically LOVE YOU
I am a total weirdo

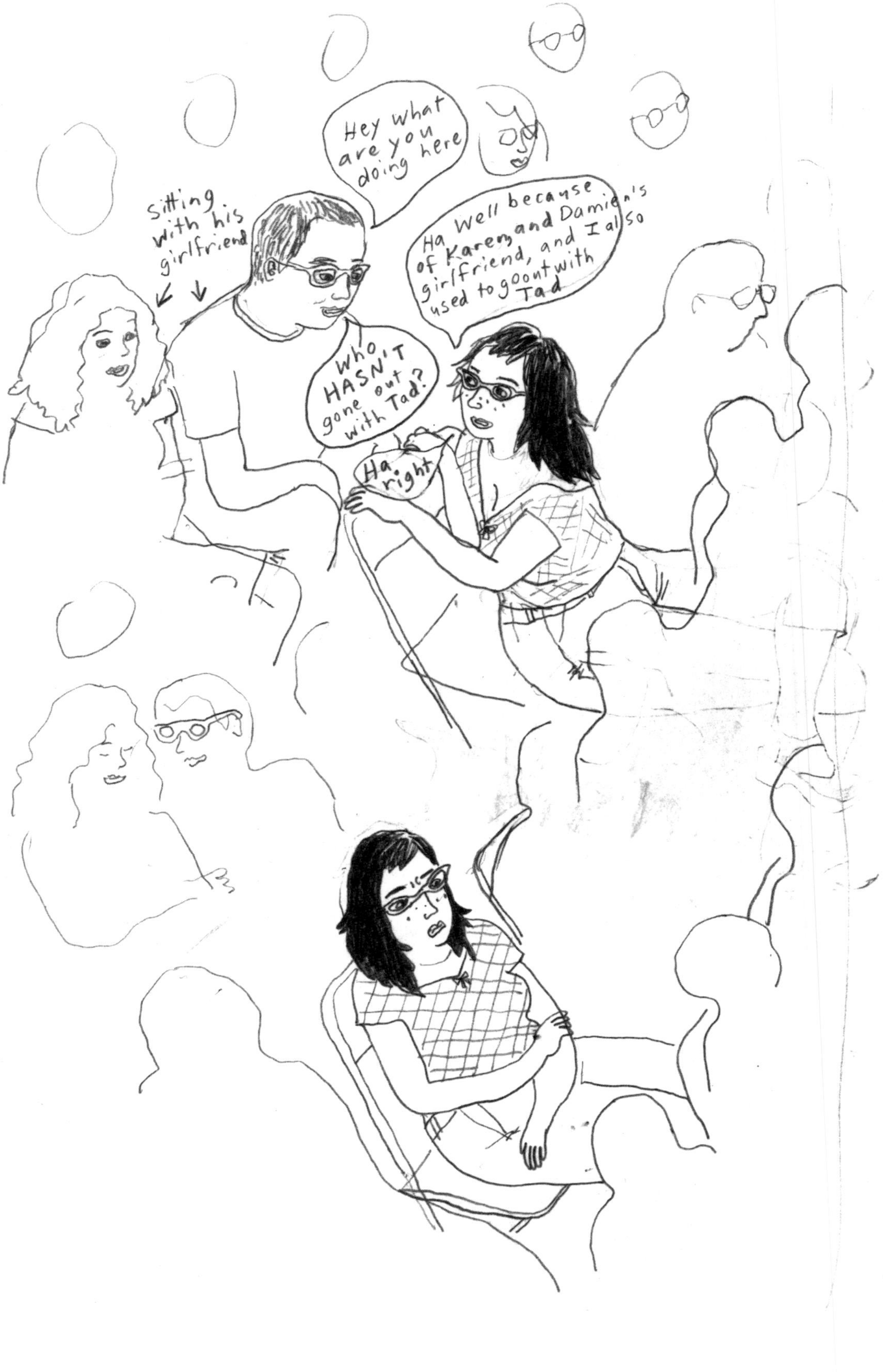
Hey what are you doing here
Sitting with his girlfriend
Ha well because of Karen and Damien's girlfriend, and I also used to go out with Tad
Who HASN'T gone out with Tad?
Ha right

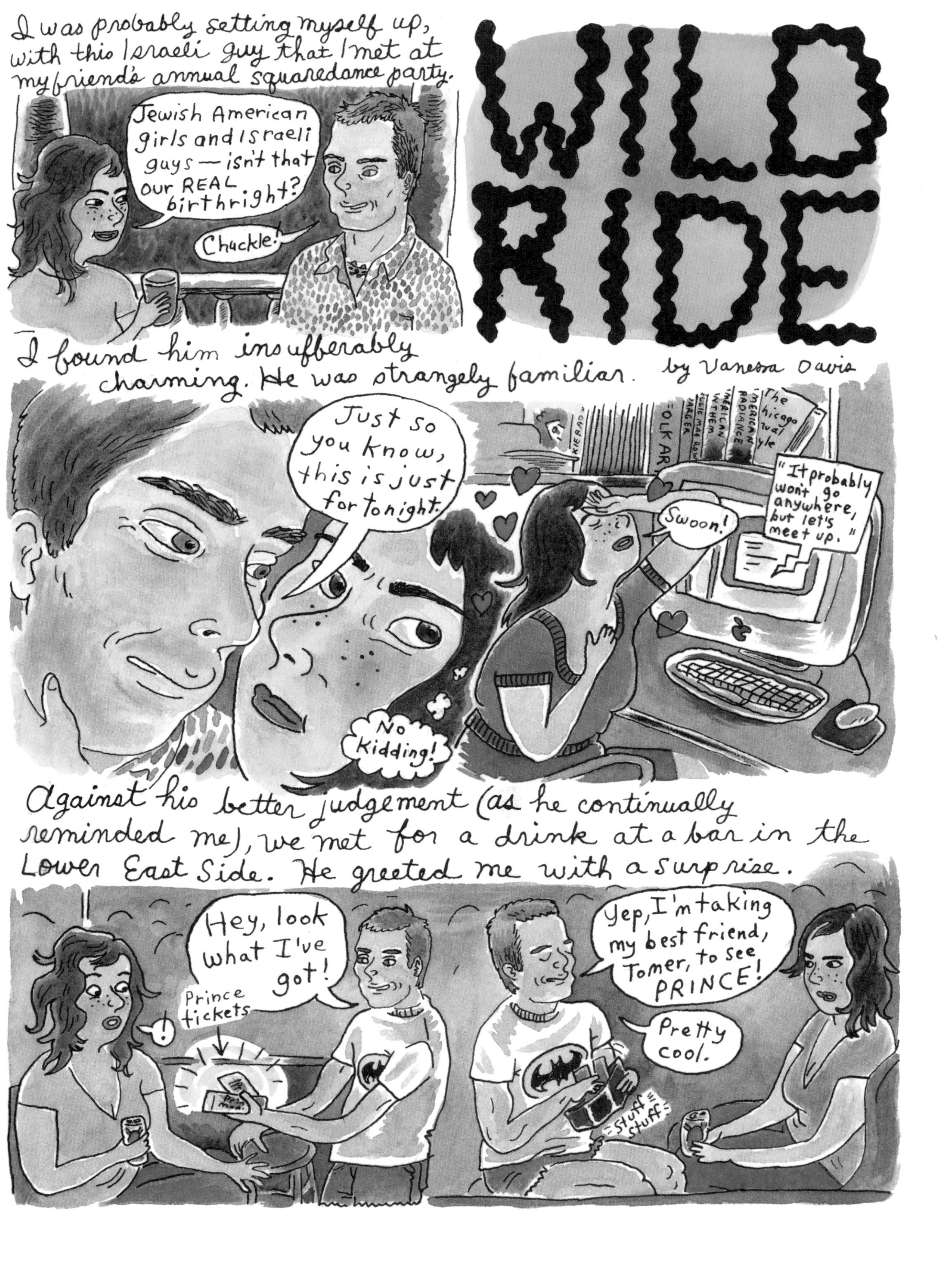

I was probably setting myself up, with this Israeli guy that I met at my friend's annual squaredance party.
WILD RIDE
Jewish American girls and Israeli guys — isn't that our REAL birthright?
Chuckle!
I found him insufferably charming. He was strangely familiar.
by Vanessa Davis
Just so you know, this is just for tonight.
No kidding!
Swoon!
"It probably won't go anywhere, but let's meet up."
Against his better judgement (as he continually reminded me), we met for a drink at a bar in the Lower East Side. He greeted me with a surprise.
Hey, look what I've got!
Prince tickets
!
Yep, I'm taking my best friend, Tomer, to see PRINCE!
Pretty cool.
Stuff Stuff

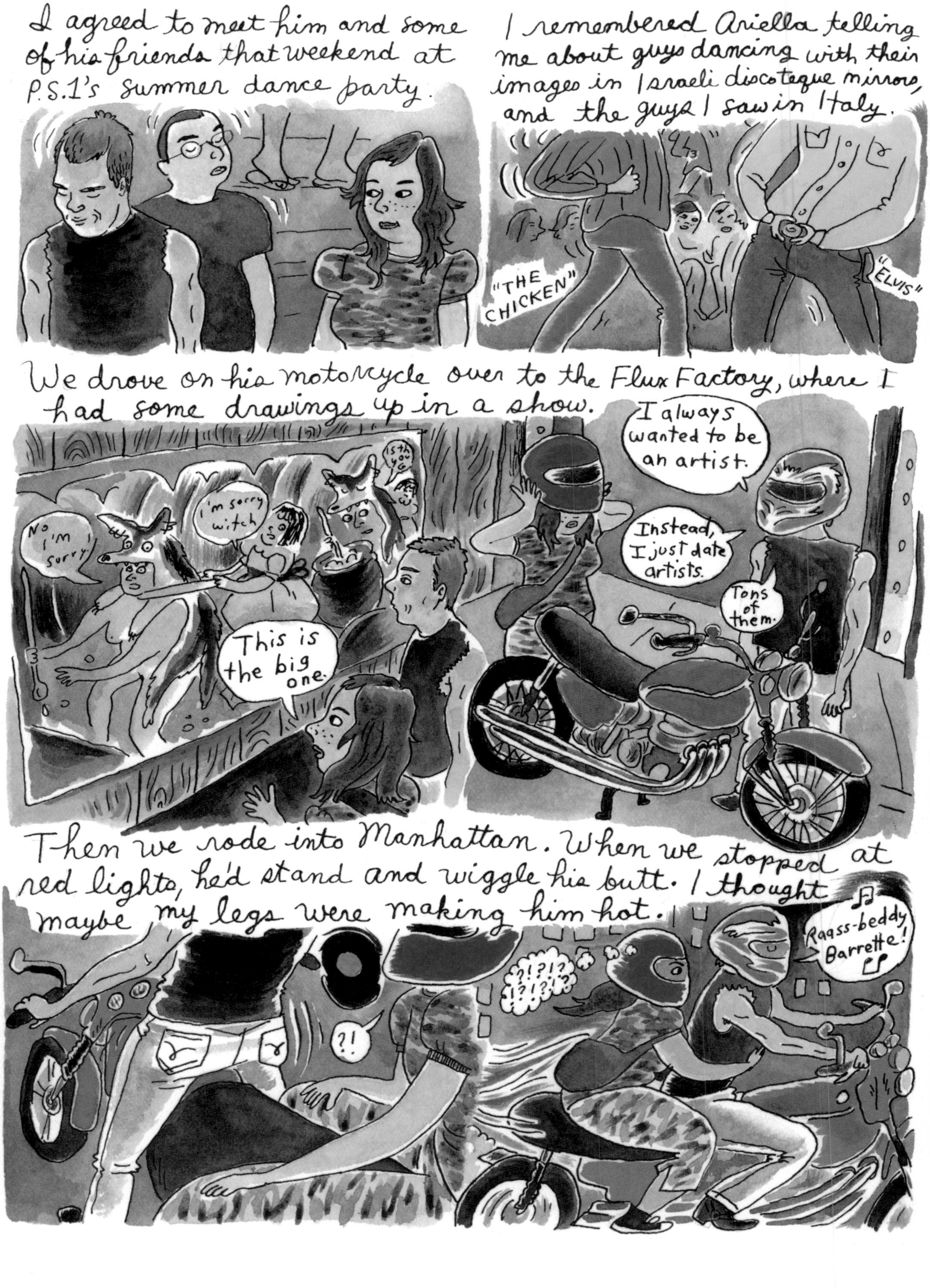
I agreed to meet him and some of his friends that weekend at P.S.1's summer dance party.
I remembered Ariella telling me about guys dancing with their images in Israeli discotheque mirrors, and the guys I saw in Italy.
"THE CHICKEN"
"ELVIS"
We drove on his motorcycle over to the Flux Factory, where I had some drawings up in a show.
No I'm sorry
I'm sorry witch
Is that you?
This is the big one.
I always wanted to be an artist.
Instead, I just date artists.
Tons of them.
Then we rode into Manhattan. When we stopped at red lights, he'd stand and wiggle his butt. I thought maybe my legs were making him hot.
?!
?!?!?
!?!?!?
Raass-beddy Barrette!

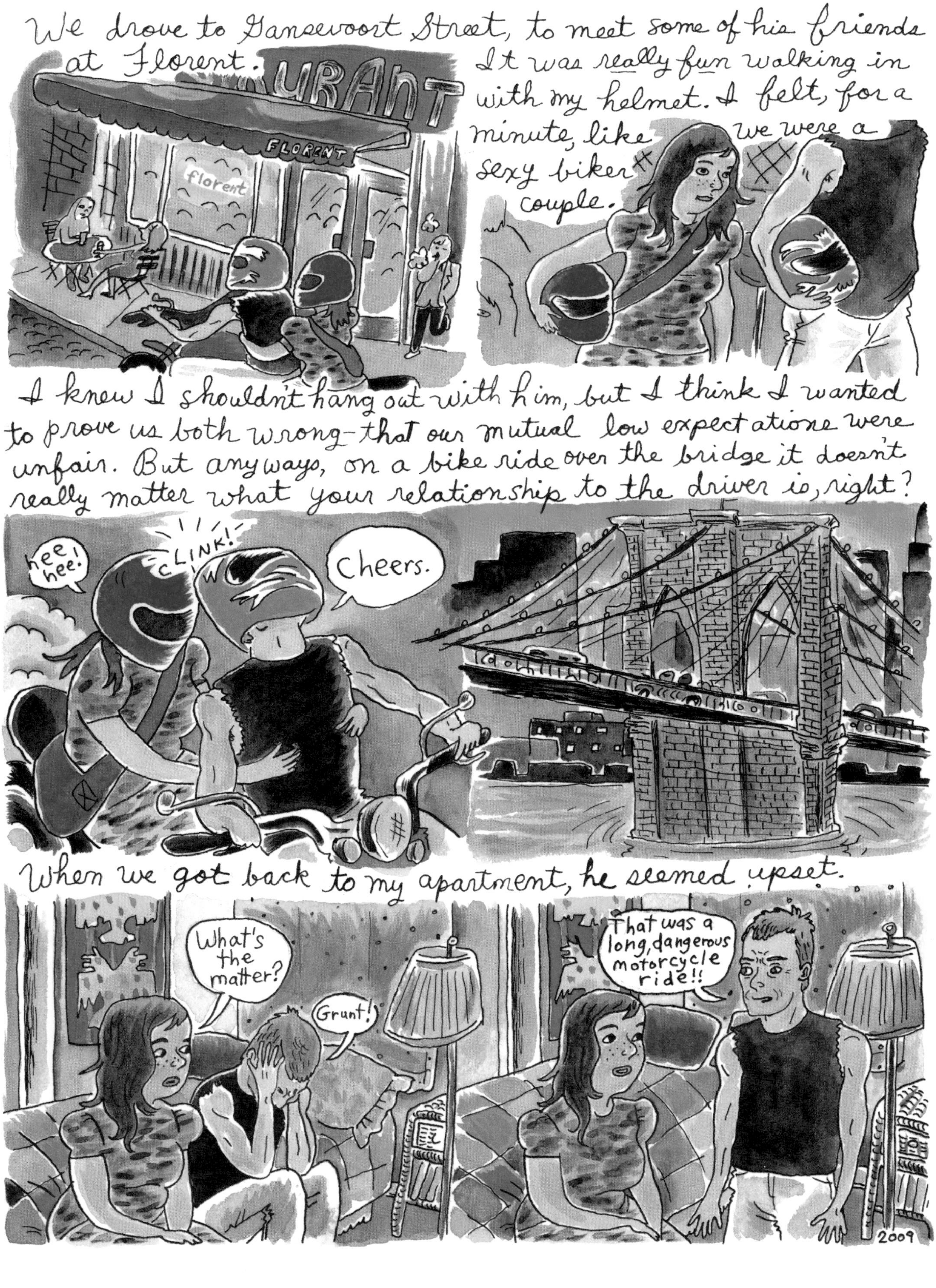
We drove to Gansevoort Street, to meet some of his friends at Florent.
URANT
FLORENT
florent
It was really fun walking in with my helmet. I felt, for a minute, like we were a sexy biker couple.
I knew I shouldn't hang out with him, but I think I wanted to prove us both wrong—that our mutual low expectations were unfair. But anyways, on a bike ride over the bridge it doesn't really matter what your relationship to the driver is, right?
hee! hee!
CLINK!
Cheers.
When we got back to my apartment, he seemed upset.
What's the matter?
Grunt!
That was a long, dangerous motorcycle ride!!
2009

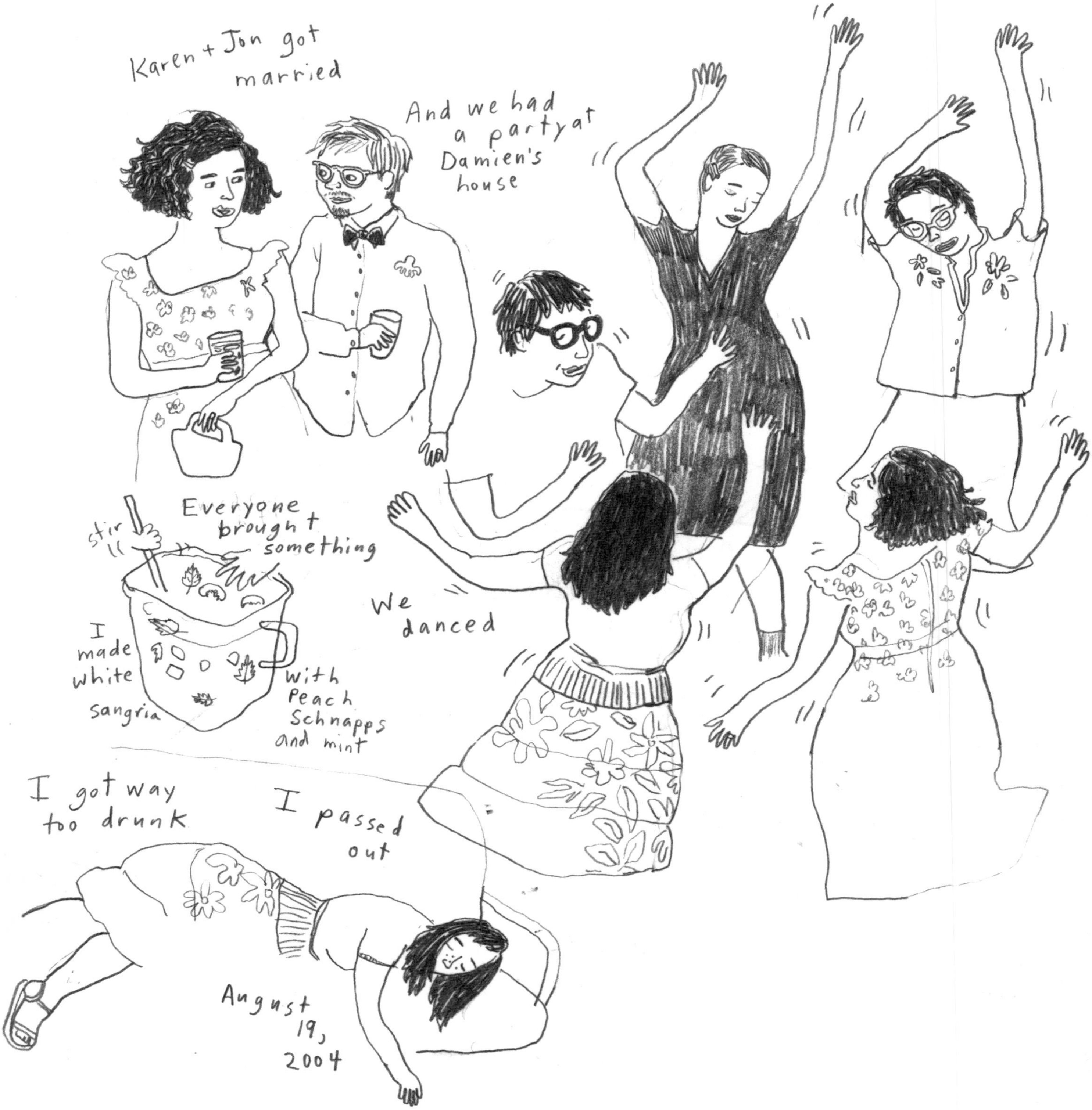
Karen + Jon got married
And we had a party at Damien's house
Everyone brought something
stir
I made white sangria
with Peach Schnapps and mint
We danced
I got way too drunk
I passed out
August 19, 2004

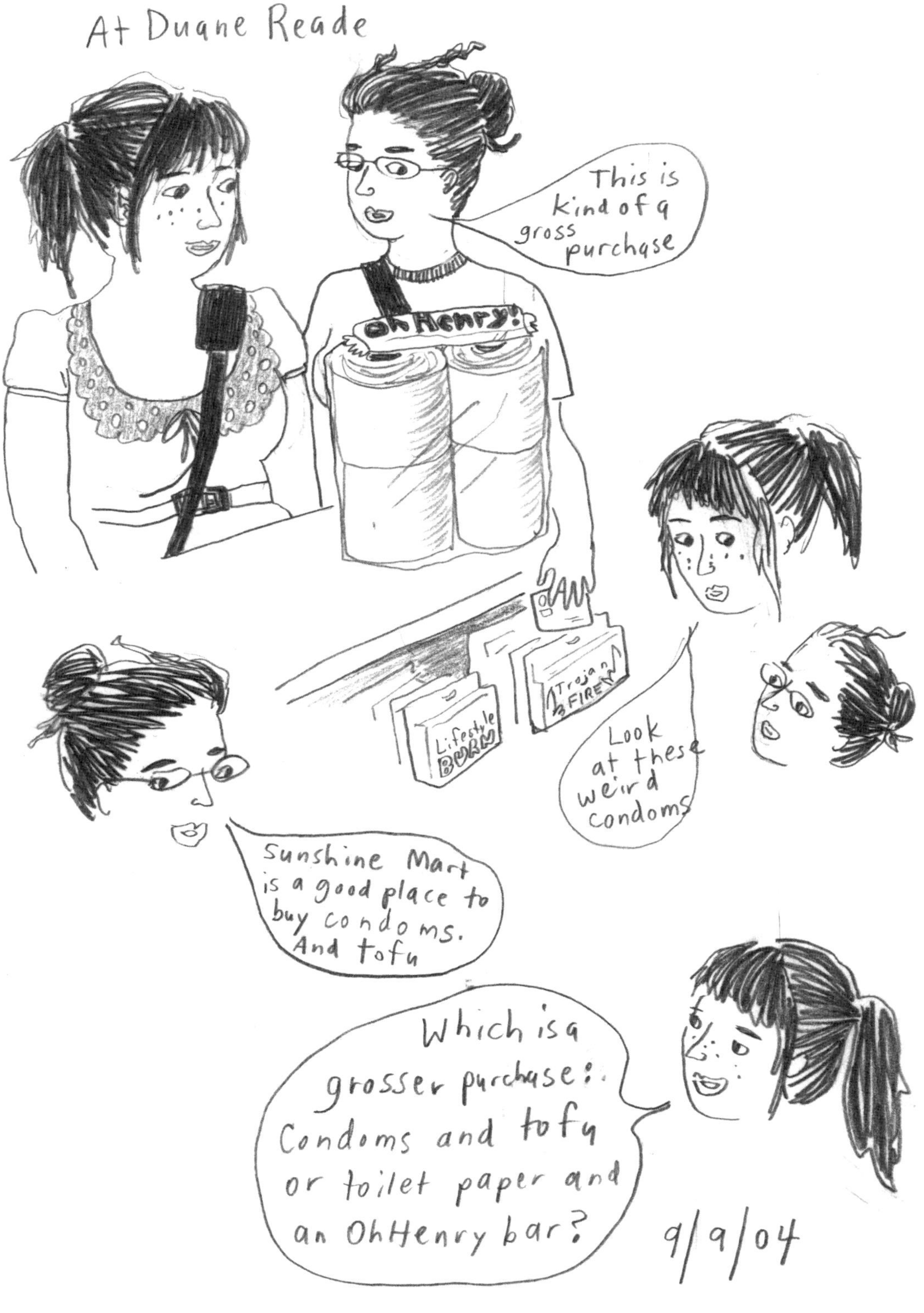
At Duane Reade
This is kind of a gross purchase
OhHenry!
Trojan FIRE
Lifestyle
Look at these weird condoms
Sunshine Mart is a good place to buy condoms. And tofu
Which is a grosser purchase: Condoms and tofu or toilet paper and an OhHenry bar?
9/9/04

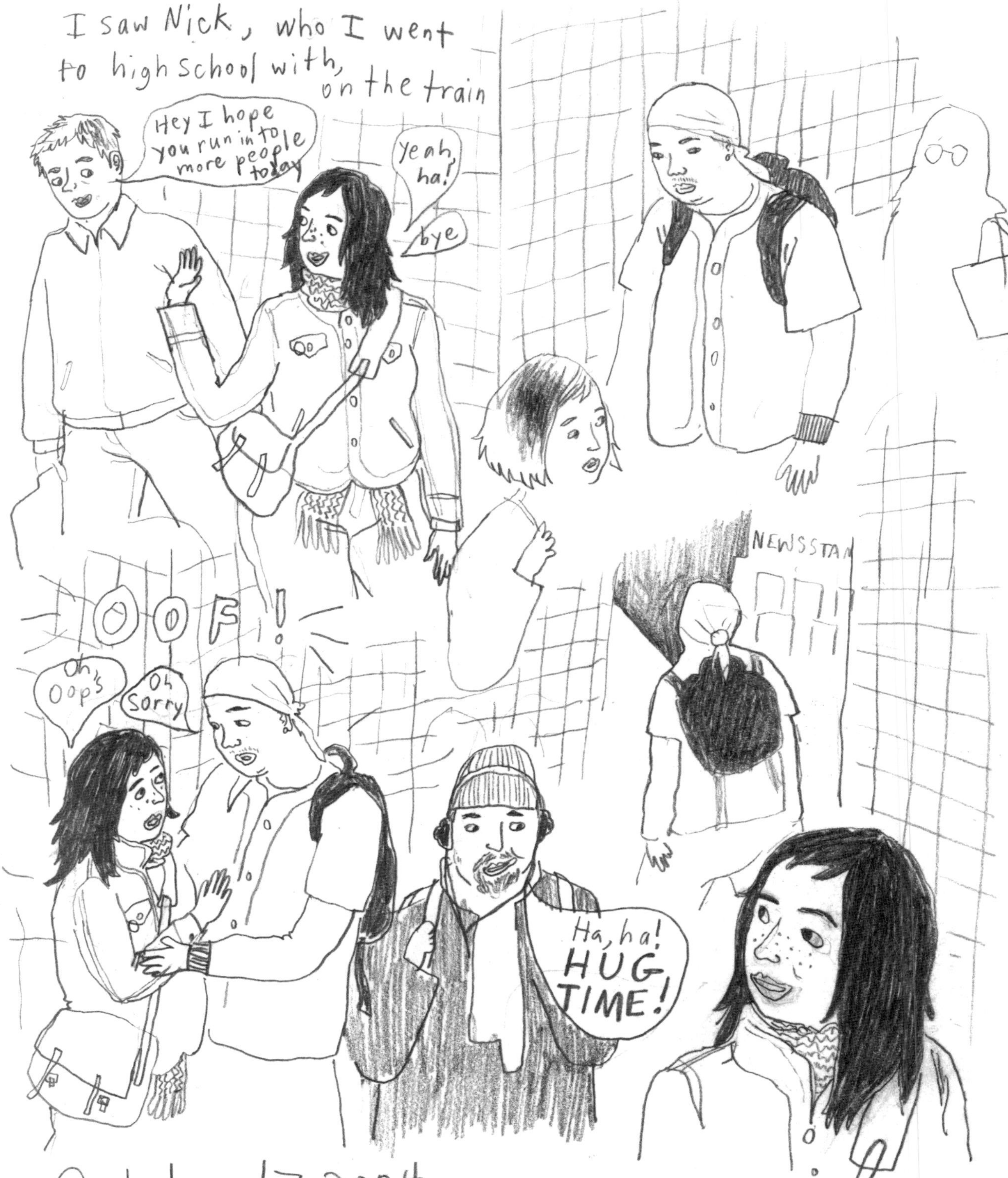

October 17, 2004

In the elevator:

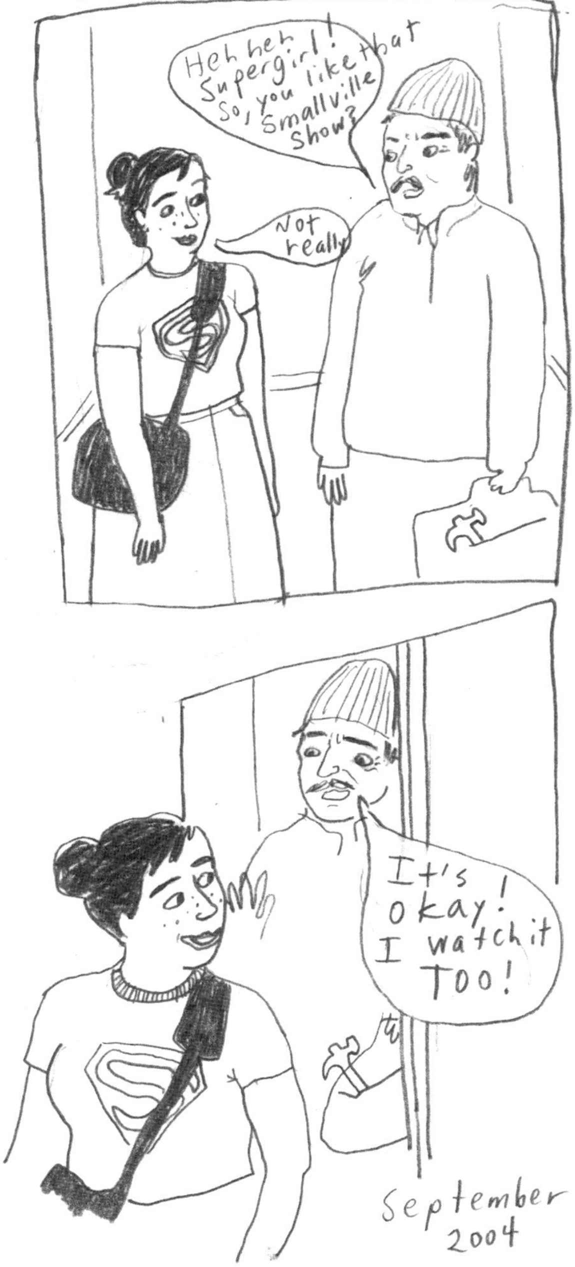
Heh heh! Supergirl! So, you like that Smallville Show?
Not really
It's okay! I watch it TOO!
September 2004

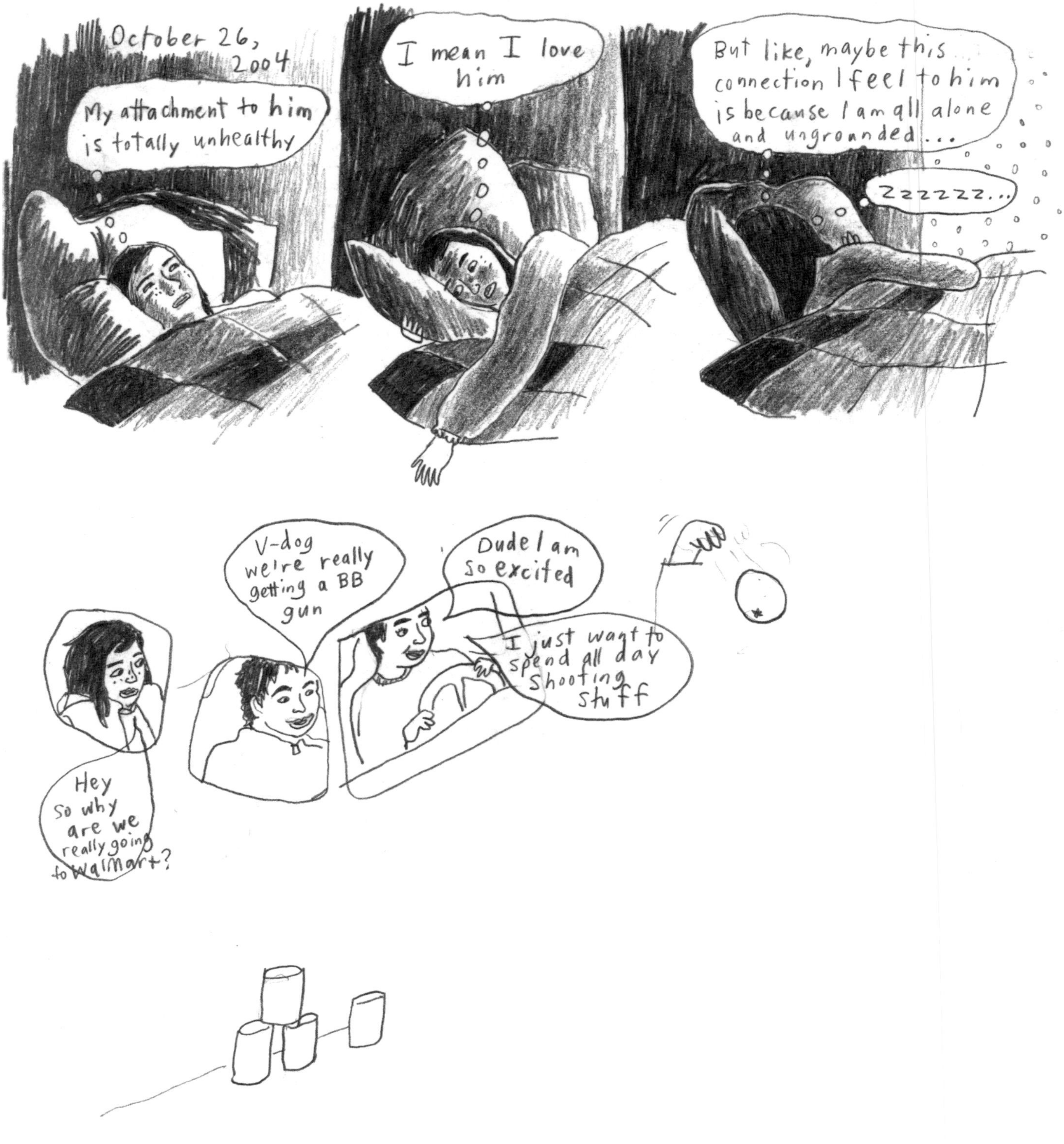
October 26, 2004
My attachment to him is totally unhealthy
I mean I love him
But like, maybe this connection I feel to him is because I am all alone and ungrounded...
Zzzzzz...
V-dog we're really getting a BB gun
Dude I am so excited
I just want to spend all day shooting stuff
Hey so why are we really going to Walmart?

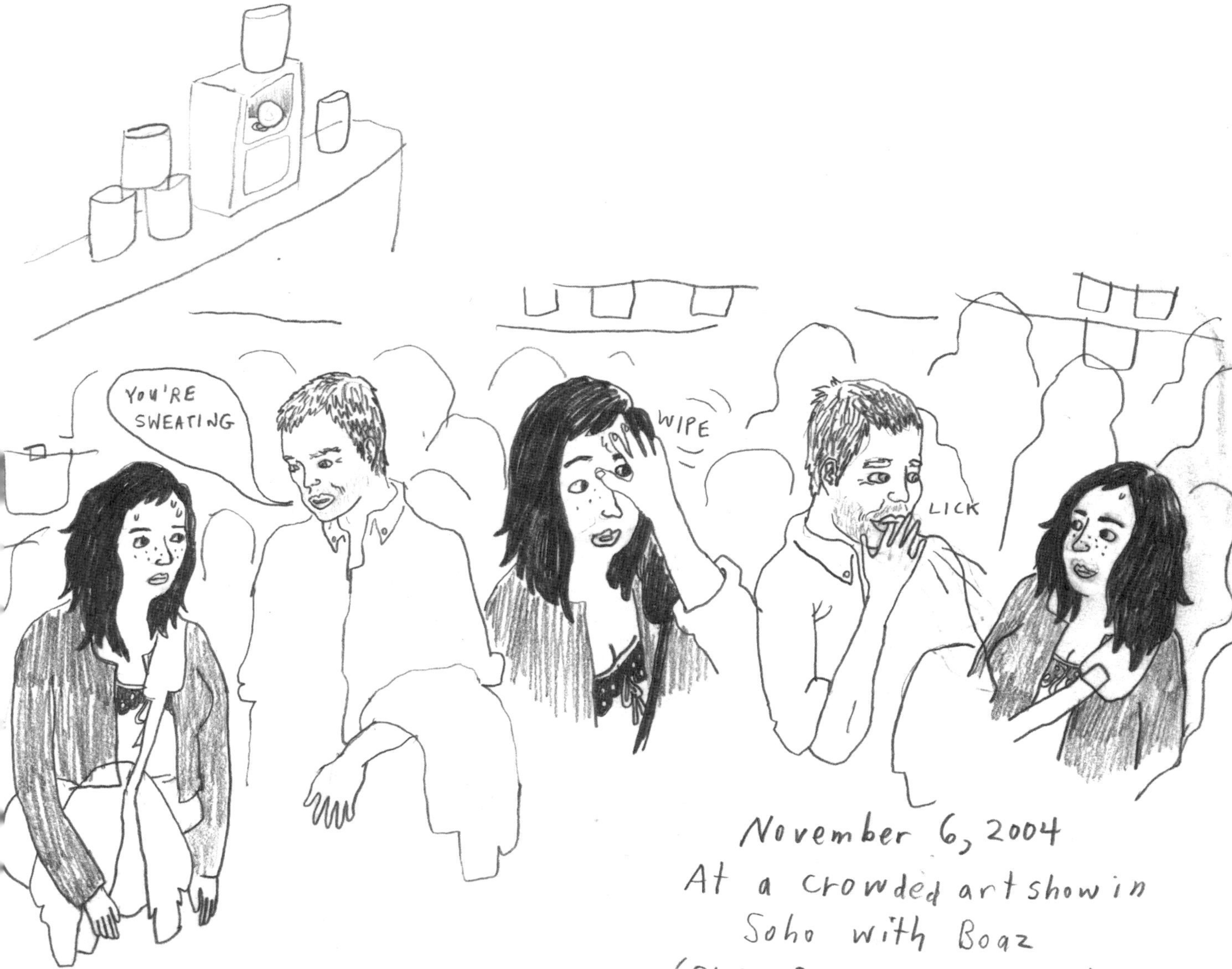
YOU'RE SWEATING
WIPE
LICK

November 6, 2004
At a crowded art show in
Soho with Boaz
(Claire Danes was there too)
(Night of 10,000 drawings at Art Space)

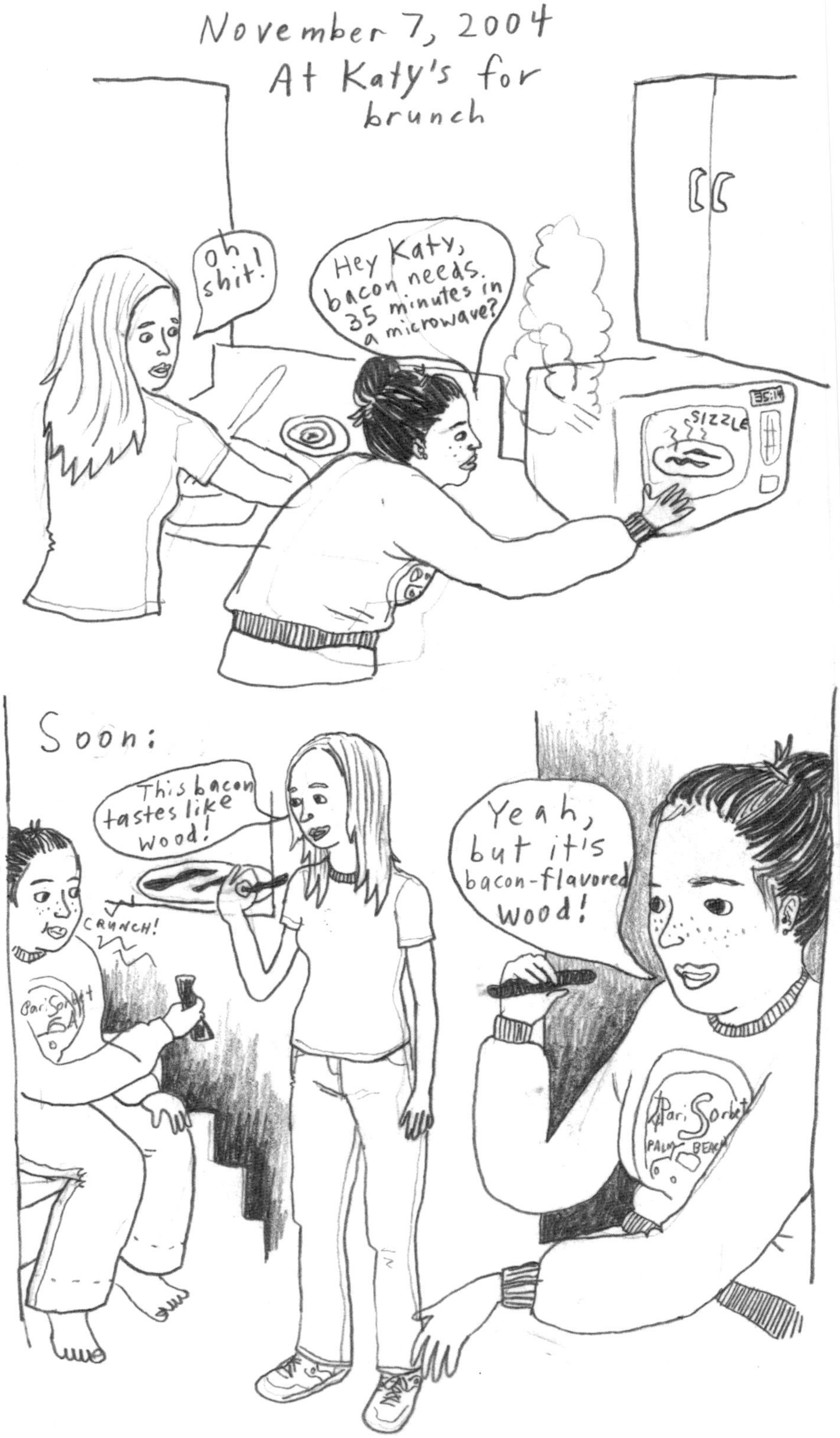
November 7, 2004
At Katy's for brunch
oh shit!
Hey Katy, bacon needs 35 minutes in a microwave?
SIZZLE
Soon:
This bacon tastes like wood!
CRUNCH!
Yeah, but it's bacon-flavored wood!

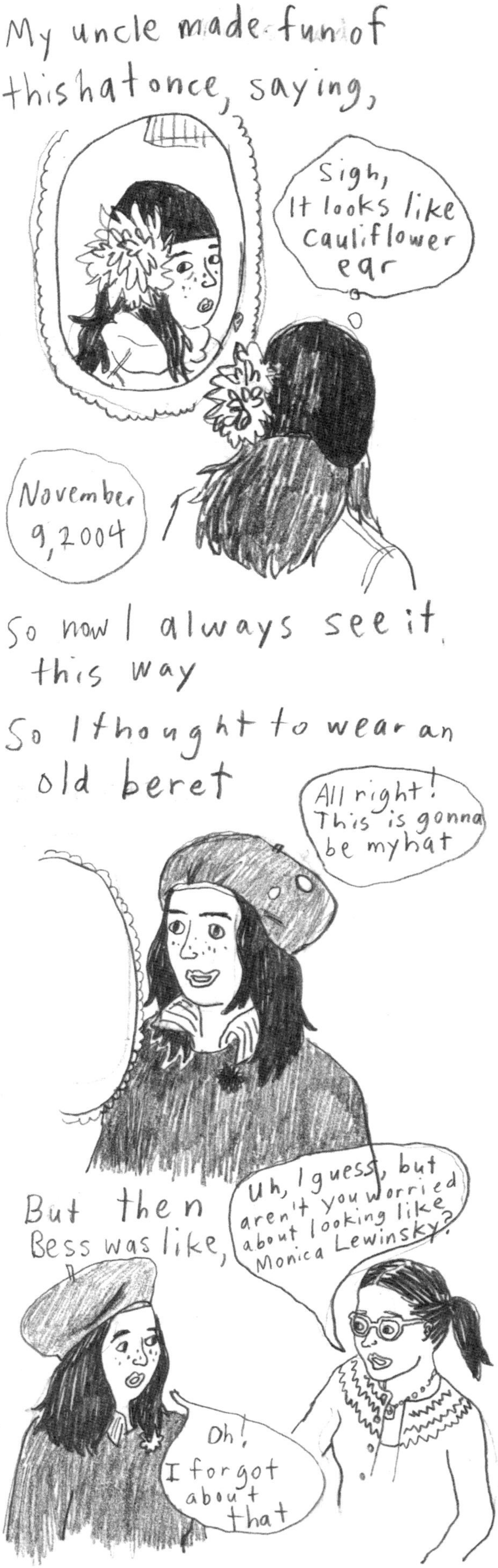
My uncle made fun of this hat once, saying,
Sigh, It looks like cauliflower ear
November 9, 2004
So now I always see it this way
So I thought to wear an old beret
All right! This is gonna be my hat
But then Bess was like,
Uh, I guess, but aren't you worried about looking like Monica Lewinsky?
Oh! I forgot about that

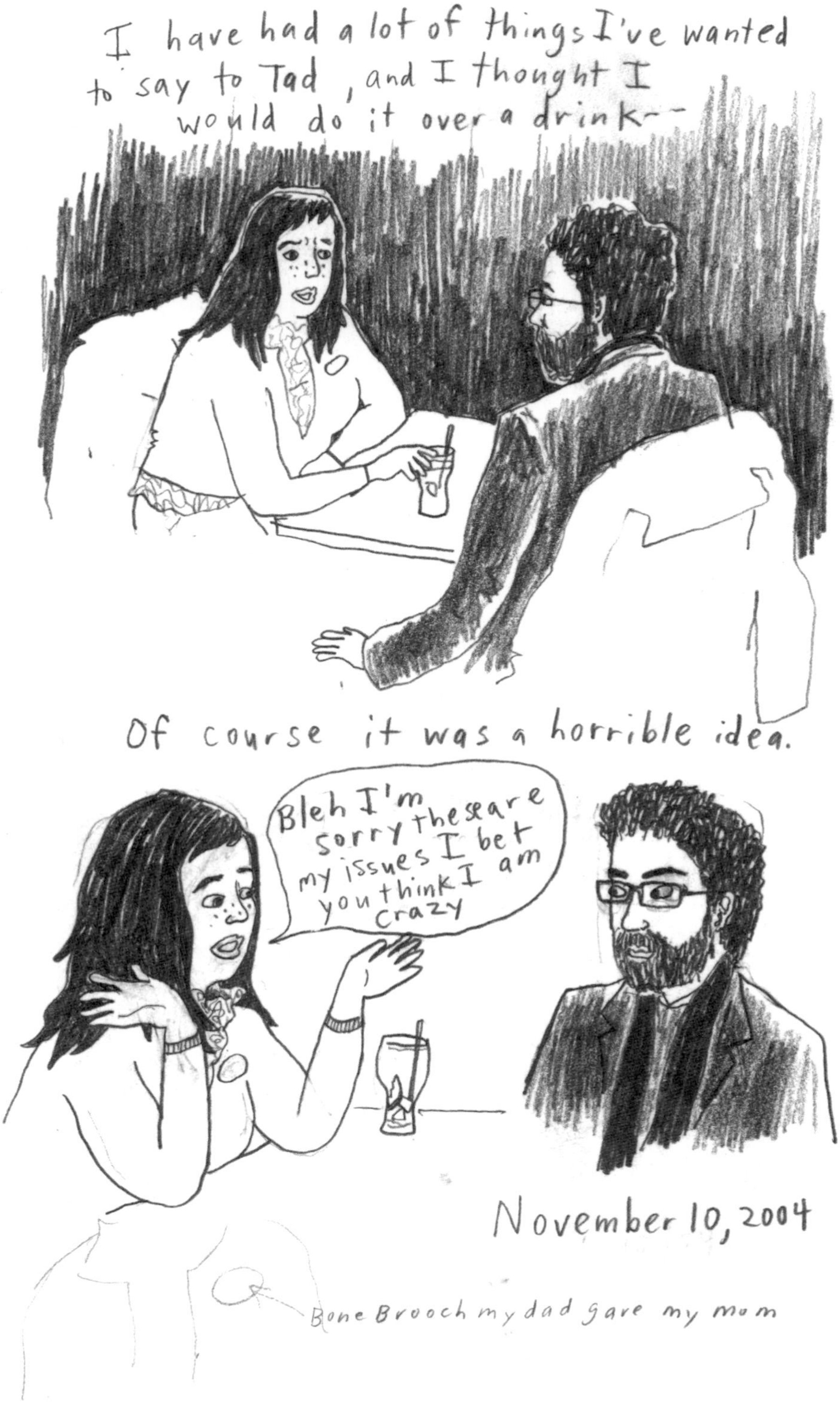
I have had a lot of things I've wanted to say to Tad, and I thought I would do it over a drink--
Of course it was a horrible idea.
Bleh I'm sorry these are my issues I bet you think I am crazy
November 10, 2004
Bone Brooch my dad gave my mom

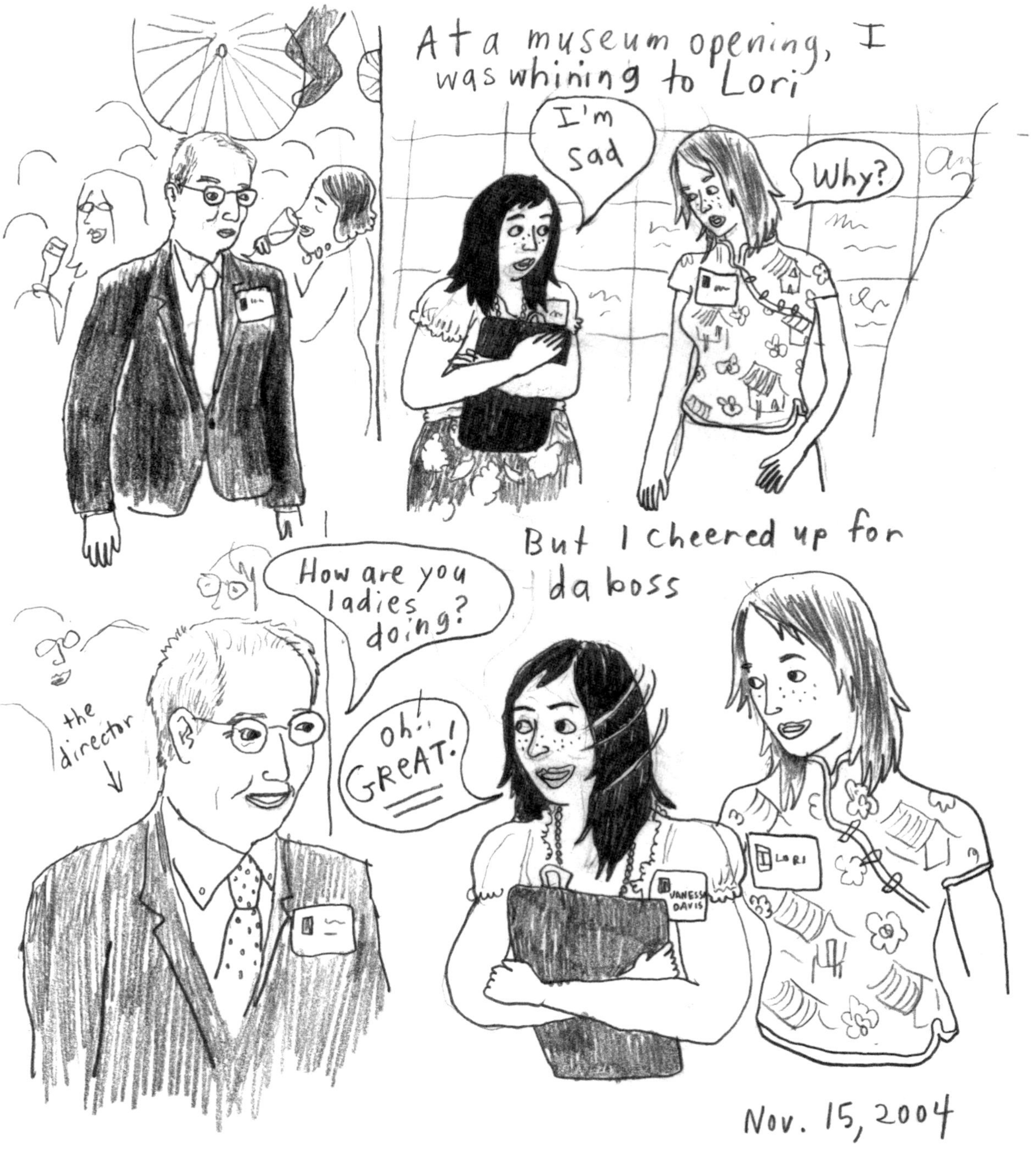

At a museum opening, I was whining to Lori
I'm sad
Why?
But I cheered up for da boss
How are you ladies doing?
the director
Oh! GREAT!
VANESSA DAVIS
LORI
Nov. 15, 2004

My mouth has really been hurting me lately, like, it hurts to open it. I think it's my wisdom teeth
MANGIA
I know it's pathetic and whiny, but it is making me FREAK OUT
oh Vanessa
sniff
I can't open my mouth wide enough to swallow this soggy bread
November 16, 2004

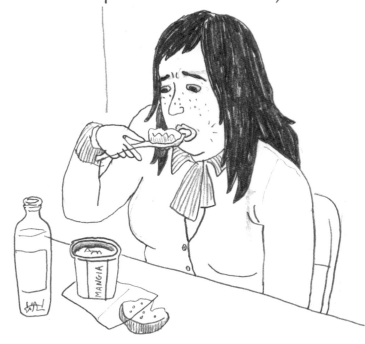

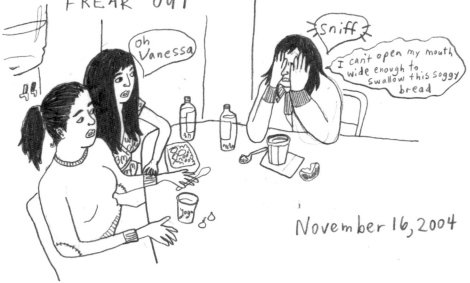

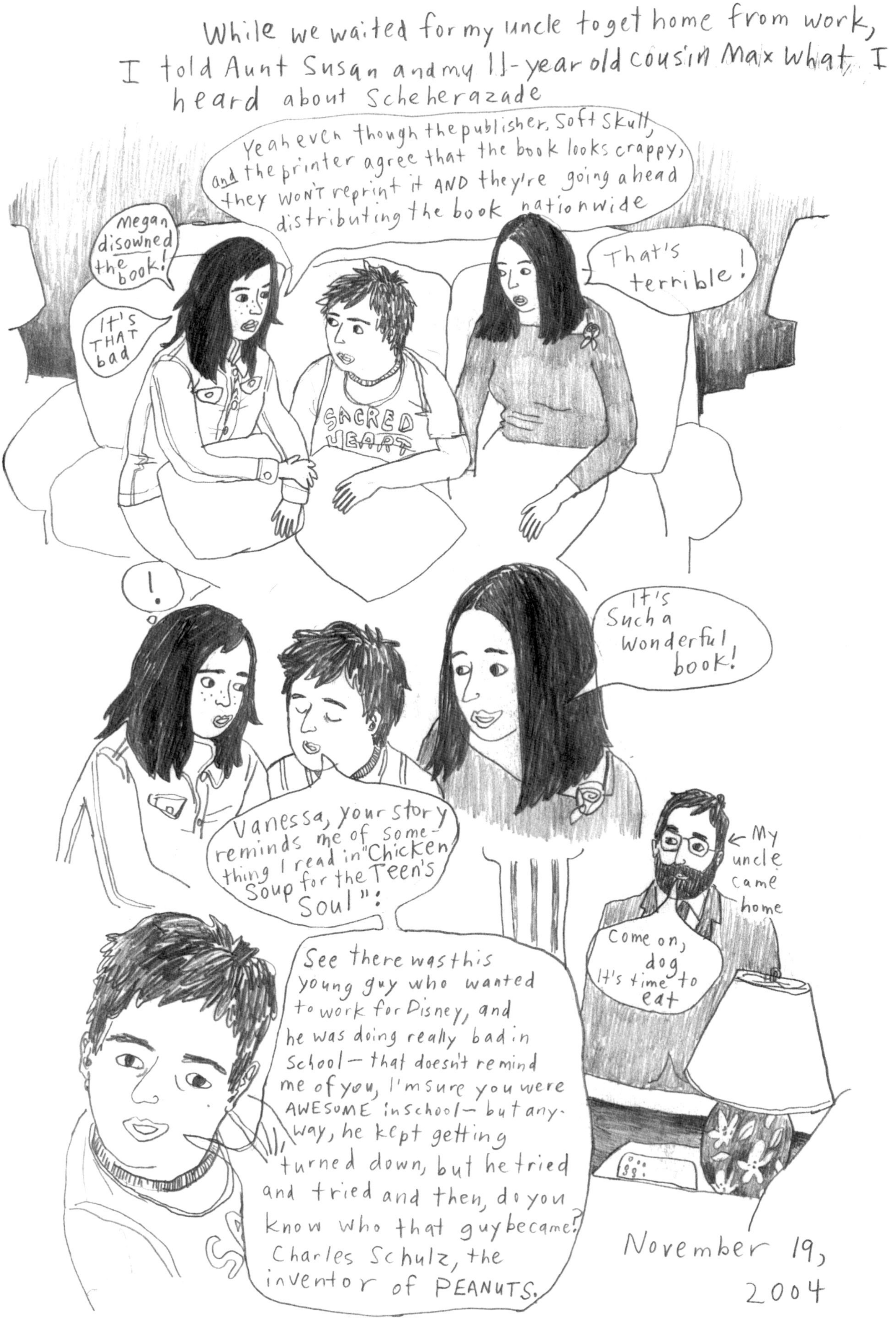
While we waited for my uncle to get home from work, I told Aunt Susan and my 11-year old cousin Max what I heard about Scheherazade
Yeah even though the publisher, Soft Skull, and the printer agree that the book looks crappy, they won't reprint it AND they're going ahead distributing the book nationwide
Megan disowned the book!
It's THAT bad
That's terrible!
SACRED HEART
!
It's such a wonderful book!
Vanessa, your story reminds me of something I read in "Chicken Soup for the Teen's Soul":
See there was this young guy who wanted to work for Disney, and he was doing really bad in school — that doesn't remind me of you, I'm sure you were AWESOME in school — but anyway, he kept getting turned down, but he tried and tried and then, do you know who that guy became? Charles Schulz, the inventor of PEANUTS.
← My uncle came home
Come on, dog It's time to eat
November 19, 2004

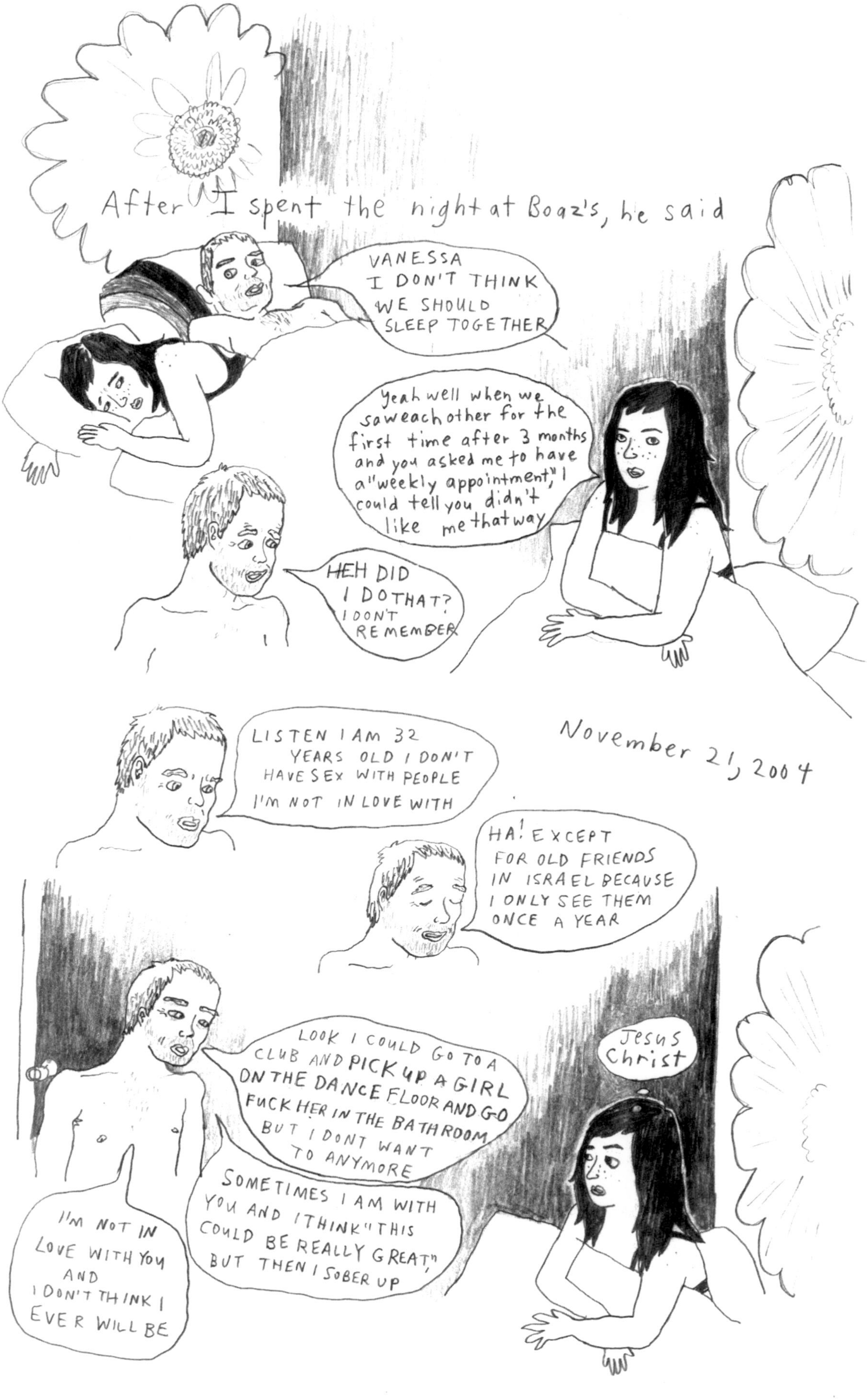
After I spent the night at Boaz's, he said
VANESSA I DON'T THINK WE SHOULD SLEEP TOGETHER
Yeah well when we saw each other for the first time after 3 months and you asked me to have a "weekly appointment," I could tell you didn't like me that way
HEH DID I DO THAT? I DON'T REMEMBER
November 21, 2004
LISTEN I AM 32 YEARS OLD I DON'T HAVE SEX WITH PEOPLE I'M NOT IN LOVE WITH
HA! EXCEPT FOR OLD FRIENDS IN ISRAEL BECAUSE I ONLY SEE THEM ONCE A YEAR
LOOK I COULD GO TO A CLUB AND PICK UP A GIRL ON THE DANCE FLOOR AND GO FUCK HER IN THE BATHROOM BUT I DONT WANT TO ANYMORE
Jesus Christ
SOMETIMES I AM WITH YOU AND I THINK "THIS COULD BE REALLY GREAT," BUT THEN I SOBER UP
I'M NOT IN LOVE WITH YOU AND I DON'T THINK I EVER WILL BE

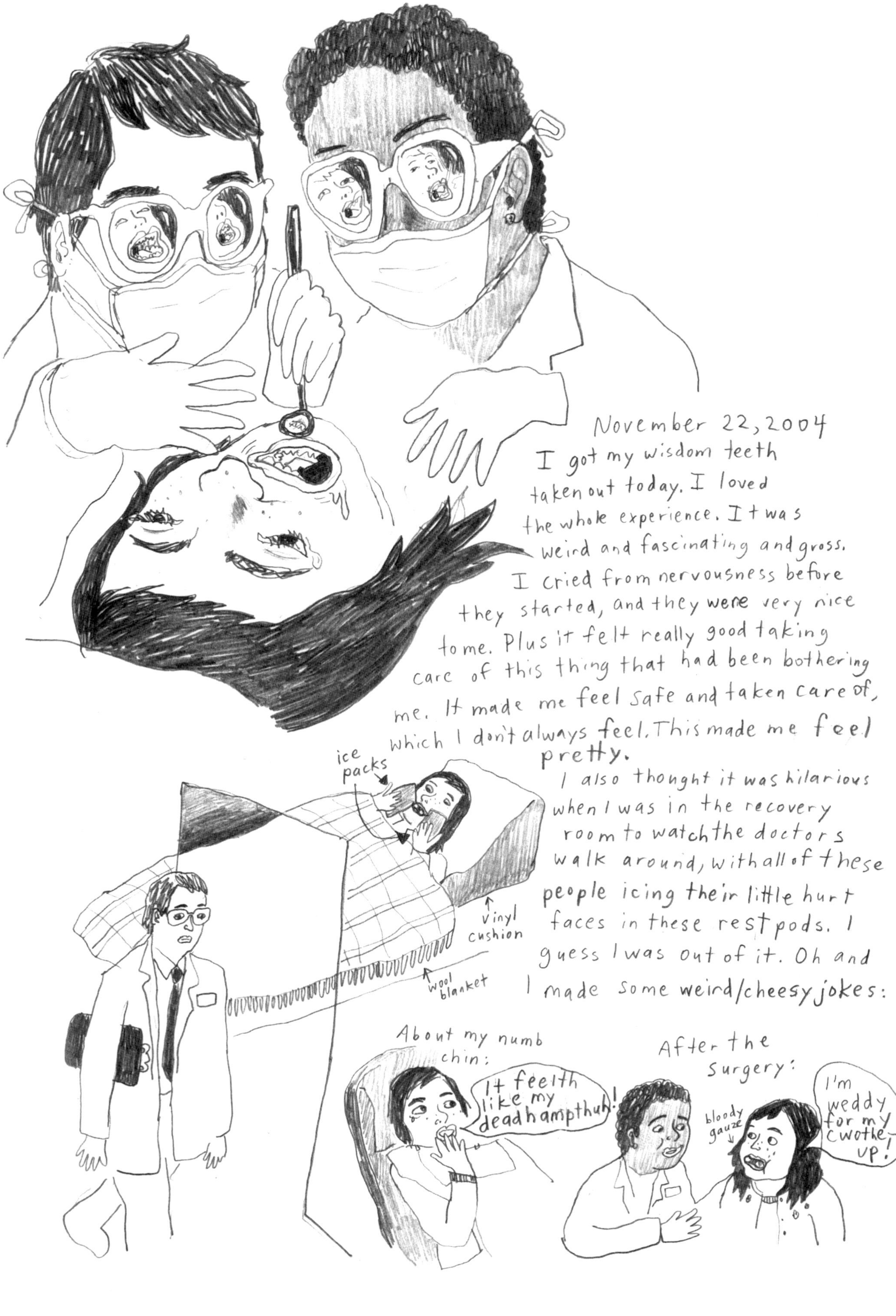
November 22, 2004
I got my wisdom teeth taken out today. I loved the whole experience. It was weird and fascinating and gross. I cried from nervousness before they started, and they were very nice to me. Plus it felt really good taking care of this thing that had been bothering me. It made me feel safe and taken care of, which I don't always feel. This made me feel pretty.
I also thought it was hilarious when I was in the recovery room to watch the doctors walk around, with all of these people icing their little hurt faces in these rest pods. I guess I was out of it. Oh and I made some weird/cheesy jokes:
ice packs
vinyl cushion
wool blanket
About my numb chin:
It feelth like my deadhampthuh!
After the surgery:
bloody gauze
I'm weddy for my cwothe-up!

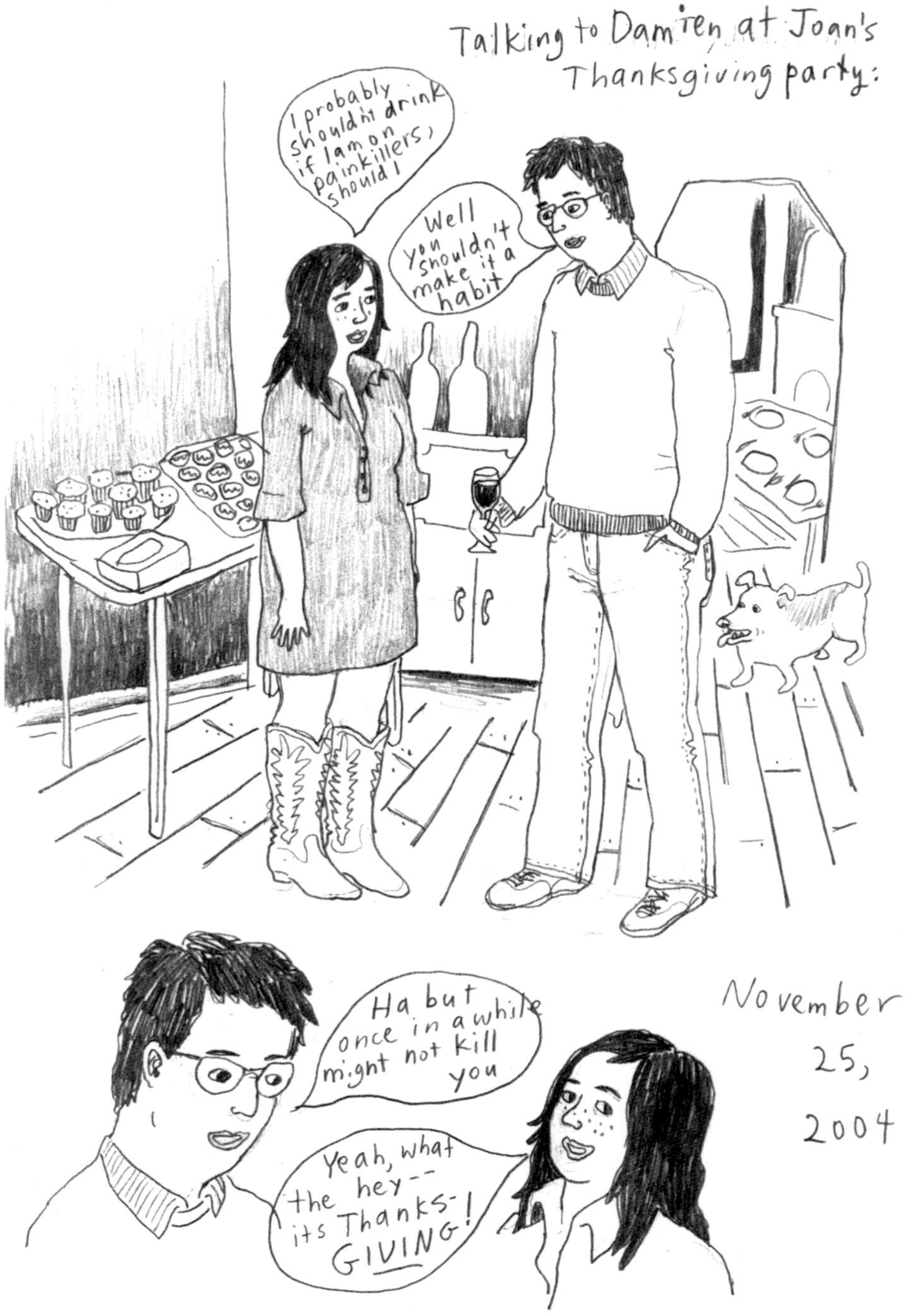
Talking to Damien at Joan's Thanksgiving party:
I probably shouldn't drink if I am on painkillers, should I
Well you shouldn't make it a habit
Ha but once in a while might not kill you
Yeah, what the hey-- its Thanks-GIVING!
November 25, 2004

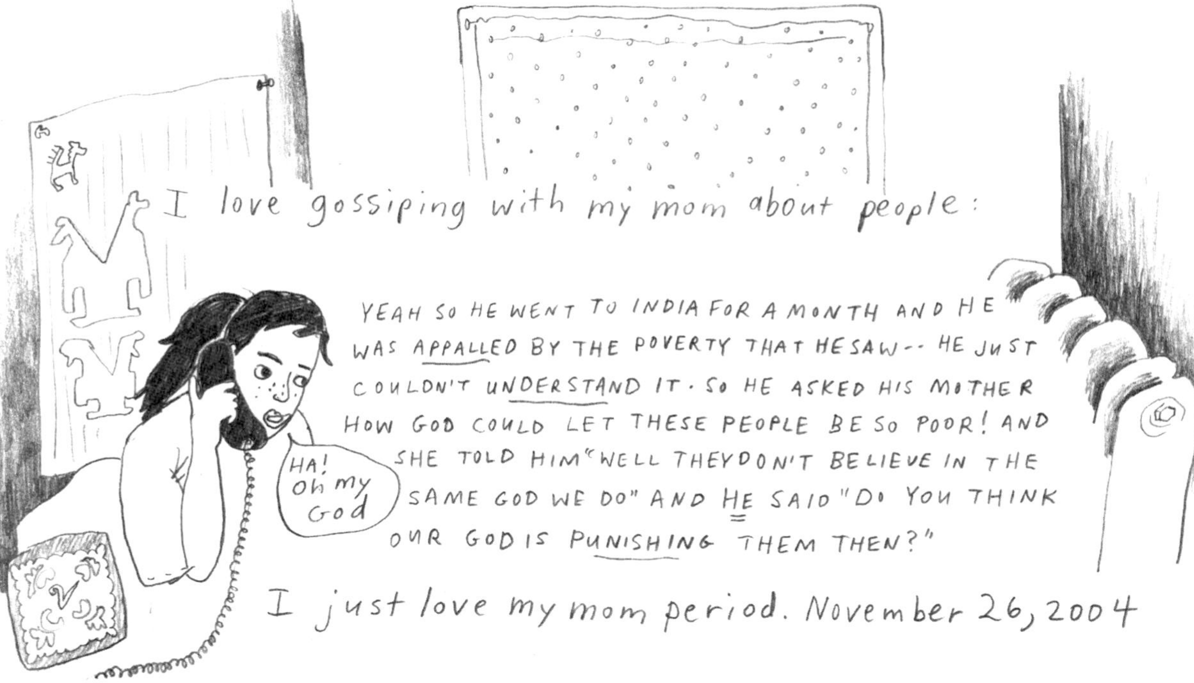
I love gossiping with my mom about people:
YEAH SO HE WENT TO INDIA FOR A MONTH AND HE WAS APPALLED BY THE POVERTY THAT HE SAW -- HE JUST COULDN'T UNDERSTAND IT. SO HE ASKED HIS MOTHER HOW GOD COULD LET THESE PEOPLE BE SO POOR! AND SHE TOLD HIM "WELL THEY DON'T BELIEVE IN THE SAME GOD WE DO" AND HE SAID "DO YOU THINK OUR GOD IS PUNISHING THEM THEN?"
HA! Oh my God
I just love my mom period. November 26, 2004

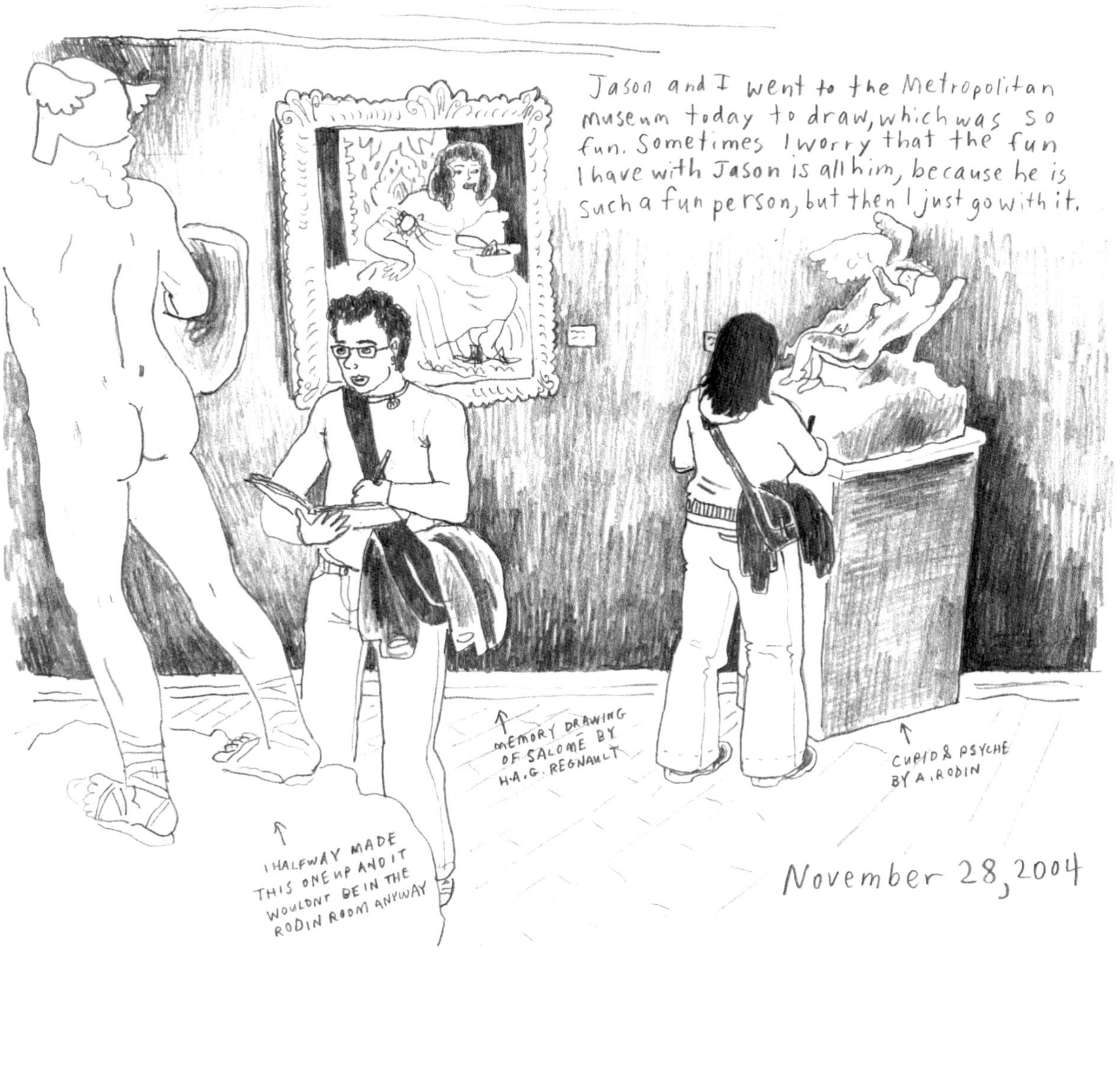
Jason and I went to the Metropolitan museum today to draw, which was so fun. Sometimes I worry that the fun I have with Jason is all him, because he is such a fun person, but then I just go with it.
MEMORY DRAWING OF SALOMÉ BY H.A.G. REGNAULT
CUPID & PSYCHE BY A. RODIN
I HALFWAY MADE THIS ONE UP AND IT WOULDN'T BE IN THE RODIN ROOM ANYWAY
November 28, 2004

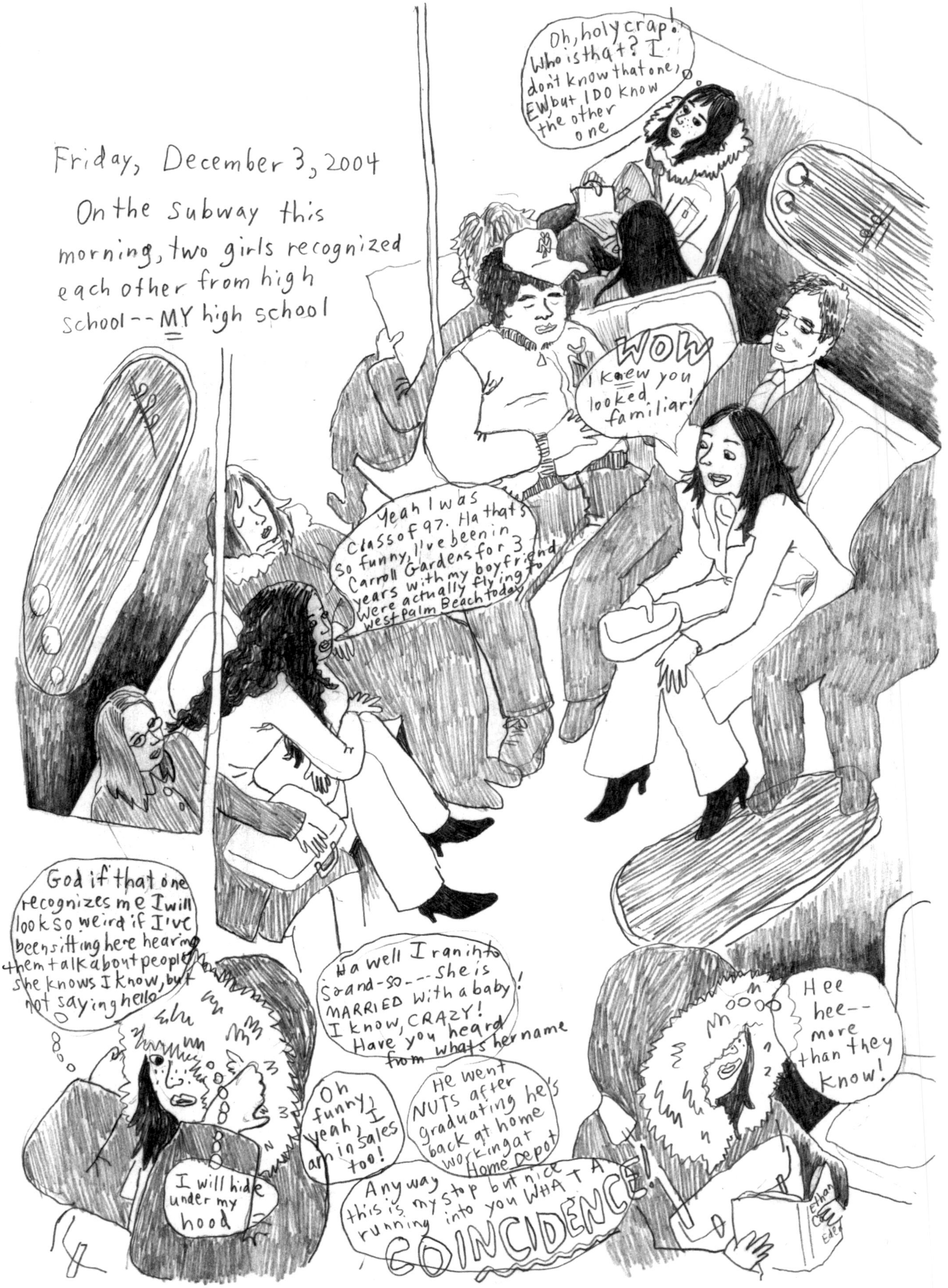
Friday, December 3, 2004
On the subway this morning, two girls recognized each other from high school -- MY high school
Oh, holy crap! Who is that? I don't know that one, EW but I DO know the other one
WOW I knew you looked familiar!
Yeah I was class of 97. Ha that's so funny, I've been in Carroll Gardens for 3 years with my boyfriend we're actually flying to West Palm Beach today
God if that one recognizes me I will look so weird if I've been sitting here hearing them talk about people she knows I know, but not saying hello
Ha well I ran into So-and-so--- she is MARRIED with a baby! I know, CRAZY! Have you heard from whats her name
Oh funny, yeah, I am in sales too!
He went NUTS after graduating he's back at home working at Home Depot
I will hide under my hood
Anyway this is my stop but nice running into you WHAT A COINCIDENCE!
Hee hee-- more than they know!

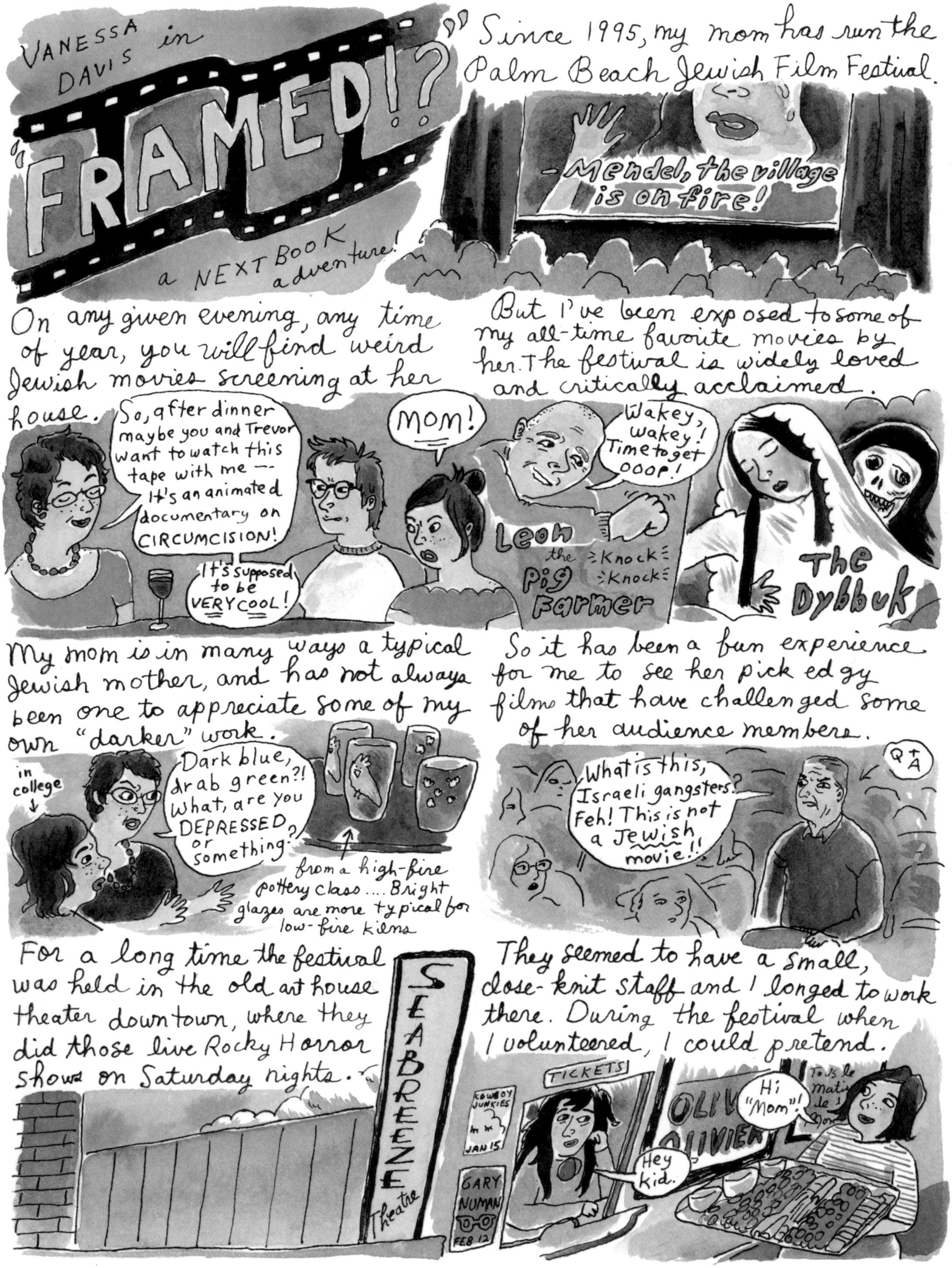
VANESSA DAVIS in
FRAMED!?
a NEXTBOOK adventure!
Since 1995, my mom has run the Palm Beach Jewish Film Festival.
-Mendel, the village is on fire!
On any given evening, any time of year, you will find weird Jewish movies screening at her house.
So, after dinner maybe you and Trevor want to watch this tape with me — It's an animated documentary on CIRCUMCISION!
It's supposed to be VERY COOL!
MOM!
But I've been exposed to some of my all-time favorite movies by her. The festival is widely loved and critically acclaimed.
Wakey, wakey! Time to get ooop!
Knock Knock
Leon the Pig Farmer
The Dybbuk
My mom is in many ways a typical Jewish mother, and has not always been one to appreciate some of my own "darker" work.
in college
Dark blue, drab green?! What, are you DEPRESSED or something?
from a high-fire pottery class.... Bright glazes are more typical for low-fire kilns
So it has been a fun experience for me to see her pick edgy films that have challenged some of her audience members.
Q+A
What is this, Israeli gangsters? Feh! This is not a JEWISH movie!!
For a long time the festival was held in the old art house theater downtown, where they did those live Rocky Horror shows on Saturday nights.
SEABREEZE Theatre
They seemed to have a small, close-knit staff and I longed to work there. During the festival when I volunteered, I could pretend.
TICKETS
KOWBOY JUNKIES
JAN 15
GARY NUMAN
FEB 12
OLIVIER
Hi "Mom"!
Hey kid.

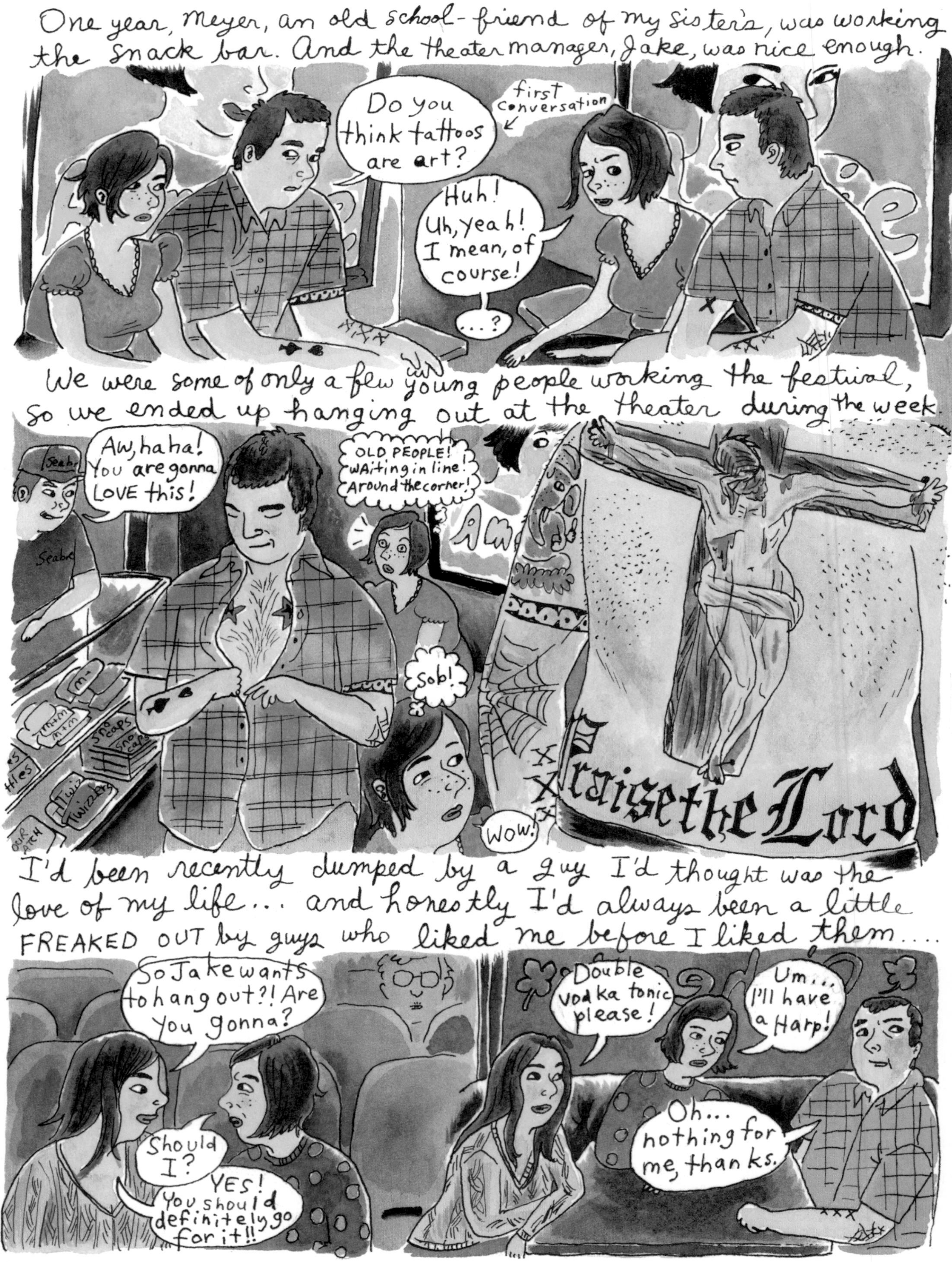
One year, Meyer, an old school-friend of my sister's, was working the snack bar. And the theater manager, Jake, was nice enough.
Do you think tattoos are art?
first conversation
Huh! Uh, yeah! I mean, of course!
...?
We were some of only a few young people working the festival, so we ended up hanging out at the theater during the week.
Aw, haha! You are gonna LOVE this!
OLD PEOPLE! Waiting in line! Around the corner!
Sob!
WOW!
Praise the Lord
I'd been recently dumped by a guy I'd thought was the love of my life... and honestly I'd always been a little FREAKED OUT by guys who liked me before I liked them....
So Jake wants to hang out?! Are you gonna?
Should I?
YES! You should definitely go for it!!
Double vodka tonic please!
Um... I'll have a Harp!
Oh... nothing for me, thanks.

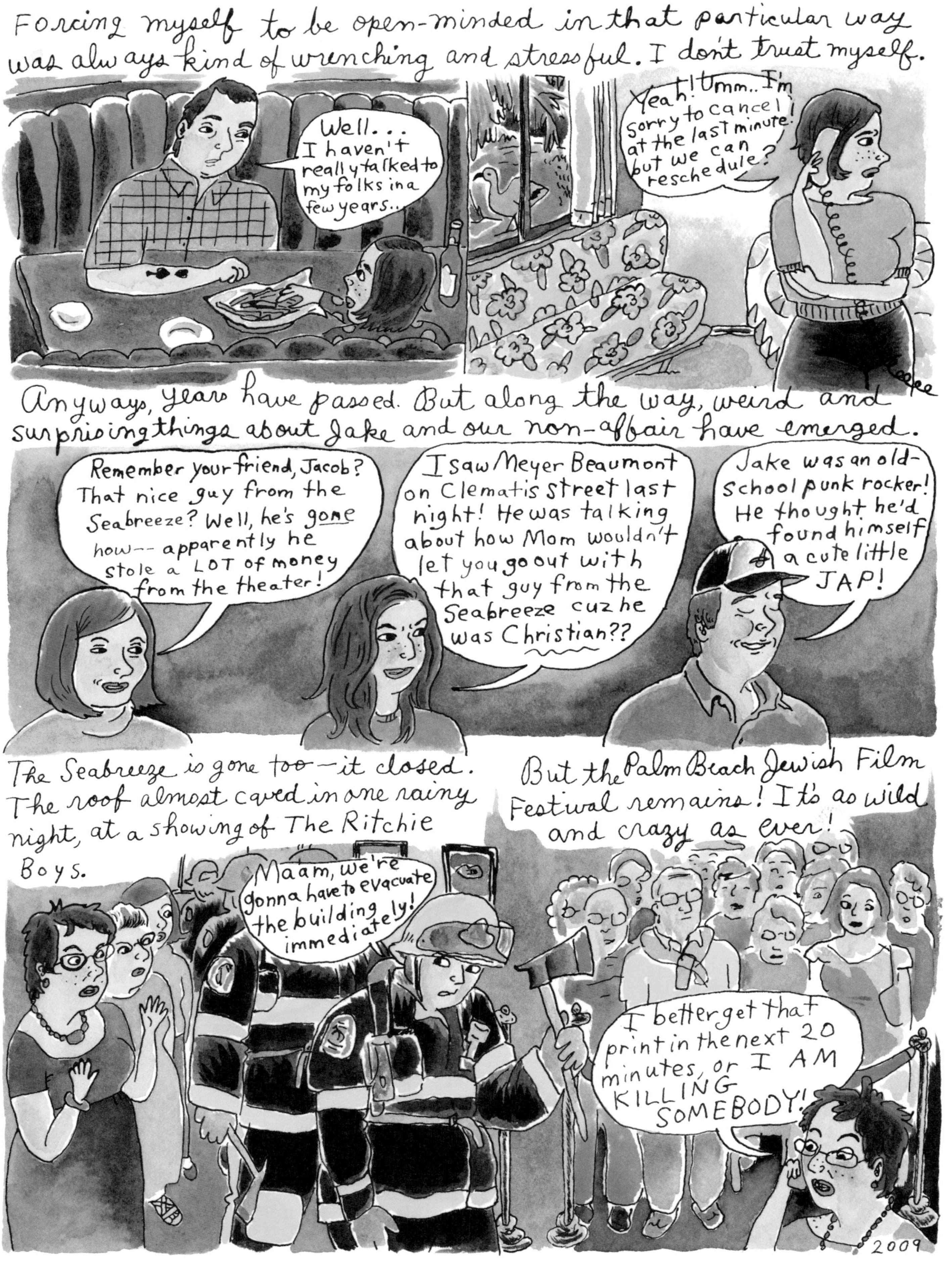

Forcing myself to be open-minded in that particular way was always kind of wrenching and stressful. I don't trust myself.
Well... I haven't really talked to my folks in a few years...
Yeah! Umm.. I'm sorry to cancel at the last minute! but we can reschedule?
Anyways, years have passed. But along the way, weird and surprising things about Jake and our non-affair have emerged.
Remember your friend, Jacob? That nice guy from the Seabreeze? Well, he's gone now-- apparently he stole a LOT of money from the theater!
I saw Meyer Beaumont on Clematis street last night! He was talking about how Mom wouldn't let you go out with that guy from the Seabreeze cuz he was Christian??
Jake was an old-school punk rocker! He thought he'd found himself a cute little JAP!
The Seabreeze is gone too—it closed. The roof almost caved in one rainy night, at a showing of The Ritchie Boys.
But the Palm Beach Jewish Film Festival remains! It's as wild and crazy as ever!
Ma'am, we're gonna have to evacuate the building immediately!
I better get that print in the next 20 minutes, or I AM KILLING SOMEBODY!
2009

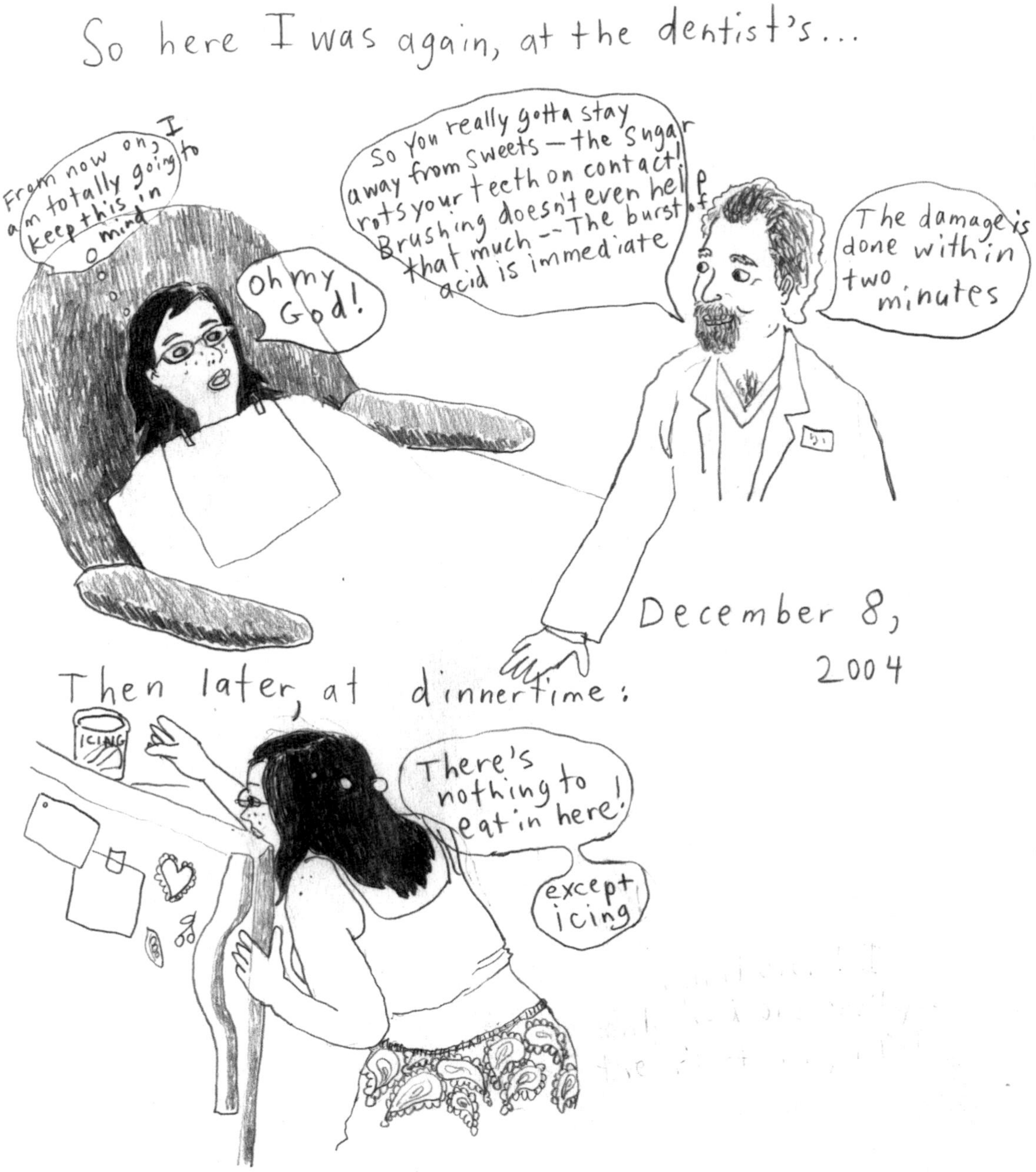
So here I was again, at the dentist's...
From now on, I am totally going to keep this in mind
Oh my God!
So you really gotta stay away from sweets — the sugar rots your teeth on contact! Brushing doesn't even help that much -- The burst of acid is immediate
The damage is done within two minutes
December 8, 2004
Then later, at dinnertime:
ICING
There's nothing to eat in here!
except icing

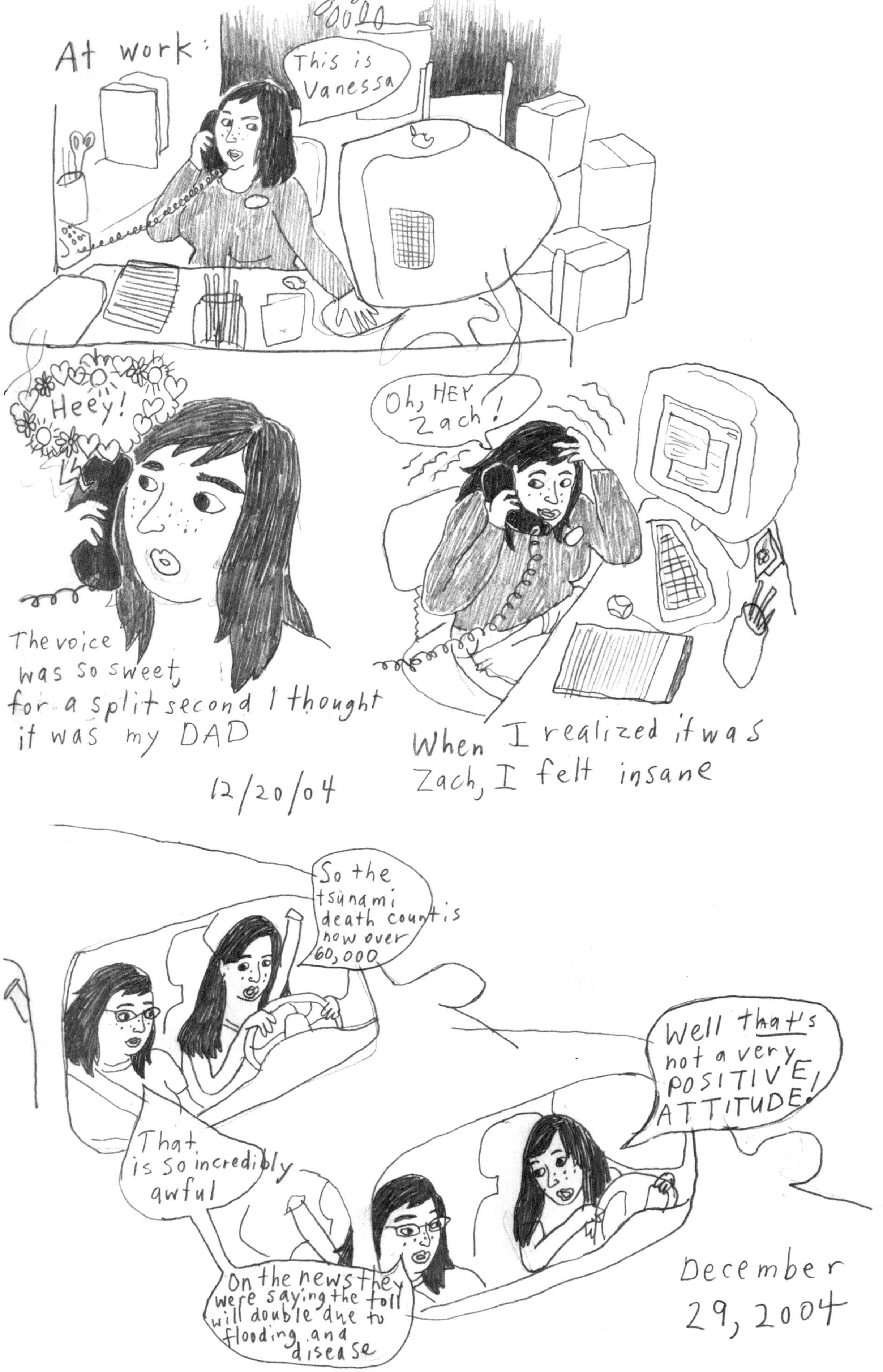
At work:
This is Vanessa
Heey!
The voice was so sweet, for a split second I thought it was my DAD
Oh, HEY Zach!
When I realized it was Zach, I felt insane
12/20/04
So the tsunami death count is now over 60,000
That is so incredibly awful
Well that's not a very POSITIVE ATTITUDE!
On the news they were saying the toll will double due to flooding and disease
December 29, 2004

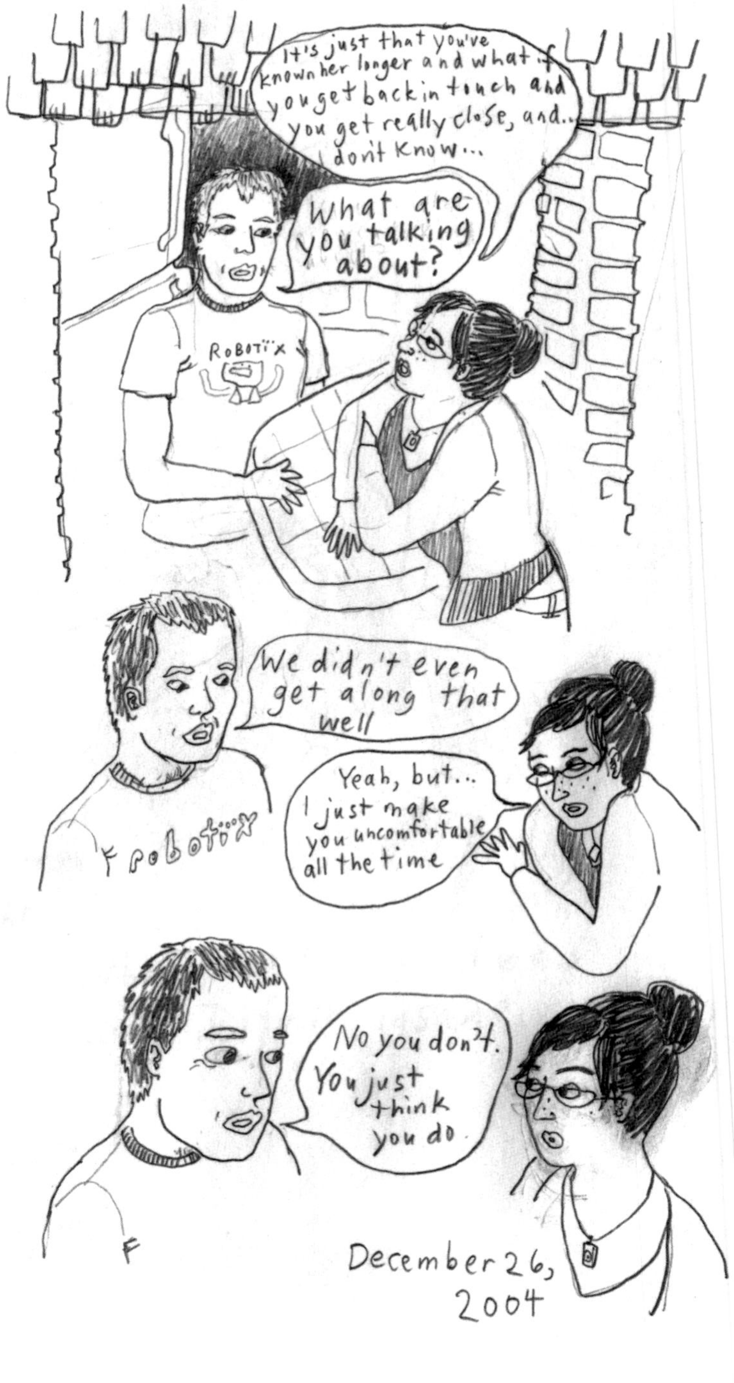
It's just that you've known her longer and what if you get back in touch and you get really close, and... I don't know...
What are you talking about?
ROBOTIX
We didn't even get along that well
Yeah, but... I just make you uncomfortable all the time
No you don't. You just think you do.
December 26, 2004

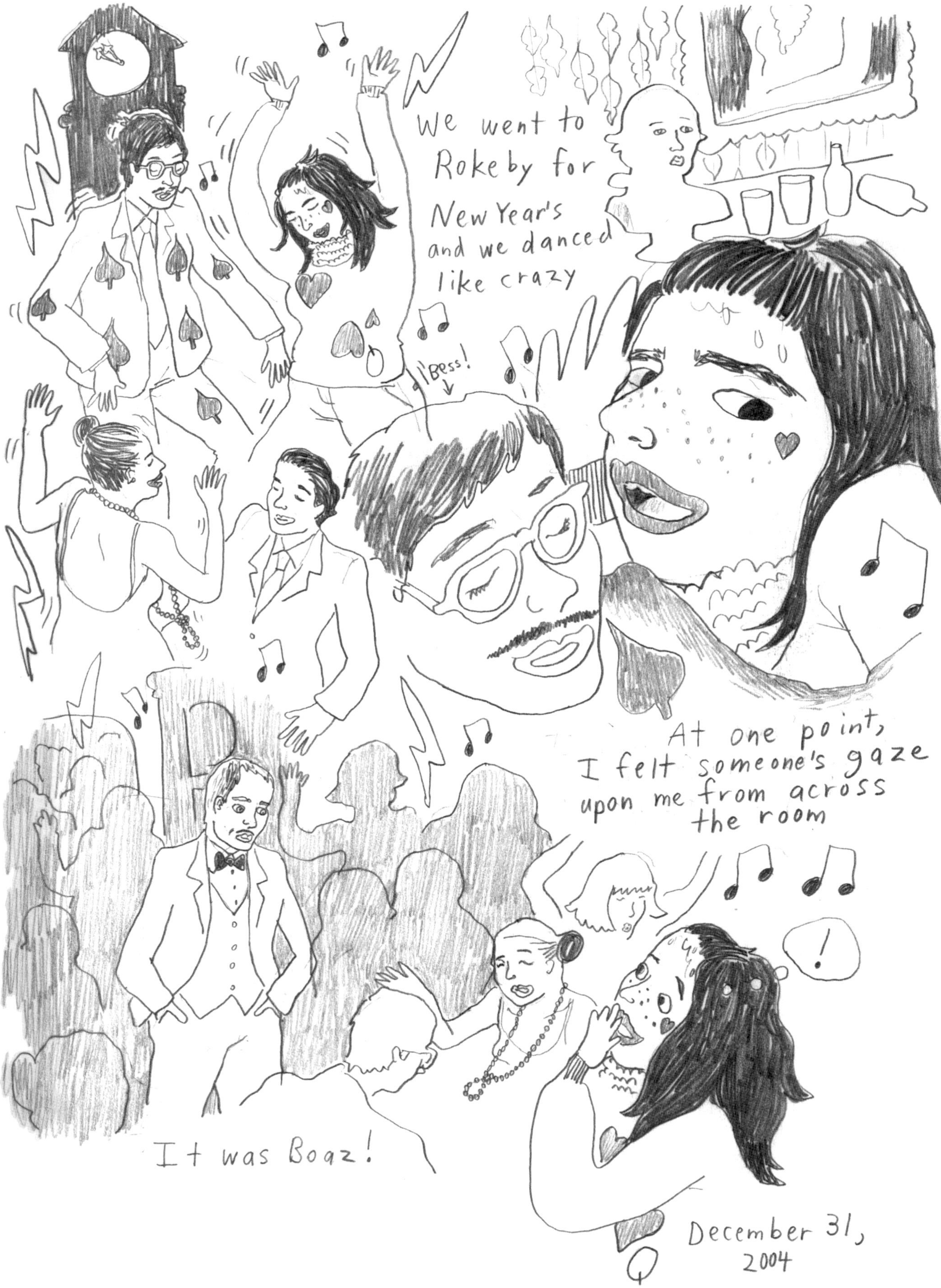
We went to Rokeby for New Year's and we danced like crazy
Bess!
At one point, I felt someone's gaze upon me from across the room
!
It was Boaz!
December 31, 2004

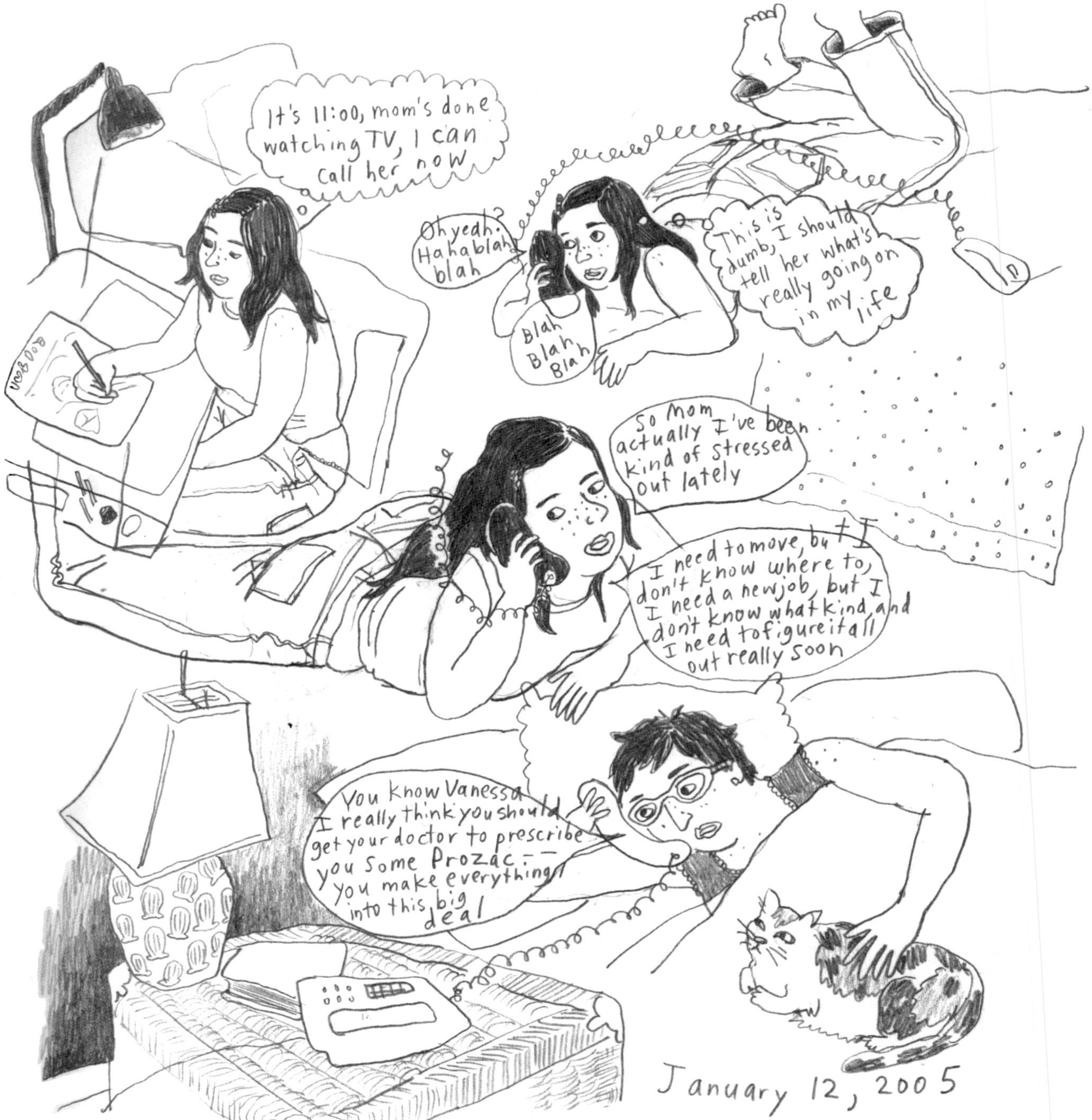
It's 11:00, mom's done watching TV, I can call her now
Oh yeah? Hahablah blah
Blah Blah Blah
This is dumb, I should tell her what's really going on in my life
So Mom actually I've been kind of stressed out lately
I need to move, but I don't know where to, I need a new job, but I don't know what kind and I need to figure it all out really soon
You know Vanessa I really think you should get your doctor to prescribe you some Prozac.— you make everything into this big deal
January 12, 2005

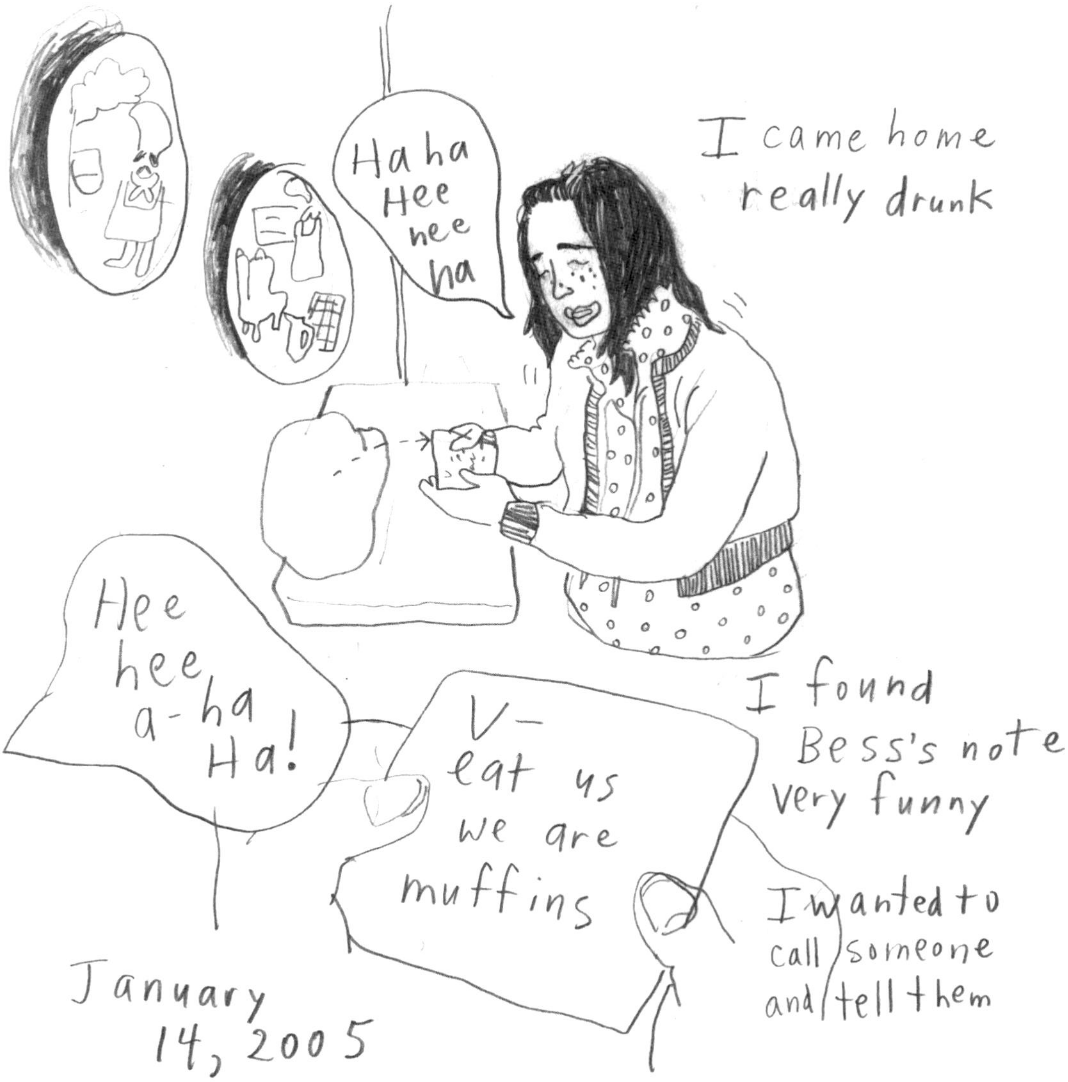
I came home really drunk
Haha Hee hee ha
Hee hee a-ha Ha!
V- eat us we are muffins
I found Bess's note very funny
I wanted to call someone and tell them
January 14, 2005

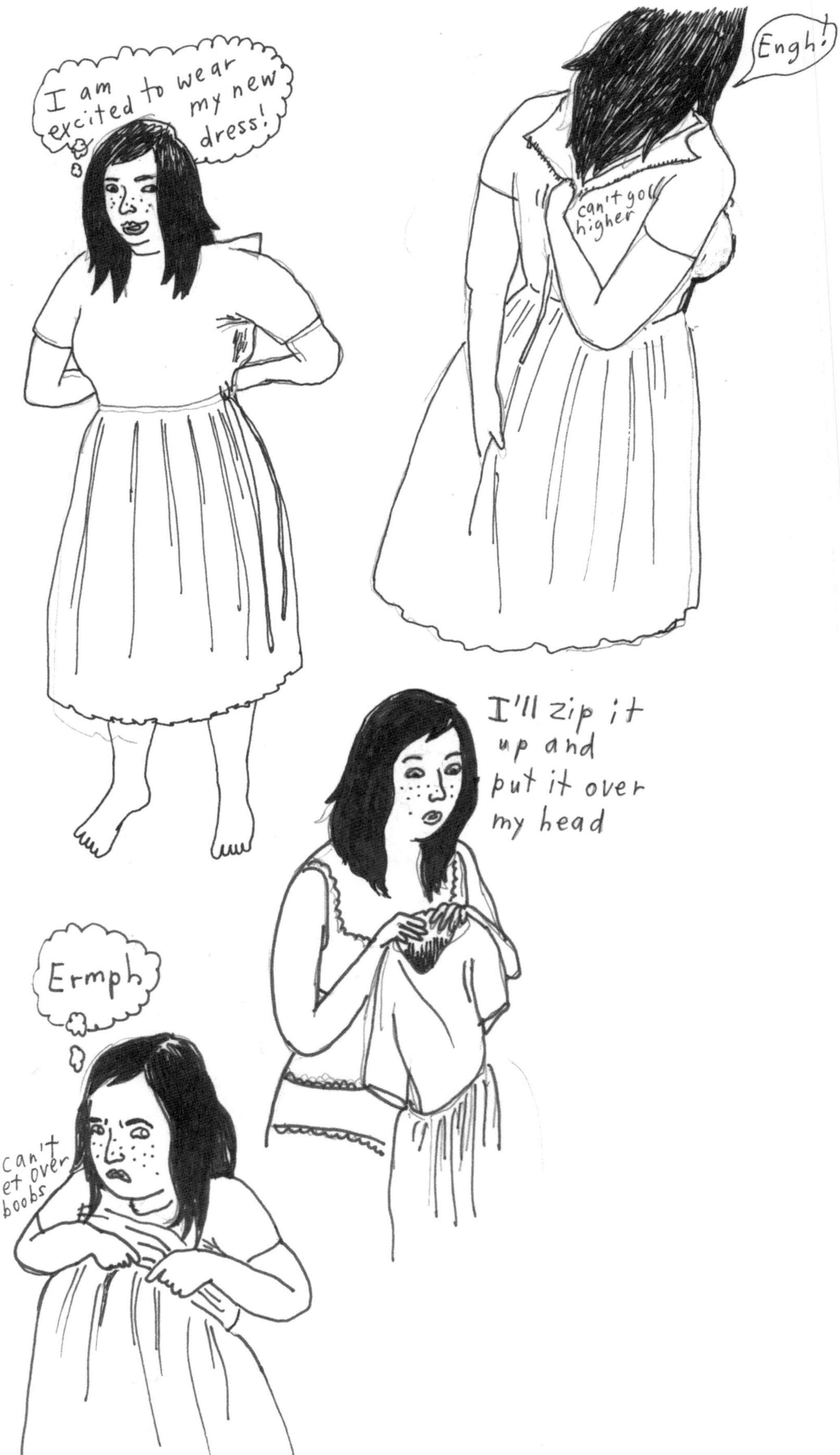

I am excited to wear my new dress!
Engh!
can't go higher
I'll zip it up and put it over my head
Ermph
can't get over boobs

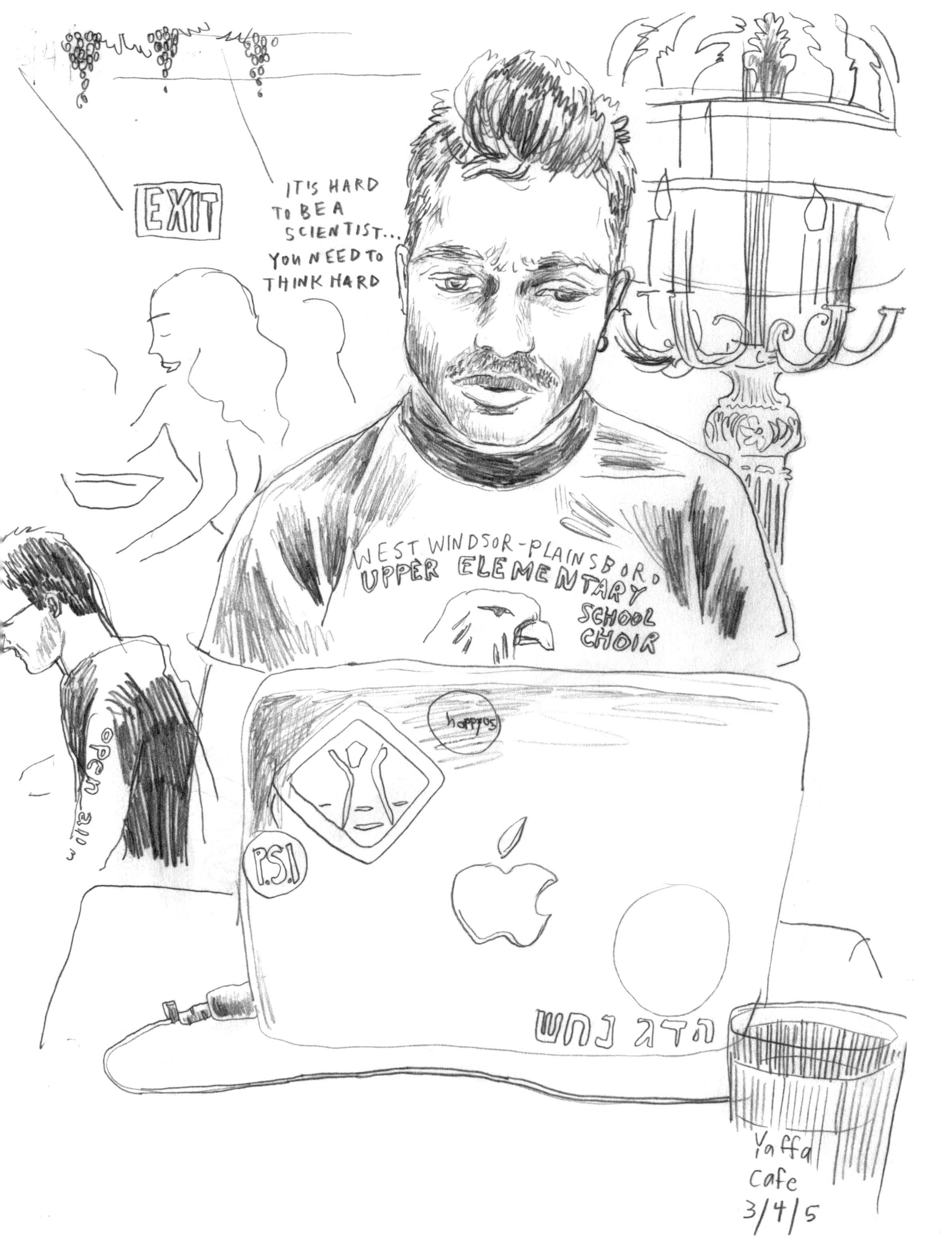

EXIT
IT'S HARD TO BE A SCIENTIST... YOU NEED TO THINK HARD
WEST WINDSOR-PLAINSBORO UPPER ELEMENTARY SCHOOL CHOIR
open
happyos
P.S.I
הדג נחש
Yaffa Cafe 3/4/5

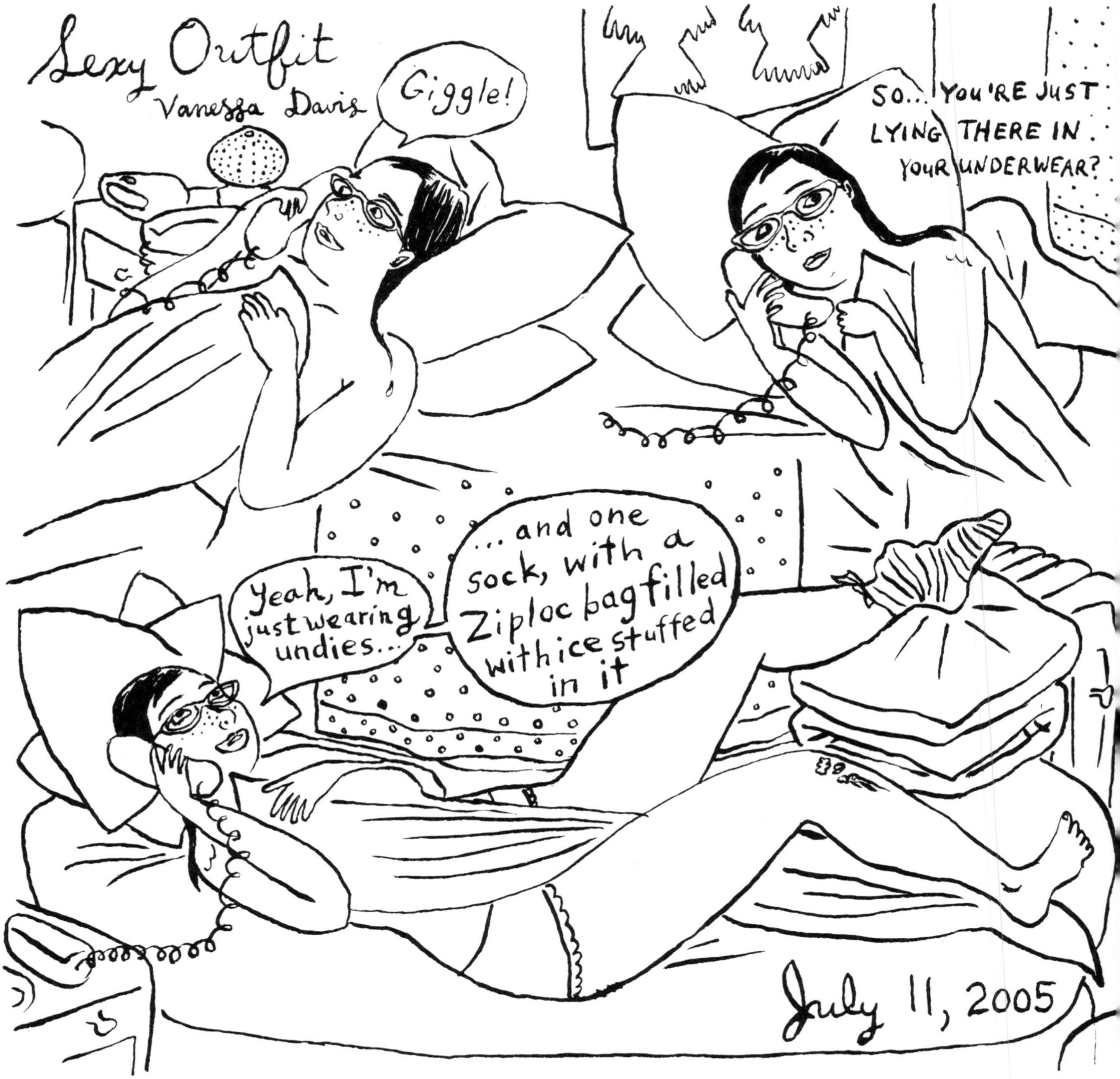

Sexy Outfit
Vanessa Davis
Giggle!
SO... YOU'RE JUST LYING THERE IN YOUR UNDERWEAR?
Yeah, I'm just wearing undies...
...and one sock, with a Ziploc bag filled with ice stuffed in it
July 11, 2005

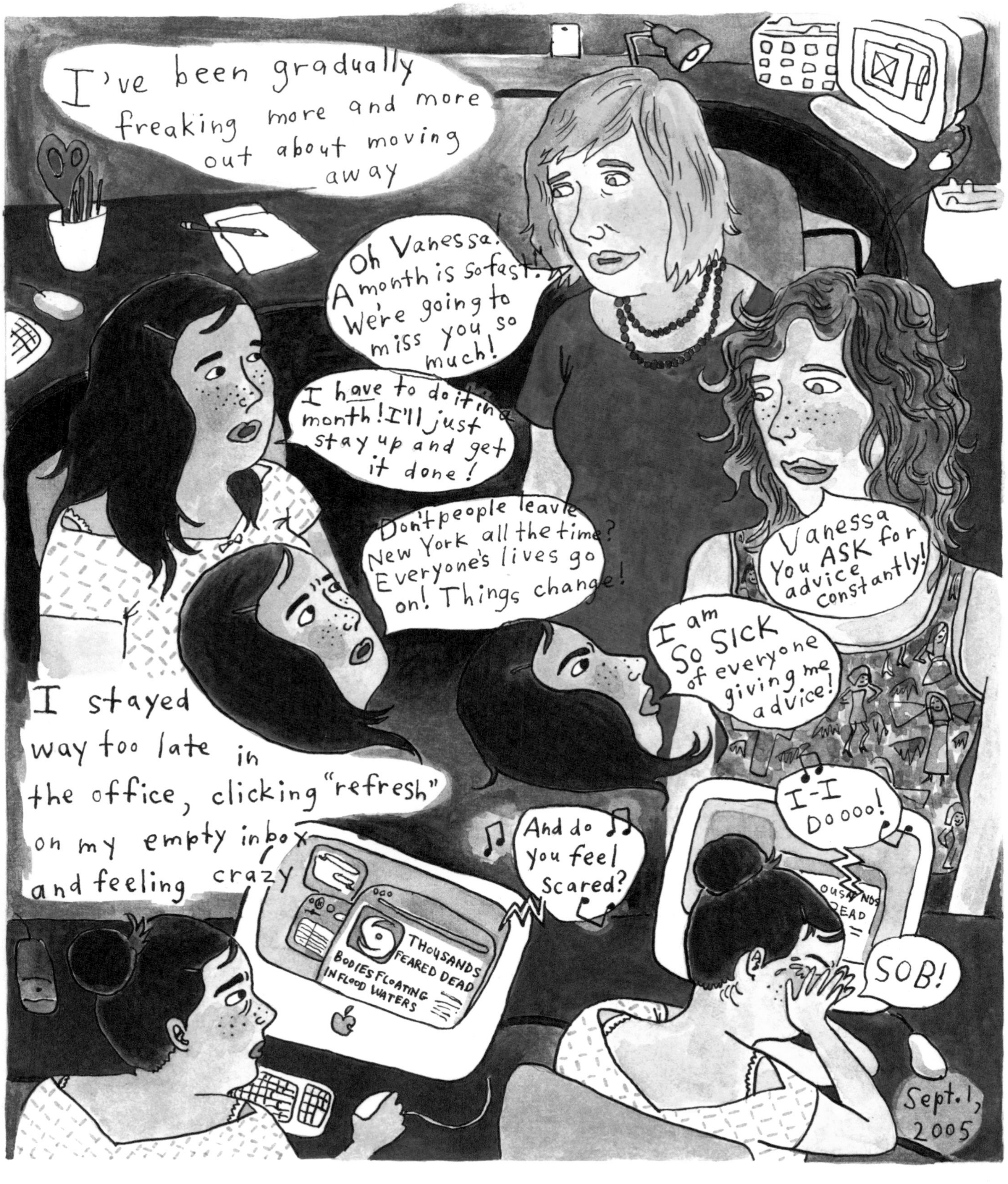
I've been gradually freaking more and more out about moving away
Oh Vanessa! A month is so fast! We're going to miss you so much!
I have to do it in a month! I'll just stay up and get it done!
Don't people leave New York all the time? Everyone's lives go on! Things change!
Vanessa You ASK for advice constantly!
I am So SICK of everyone giving me advice!
I stayed way too late in the office, clicking "refresh" on my empty inbox and feeling crazy
THOUSANDS FEARED DEAD
BODIES FLOATING IN FLOOD WATERS
And do you feel scared?
I-I Doooo!
SOB!
Sept. 1, 2005

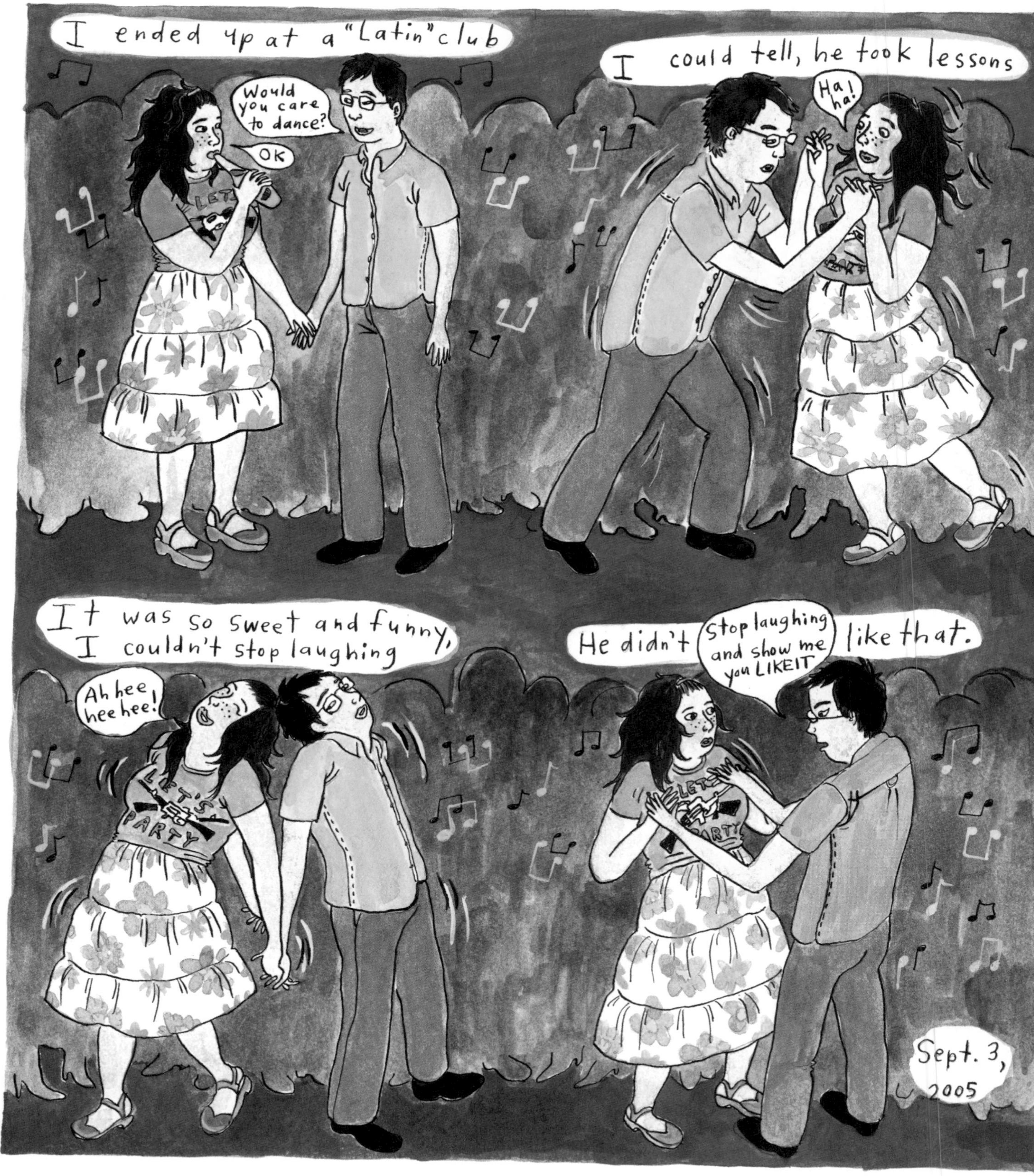
I ended up at a "Latin" club
Would you care to dance?
OK
I could tell, he took lessons
Ha! ha!
It was so sweet and funny, I couldn't stop laughing
Ah hee hee hee!
LET'S PARTY
He didn't like that.
Stop laughing and show me you LIKE IT
Sept. 3, 2005

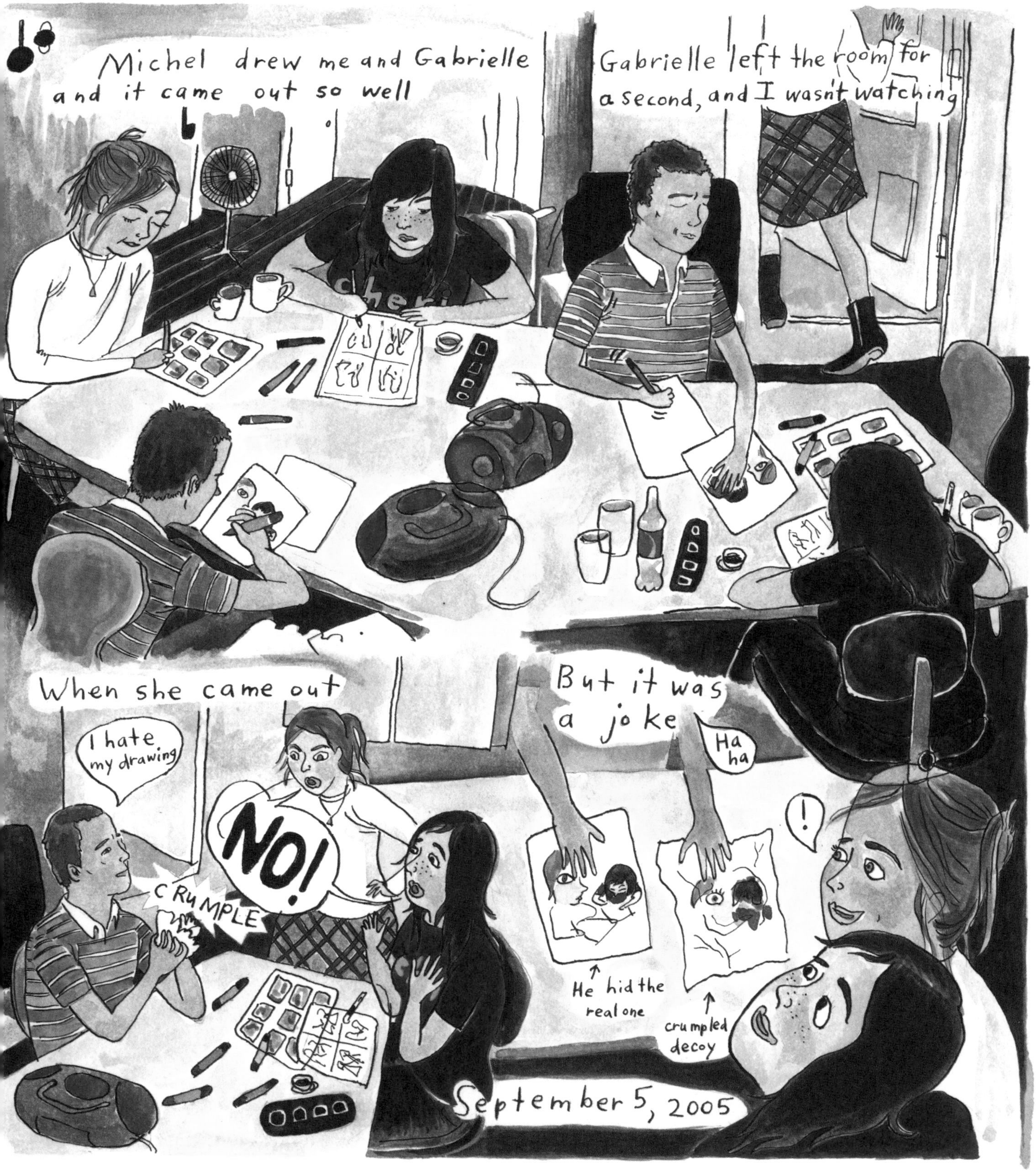

Michel drew me and Gabrielle and it came out so well
Gabrielle left the room for a second, and I wasn't watching
When she came out
I hate my drawing
CRUMPLE
NO!
But it was a joke
Ha ha
!
He hid the real one
crumpled decoy
September 5, 2005

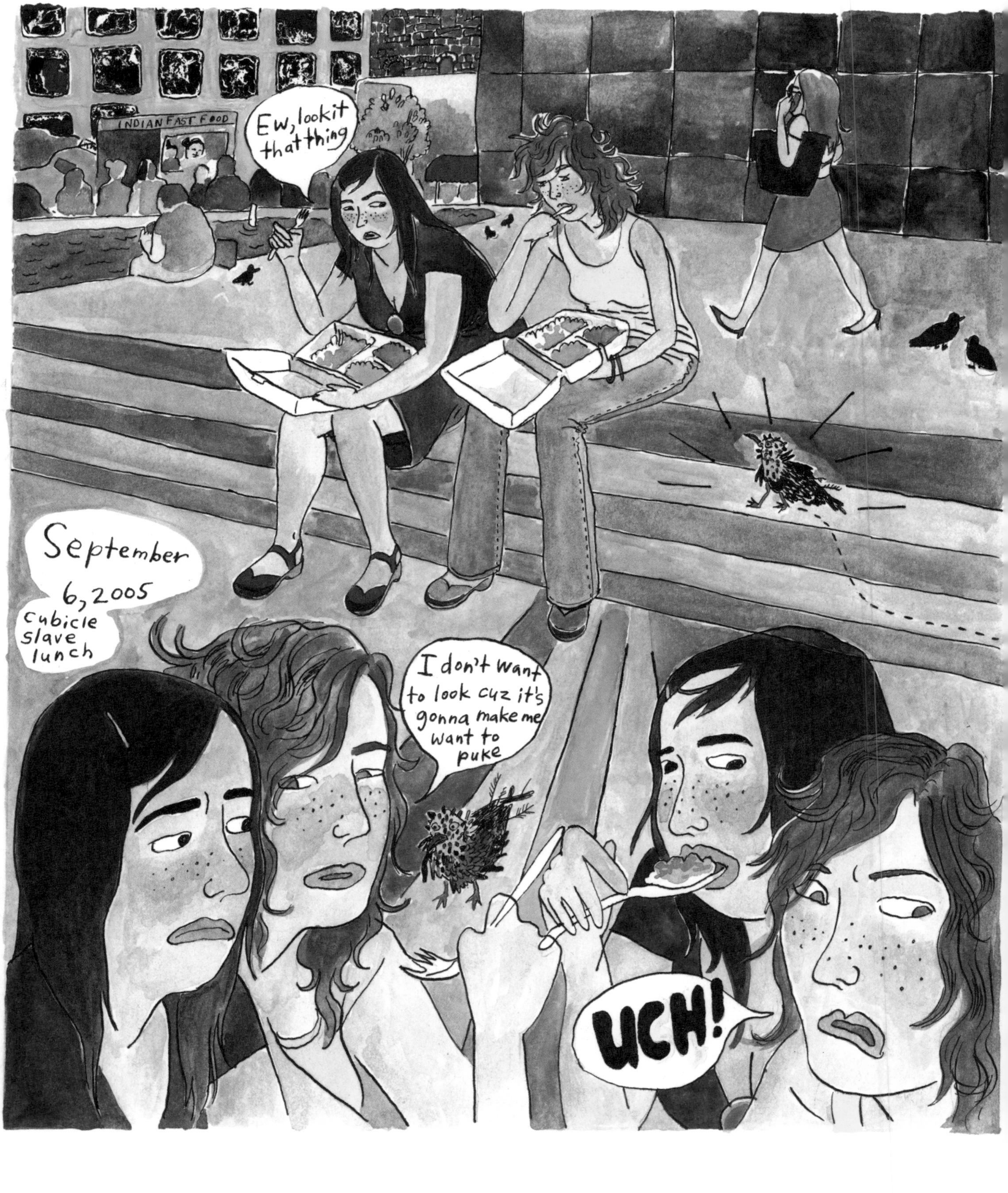
Ew, lookit that thing
INDIAN FAST FOOD
September 6, 2005
cubicle slave lunch
I don't want to look cuz it's gonna make me want to puke
UCH!

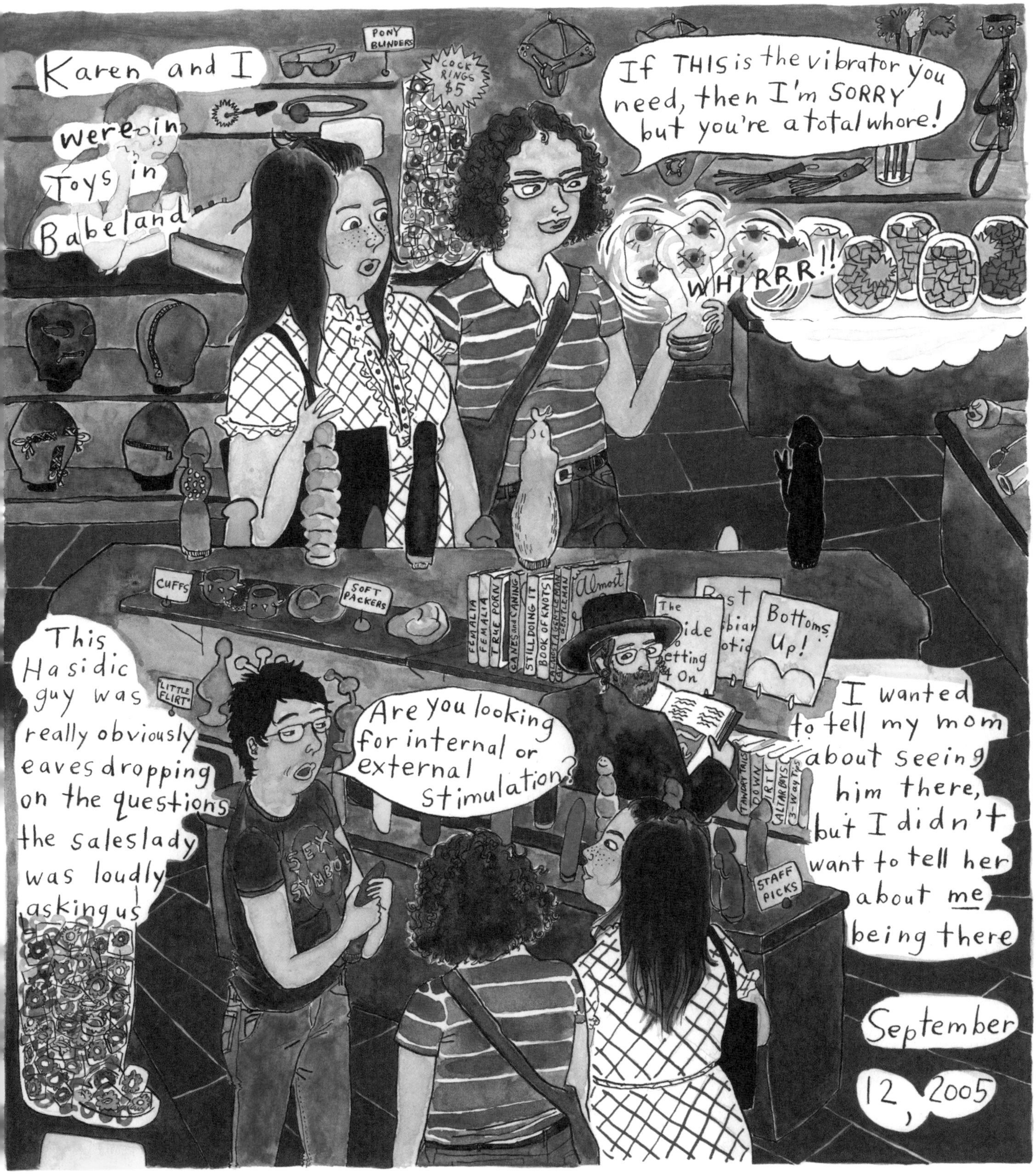
Karen and I were in Toys in Babeland
PONY BLINDERS
COCK RINGS $5
If THIS is the vibrator you need, then I'm SORRY but you're a total whore!
WHIRRR!!
CUFFS
SOFT PACKERS
FEMALIA
FEMALIA
TRUE PORN
CANES and CANING
STILL DOING IT
BOOK OF KNOTS
Almost
Bottoms Up!
This Hasidic guy was really obviously eavesdropping on the questions the saleslady was loudly asking us
"LITTLE FLIRT"
Are you looking for internal or external stimulation?
SEX SYMBOL
I wanted to tell my mom about seeing him there, but I didn't want to tell her about me being there
STAFF PICKS
September 12, 2005

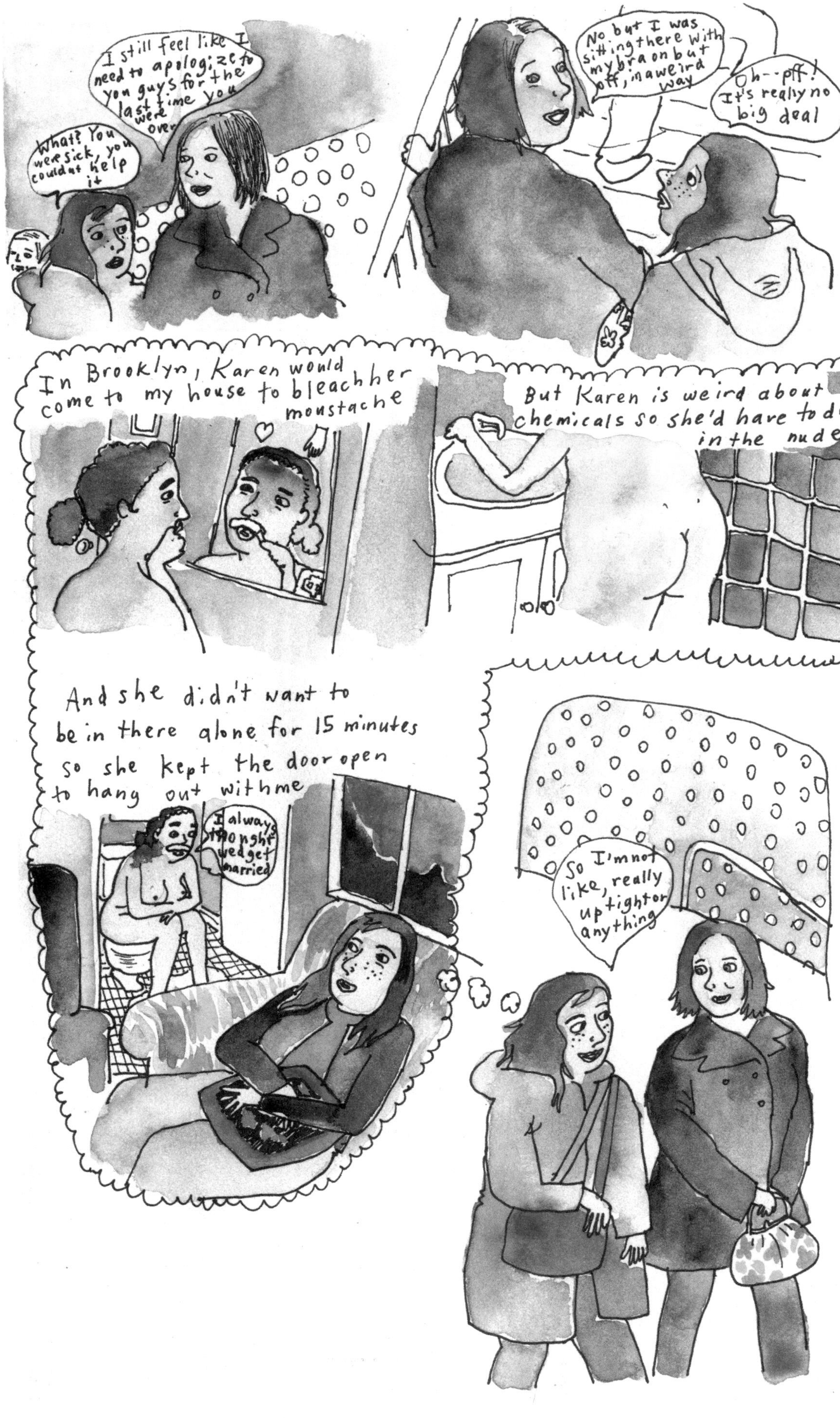

I still feel like I need to apologize to you guys for the last time you were over
What? You were sick, you couldn't help it
No but I was sitting there with my bra on but off, in a weird way
Oh--pff! It's really no big deal
In Brooklyn, Karen would come to my house to bleach her moustache
But Karen is weird about chemicals so she'd have to do it in the nude
And she didn't want to be in there alone for 15 minutes so she kept the door open to hang out with me
I always thought we'd get married
So I'm not like, really uptight or anything

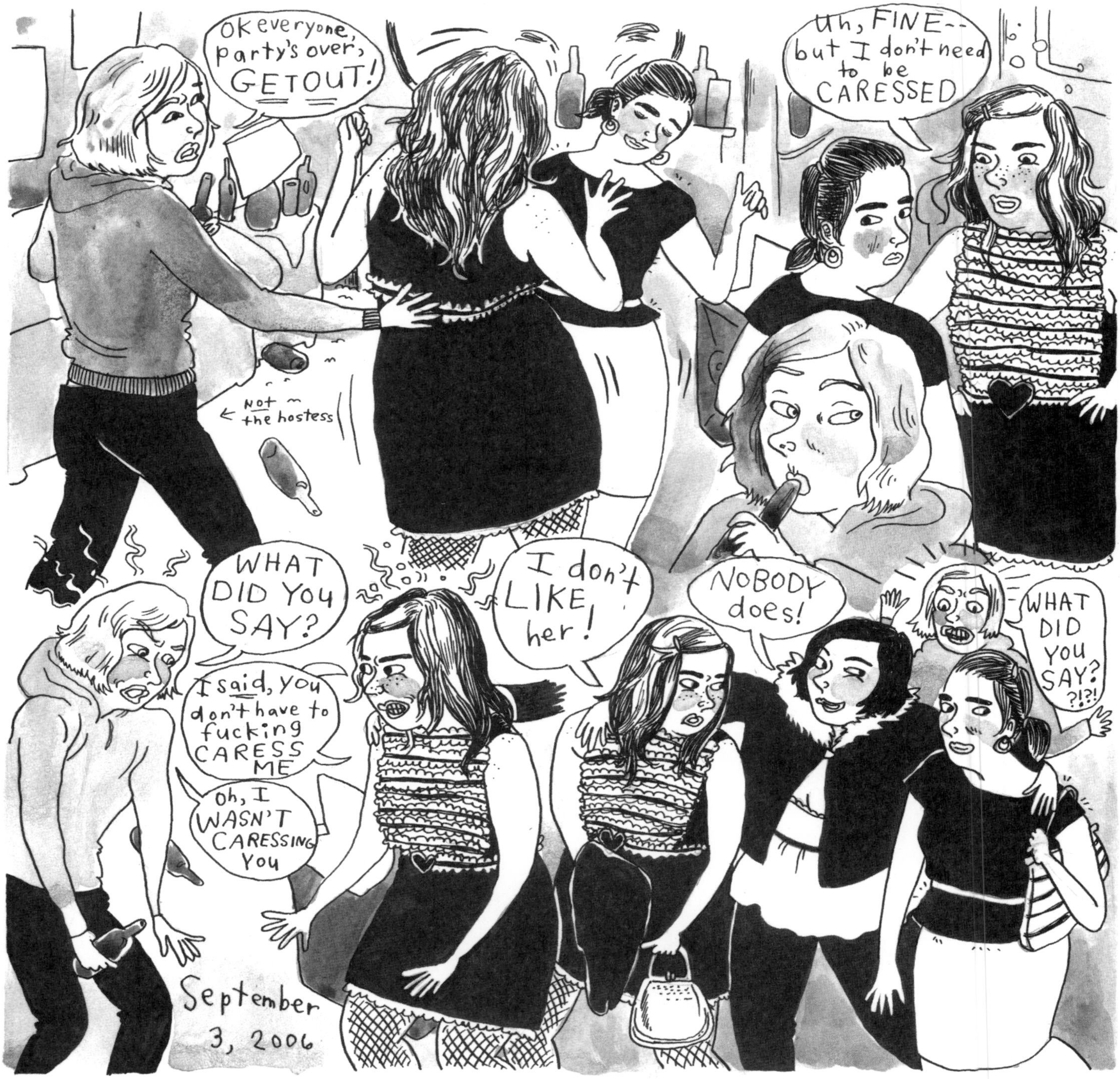
Ok everyone, party's over, GETOUT!
Uh, FINE-- but I don't need to be CARESSED
← NOT ~ the hostess
WHAT DID YOU SAY?
I don't LIKE her!
NOBODY does!
WHAT DID YOU SAY? ?!?!
I said, you don't have to fucking CARESS ME
Oh, I WASN'T CARESSING YOU
September 3, 2006

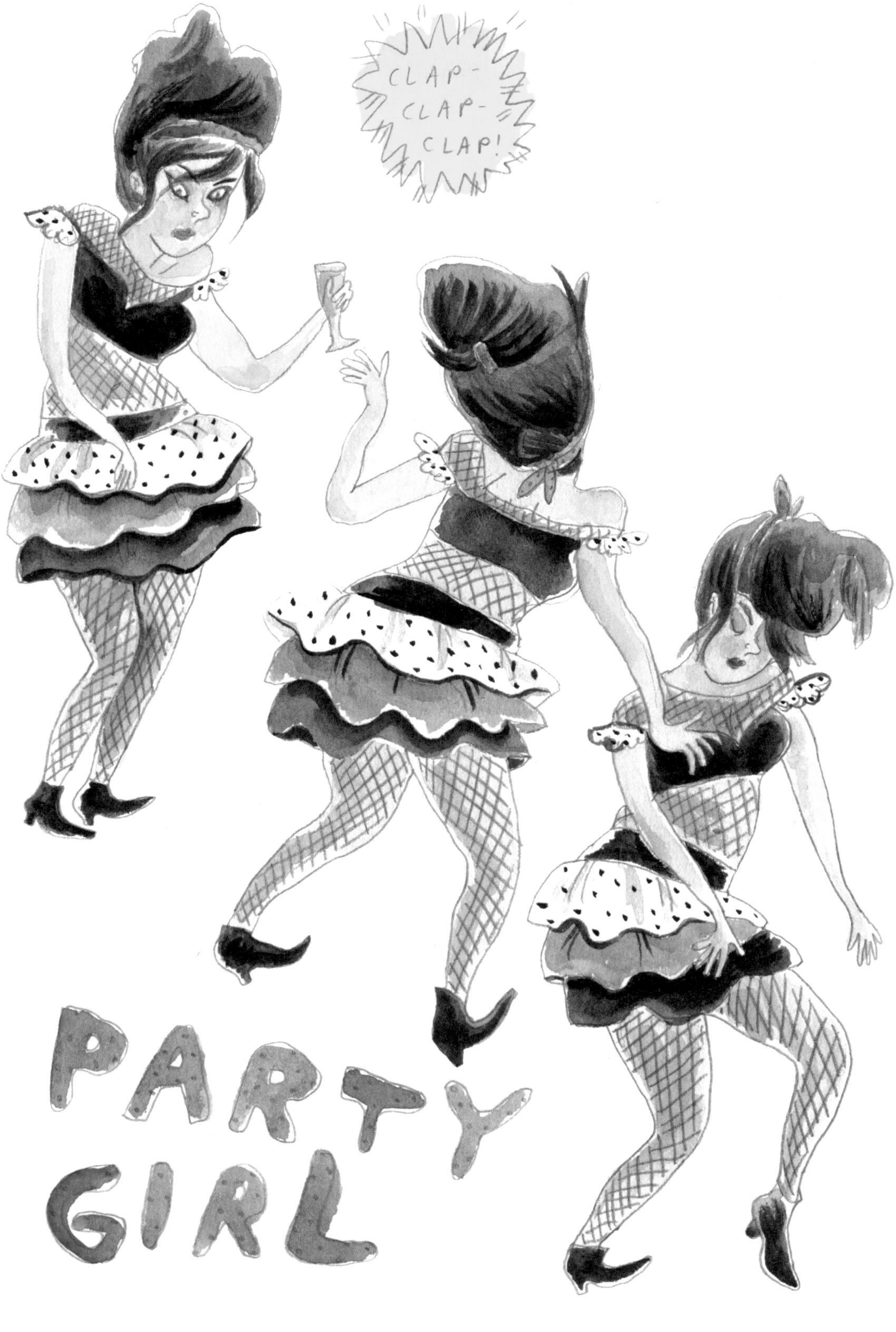
CLAP-
CLAP-
CLAP!
PARTY
GIRL

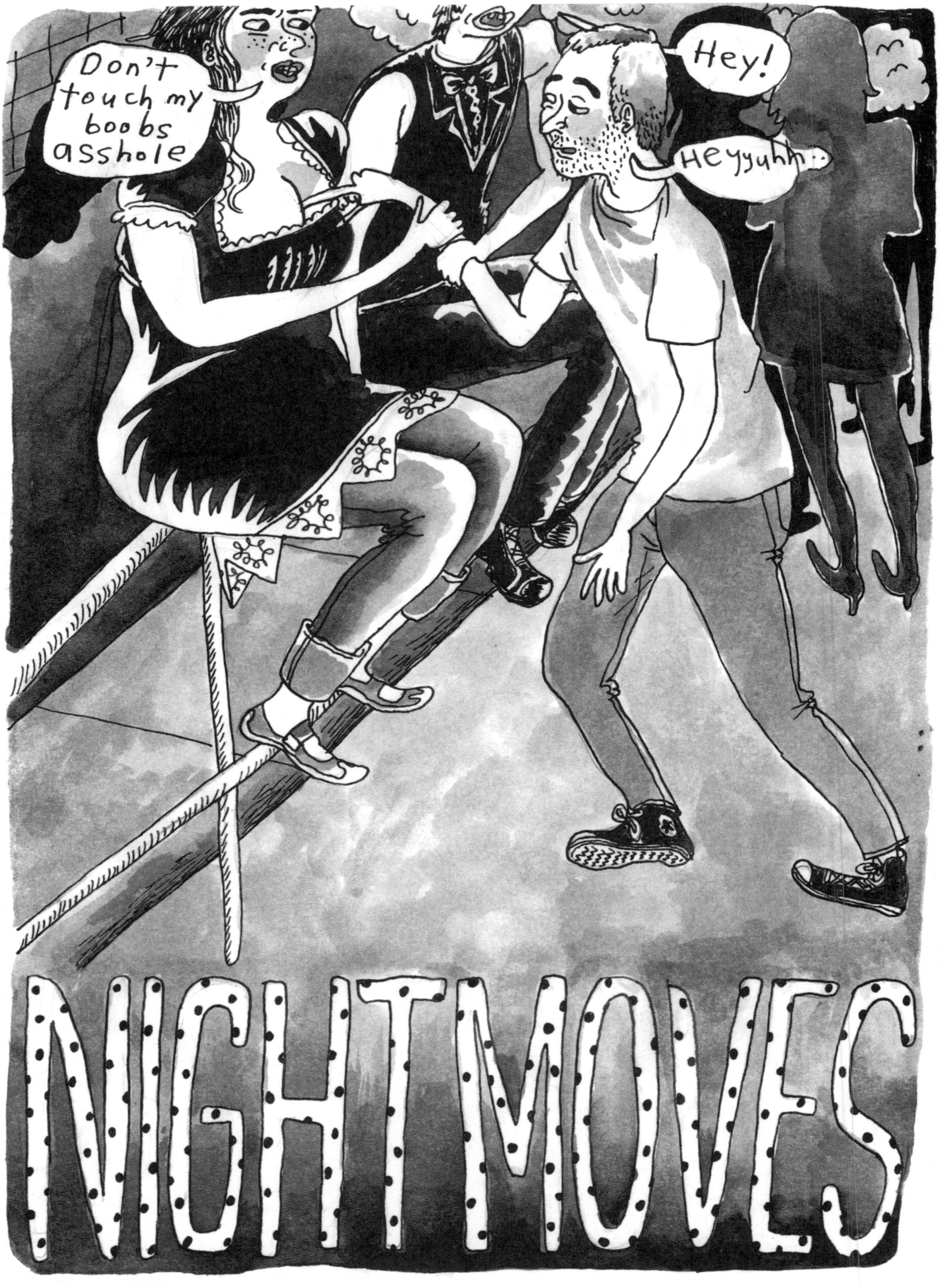
Don't touch my boobs asshole
Hey!
Heyyuhh
NIGHT MOVES

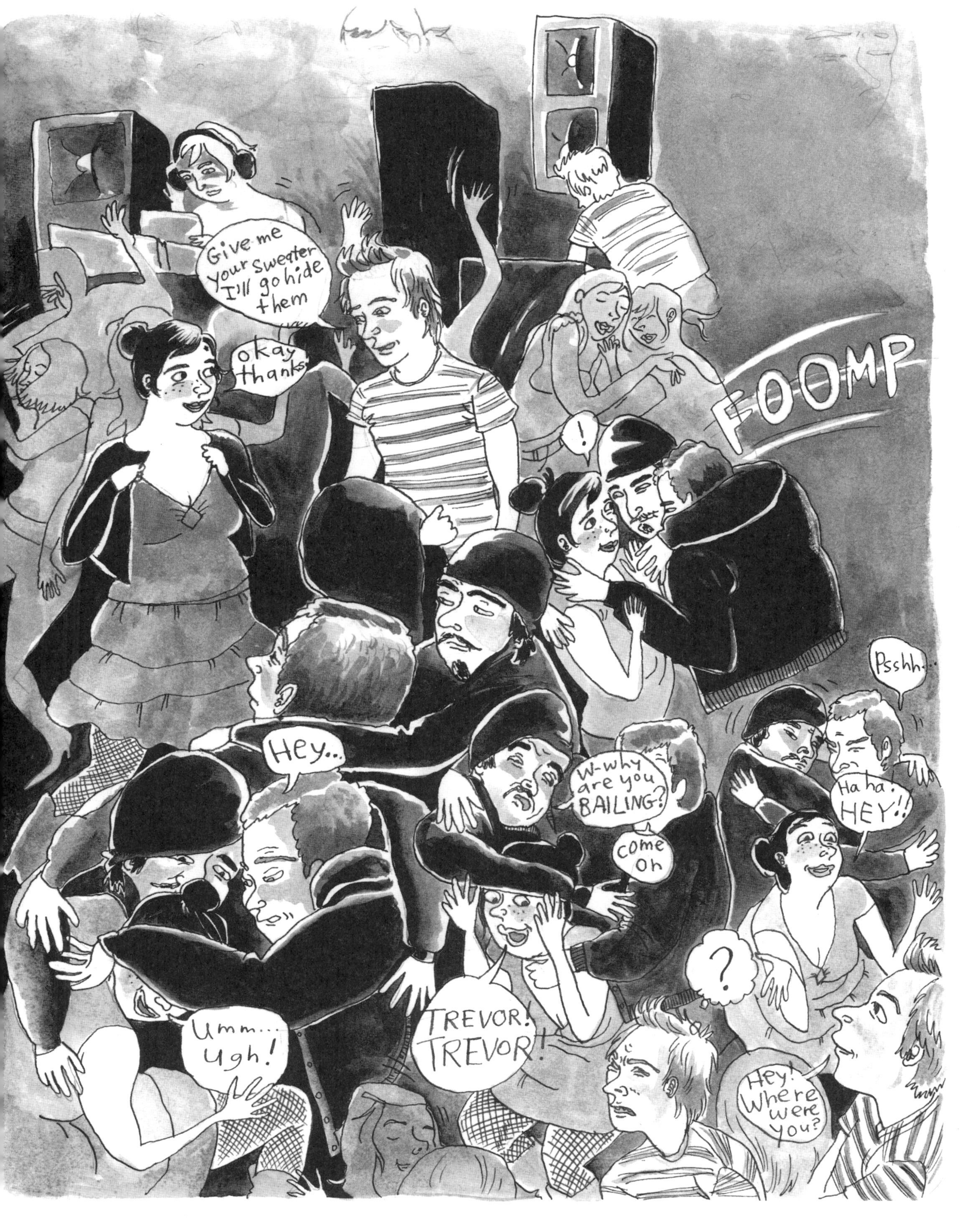
Give me your sweater I'll go hide them
okay thanks
!
FOOMP
Psshh...
Hey...
W-why are you BAILING?
Ha ha! HEY!!
come on
?
Umm... Ugh!
TREVOR! TREVOR!
Hey! Where were you?

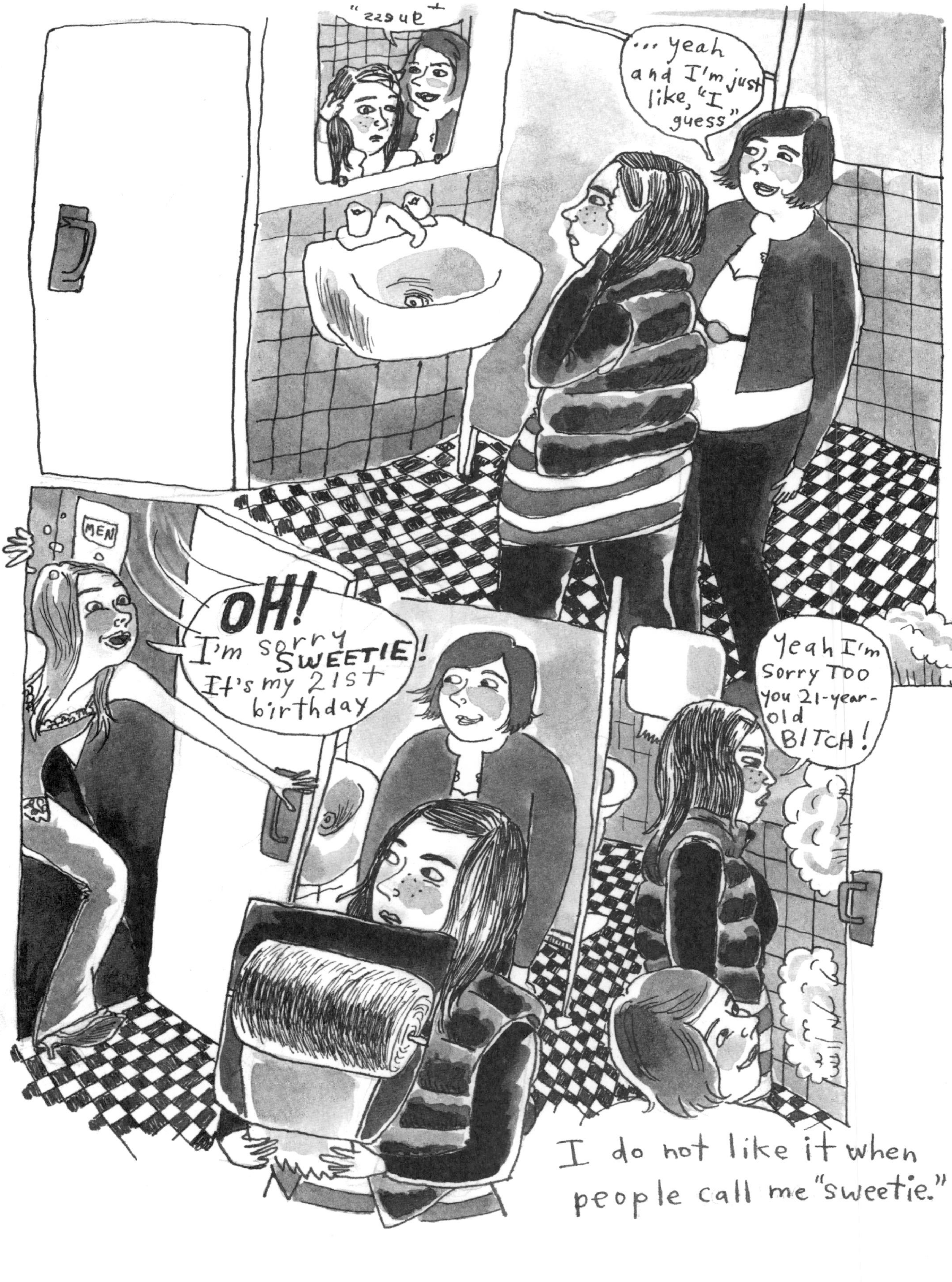
... yeah and I'm just like, "I guess"
MEN
OH! I'm sorry SWEETIE! It's my 21st birthday
Yeah I'm sorry TOO you 21-year-old BITCH!
I do not like it when people call me "sweetie."

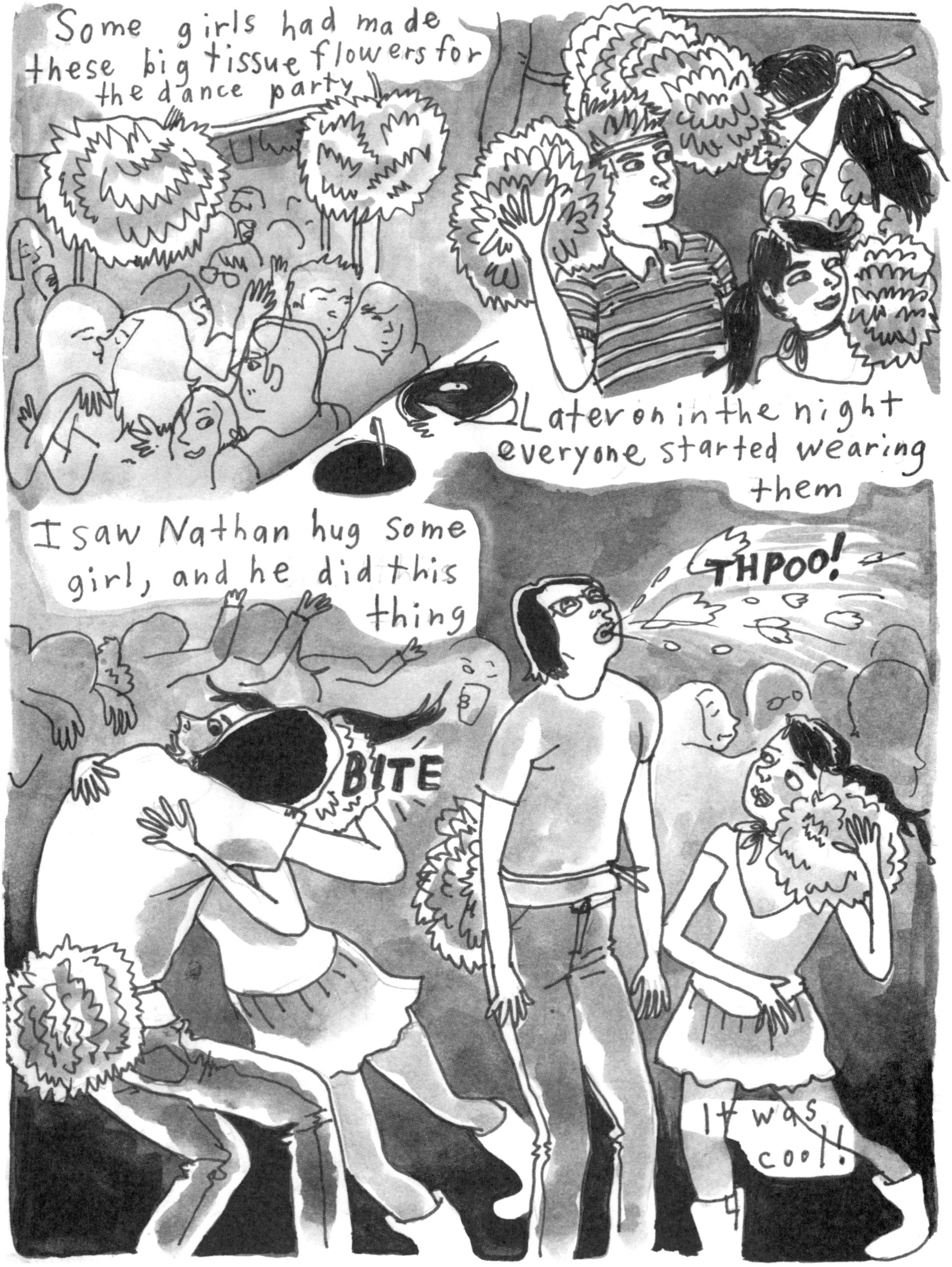

Some girls had made these big tissue flowers for the dance party
Later on in the night everyone started wearing them
I saw Nathan hug some girl, and he did this thing
THPOO!
BITE
It was cool!

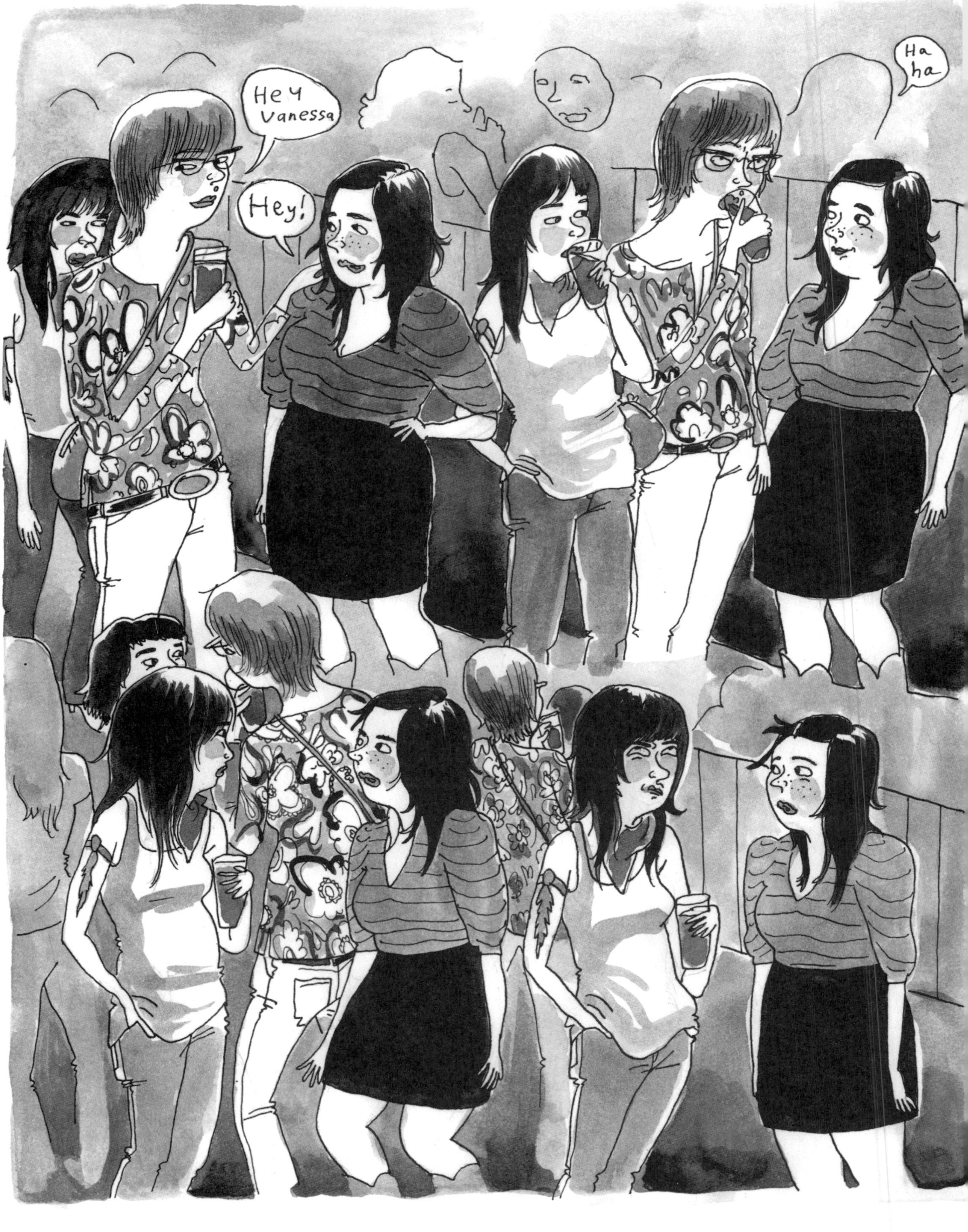
Hey Vanessa
Hey!
Ha ha

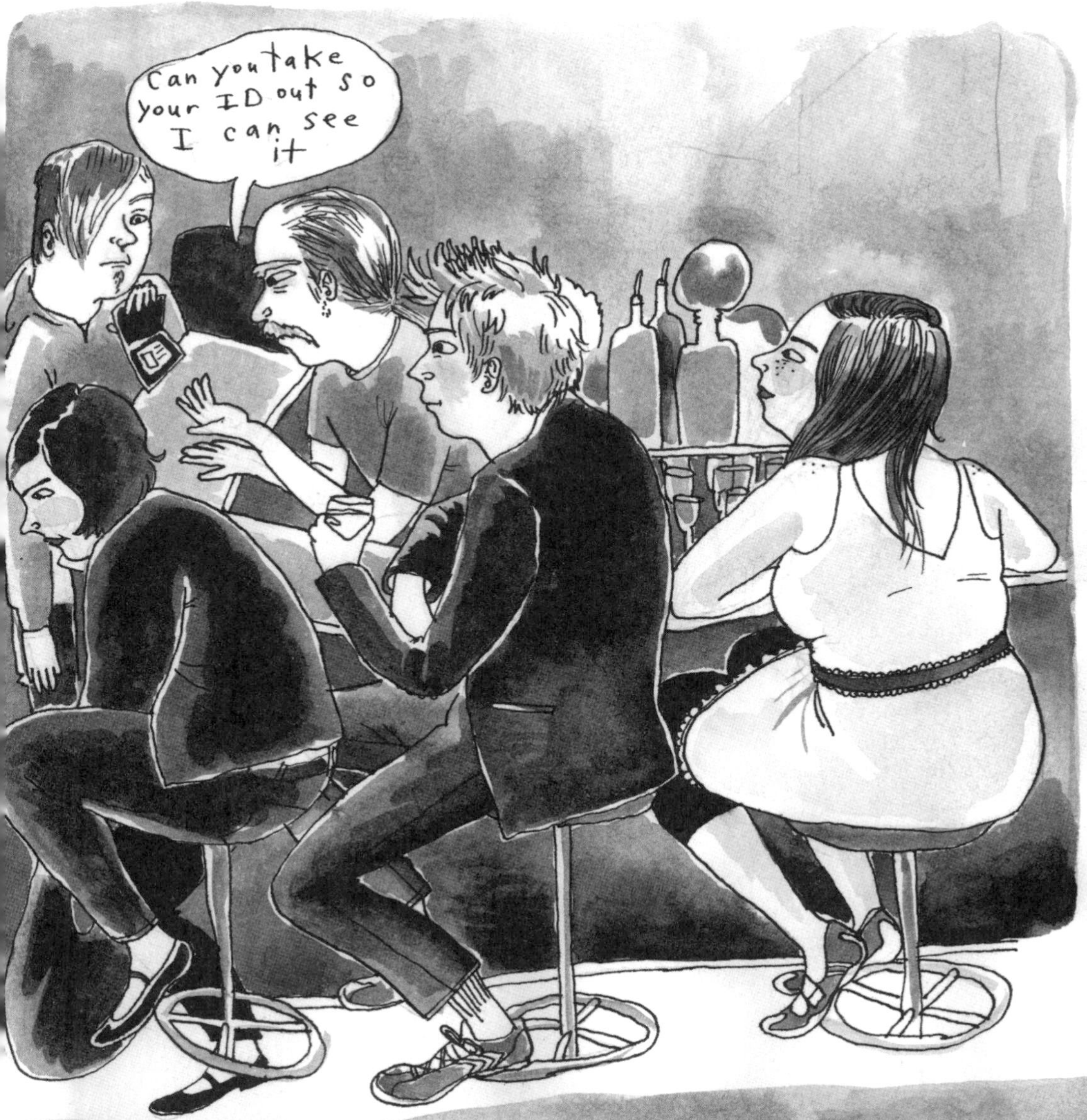
Can you take your ID out so I can see it

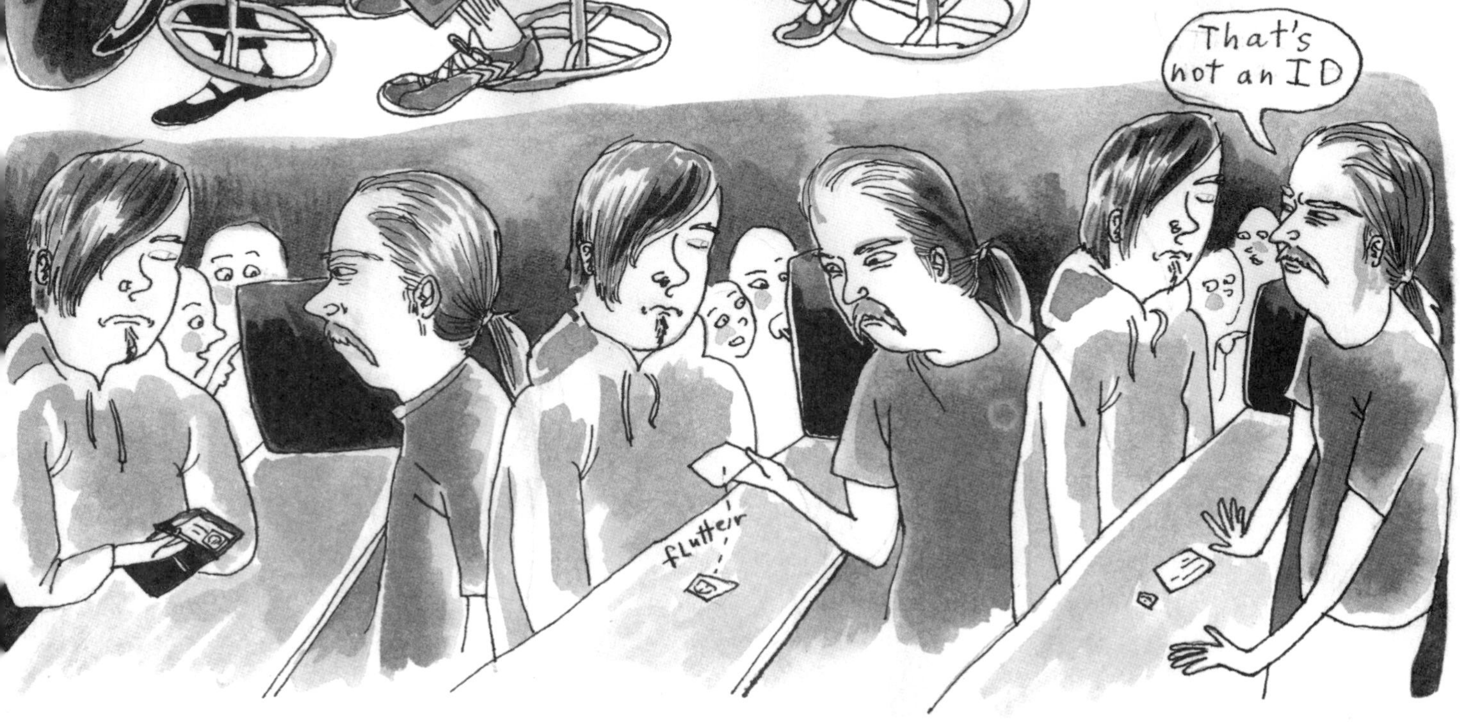
That's not an ID
flutter

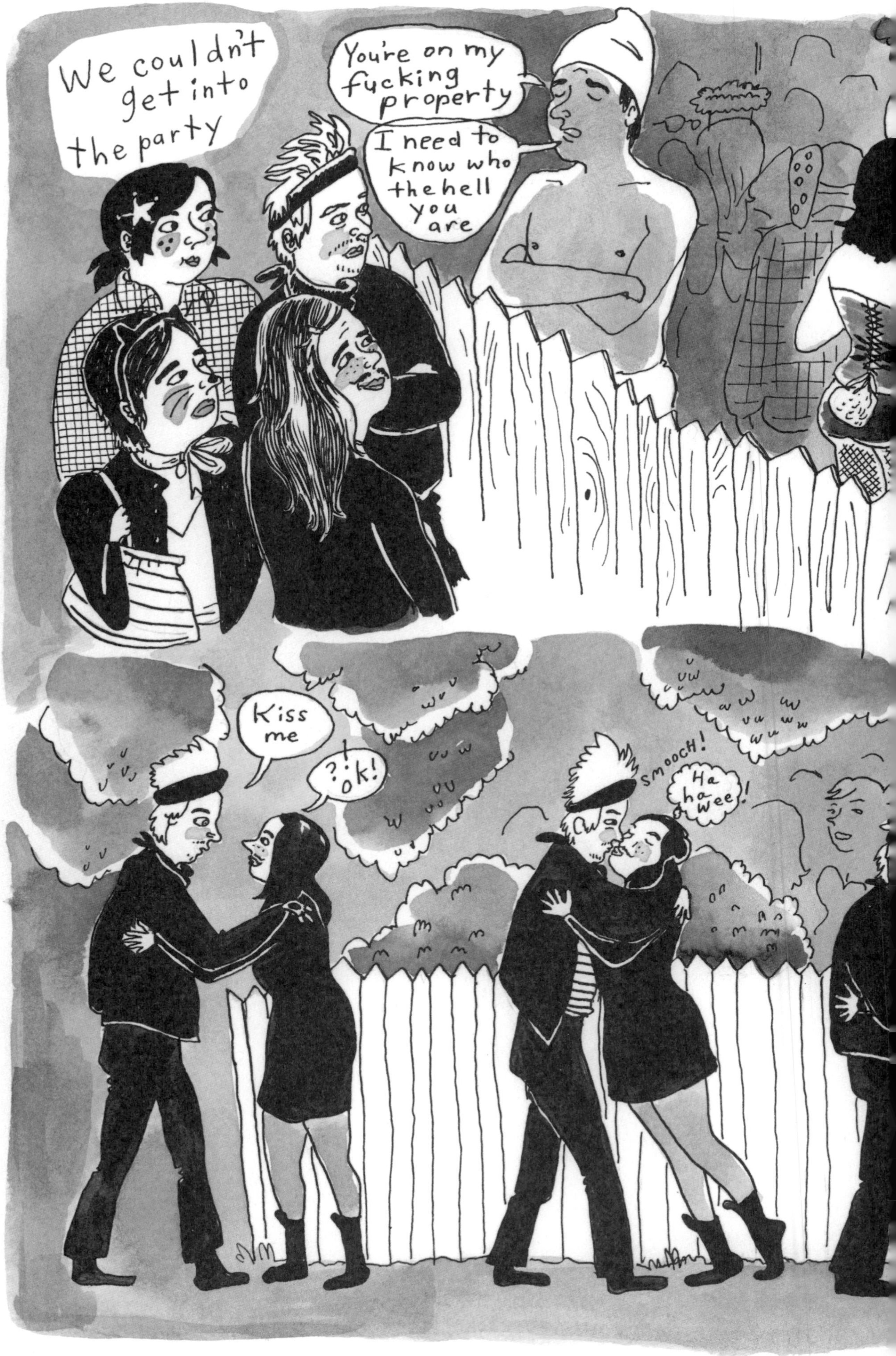
We couldn't get into the party
You're on my fucking property
I need to know who the hell you are
Kiss me
?! ok!
SMOOCH!
Ha ha wee!

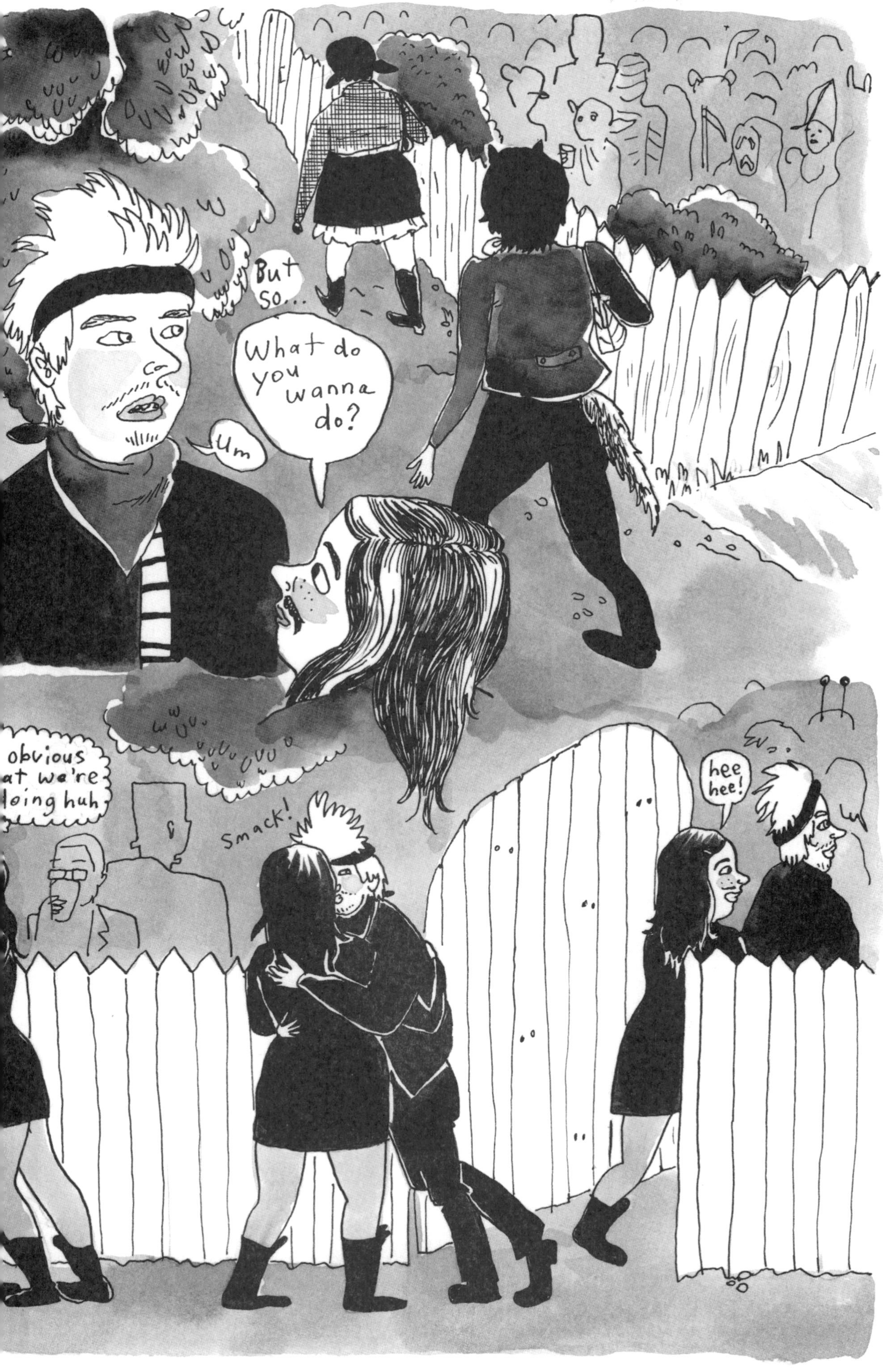

But so...
What do you wanna do?
Um
obvious
at we're
doing huh
Smack!
hee hee!

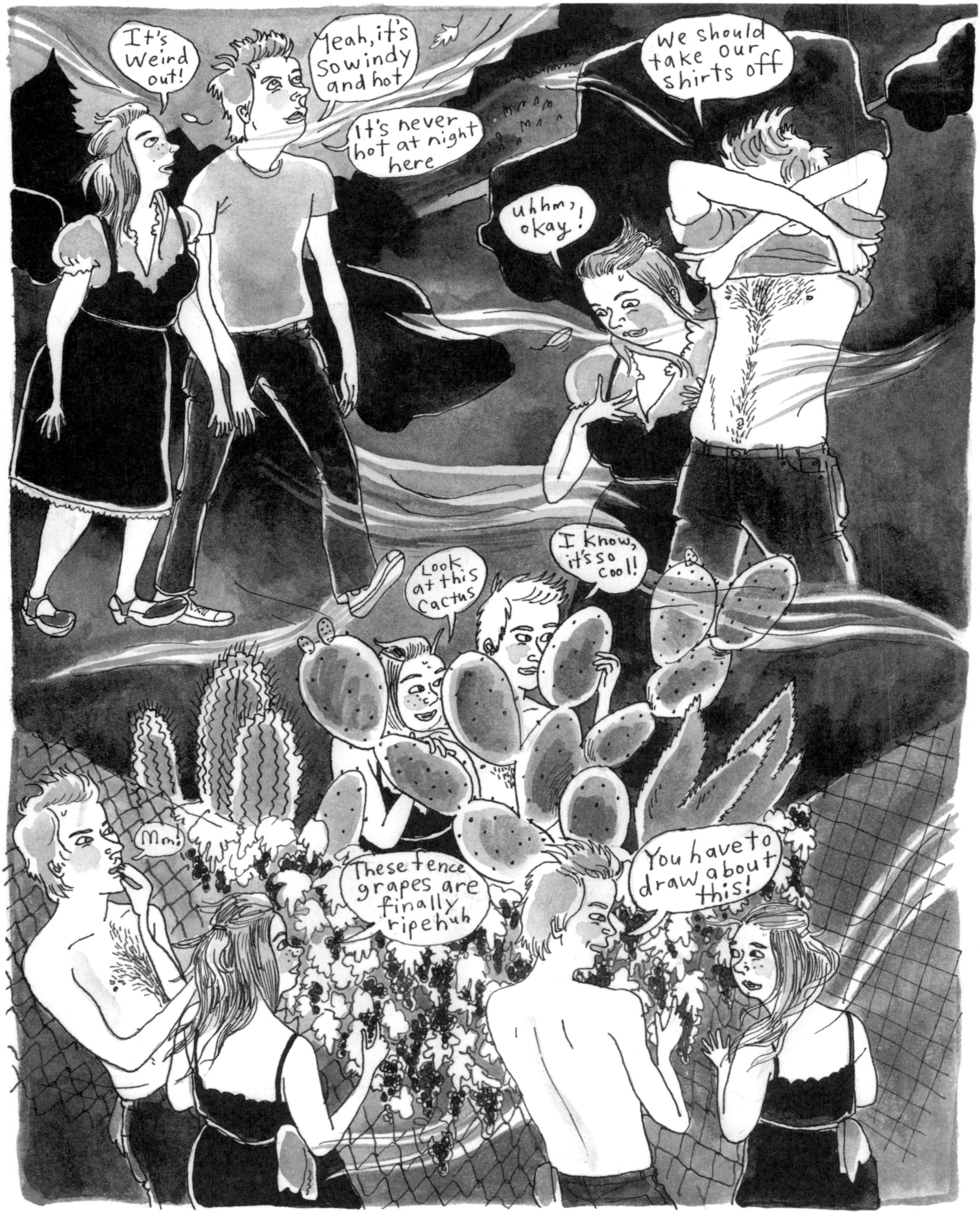
It's weird out!
Yeah, it's so windy and hot
It's never hot at night here
We should take our shirts off
Uhhm, okay!
Look at this cactus
I know, it's so cool!
Mm!
These fence grapes are finally ripe huh
You have to draw about this!

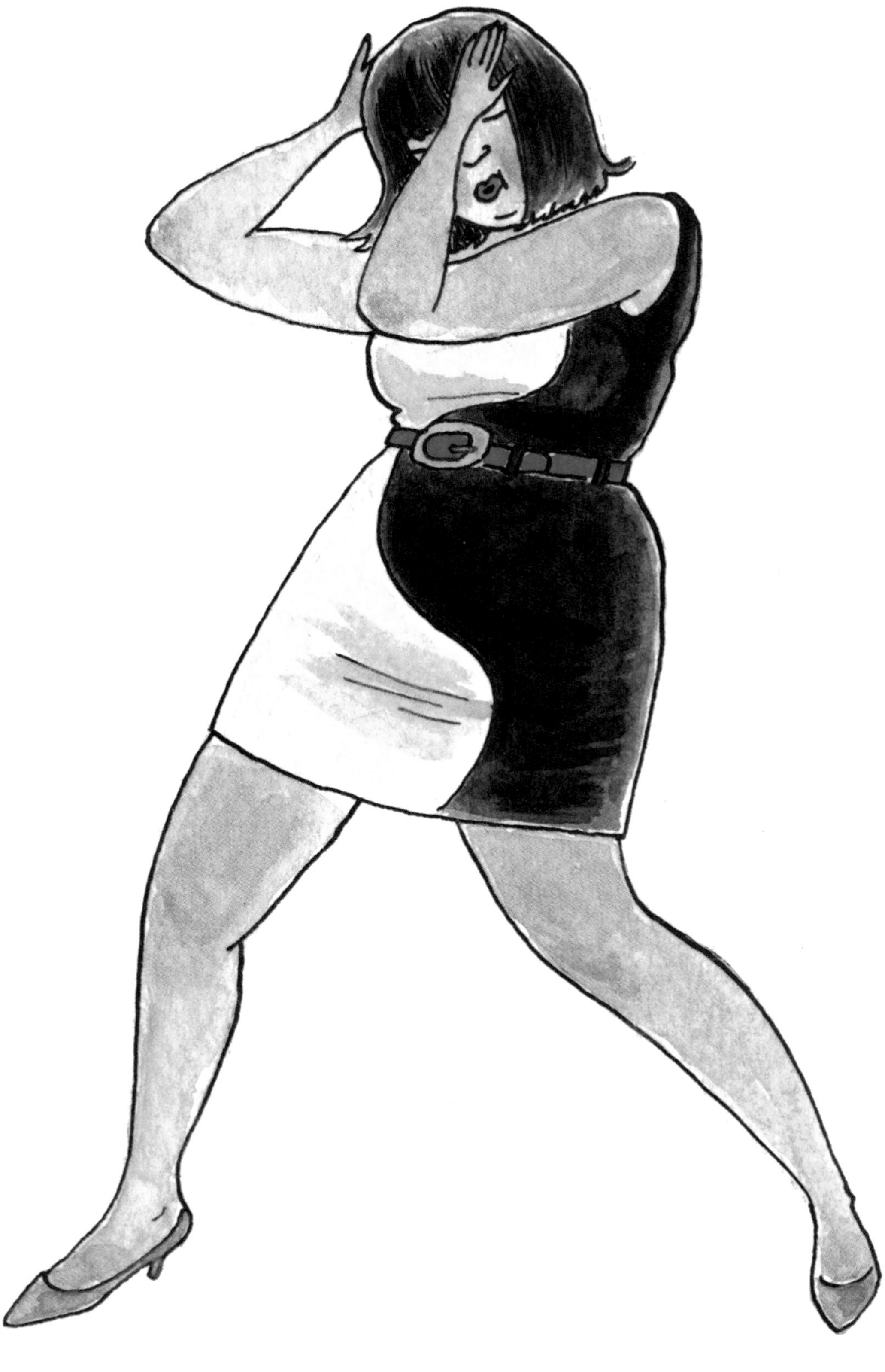

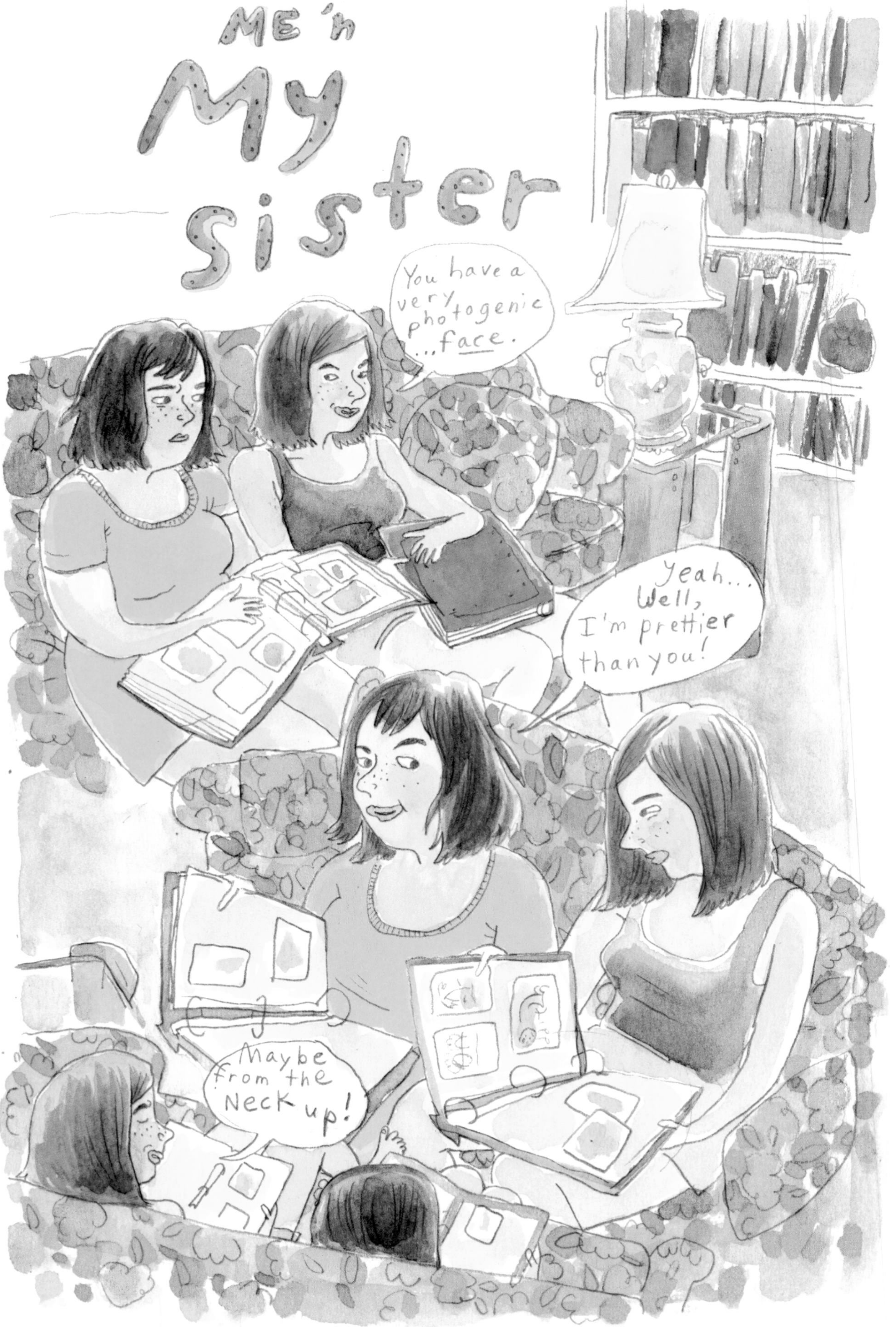
ME 'n My sister
You have a very photogenic ...face.
Yeah... Well, I'm prettier than you!
Maybe from the Neck up!

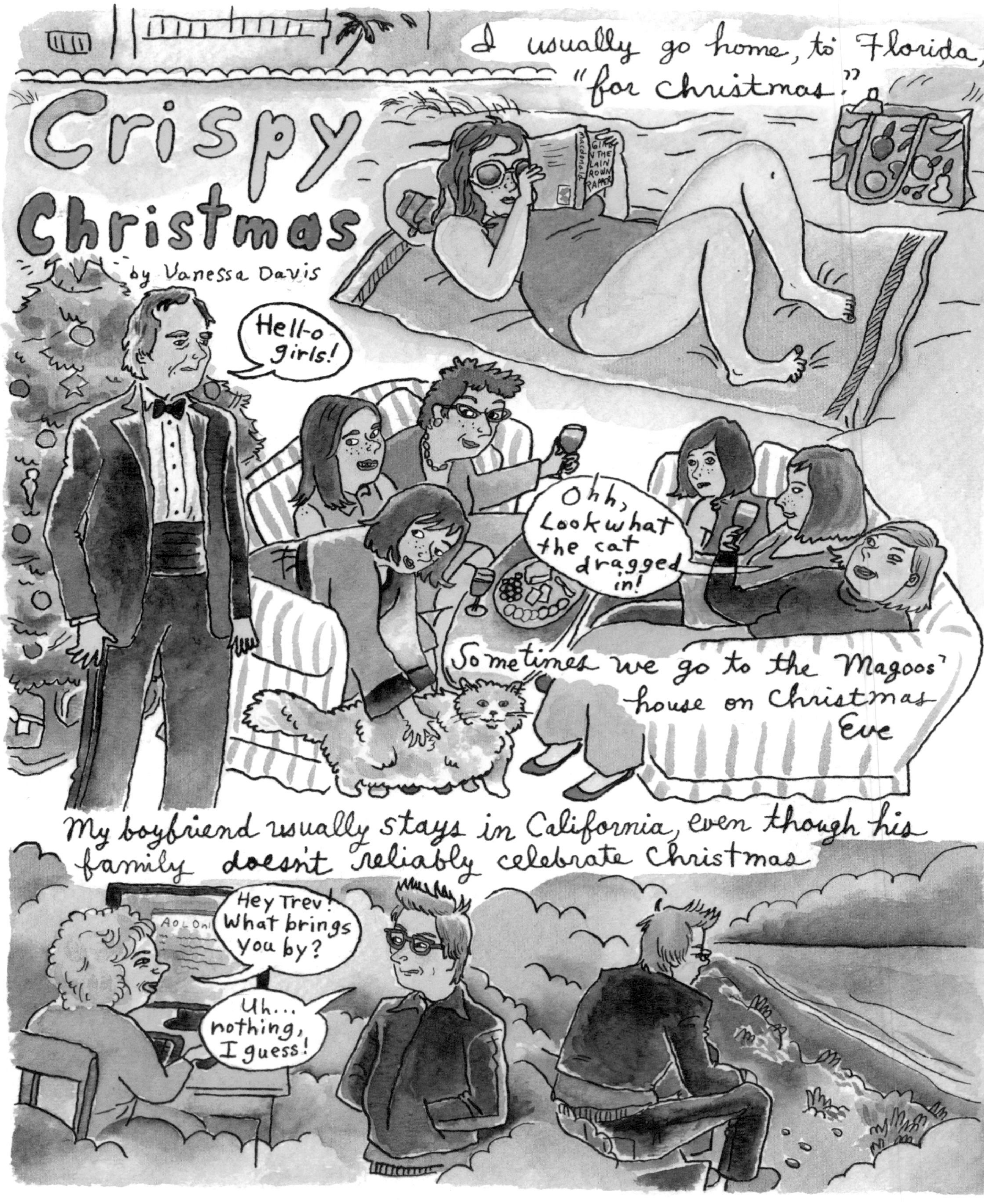
I usually go home, to Florida, "for Christmas."
Crispy Christmas
by Vanessa Davis
Hell-o girls!
Ohh, Look what the cat dragged in!
Sometimes we go to the Magoos' house on Christmas Eve
My boyfriend usually stays in California, even though his family doesn't reliably celebrate Christmas
Hey Trev! What brings you by?
Uh... nothing, I guess!

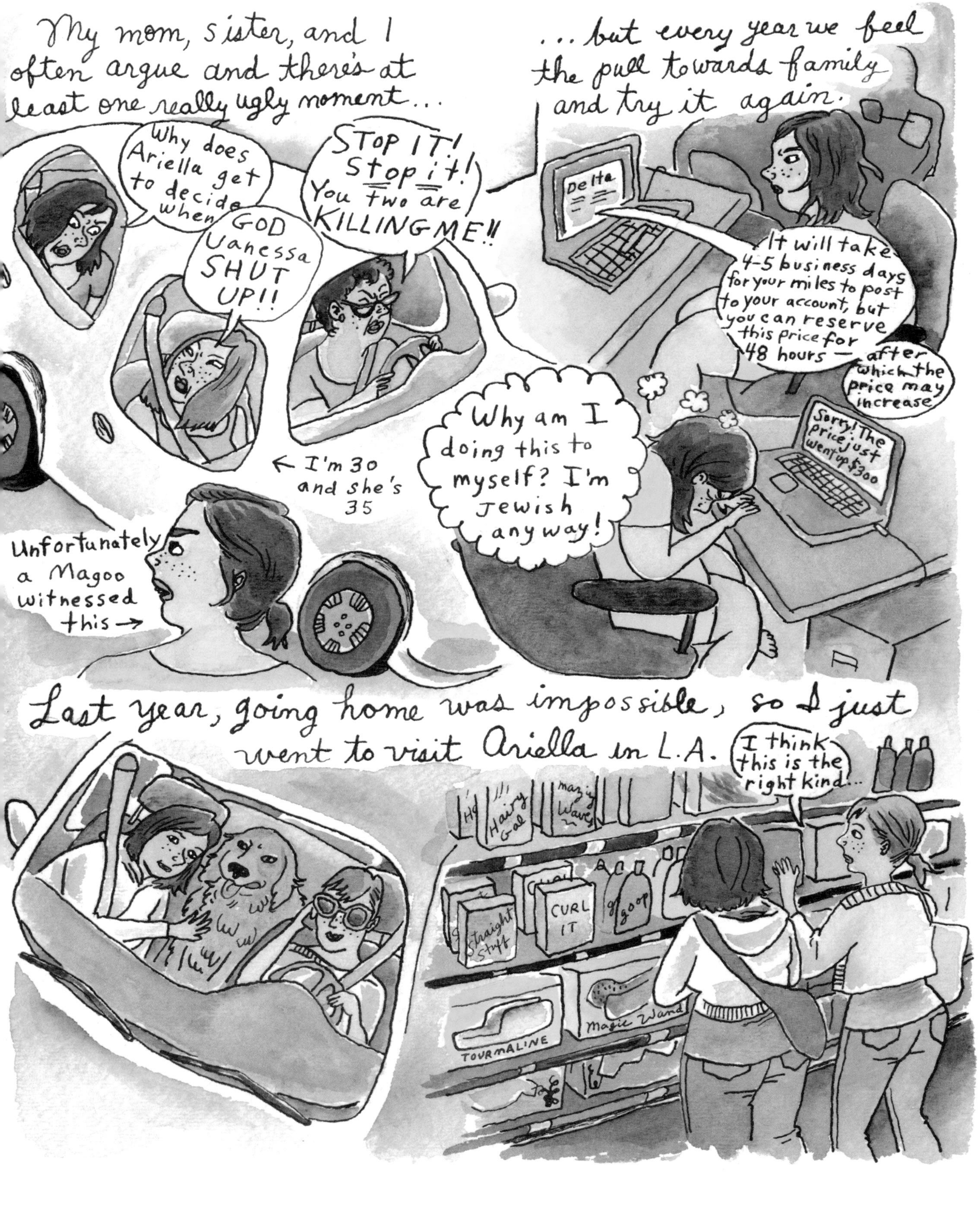

My mom, sister, and I often argue and there's at least one really ugly moment...
Why does Ariella get to decide when
STOP IT! Stop it! You two are KILLINGME!!
GOD Vanessa SHUT UP!!
← I'm 30 and she's 35
Unfortunately a Magoo witnessed this →
... but every year we feel the pull towards family and try it again.
Delta
It will take 4-5 business days for your miles to post to your account, but you can reserve this price for 48 hours — after which the price may increase
Why am I doing this to myself? I'm Jewish anyway!
Sorry! The price just went up $300
Last year, going home was impossible, so I just went to visit Ariella in L.A.
I think this is the right kind...
Hairy Gal
Wavy
Straight Stuff
CURL IT
goop
TOURMALINE
Magic Wand

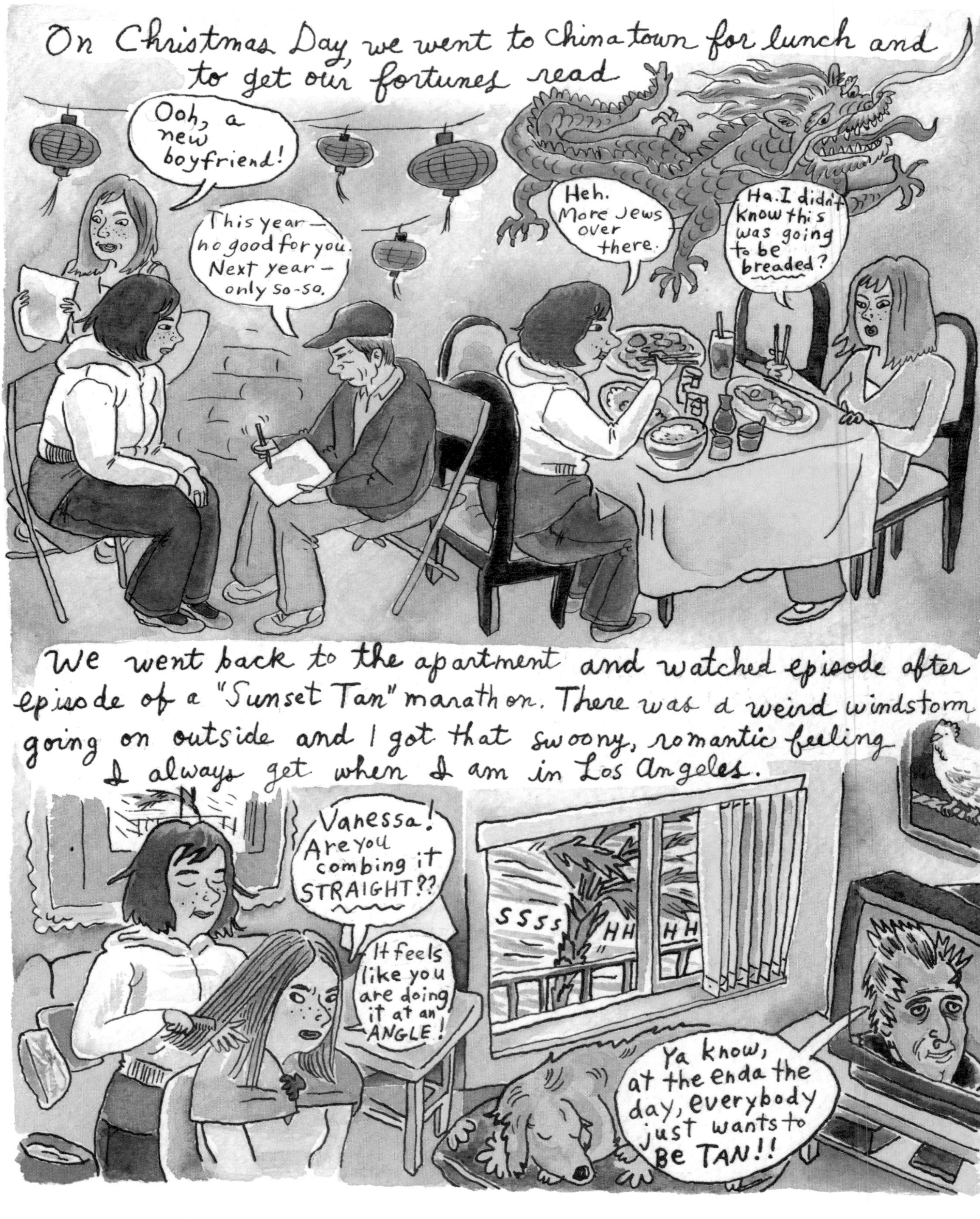
On Christmas Day, we went to Chinatown for lunch and to get our fortunes read
Ooh, a new boyfriend!
This year— no good for you. Next year— only so-so.
Heh. More Jews over there.
Ha. I didn't know this was going to be breaded?
We went back to the apartment and watched episode after episode of a "Sunset Tan" marathon. There was a weird windstorm going on outside and I got that swoony, romantic feeling I always get when I am in Los Angeles.
Vanessa! Are you combing it STRAIGHT??
It feels like you are doing it at an ANGLE!
SSSS HH HH
Ya know, at the enda the day, everybody just wants to BE TAN!!

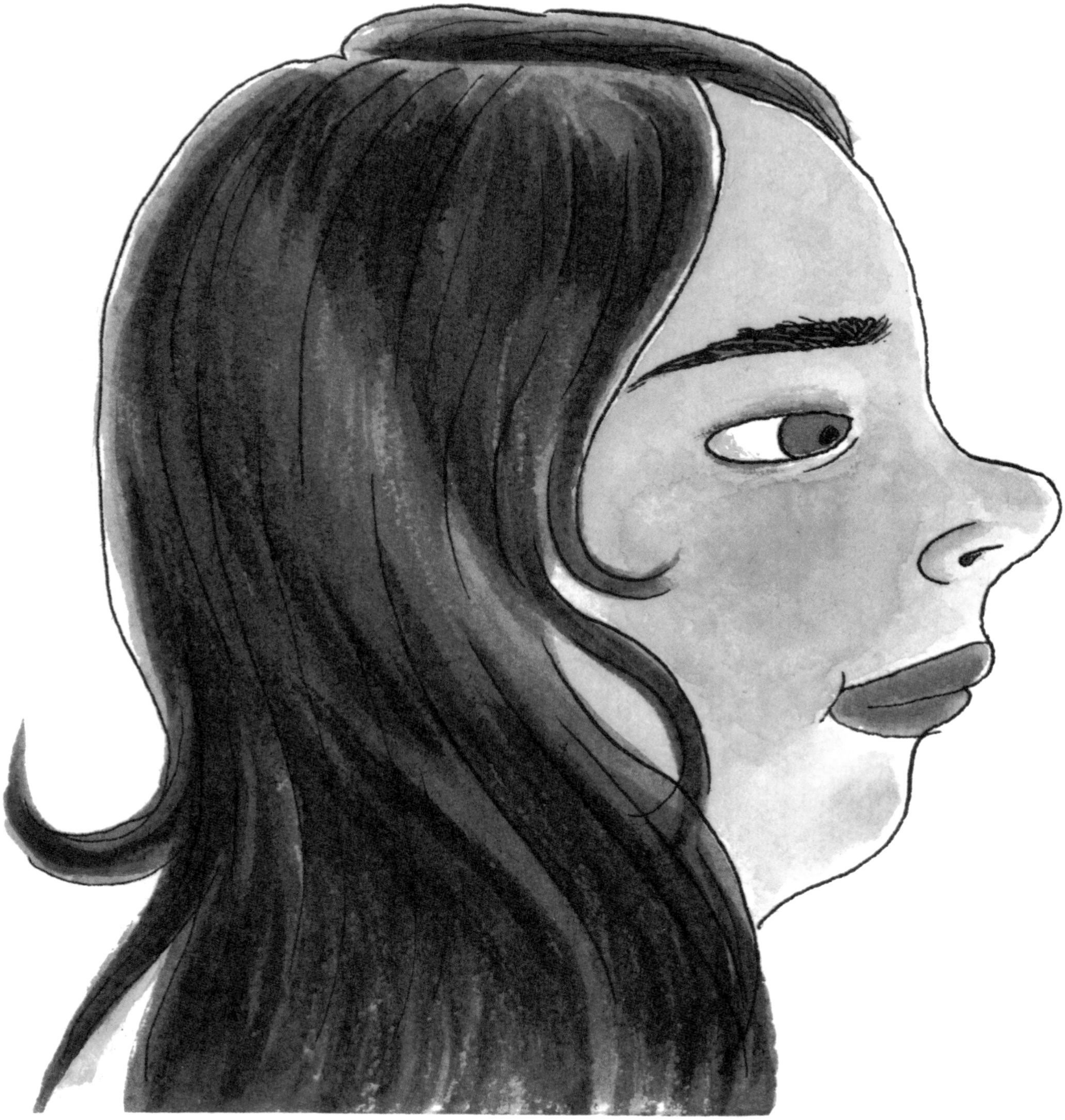

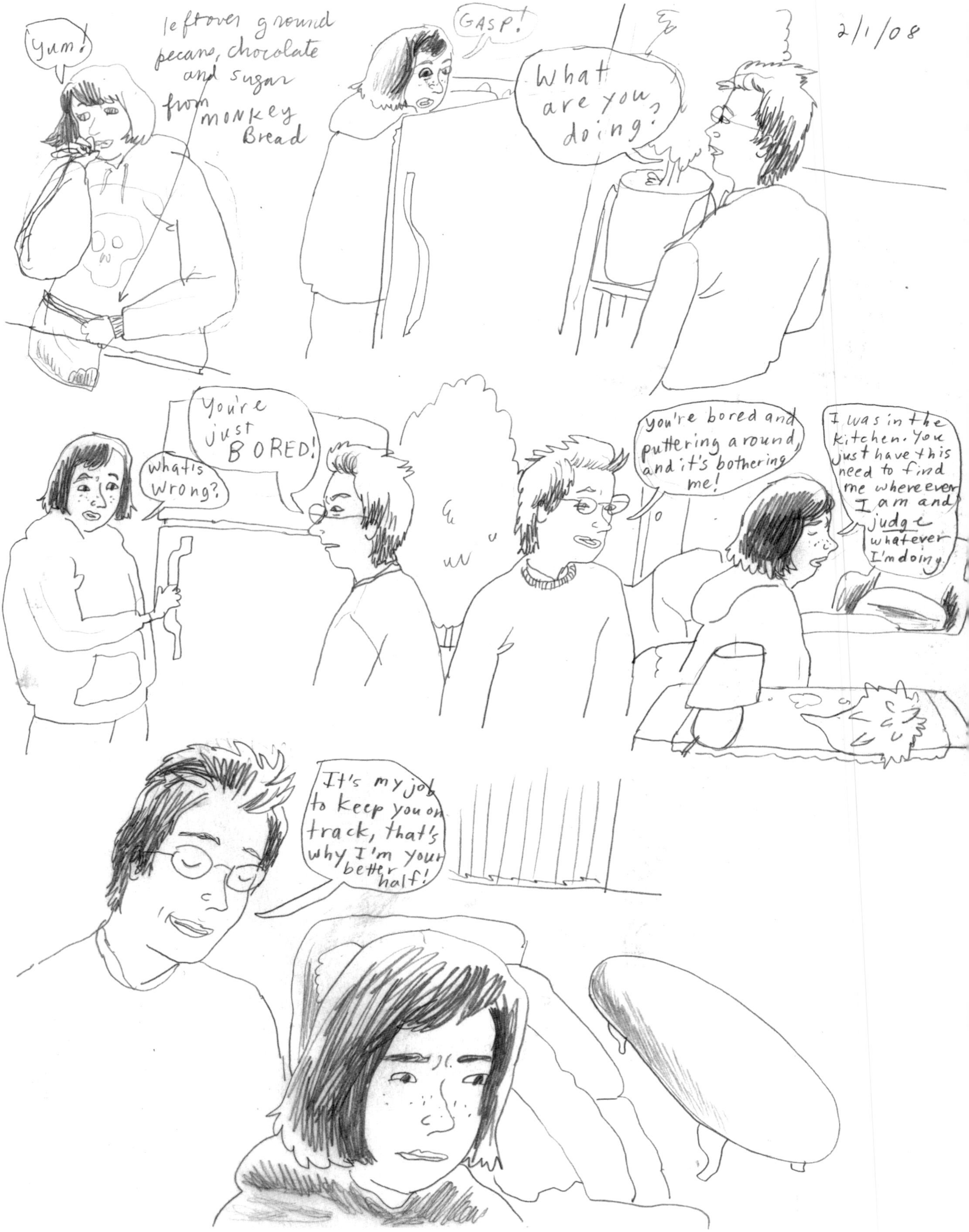
2/1/08
Yum!
leftover ground pecans, chocolate and sugar from Monkey Bread
GASP!
What are you doing?
You're just BORED!
what's wrong?
You're bored and puttering around, and it's bothering me!
I was in the kitchen. You just have this need to find me where ever I am and judge whatever I'm doing.
It's my job to keep you on track, that's why I'm your better half!

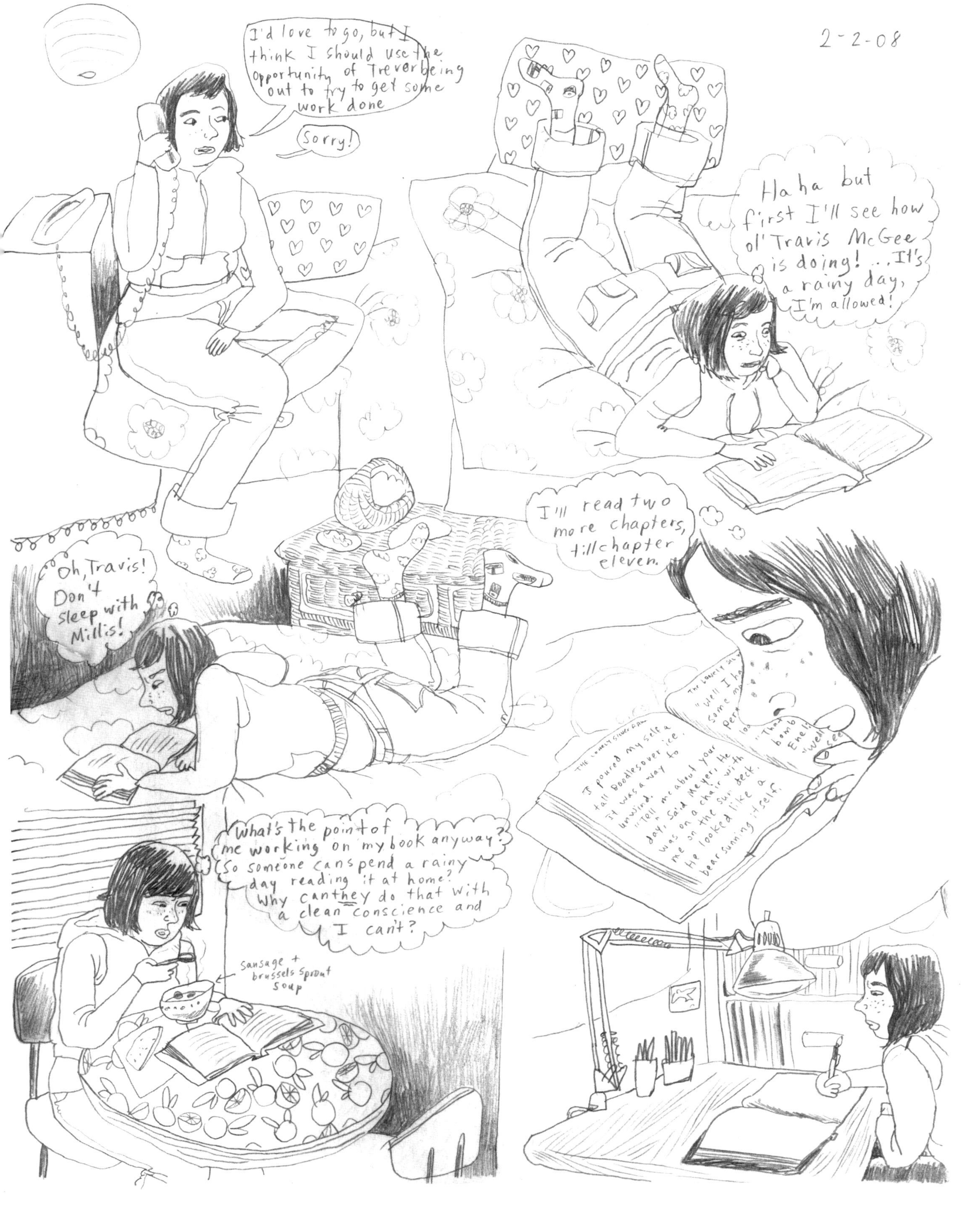
2-2-08
I'd love to go, but I think I should use the opportunity of Trever being out to try to get some work done
Sorry!
Ha ha but first I'll see how ol' Travis McGee is doing! ...It's a rainy day, I'm allowed!
I'll read two more chapters, till chapter eleven.
Oh, Travis! Don't sleep with Millis!
THE LONELY SILVER RAIN
I poured myself a tall Boodles over ice. It was a way to unwind. "Tell me about your day," said Meyer. He was on a chair with me on the sun deck. He looked like a bear sunning itself.
What's the point of me working on my book anyway? So someone can spend a rainy day reading it at home? Why can they do that with a clean conscience and I can't?
sausage + brussels sprout soup

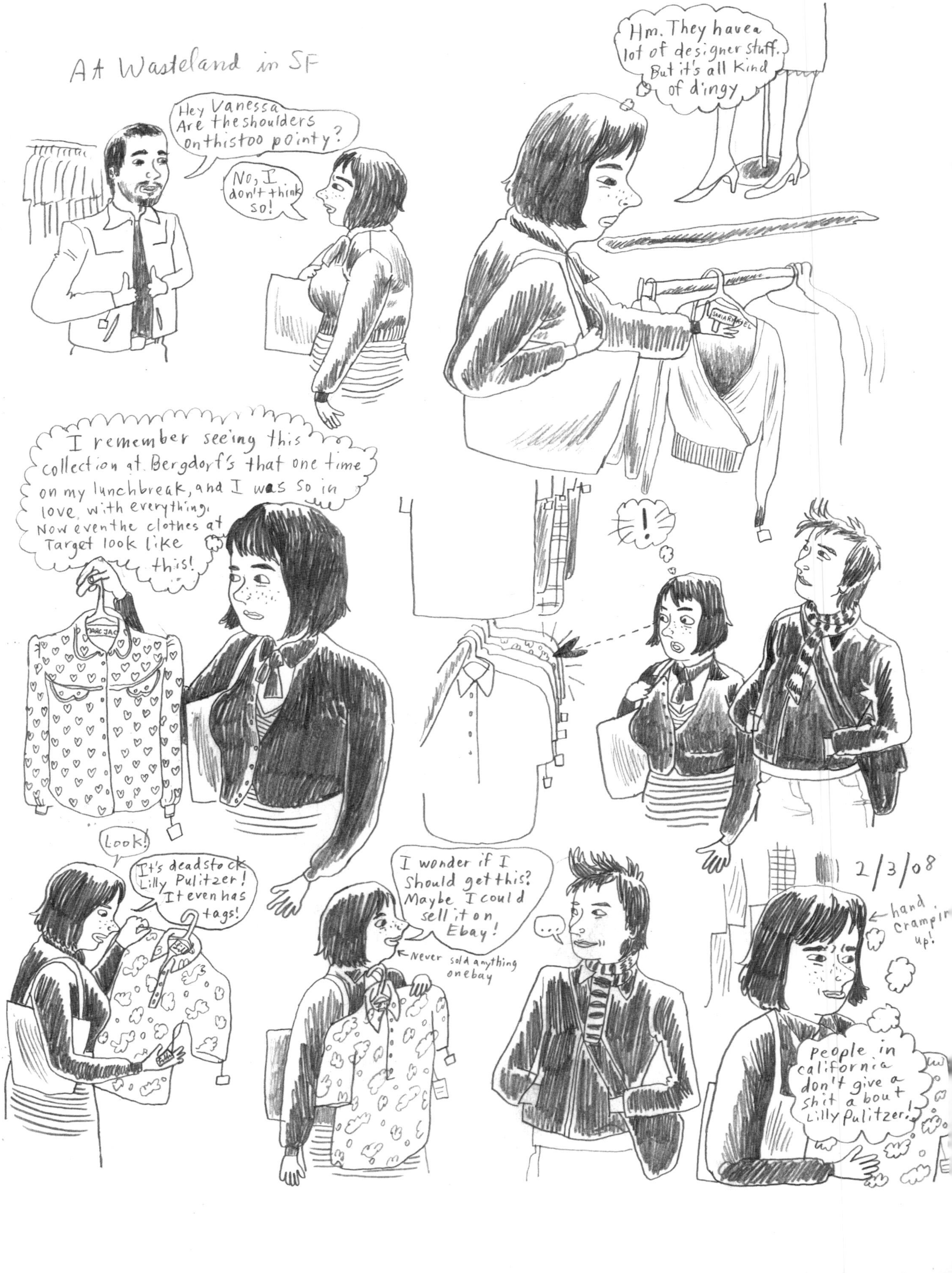
At Wasteland in SF
Hey Vanessa Are the shoulders on this too pointy?
No, I don't think so!
Hm. They have a lot of designer stuff. But it's all kind of dingy
I remember seeing this collection at Bergdorf's that one time on my lunchbreak, and I was so in love with everything. Now even the clothes at Target look like this!
MARC JAC
!
Look!
It's deadstock Lilly Pulitzer! It even has tags!
I wonder if I should get this? Maybe I could sell it on Ebay!
Never sold anything on ebay
...
2/3/08
hand crampin up!
people in california don't give a shit about Lilly Pulitzer!

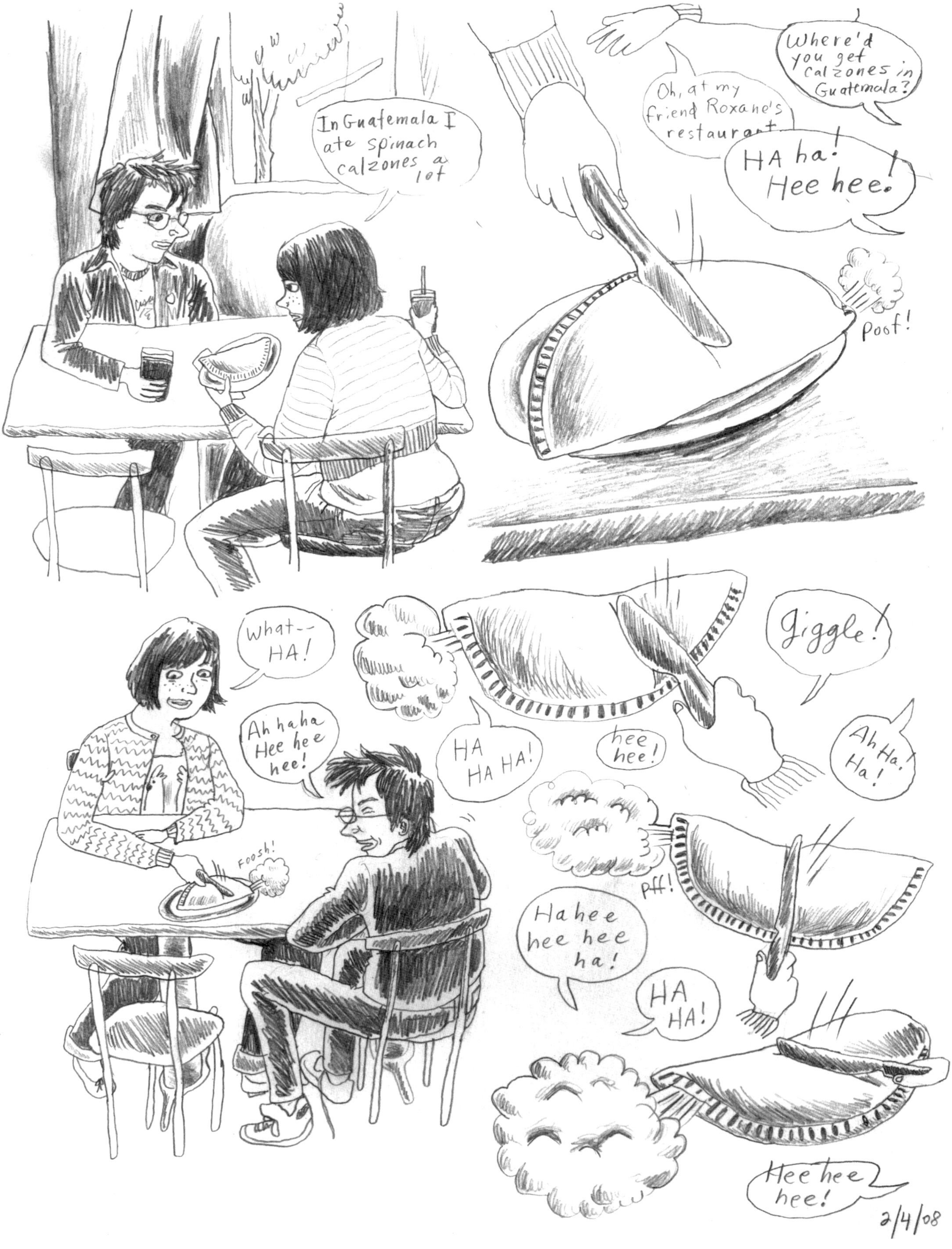
In Guatemala I ate spinach calzones a lot
Where'd you get calzones in Guatemala?
Oh, at my friend Roxane's restaurant.
HA ha! Hee hee!
Poof!
What-- HA!
Ah haha Hee hee hee!
Foosh!
HA HA HA!
Giggle!
hee hee!
Ah Ha! Ha!
Pff!
Ha hee hee hee ha!
HA HA!
Hee hee hee!
2/4/08

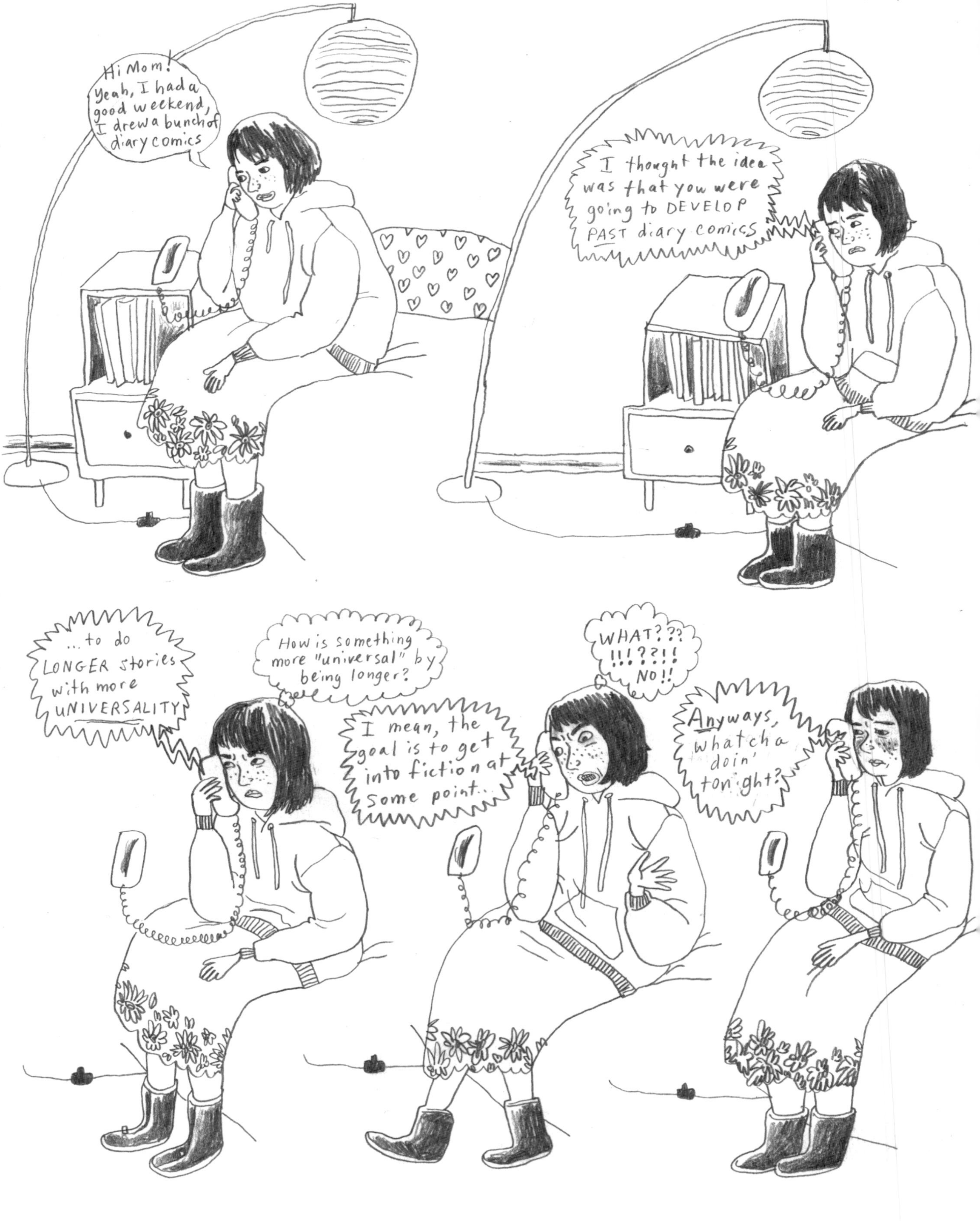
Hi Mom! Yeah, I had a good weekend, I drew a bunch of diary comics
I thought the idea was that you were going to DEVELOP PAST diary comics
...to do LONGER stories with more UNIVERSALITY
How is something more "universal" by being longer?
I mean, the goal is to get into fiction at some point...
WHAT??? !!!???!! NO!!
Anyways, whatcha doin' tonight?

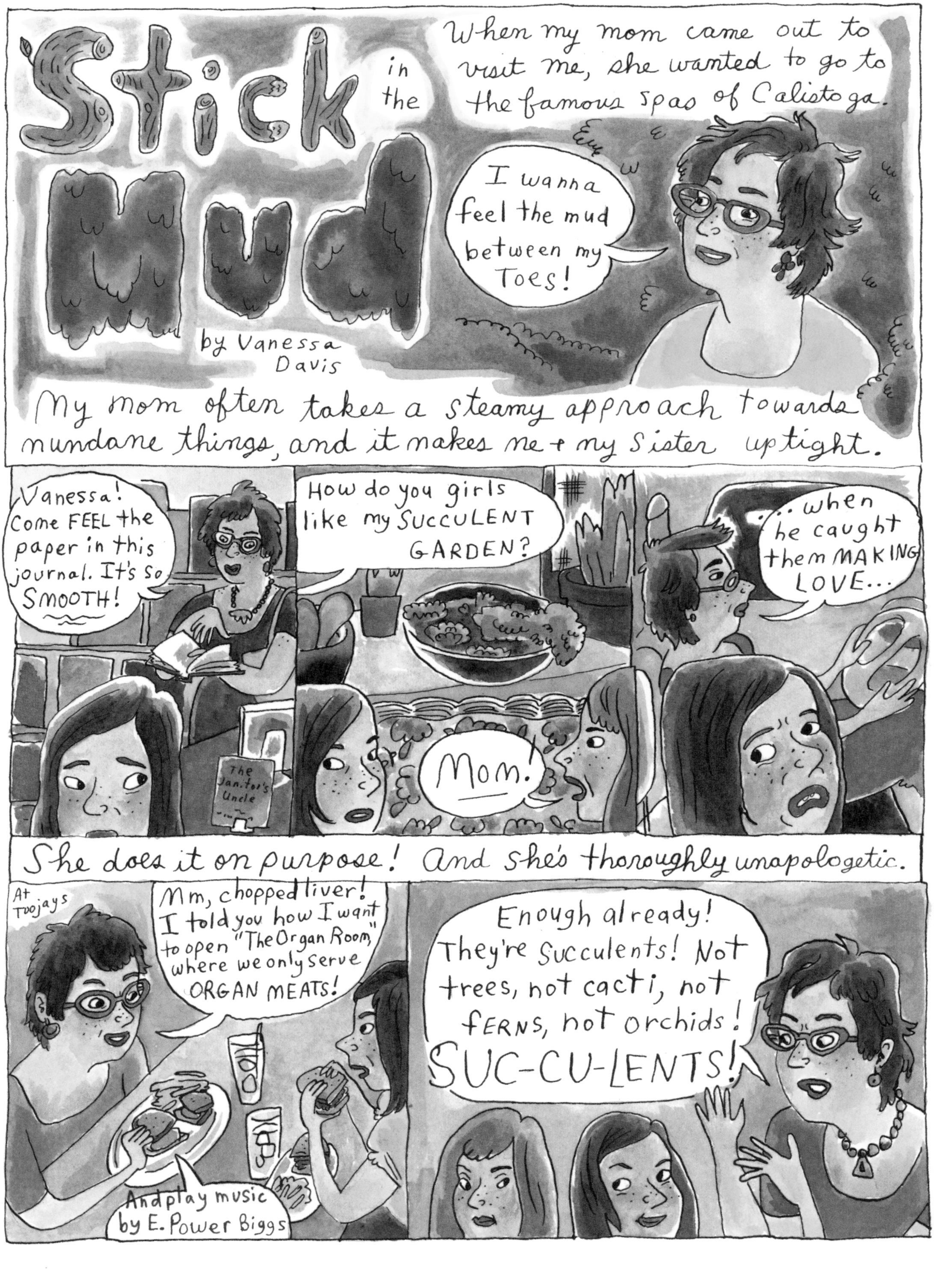
Stick in the Mud
by Vanessa Davis
When my mom came out to visit me, she wanted to go to the famous spas of Calistoga.
I wanna feel the mud between my Toes!
My mom often takes a steamy approach towards mundane things, and it makes me + my sister uptight.
Vanessa! Come FEEL the paper in this journal. It's so SMOOTH!
The Janitor's Uncle
How do you girls like my SUCCULENT GARDEN?
Mom!
...when he caught them MAKING LOVE...
She does it on purpose! And she's thoroughly unapologetic.
At Toojays
Mm, chopped liver! I told you how I want to open "The Organ Room" where we only serve ORGAN MEATS!
And play music by E. Power Biggs
Enough already! They're succulents! Not trees, not cacti, not ferns, not orchids! SUC-CU-LENTS!

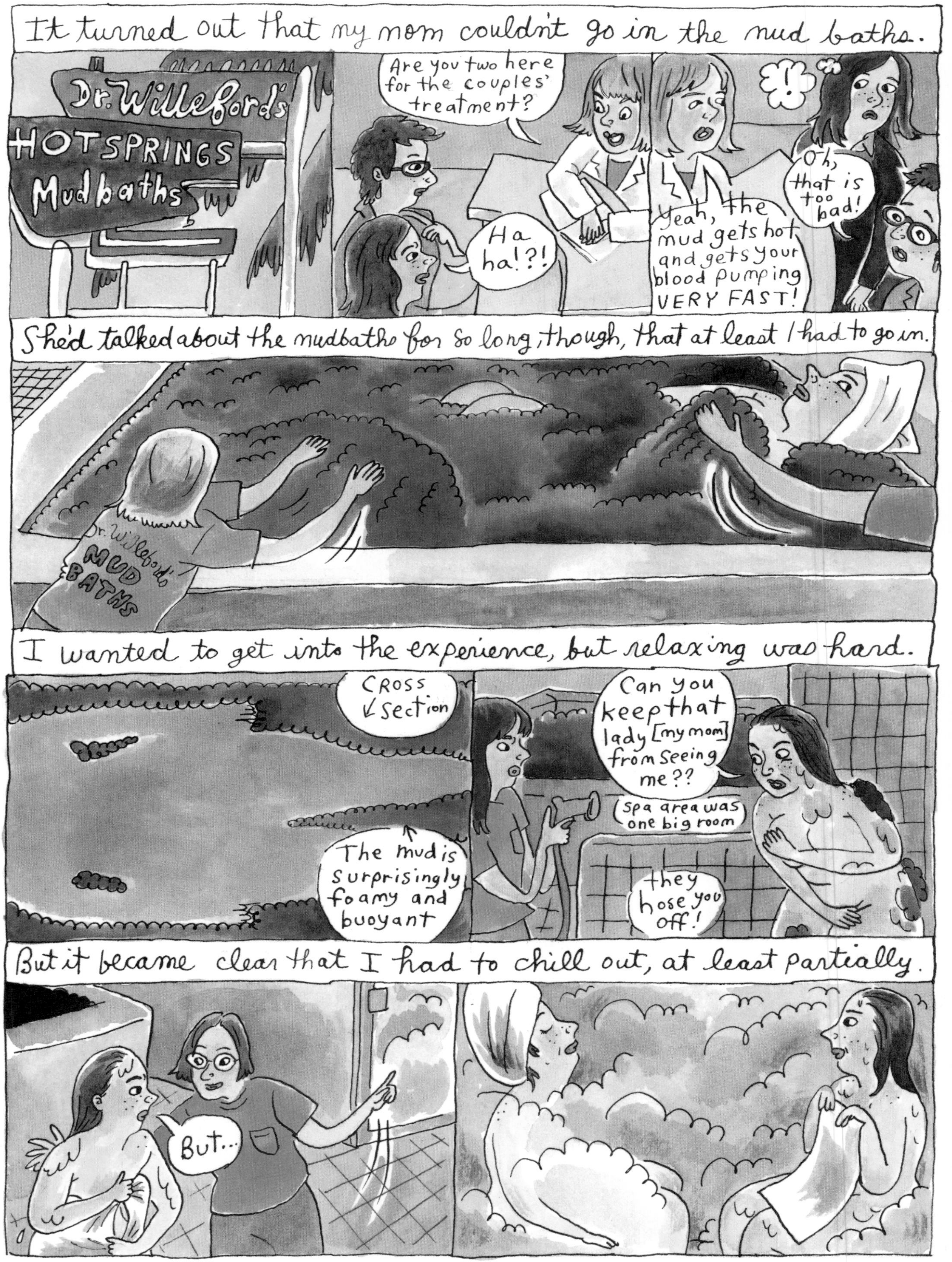
It turned out that my mom couldn't go in the mud baths.
Dr. Willeford's HOTSPRINGS Mudbaths
Are you two here for the couples' treatment?
Ha ha!?!
Yeah, the mud gets hot and gets your blood pumping VERY FAST!
!
Oh, that is too bad!
She'd talked about the mudbaths for so long, though, that at least I had to go in.
Dr. Willeford's MUD BATHS
I wanted to get into the experience, but relaxing was hard.
CROSS section
The mud is surprisingly foamy and buoyant
Can you keep that lady [my mom] from seeing me??
(spa area was one big room)
they hose you off!
But it became clear that I had to chill out, at least partially.
But...

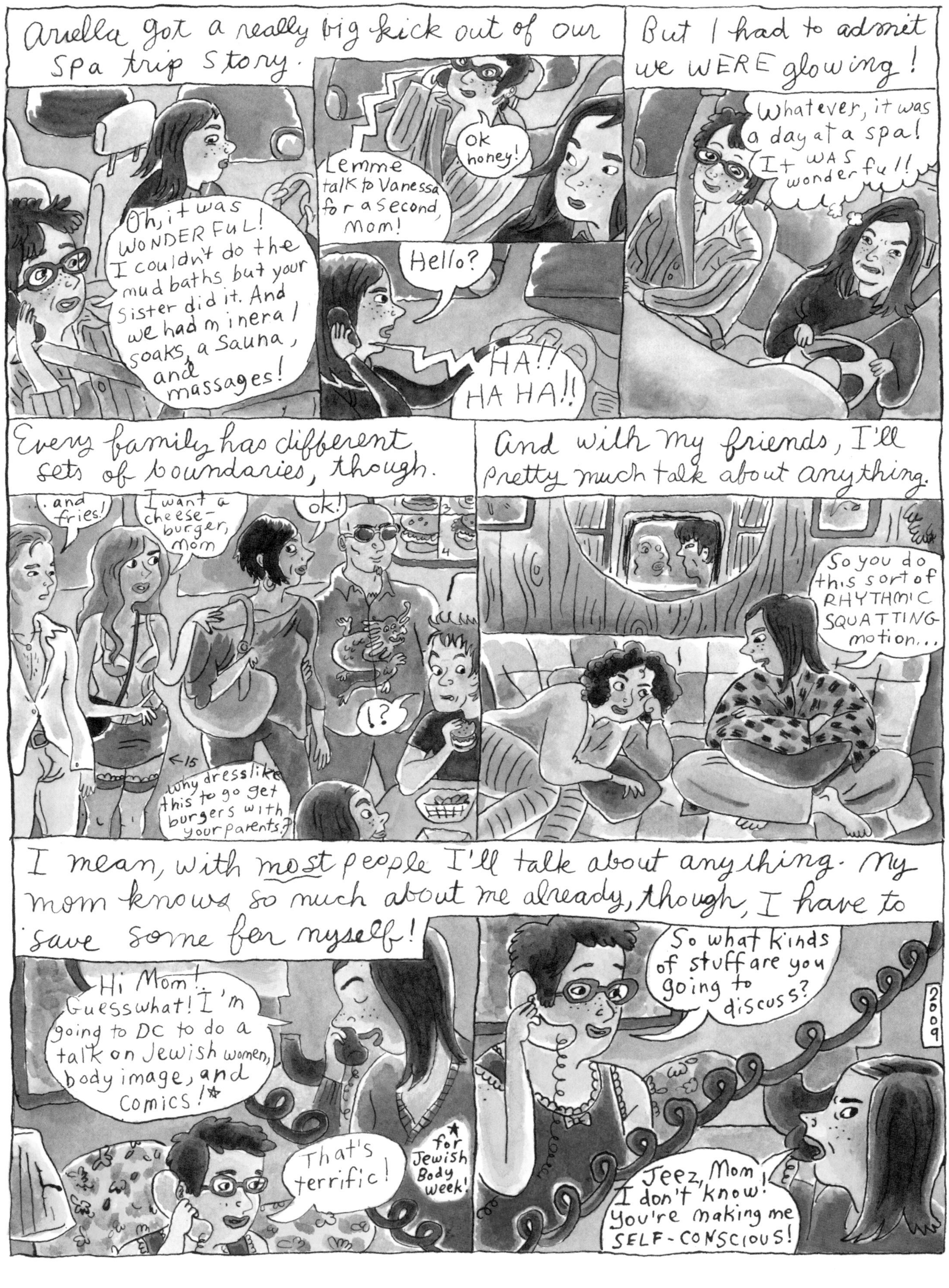
Ariella got a really big kick out of our Spa trip Story.
Oh, it was WONDERFUL! I couldn't do the mud baths but your sister did it. And we had mineral soaks, a Sauna, and massages!
Lemme talk to Vanessa for a second, mom!
Ok honey!
Hello?
HA!! HA HA!!
But I had to admit we WERE glowing!
Whatever, it was a day at a spa! It WAS wonderful!
Every family has different sets of boundaries, though.
...and fries!
I want a cheese-burger, mom
ok!
!?
←15
Why dress like this to go get burgers with your parents?
And with my friends, I'll pretty much talk about anything.
So you do this sort of RHYTHMIC SQUATTING motion...
I mean, with most people I'll talk about anything. My mom knows so much about me already, though, I have to save some for myself!
Hi Mom! Guess what! I'm going to DC to do a talk on Jewish women, body image, and comics!☆
That's terrific!
☆ for Jewish Body week!
So what kinds of stuff are you going to discuss?
Jeez, Mom! I don't know! You're making me SELF-CONSCIOUS!
2009

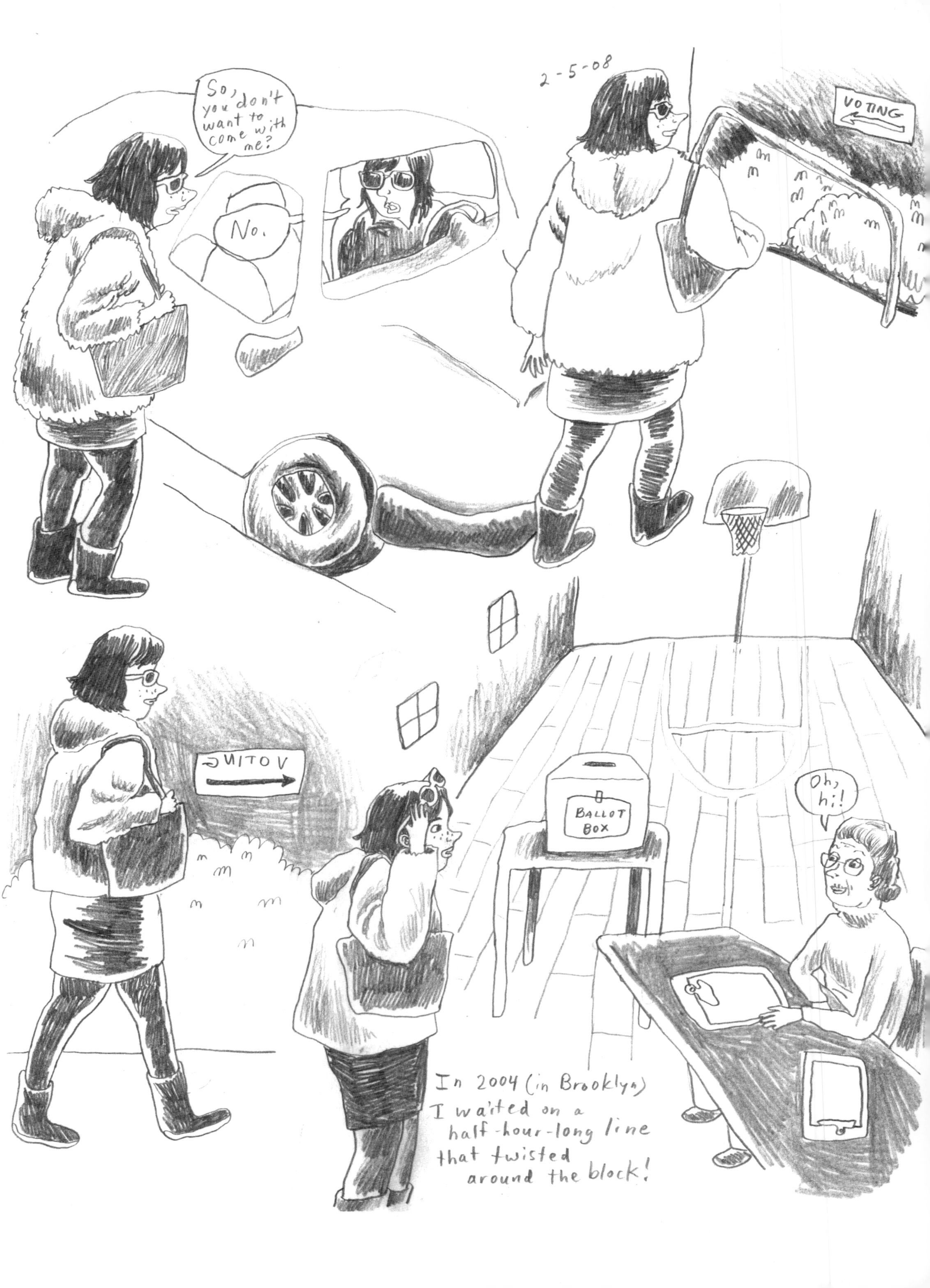
2-5-08
So, don't you want to come with me?
No.
VOTING
VOTING
BALLOT BOX
Oh, hi!
In 2004 (in Brooklyn) I waited on a half-hour-long line that twisted around the block!

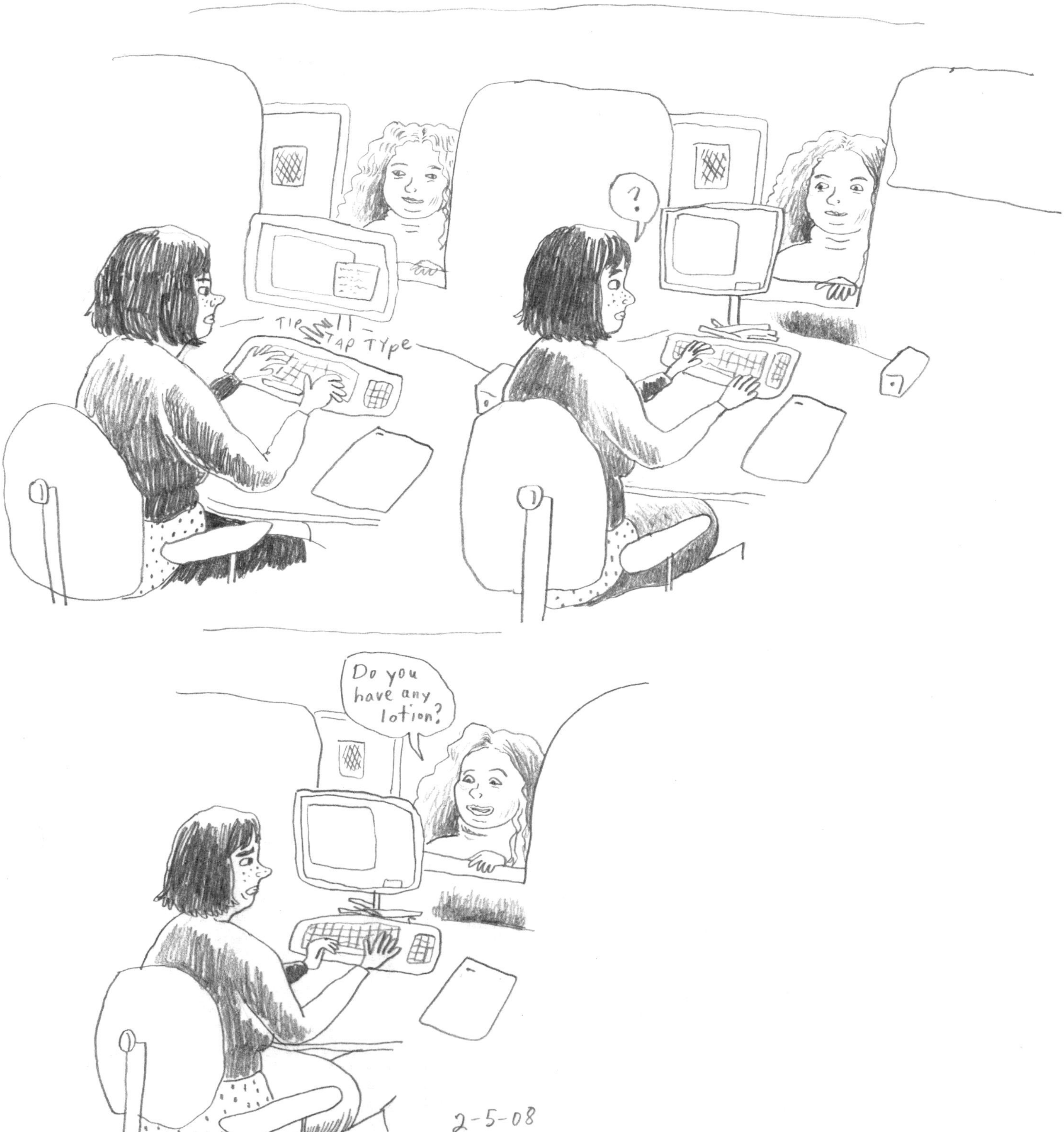
TIP TAP TYPE
?
Do you have any lotion?
2-5-08

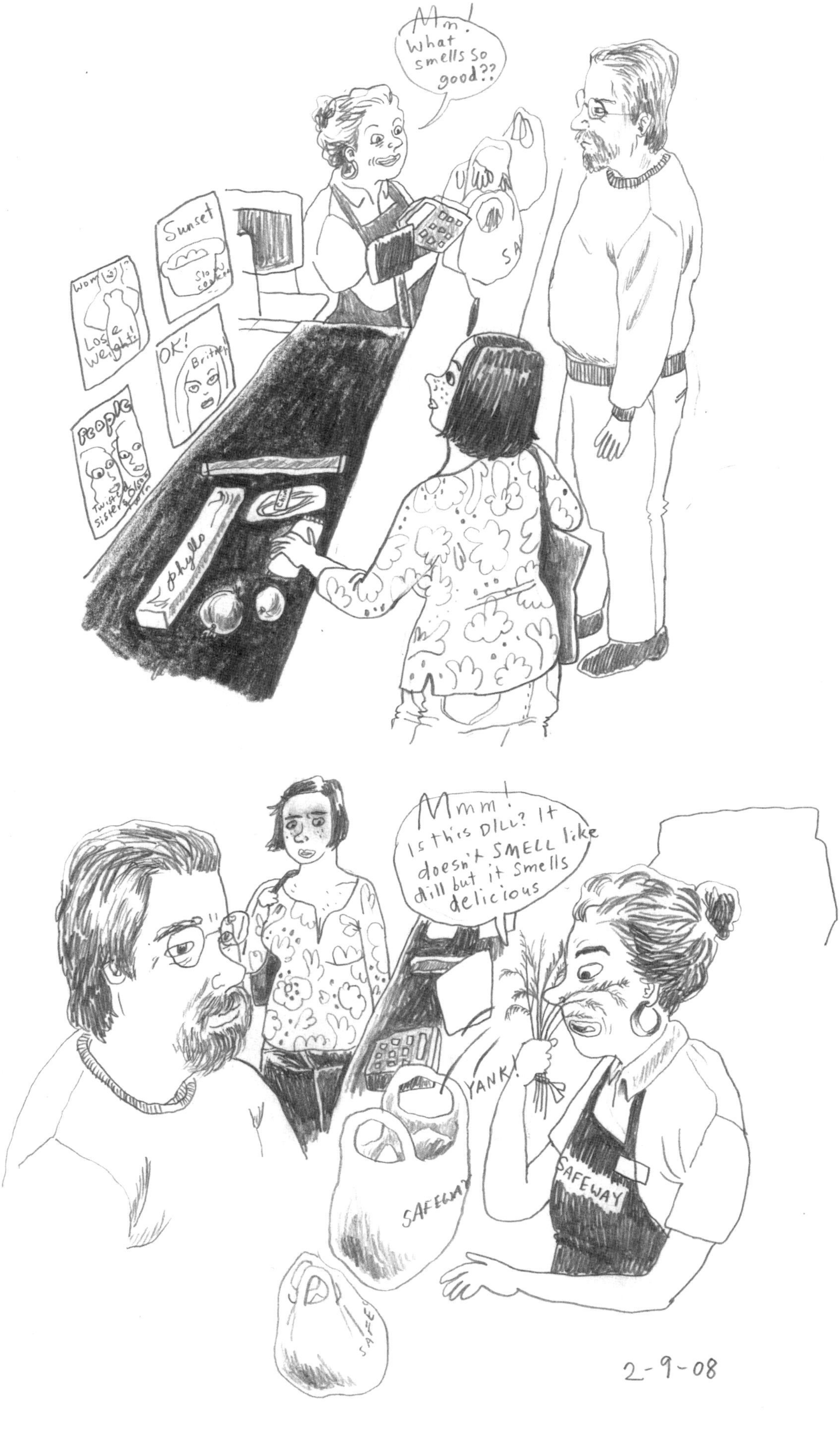
Mm! What smells so good??
Sunset
Lose weight!
OK! Britney
People
phyllo
Mmm! Is this DILL? It doesn't SMELL like dill but it smells delicious
YANK!
SAFEWAY
SAFEWAY
2-9-08

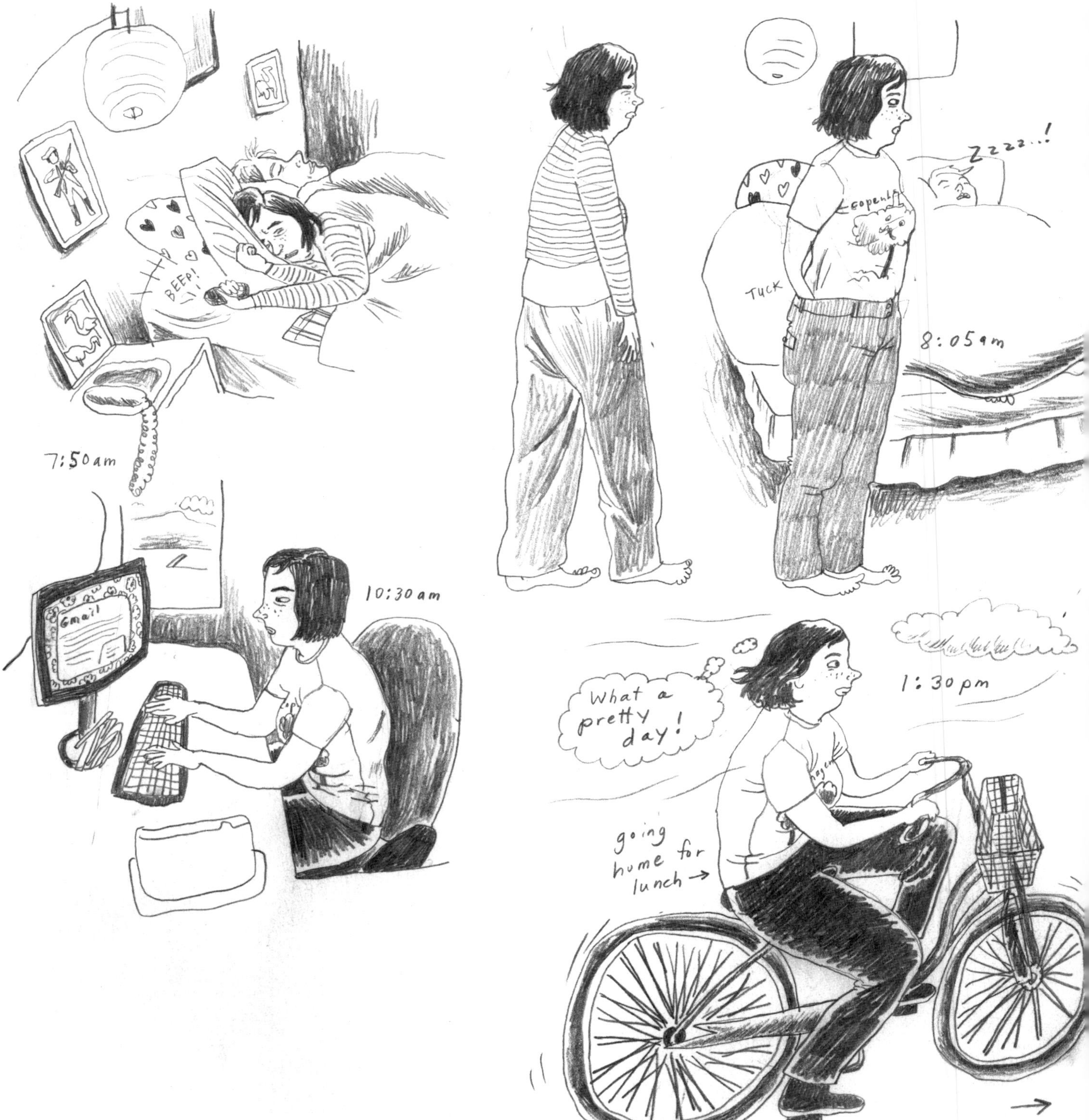
BEEP!
7:50am
Zzzz..!
TUCK
8:05am
Gmail
10:30am
What a pretty day!
1:30pm
going home for lunch →

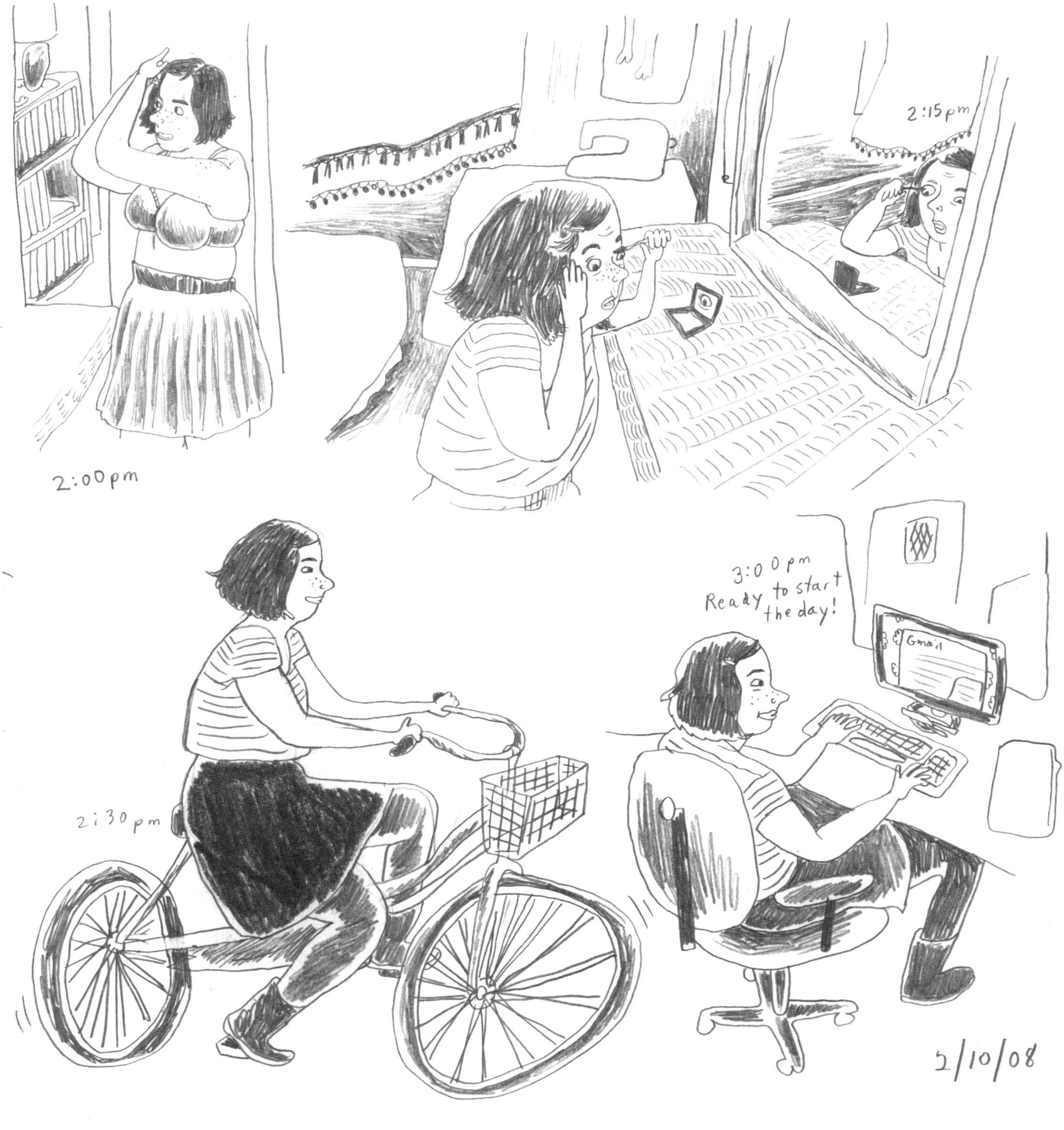

2:00pm
2:15pm
2:30pm
3:00pm
Ready to start the day!
Gmail
2/10/08

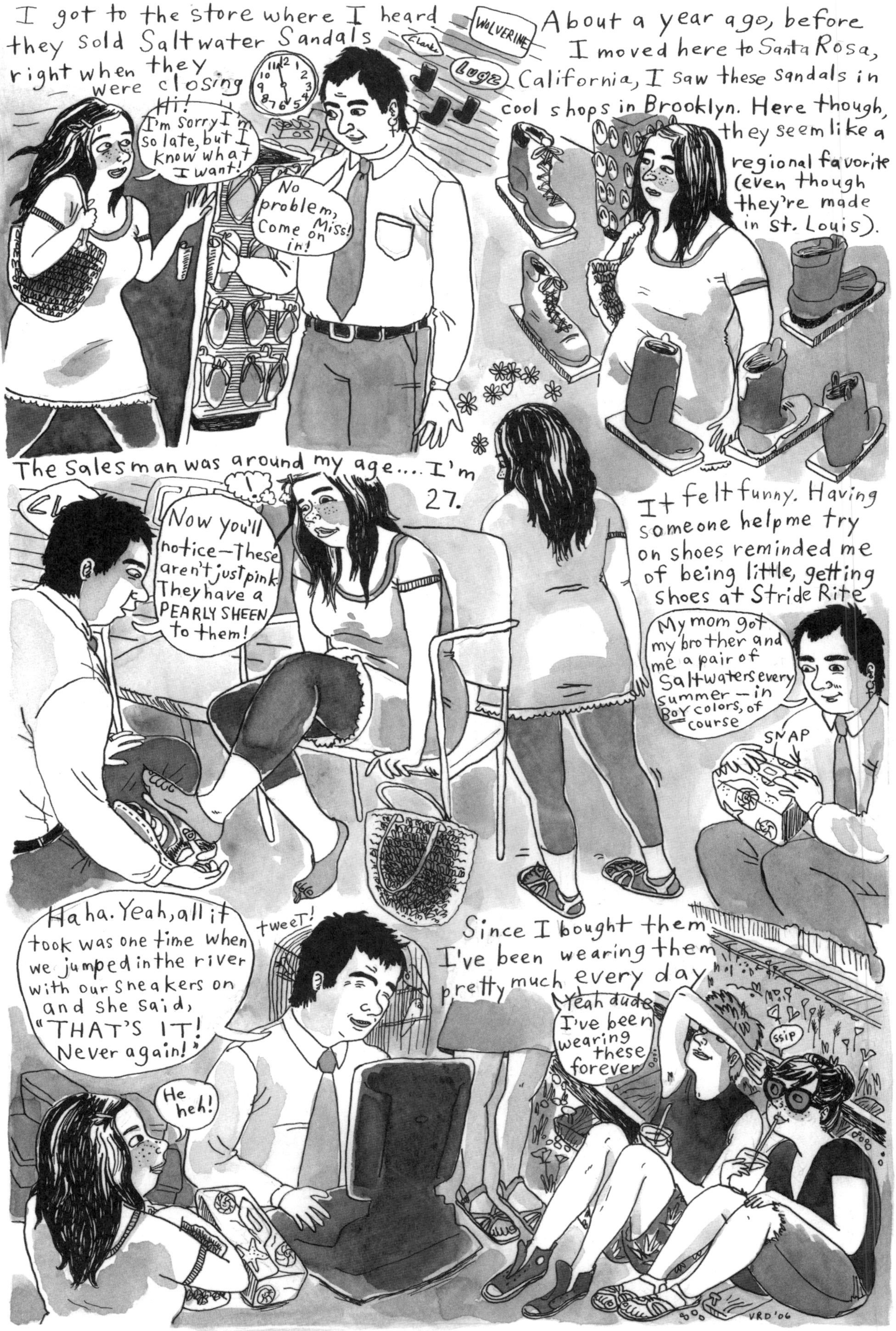
I got to the store where I heard they sold Saltwater Sandals right when they were closing
WOLVERINE
Hi! I'm sorry I'm so late, but I know what I want!
No problem, Miss! Come on in!
About a year ago, before I moved here to Santa Rosa, California, I saw these sandals in cool shops in Brooklyn. Here though, they seem like a regional favorite (even though they're made in St. Louis).
The salesman was around my age.... I'm 27.
!
Now you'll notice—these aren't just pink. They have a PEARLY SHEEN to them!
It felt funny. Having someone help me try on shoes reminded me of being little, getting shoes at Stride Rite
My mom got my brother and me a pair of Saltwaters every summer—in BOY colors, of course
SNAP
Haha. Yeah, all it took was one time when we jumped in the river with our sneakers on and she said, "THAT'S IT! Never again!"
TWEET!
He heh!
Since I bought them I've been wearing them pretty much every day
Yeah dude I've been wearing these forever
ssip
VRD '06

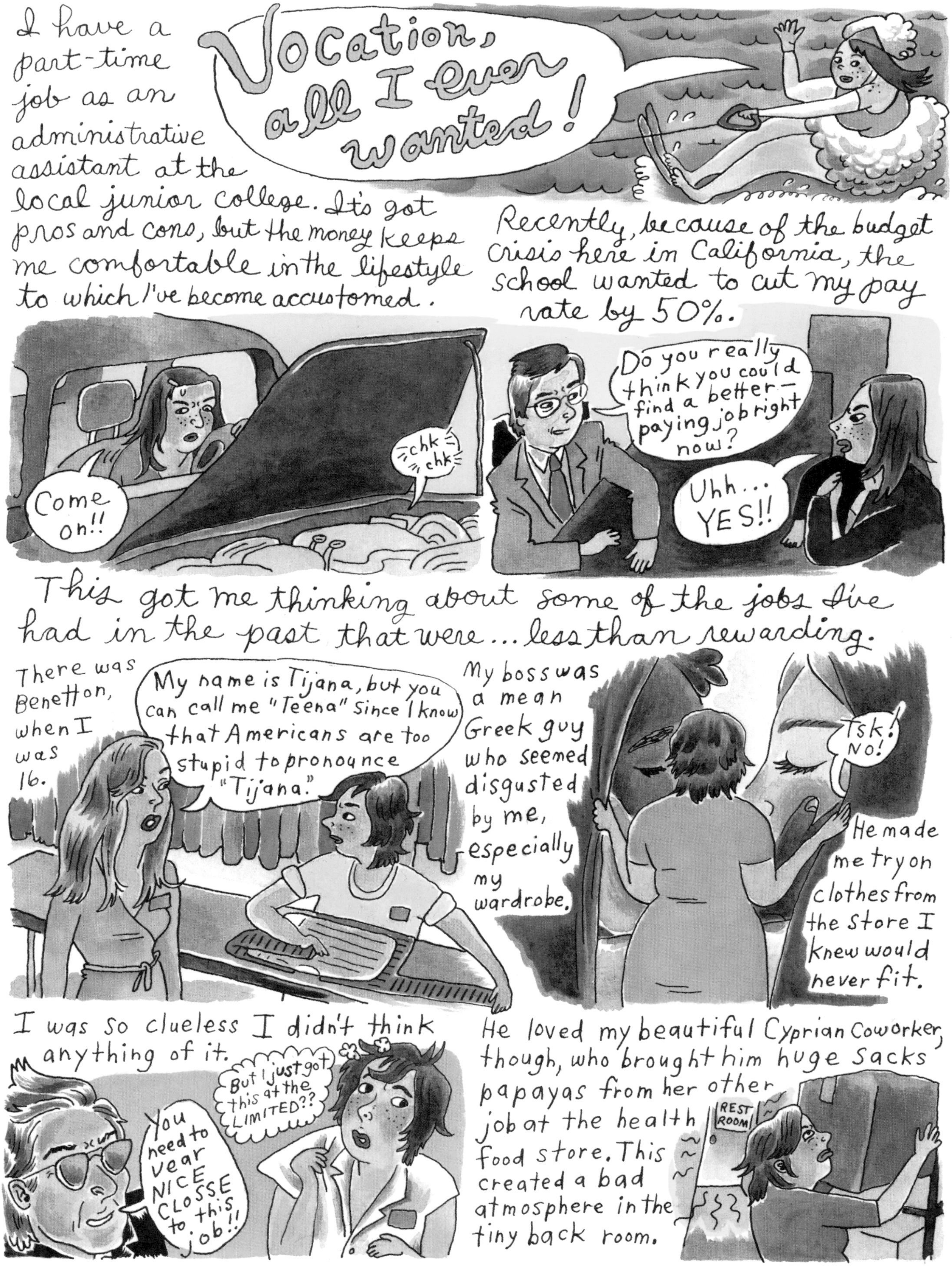

I have a part-time job as an administrative assistant at the local junior college. It's got pros and cons, but the money keeps me comfortable in the lifestyle to which I've become accustomed.
Vocation, all I ever wanted!
Recently, because of the budget crisis here in California, the school wanted to cut my pay rate by 50%.
Come on!!
chk chk
Do you really think you could find a better-paying job right now?
Uhh... YES!!
This got me thinking about some of the jobs I've had in the past that were... less than rewarding.
There was Benetton, when I was 16.
My name is Tijana, but you can call me "Teena" since I know that Americans are too stupid to pronounce "Tijana."
My boss was a mean Greek guy who seemed disgusted by me, especially my wardrobe.
Tsk! No!
He made me try on clothes from the store I knew would never fit.
I was so clueless I didn't think anything of it.
But I just got this at the LIMITED??
You need to vear NICE CLOSSE to this job!!
He loved my beautiful Cyprian coworker, though, who brought him huge sacks papayas from her other job at the health food store. This created a bad atmosphere in the tiny back room.
REST ROOM

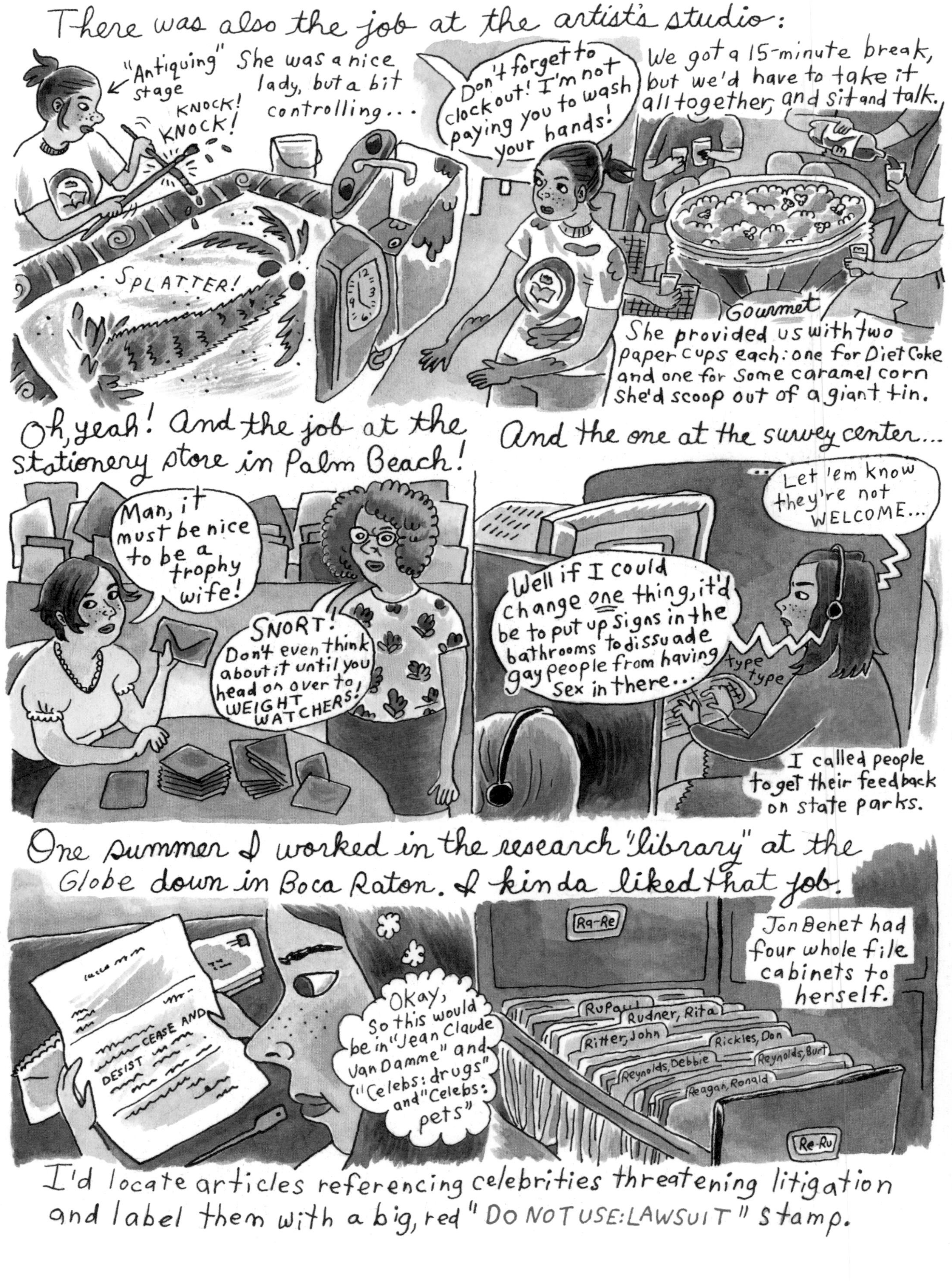
There was also the job at the artist's studio:
"Antiquing" stage
She was a nice lady, but a bit controlling...
KNOCK! KNOCK!
SPLATTER!
Don't forget to clock out! I'm not paying you to wash your hands!
We got a 15-minute break, but we'd have to take it all together, and sit and talk.
Gourmet
She provided us with two paper cups each: one for Diet Coke and one for some caramel corn she'd scoop out of a giant tin.
Oh, yeah! And the job at the stationery store in Palm Beach!
Man, it must be nice to be a trophy wife!
SNORT! Don't even think about it until you head on over to WEIGHT WATCHERS!
And the one at the survey center...
Let 'em know they're not WELCOME...
Well if I could change one thing, it'd be to put up signs in the bathrooms to dissuade gay people from having sex in there...
type type
I called people to get their feedback on state parks.
One summer I worked in the research "library" at the Globe down in Boca Raton. I kinda liked that job.
CEASE AND DESIST
Okay, so this would be in "Jean Claude Van Damme" and "Celebs: drugs" and "Celebs: pets"
Ra-Re
JonBenet had four whole file cabinets to herself.
RuPaul
Rudner, Rita
Ritter, John
Rickles, Don
Reynolds, Debbie
Reynolds, Burt
Reagan, Ronald
Re-Ru
I'd locate articles referencing celebrities threatening litigation and label them with a big, red "DO NOT USE: LAWSUIT" stamp.

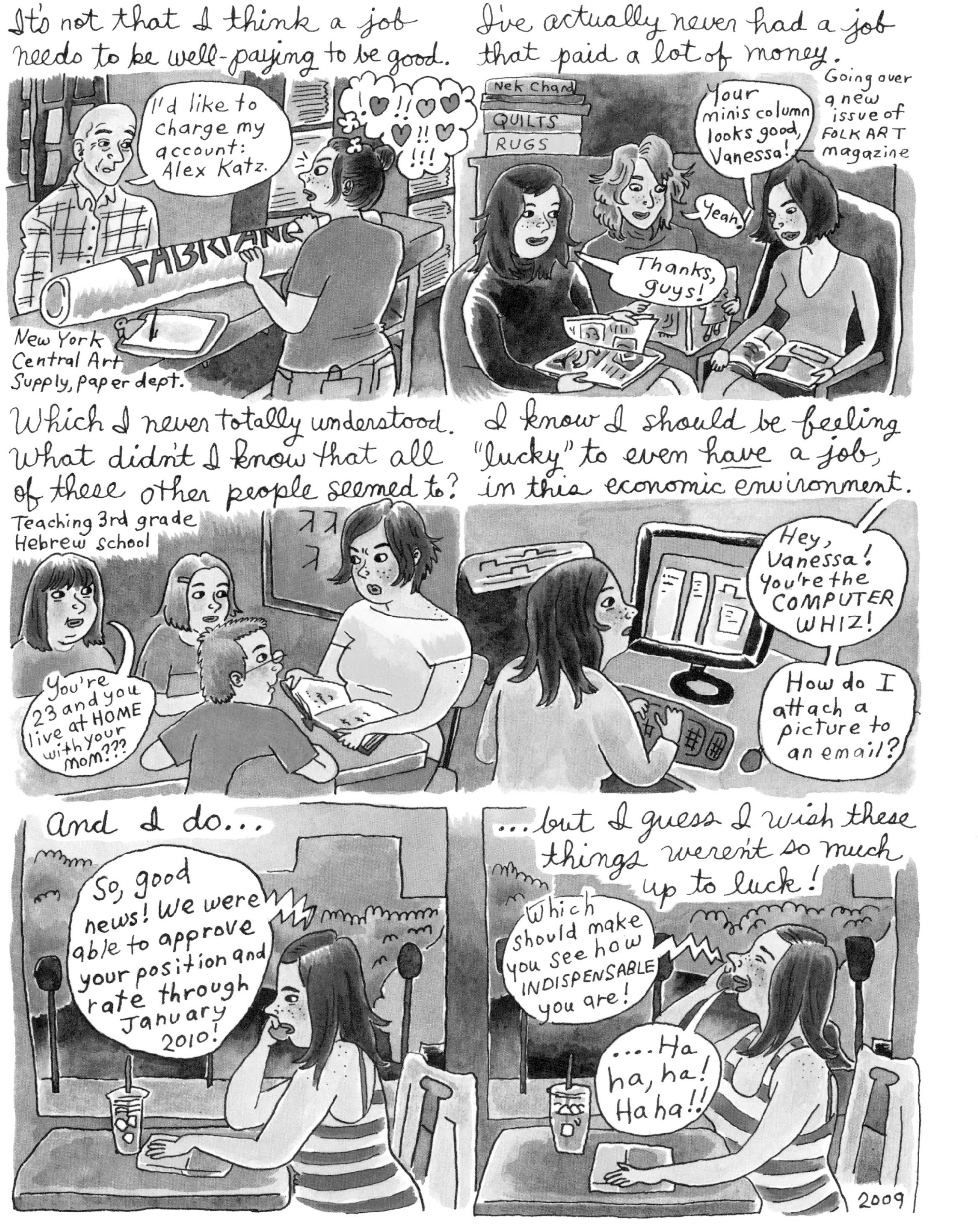
It's not that I think a job needs to be well-paying to be good.
I'd like to charge my account: Alex Katz.
FABRIANO
New York Central Art Supply, paper dept.
I've actually never had a job that paid a lot of money.
Nek Chand
QUILTS
RUGS
Going over a new issue of FOLK ART magazine
Your minis column looks good, Vanessa!
Yeah.
Thanks, guys!
Which I never totally understood. What didn't I know that all of these other people seemed to?
Teaching 3rd grade Hebrew school
You're 23 and you live at HOME with your mom???
I know I should be feeling "lucky" to even have a job, in this economic environment.
Hey, Vanessa! You're the COMPUTER WHIZ!
How do I attach a picture to an email?
And I do...
So, good news! We were able to approve your position and rate through January 2010!
...but I guess I wish these things weren't so much up to luck!
Which should make you see how INDISPENSABLE you are!
....Ha ha, ha! Ha ha!!
2009

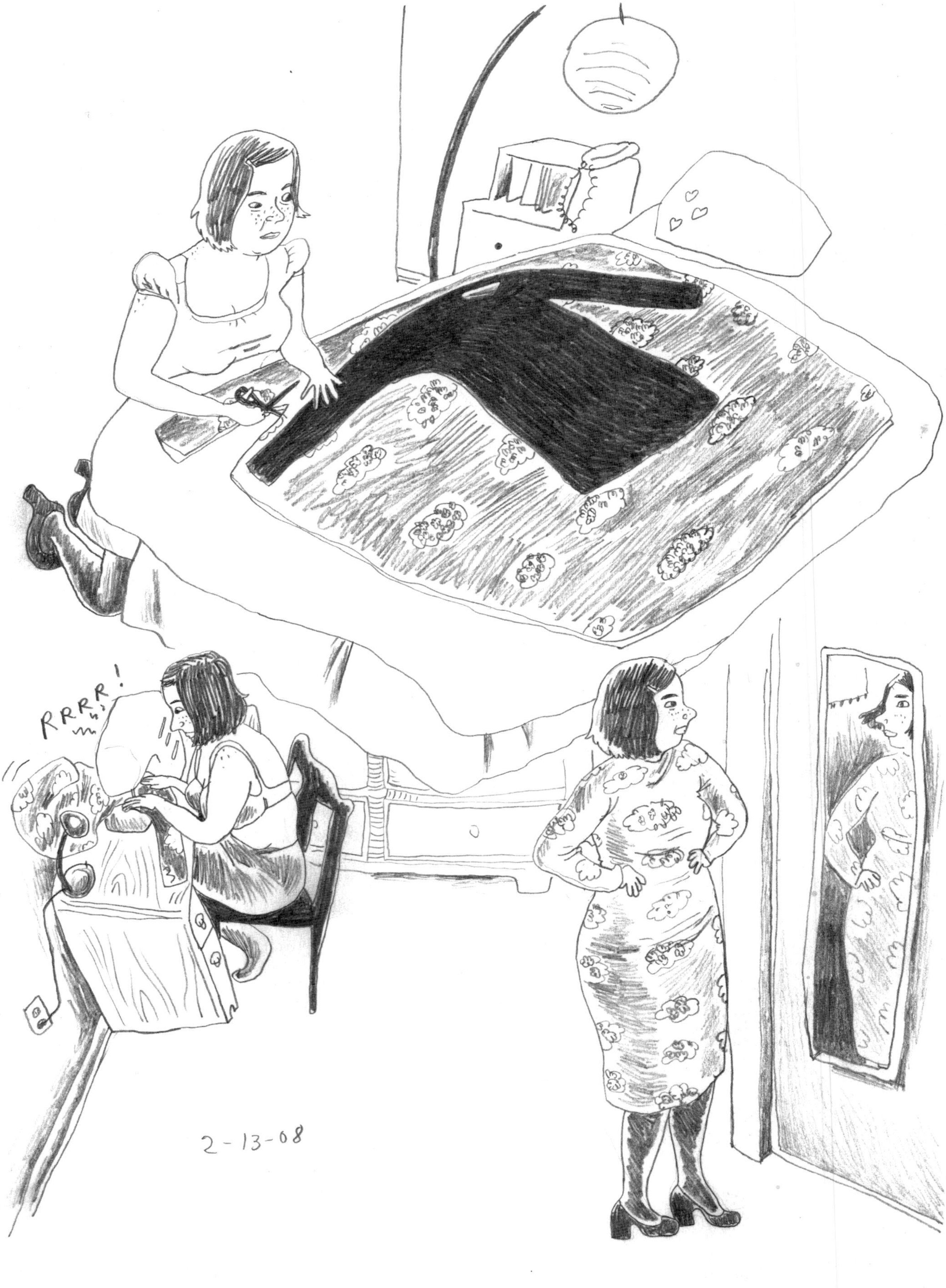
RRRR!
2-13-08

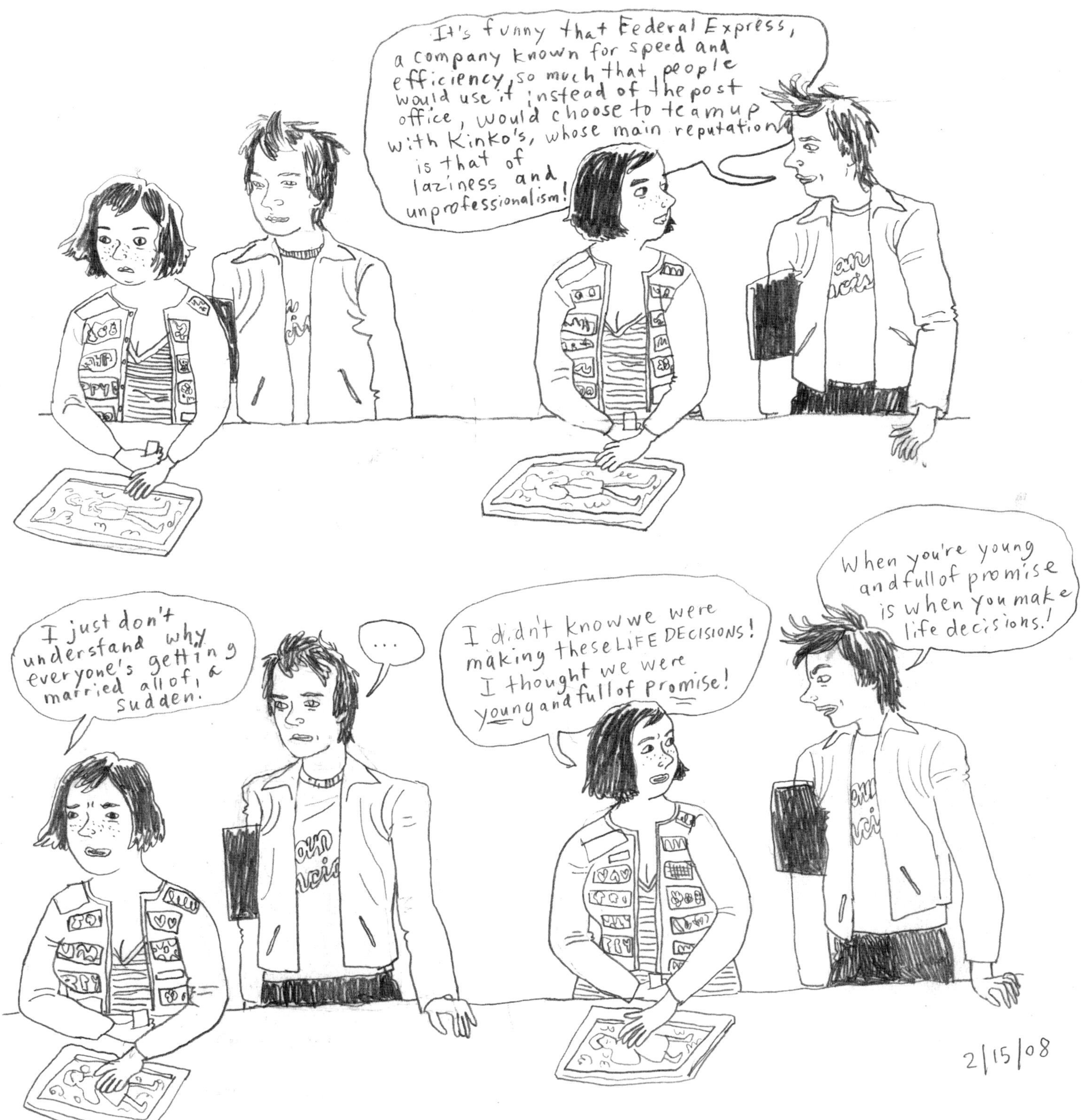
It's funny that Federal Express, a company known for speed and efficiency, so much that people would use it instead of the post office, would choose to team up with Kinko's, whose main reputation is that of laziness and unprofessionalism!
I just don't understand why everyone's getting married all of a sudden.
...
I didn't know we were making these LIFE DECISIONS! I thought we were young and full of promise!
When you're young and full of promise is when you make life decisions!
2/15/08

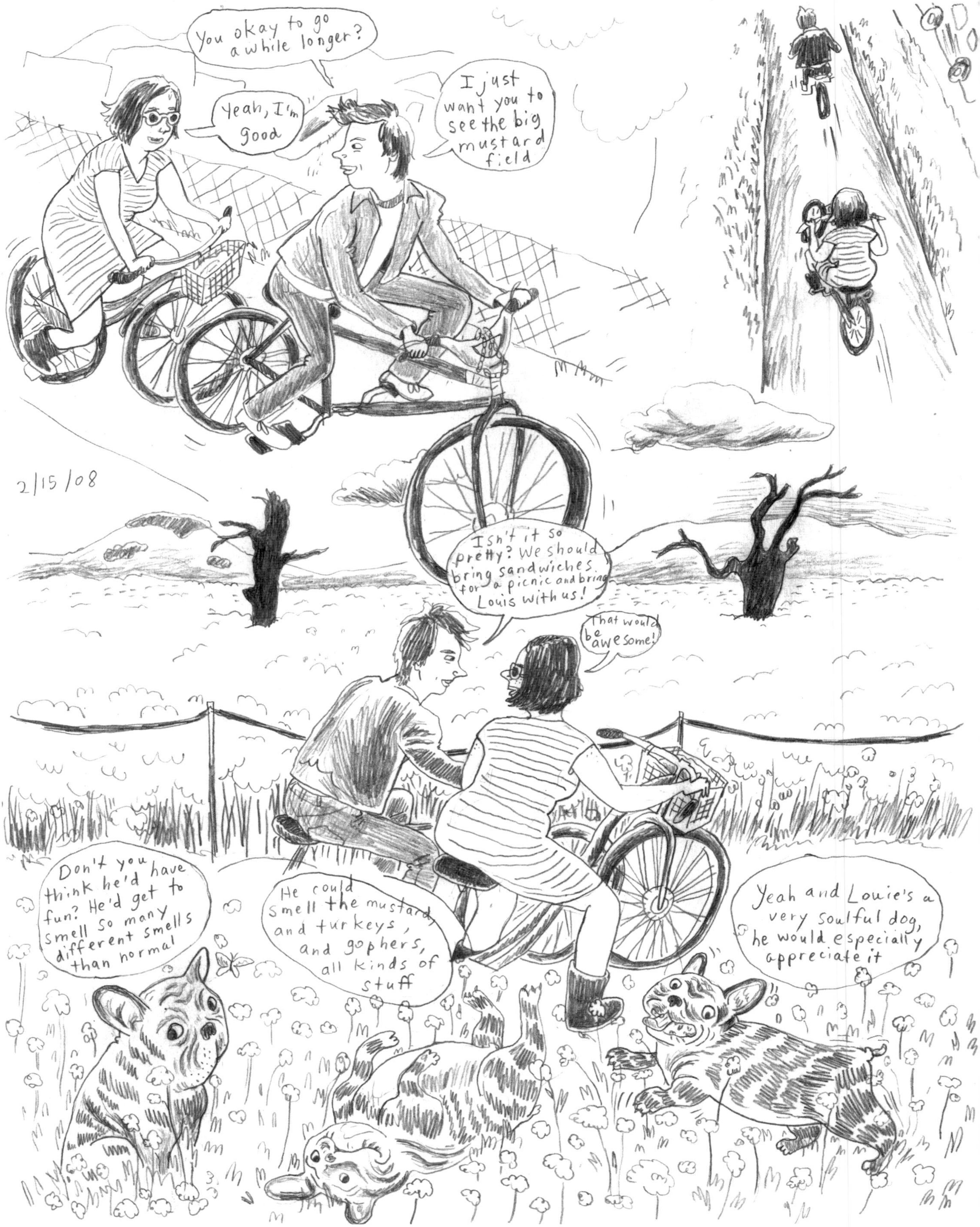
You okay to go a while longer?
Yeah, I'm good
I just want you to see the big mustard field
2/15/08
Isn't it so pretty? We should bring sandwiches for a picnic and bring Louis with us!
That would be awesome!
Don't you think he'd have fun? He'd get to smell so many different smells than normal
He could smell the mustard, and turkeys, and gophers, all kinds of stuff
Yeah and Louie's a very soulful dog, he would especially appreciate it

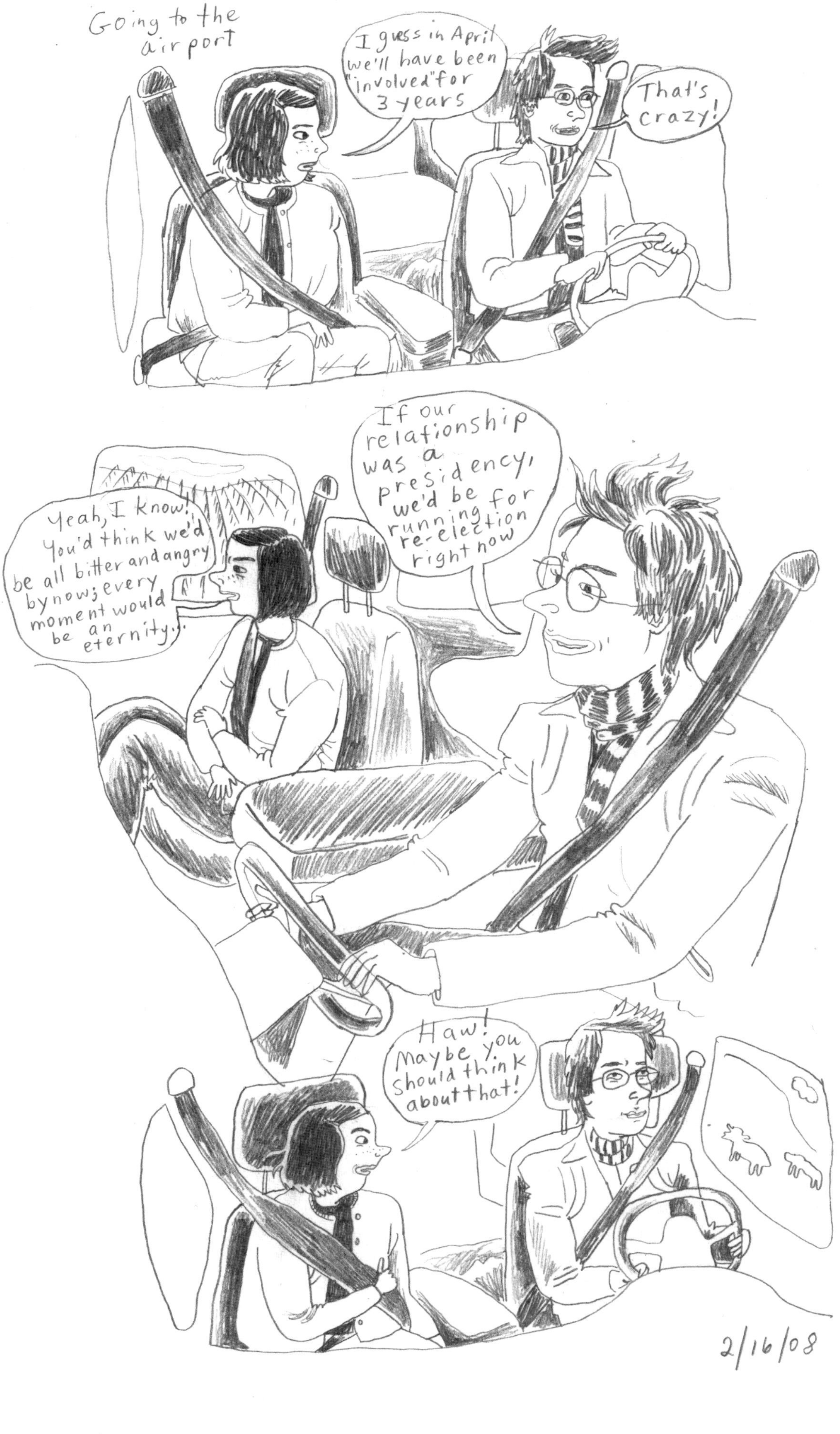
Going to the airport
I guess in April we'll have been "involved" for 3 years
That's crazy!
If our relationship was a presidency, we'd be running for re-election right now
Yeah, I know! You'd think we'd be all bitter and angry by now; every moment would be an eternity...
Haw! Maybe you should think about that!
2/16/08

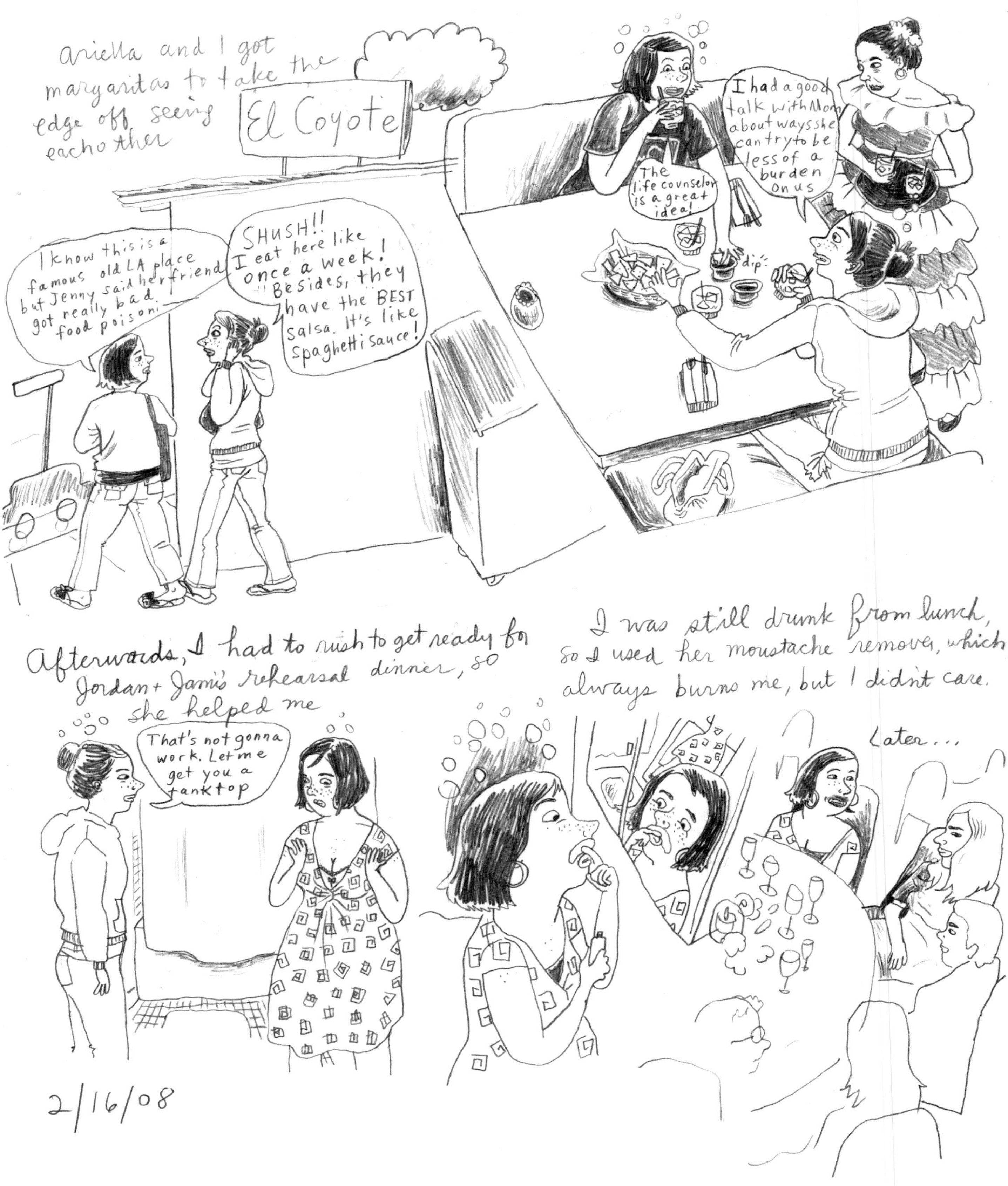
ariella and I got margaritas to take the edge off seeing eachother
El Coyote
I know this is a famous old LA place but Jenny said her friend got really bad food poisoni
SHUSH!! I eat here like once a week! Besides, they have the BEST salsa. It's like Spaghetti sauce!
The life counselor is a great idea!
I had a good talk with Mom about ways she can try to be less of a burden on us
dip
Afterwards, I had to rush to get ready for Jordan + Jami's rehearsal dinner, so she helped me
That's not gonna work. Let me get you a tank top
I was still drunk from lunch, so I used her moustache remover, which always burns me, but I didn't care.
Later...
2/16/08

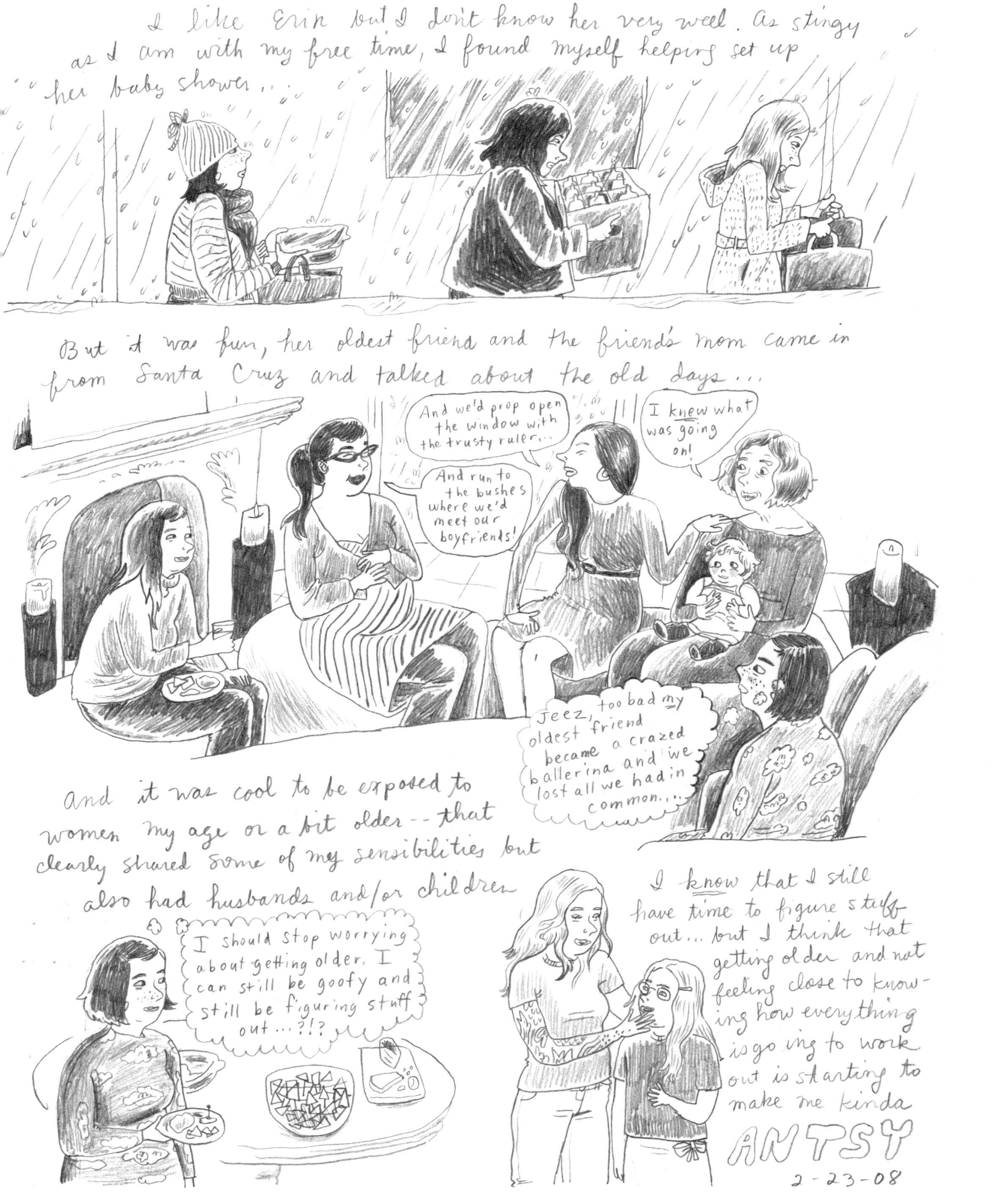
I like Erin but I don't know her very well. As stingy as I am with my free time, I found myself helping set up her baby shower...
But it was fun, her oldest friend and the friend's mom came in from Santa Cruz and talked about the old days...
And we'd prop open the window with the trusty ruler...
And run to the bushes where we'd meet our boyfriends!
I knew what was going on!
Jeez, too bad my oldest friend became a crazed ballerina and we lost all we had in common...
and it was cool to be exposed to women my age or a bit older -- that clearly shared some of my sensibilities but also had husbands and/or children
I should stop worrying about getting older. I can still be goofy and still be figuring stuff out...?!?
I know that I still have time to figure stuff out... but I think that getting older and not feeling close to knowing how everything is going to work out is starting to make me kinda
ANTSY
2-23-08

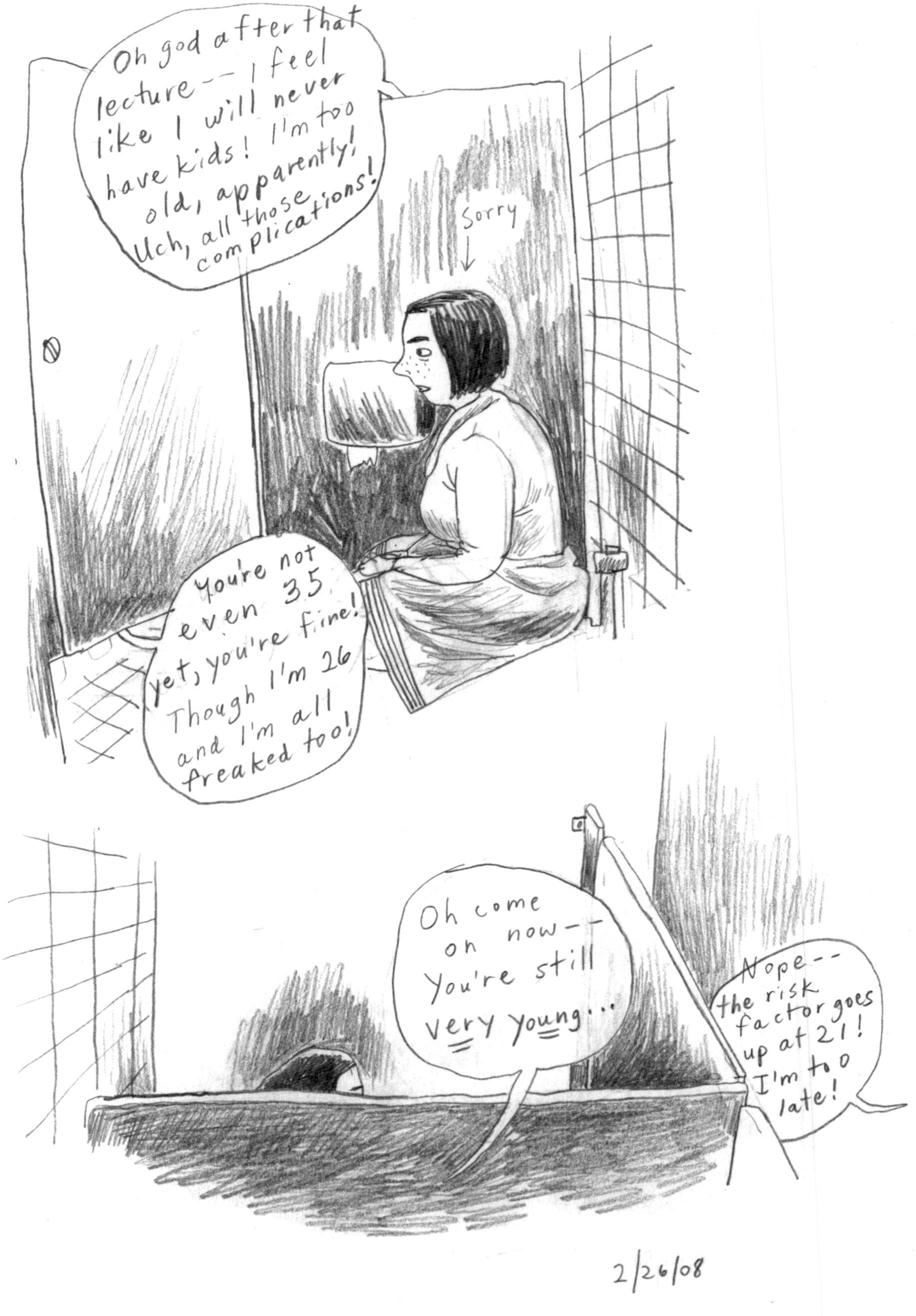
Oh god after that lecture -- I feel like I will never have kids! I'm too old, apparently! Uch, all those complications!
Sorry
You're not even 35 yet, you're fine! Though I'm 26 and I'm all freaked too!
Oh come on now-- You're still very young...
Nope-- the risk factor goes up at 21! I'm too late!

2/26/08

On line for coffee this morning,
Santa Rosa Junior College

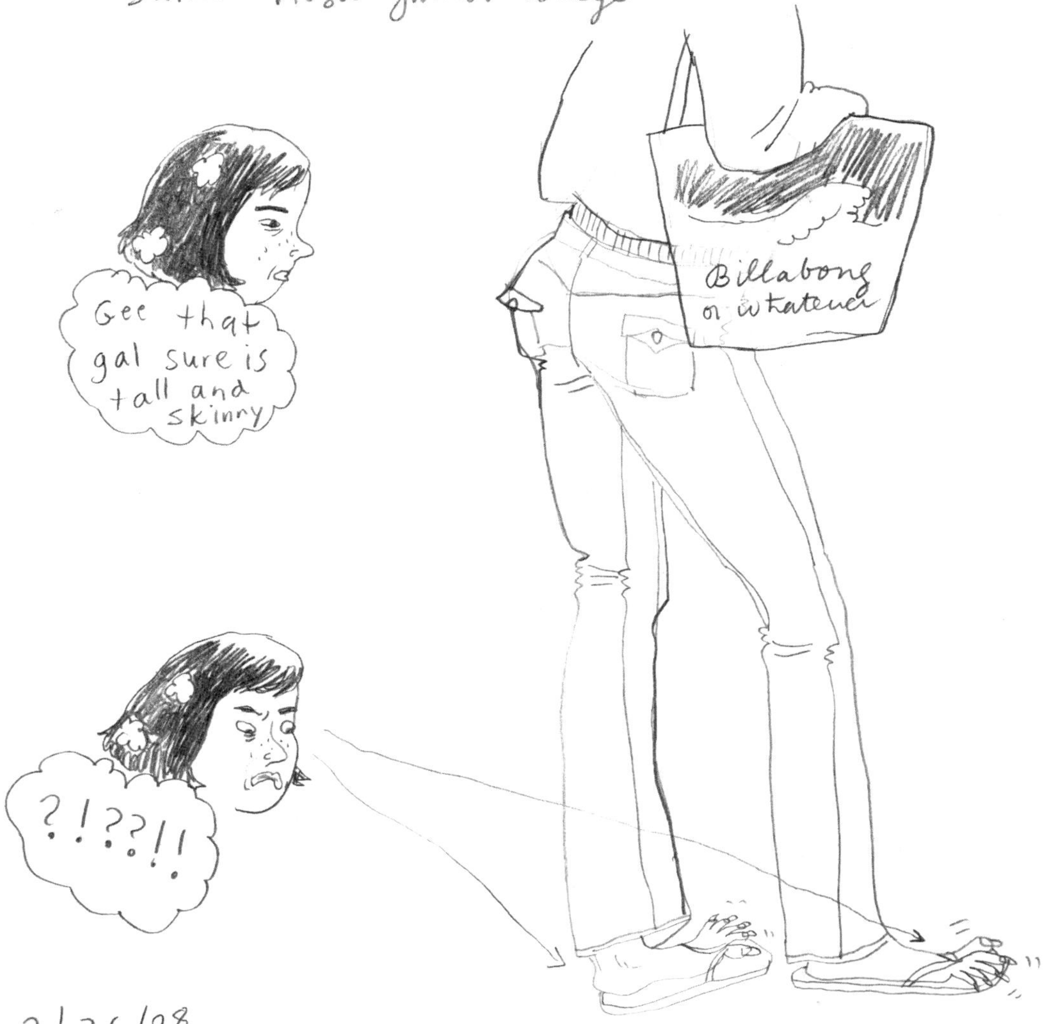
Billabong
or whatever
Gee that gal sure is tall and skinny
?!??!!

2/26/08

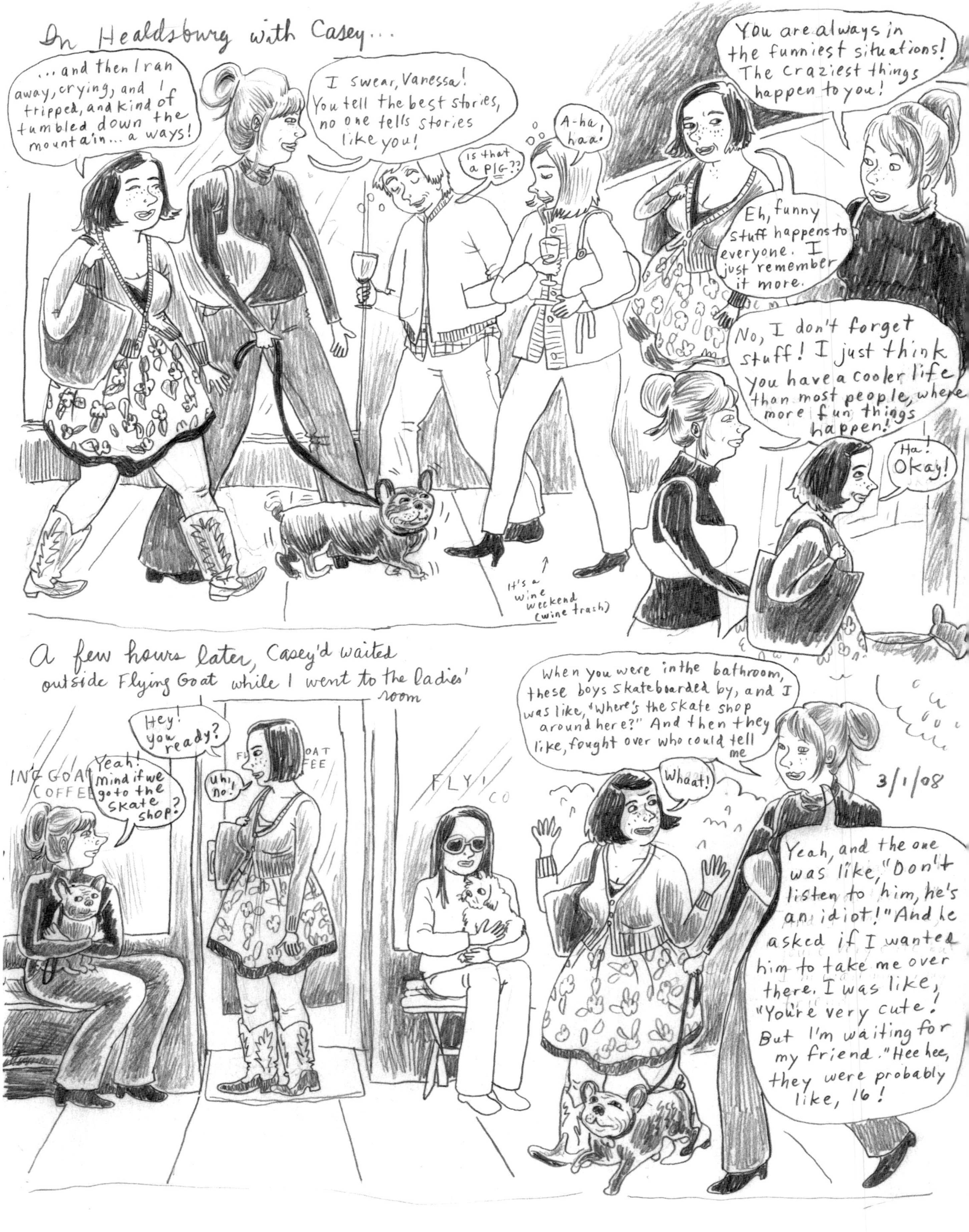

In Healdsburg with Casey...
...and then I ran away, crying, and I tripped, and kind of tumbled down the mountain... a ways!
I swear, Vanessa! You tell the best stories, no one tells stories like you!
Is that a PIG??
A-ha haa!
It's a wine weekend (wine trash)
You are always in the funniest situations! The craziest things happen to you!
Eh, funny stuff happens to everyone. I just remember it more.
No, I don't forget stuff! I just think you have a cooler life than most people, where more fun things happen!
Ha! Okay!
A few hours later, Casey'd waited outside Flying Goat while I went to the ladies' room
Hey! you ready?
Yeah! mind if we go to the skate shop?
Uh, no!
When you were in the bathroom, these boys skateboarded by, and I was like, "Where's the skate shop around here?" And then they like, fought over who could tell me
Whaat!
Yeah, and the one was like, "Don't listen to him, he's an idiot!" And he asked if I wanted him to take me over there. I was like, "You're very cute! But I'm waiting for my friend." Hee hee, they were probably like, 16!
3/1/08

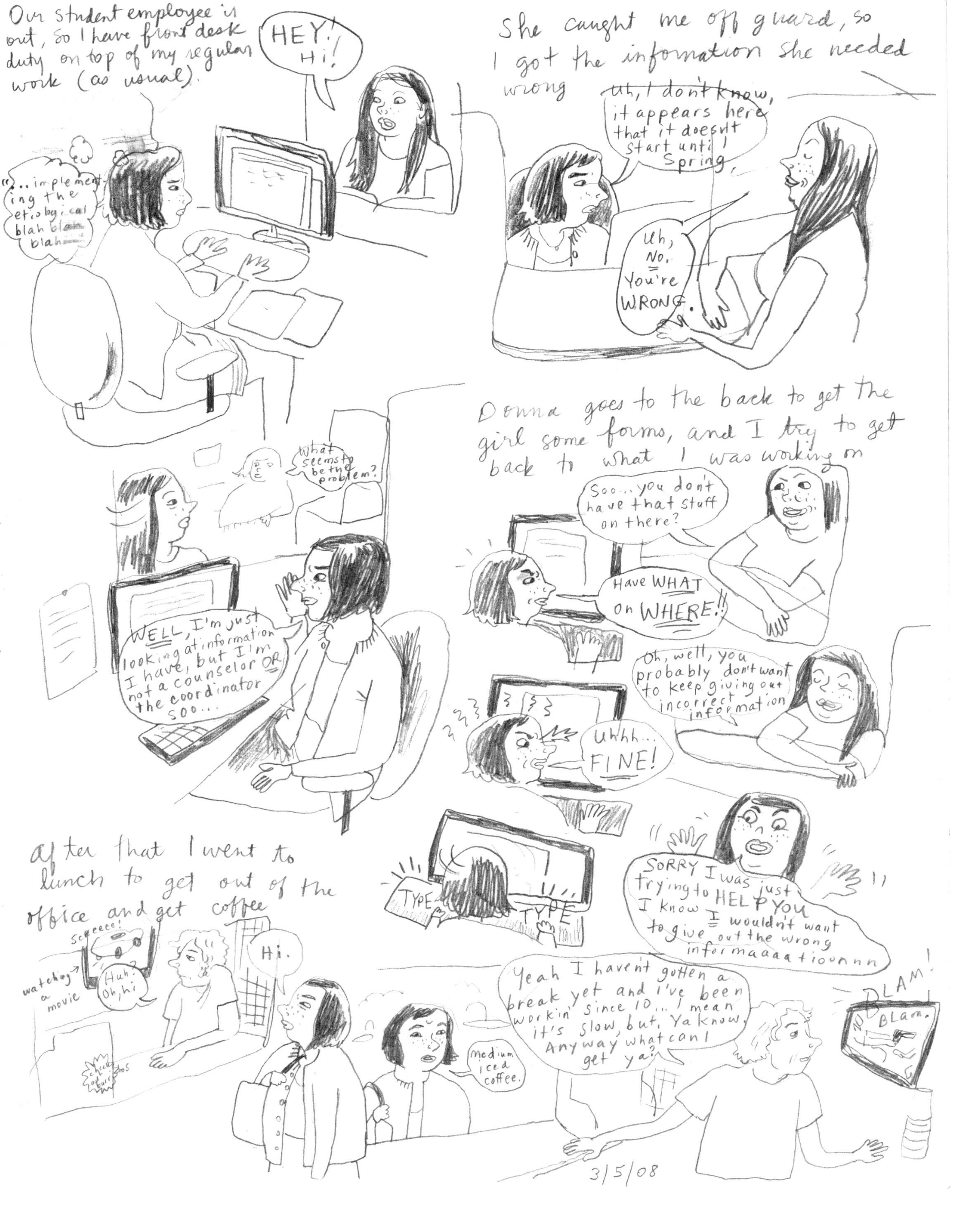
Our student employee is out, so I have front desk duty on top of my regular work (as usual).
HEY! Hi!
"...implementing the etiological blah blah blah
She caught me off guard, so I got the information she needed wrong
Uh, I don't know, it appears here that it doesn't start until Spring
Uh, No. You're WRONG.
What seems to be the problem?
WELL, I'm just looking at information I have, but I'm not a counselor OR the coordinator soo...
Donna goes to the back to get the girl some forms, and I try to get back to what I was working on
Soo... you don't have that stuff on there?
Have WHAT on WHERE!!
Oh, well, you probably don't want to keep giving out incorrect information
Uhhh... FINE!
TYPE
TYPE
SORRY I was just trying to HELP YOU I know I wouldn't want to give out the wrong informaaaatioonnn
After that I went to lunch to get out of the office and get coffee
screeeee!
watching a movie
Huh. Oh, hi
Hi.
medium iced coffee.
Yeah I haven't gotten a break yet and I've been workin' since 10... I mean it's slow, but, Ya know. Anyway what can I get ya?
BLAM!
BLAM.
3/5/08

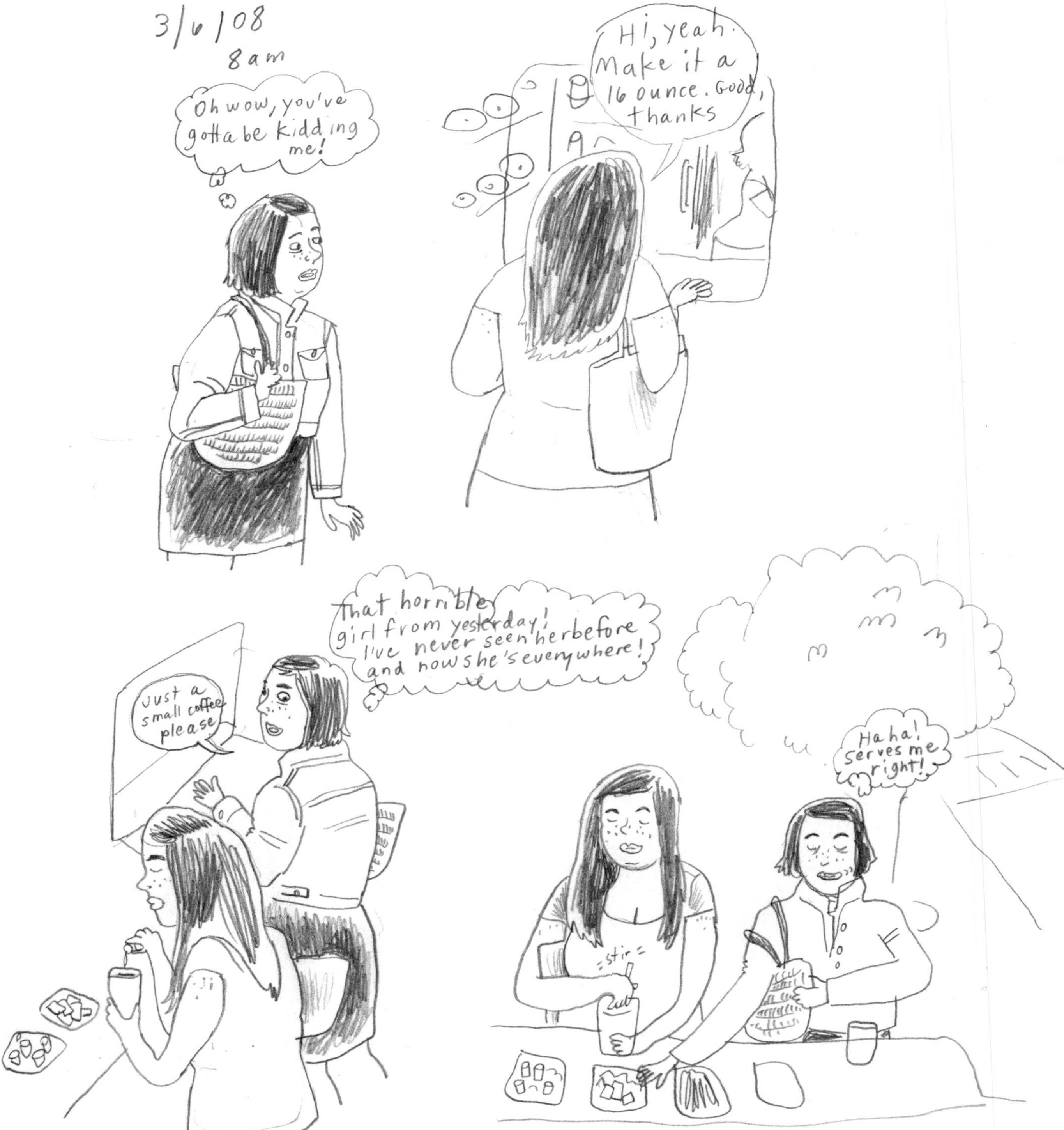
3/6/08
8am
Oh wow, you've gotta be kidding me!
Hi, yeah. Make it a 16 ounce. Good, thanks
That horrible girl from yesterday! I've never seen her before and now she's everywhere!
Just a small coffee please
Haha! Serves me right!
stir

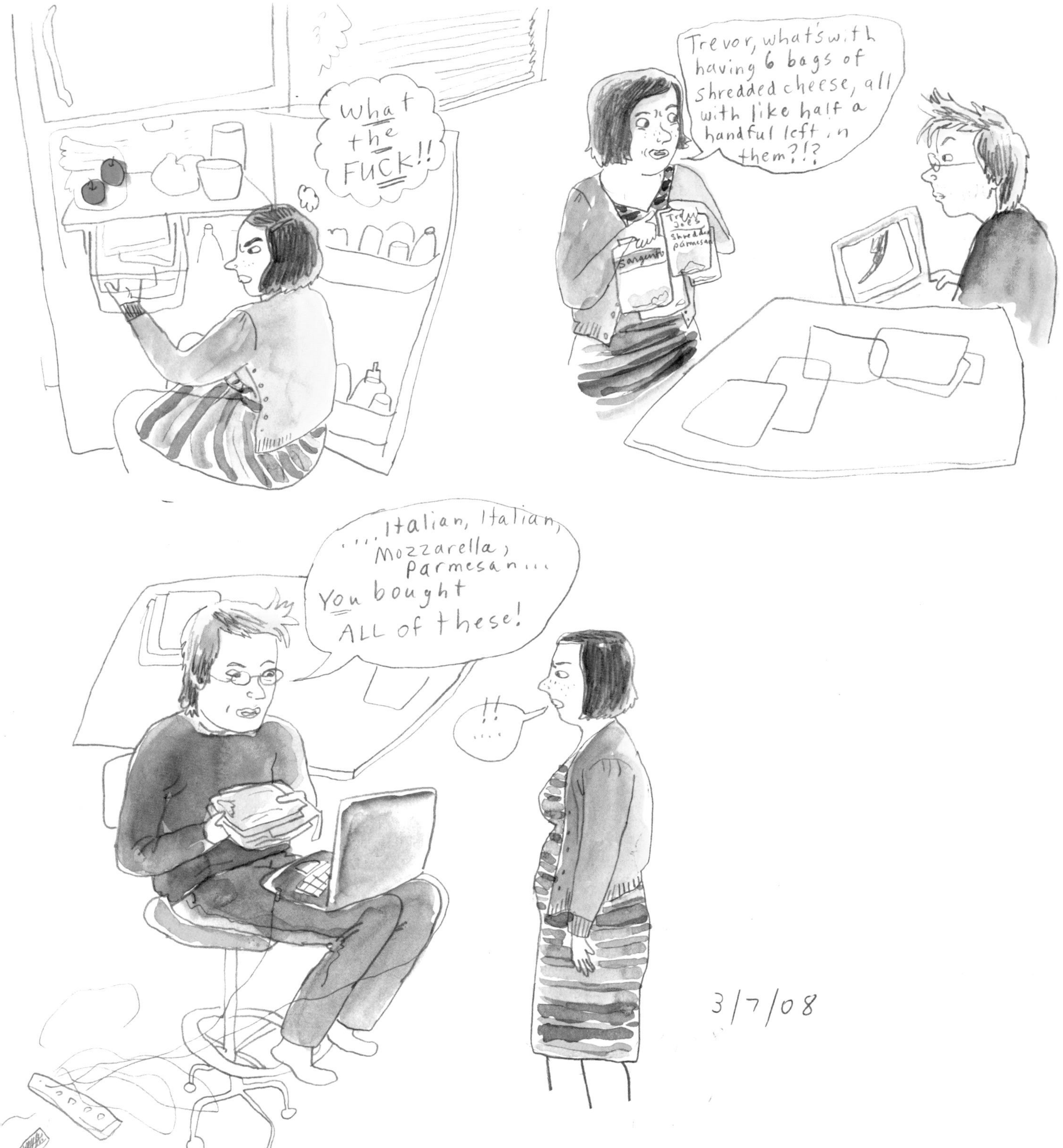
What the FUCK!!
Trevor, what's with having 6 bags of shredded cheese, all with like half a handful left in them?!?
Sargento
Shredded parmesan
....Italian, Italian, Mozzarella, parmesan... You bought ALL of these!
!! ....
3/7/08

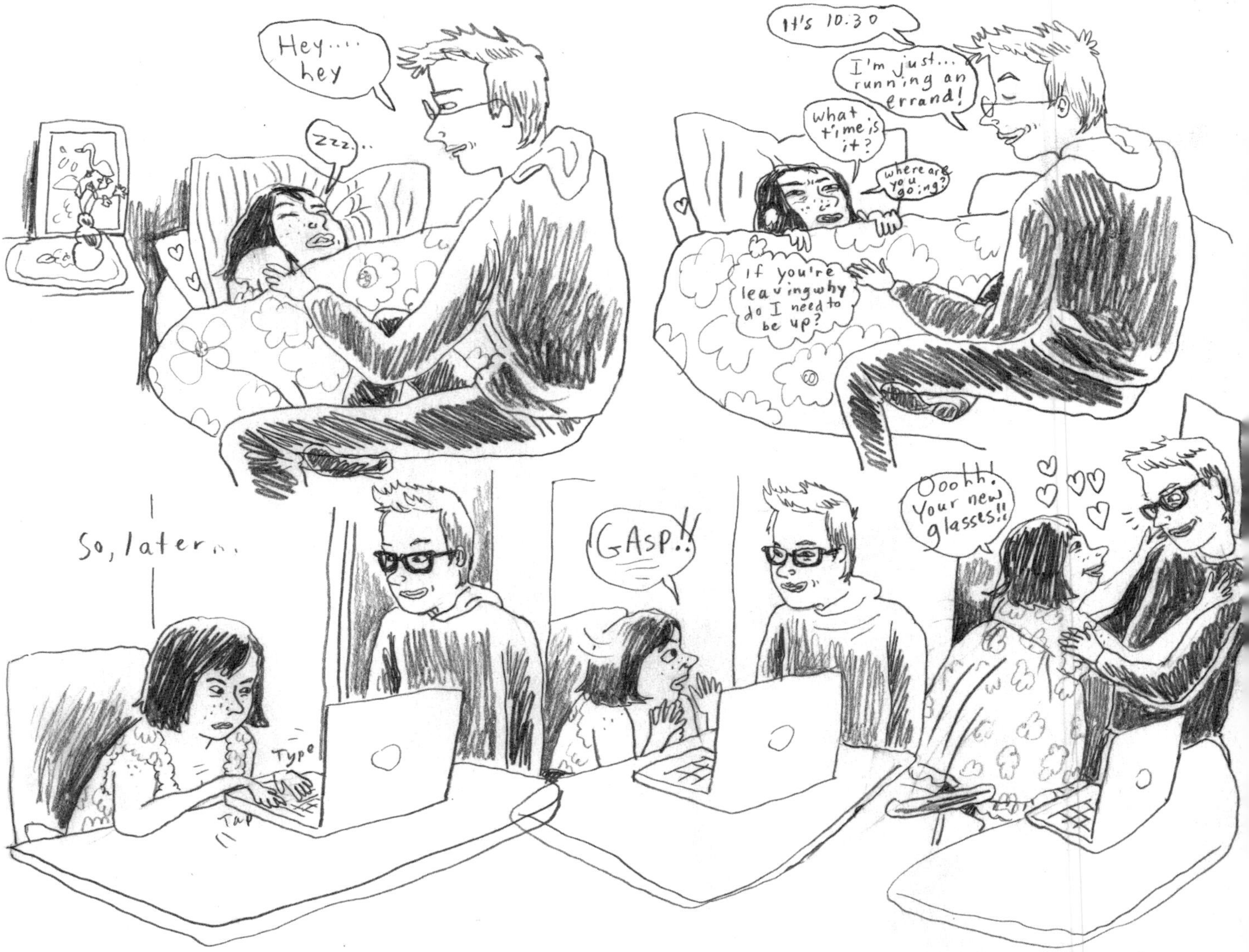
Hey... hey
zzz..
It's 10.30
I'm just... running an errand!
what time is it?
where are you going?
If you're leaving why do I need to be up?
So, later...
Type
Tap
GASP!!
Oooh! Your new glasses!!

3/14/08

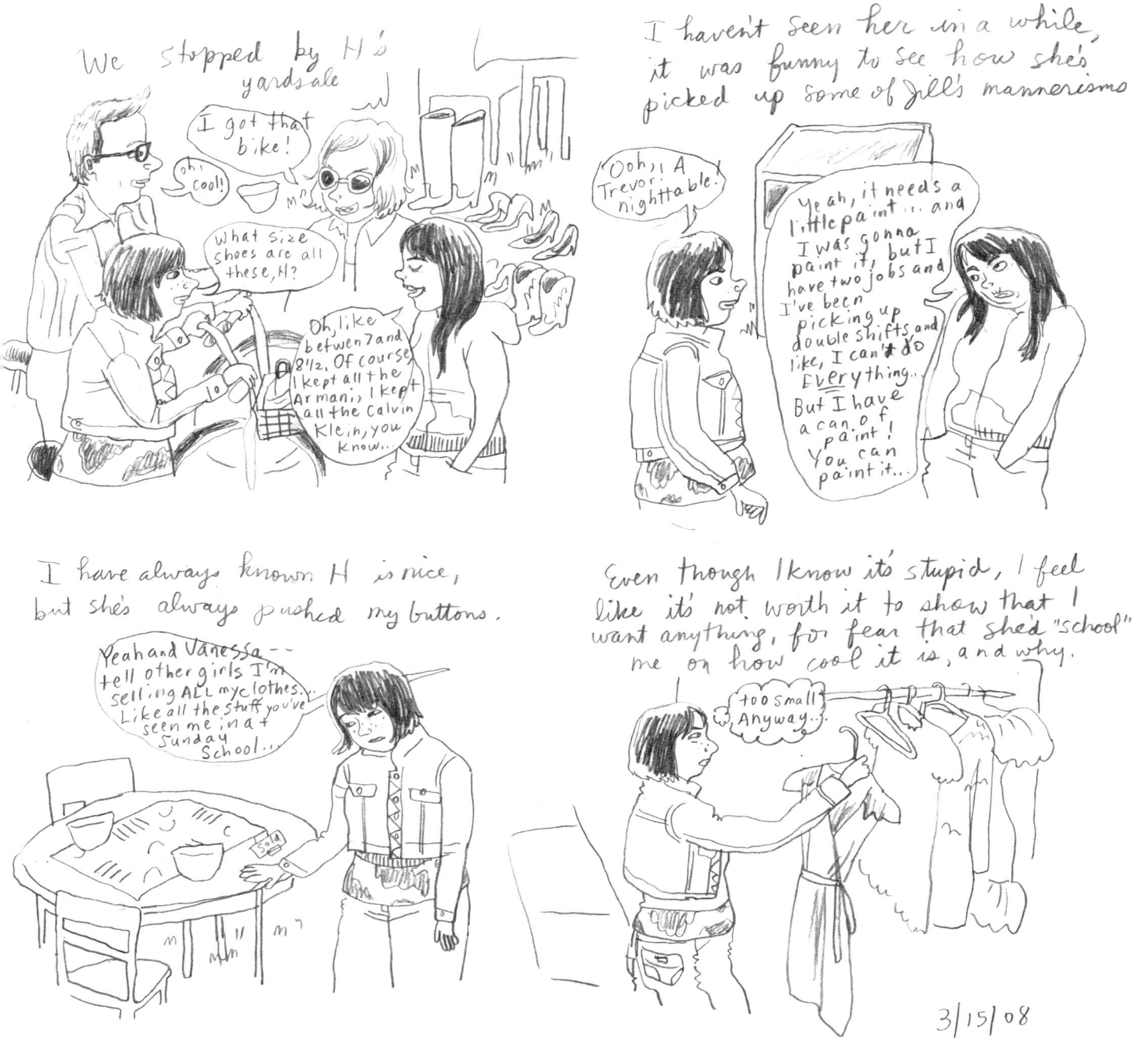
We stopped by H's yardsale
I got that bike!
oh, cool!
What size shoes are all these, H?
Oh, like betwen 7 and 8½. Of course, I kept all the Armani, I kept all the Calvin Klein, you know...
I haven't seen her in a while, it was funny to see how she's picked up some of Jill's mannerisms
Ooh, A Trevor nighttable!
Yeah, it needs a little paint... and I was gonna paint it, but I have two jobs and I've been picking up double shifts and like, I can't do EVERYthing.. But I have a can of paint! You can paint it...
I have always known H is nice, but she's always pushed my buttons.
Yeah and Vanessa -- tell other girls I'm selling ALL my clothes.. Like all the stuff you've seen me in at Sunday School...
Sold
Even though I know it's stupid, I feel like it's not worth it to show that I want anything, for fear that she'd "school" me on how cool it is, and why.
too small Anyway...
3/15/08

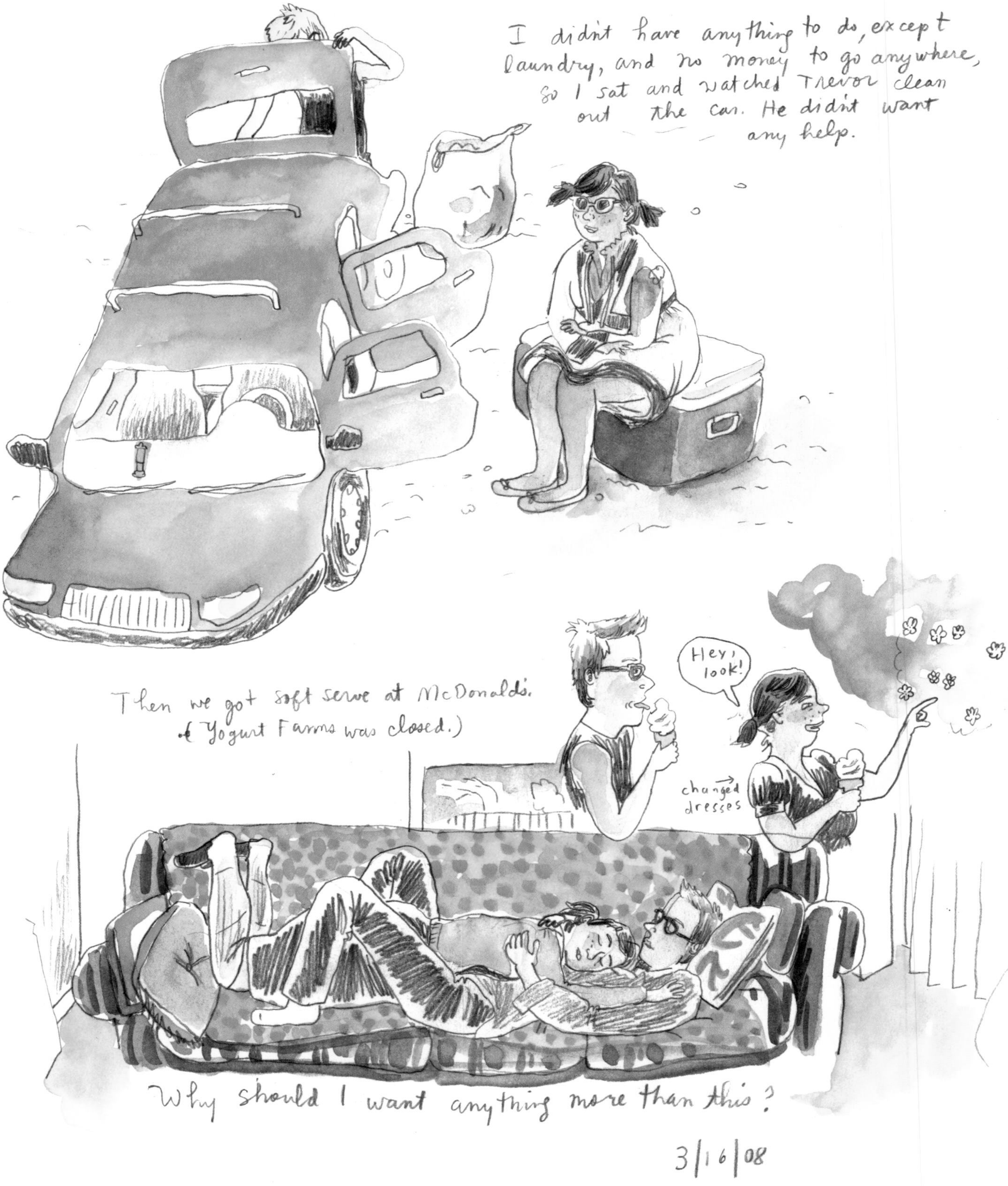
I didn't have anything to do, except laundry, and no money to go anywhere, so I sat and watched Trevor clean out the car. He didn't want any help.
Then we got soft serve at McDonald's. (Yogurt Farms was closed.)
Hey, look!
changed dresses
Why should I want anything more than this?
3/16/08

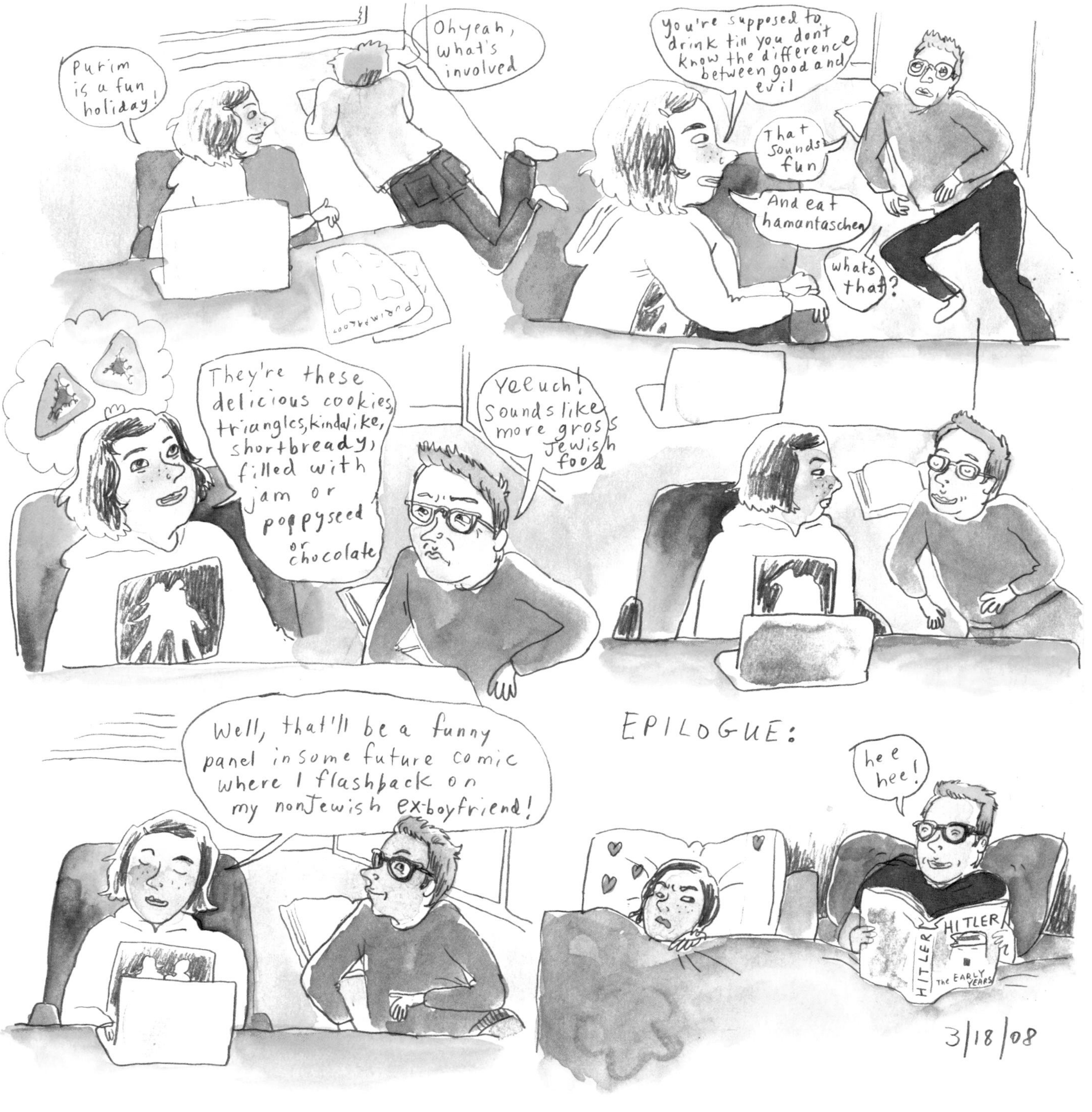
Purim is a fun holiday!
Oh yeah, what's involved
You're supposed to drink till you don't know the difference between good and evil
That sounds fun
And eat hamantaschen
what's that?
PURIMPALOOZA
They're these delicious cookies, triangles, kinda like, shortbready, filled with jam or poppyseed or chocolate
Yeeuch! Sounds like more gross Jewish food
Well, that'll be a funny panel in some future comic where I flashback on my nonJewish ex-boyfriend!
EPILOGUE:
hee hee!
HITLER
HITLER
HITLER
The EARLY YEARS
3/18/08

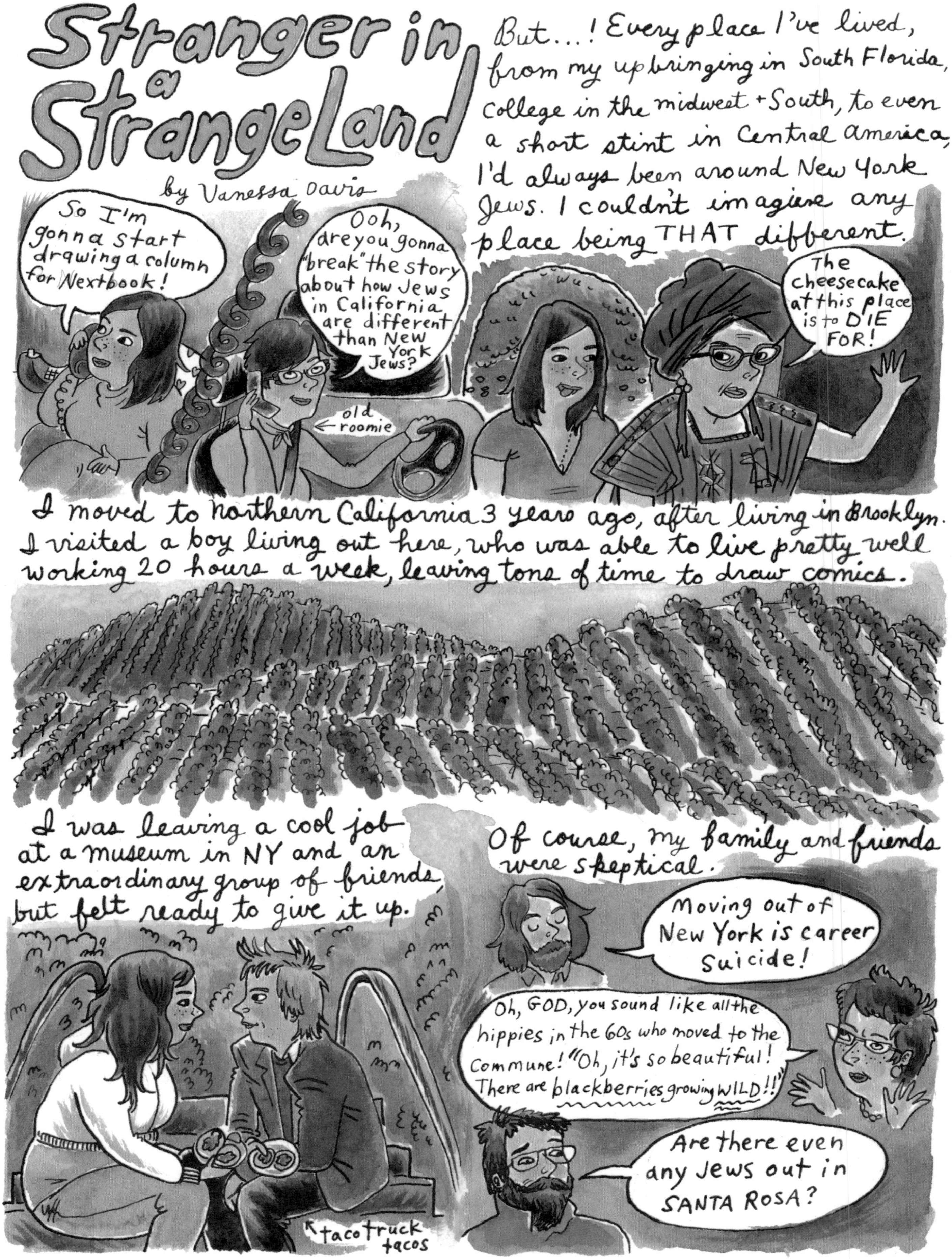
Stranger in a Strange Land
by Vanessa Davis
But...! Every place I've lived, from my upbringing in South Florida, college in the midwest + South, to even a short stint in Central america, I'd always been around New York Jews. I couldn't imagine any place being THAT different.
So I'm gonna start drawing a column for Nextbook!
Ooh, are you gonna "break" the story about how Jews in California are different than New York Jews?
old roomie
The cheesecake at this place is to DIE FOR!
I moved to northern California 3 years ago, after living in Brooklyn. I visited a boy living out here, who was able to live pretty well working 20 hours a week, leaving tons of time to draw comics.
I was leaving a cool job at a museum in NY and an extraordinary group of friends, but felt ready to give it up.
taco truck tacos
Of course, my family and friends were skeptical.
Moving out of New York is career suicide!
Oh, GOD, you sound like all the hippies in the 60s who moved to the commune! "Oh, it's so beautiful! There are blackberries growing WILD!!"
Are there even any Jews out in SANTA ROSA?

Santa Rosa is a funny place with a party atmosphere. There's a group of young people living a big-city-style singleton lifestyle, but within a sort of small town with a limited number of professional opportunities, bars, and guys to date.

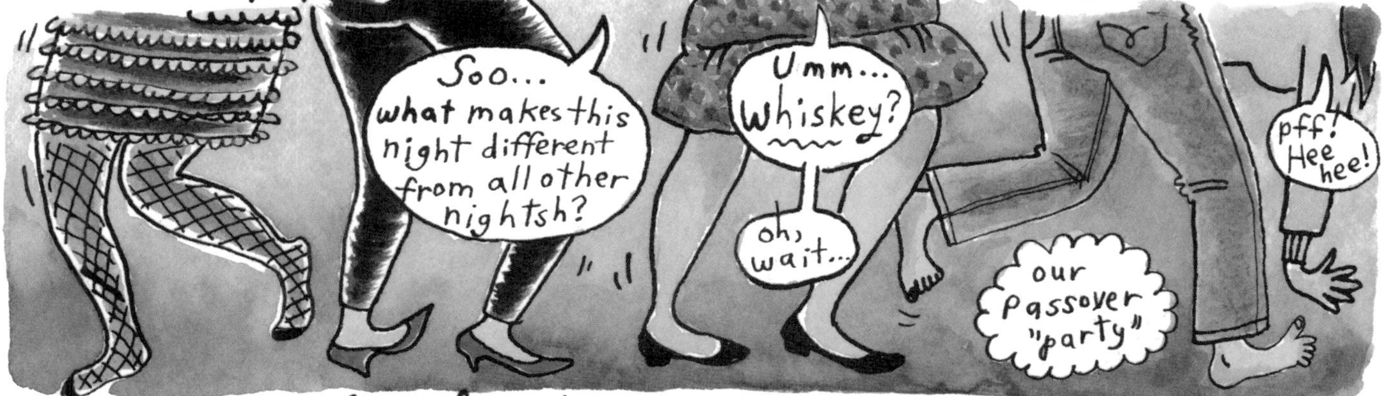
Soo... what makes this night different from all other nightsh?
Umm... Whiskey?
oh, wait...
our Passover "party"
pff! Hee hee!

There are some Jews here though, and they're my friends. I think that they might connect with their Judaism in a different way than me— I've never been in a situation where I had to feel like it made me different. I've definitely come to take it for granted.

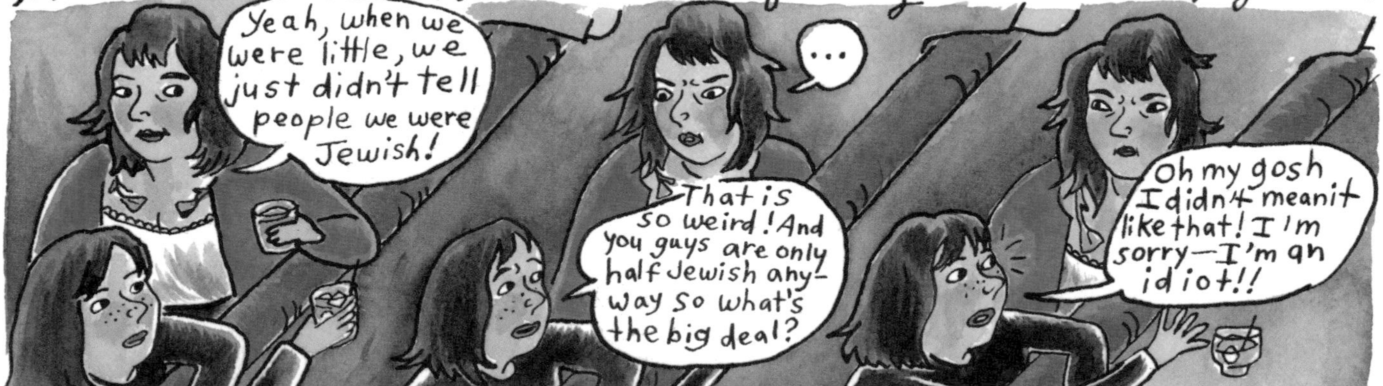
Yeah, when we were little, we just didn't tell people we were Jewish!
...
That is so weird! And you guys are only half Jewish anyway so what's the big deal?
Oh my gosh I didn't mean it like that! I'm sorry—I'm an idiot!!

The brand of East Coast Jewishness that I grew up with, however, is not the norm out here. My mom came out to visit me a while ago, and even on her short trip, she could tell the "vibe" was different.

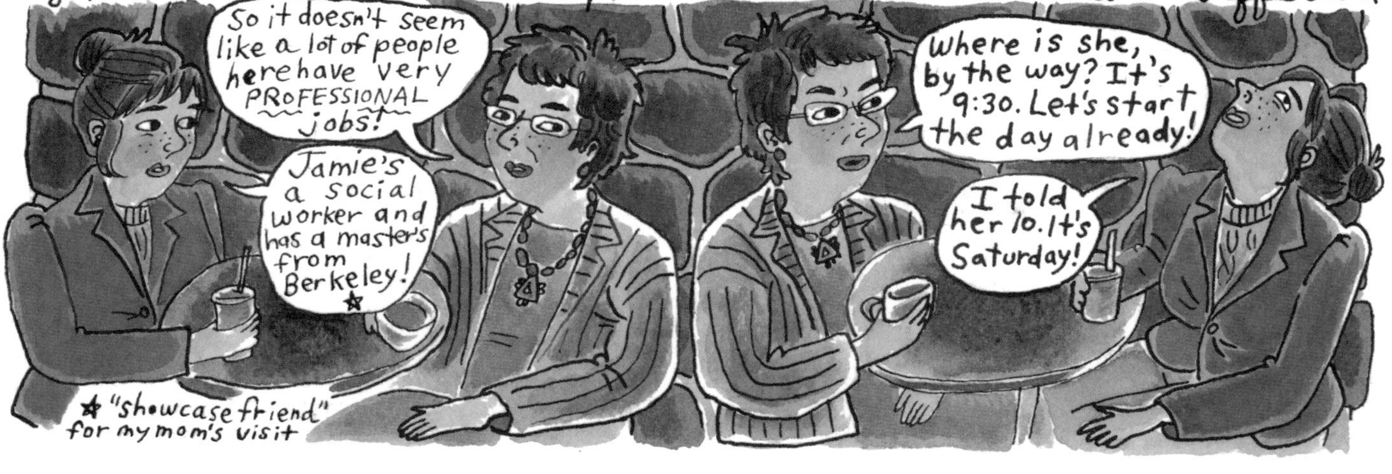
So it doesn't seem like a lot of people here have very PROFESSIONAL jobs!
Jamie's a social worker and has a master's from Berkeley! ★
Where is she, by the way? It's 9:30. Let's start the day already!
I told her 10. It's Saturday!

★ "showcase friend" for my mom's visit

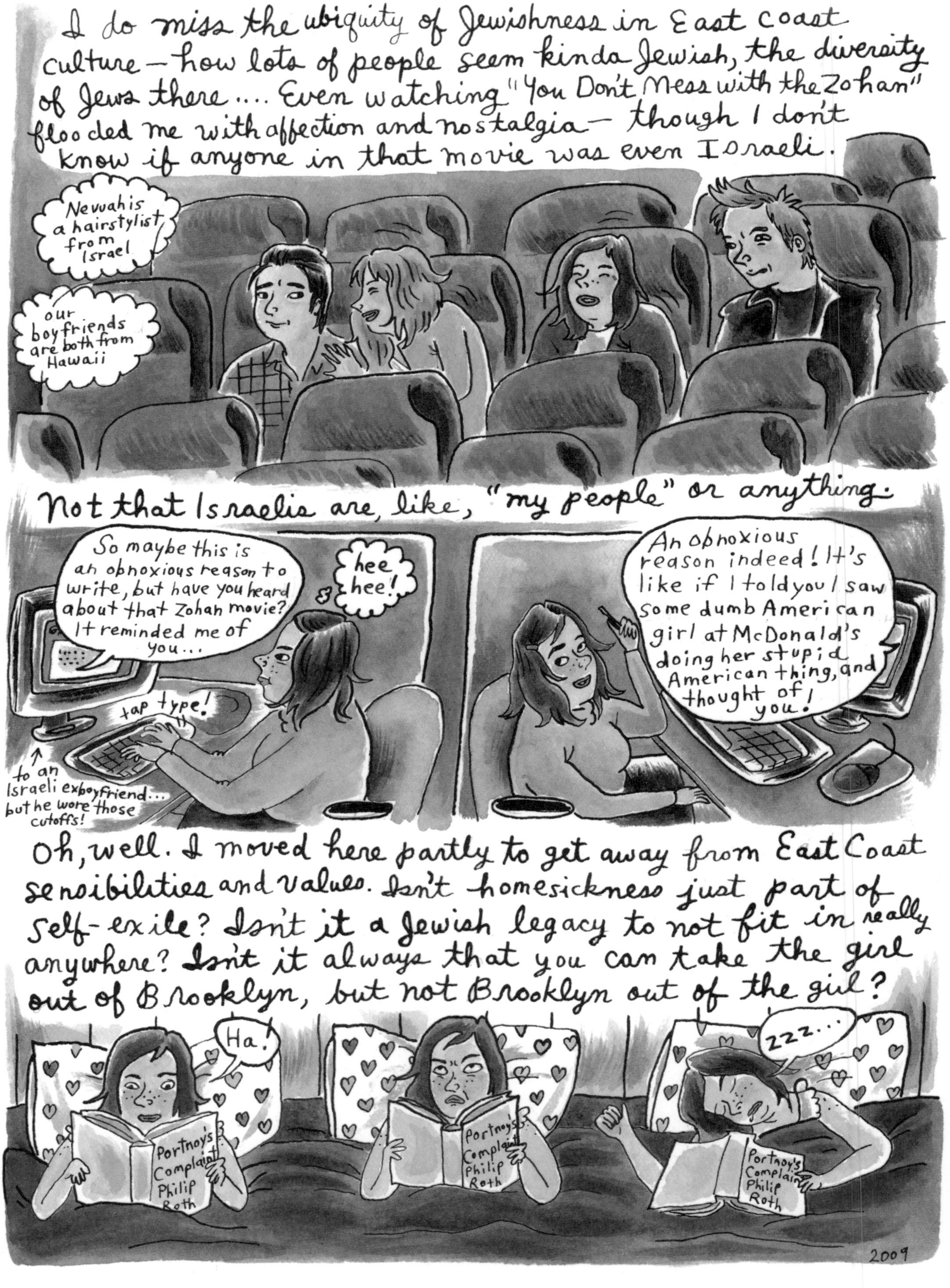
I do miss the ubiquity of Jewishness in East coast culture—how lots of people seem kinda Jewish, the diversity of Jews there.... Even watching "You Don't Mess with the Zohan" flooded me with affection and nostalgia—though I don't know if anyone in that movie was even Israeli.
Newah is a hairstylist from Israel
our boyfriends are both from Hawaii
Not that Israelis are, like, "my people" or anything.
So maybe this is an obnoxious reason to write, but have you heard about that Zohan movie? It reminded me of you...
hee hee!
tap type!
↑ to an Israeli exboyfriend... but he wore those cutoffs!
An obnoxious reason indeed! It's like if I told you I saw some dumb American girl at McDonald's doing her stupid American thing, and thought of you!
Oh, well. I moved here partly to get away from East Coast sensibilities and values. Isn't homesickness just part of self-exile? Isn't it a Jewish legacy to not fit in really anywhere? Isn't it always that you can take the girl out of Brooklyn, but not Brooklyn out of the girl?
Ha!
Portnoy's Complaint Philip Roth
Portnoy's Complaint Philip Roth
zzz...
Portnoy's Complaint Philip Roth
2009

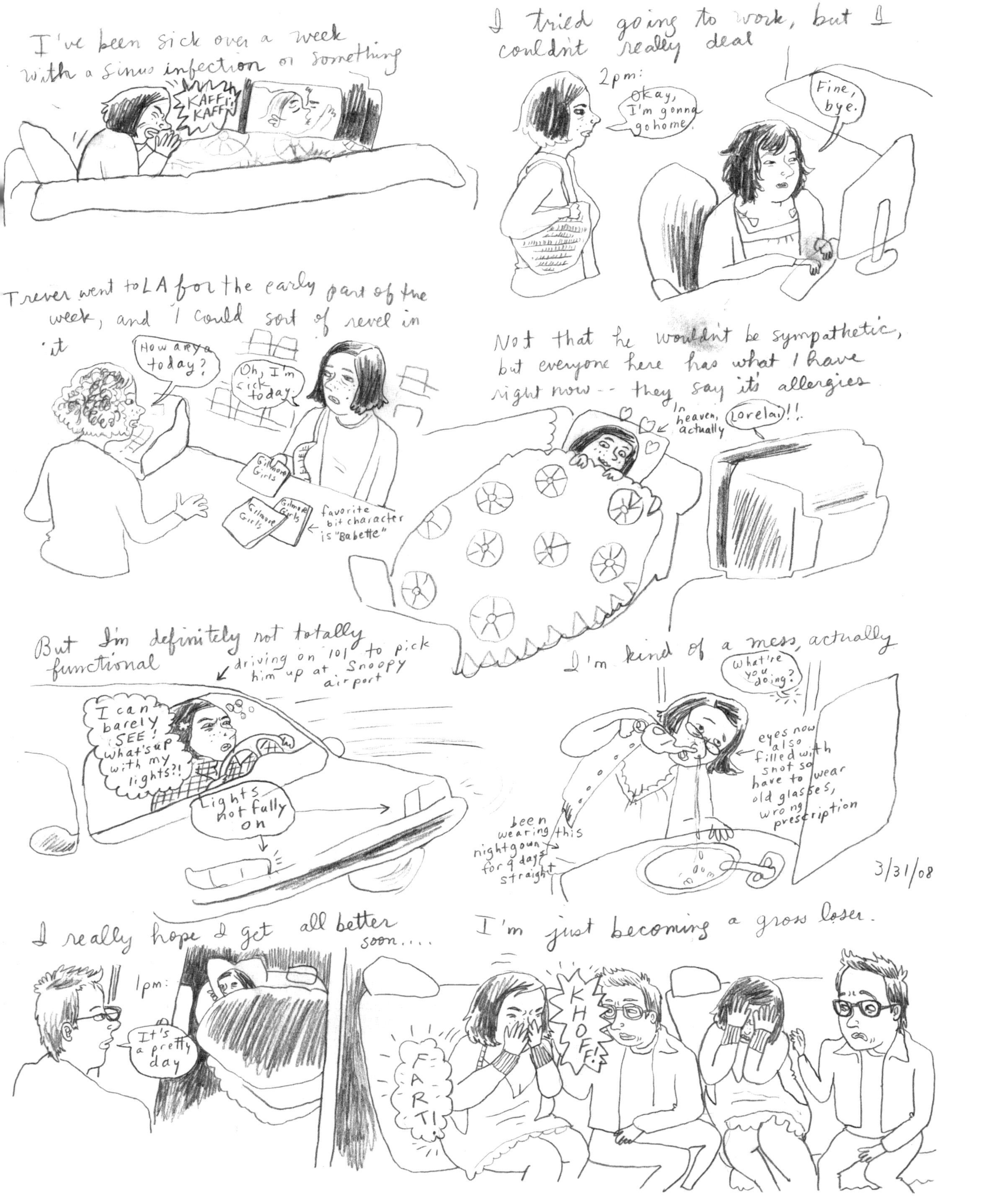

I've been sick over a week with a sinus infection or something
KAFF! KAFF!
I tried going to work, but I couldn't really deal
2pm:
Okay, I'm gonna go home.
Fine, bye.
Trever went to LA for the early part of the week, and I could sort of revel in it
How are ya today?
Oh, I'm sick today.
Gilmore Girls
Gilmore Girls
Gilmore Girls
favorite bit character is "Babette"
Not that he wouldn't be sympathetic, but everyone here has what I have right now -- they say it's allergies
In heaven, actually
Lorelai!!
But I'm definitely not totally functional
driving on 101 to pick him up at Snoopy airport
I can barely SEE! what's up with my lights?!
Lights not fully on
I'm kind of a mess, actually
What're you doing?
eyes now also filled with snot so have to wear old glasses, wrong prescription
been wearing this nightgown for 9 days straight
3/31/08
I really hope I get all better soon....
1pm:
It's a pretty day
I'm just becoming a gross loser.
FART!
KHOFF!

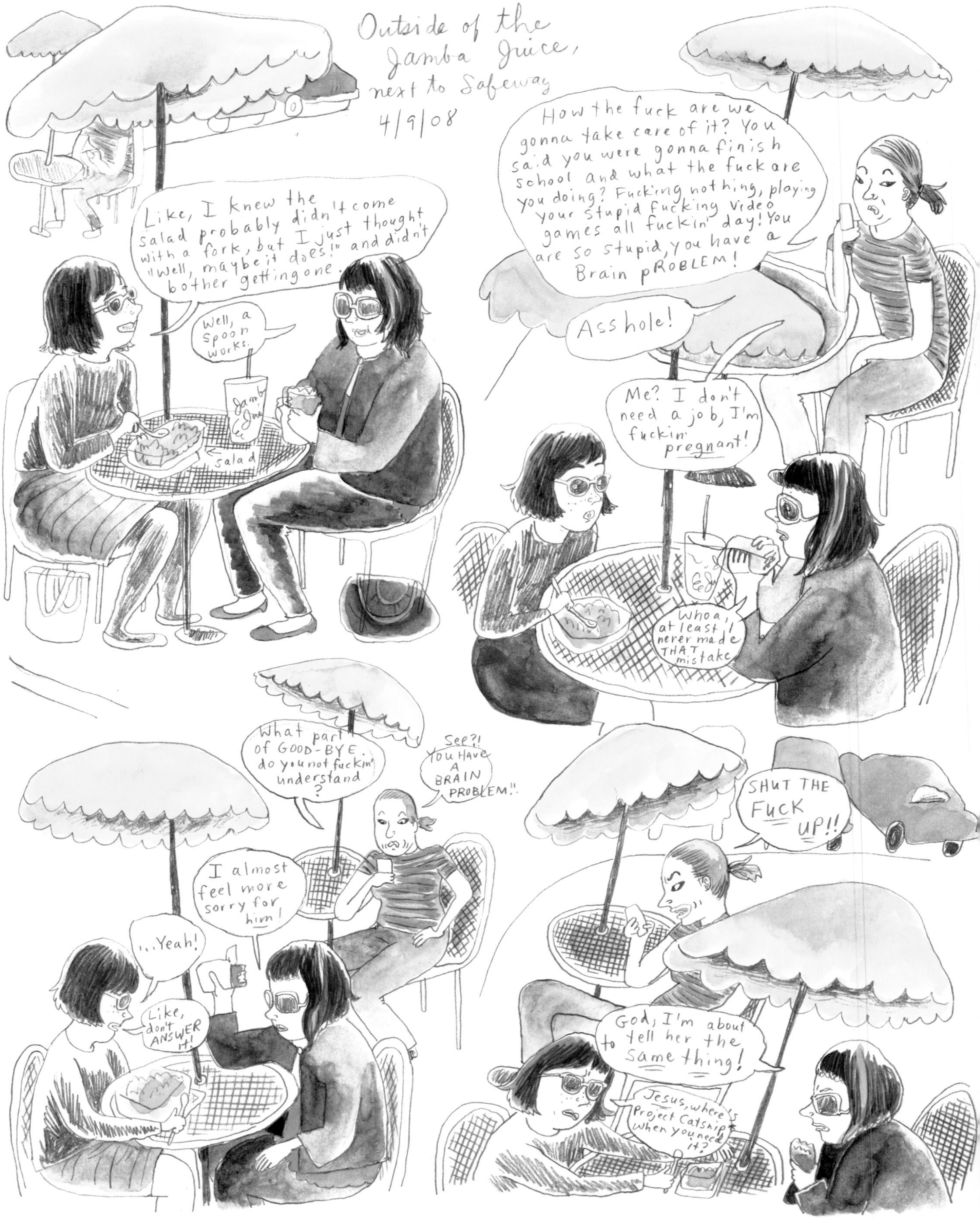
Outside of the Jamba Juice, next to Safeway 4/9/08
Like, I knew the salad probably didn't come with a fork, but I just thought "Well, maybe it does!" and didn't bother getting one.
Well, a spoon works.
salad
How the fuck are we gonna take care of it? You said you were gonna finish school and what the fuck are you doing? Fucking nothing, playing your stupid fucking video games all fuckin' day! You are so stupid, you have a Brain PROBLEM!
Asshole!
Me? I don't need a job, I'm fuckin' pregnant!
Whoa, at least I never made THAT mistake
What part of GOOD-BYE do you not fuckin' understand?
See?! You have a BRAIN PROBLEM!!
I almost feel more sorry for him!
...Yeah!
Like, don't ANSWER it!
SHUT THE FUCK UP!!
God, I'm about to tell her the same thing!
Jesus, where's Project Catship* when you need it?

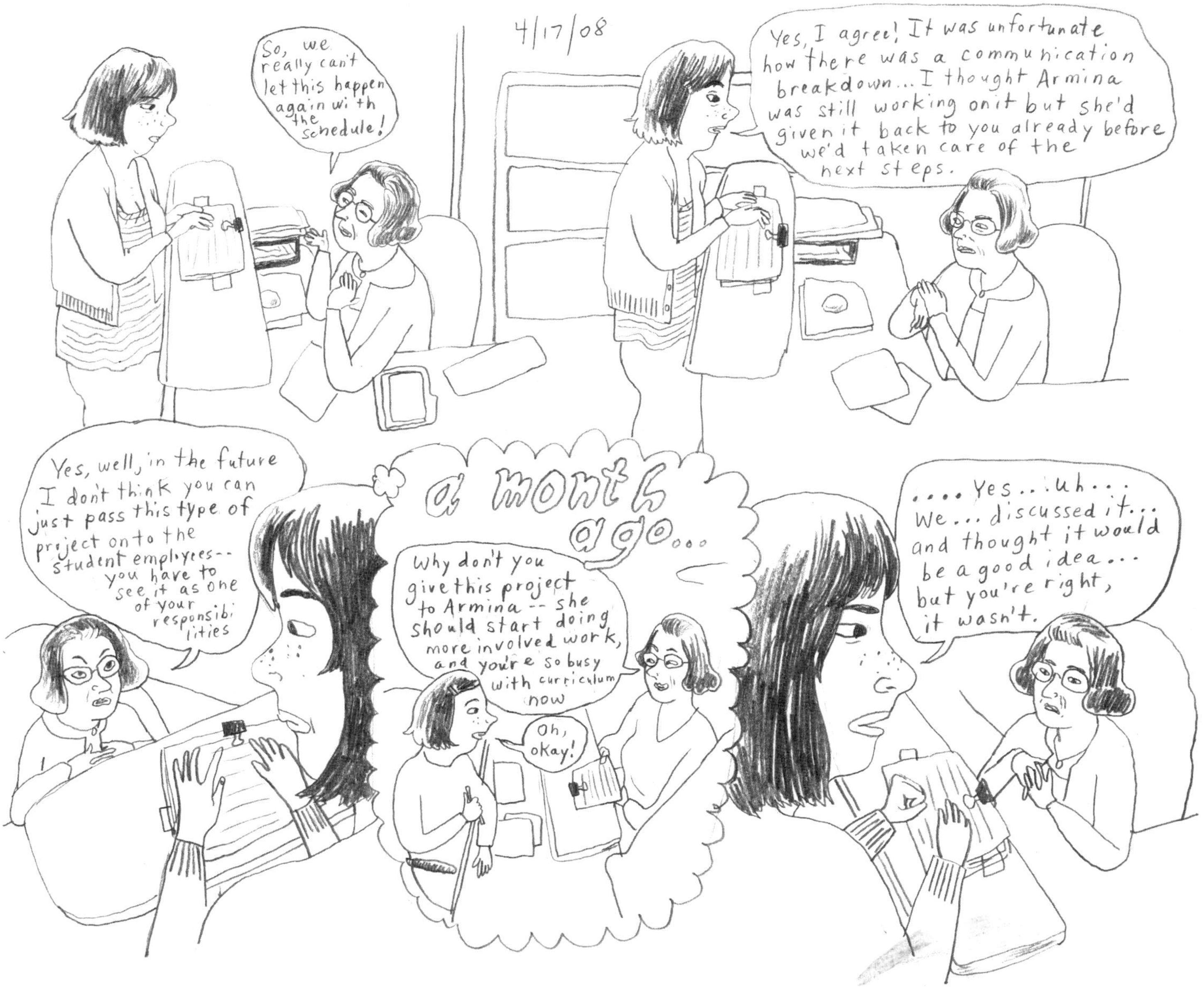
4/17/08
So, we really can't let this happen again with the schedule!
Yes, I agree! It was unfortunate how there was a communication breakdown... I thought Armina was still working on it but she'd given it back to you already before we'd taken care of the next steps.
Yes, well, in the future I don't think you can just pass this type of project on to the student employees-- you have to see it as one of your responsibilities
a month ago...
Why don't you give this project to Armina -- she should start doing more involved work, and you're so busy with curriculum now
Oh, okay!
....Yes...uh... We...discussed it... and thought it would be a good idea... but you're right, it wasn't.

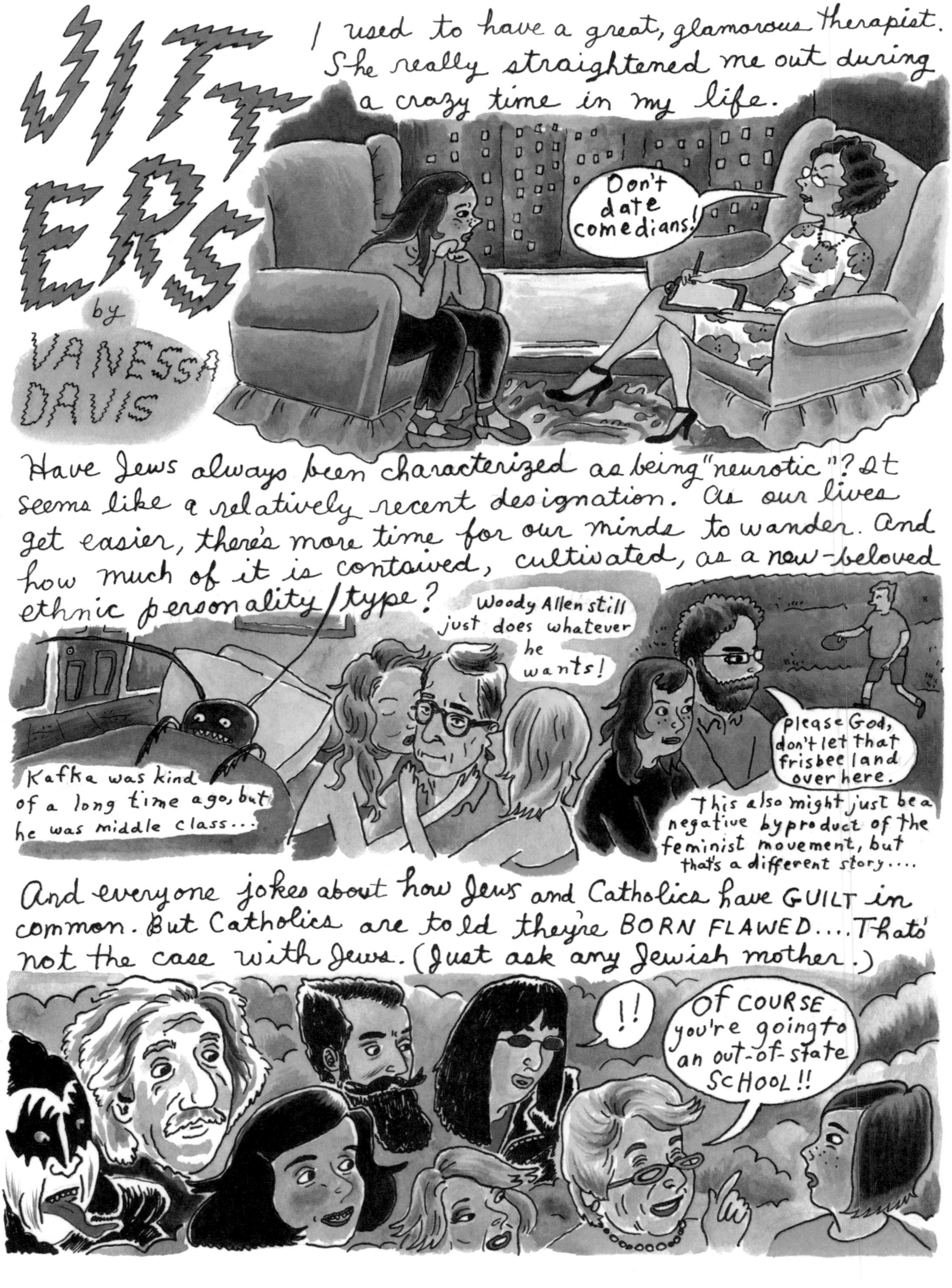
JITTERS
by
VANESSA DAVIS
I used to have a great, glamorous therapist. She really straightened me out during a crazy time in my life.
Don't date comedians!
Have Jews always been characterized as being "neurotic"? It seems like a relatively recent designation. As our lives get easier, there's more time for our minds to wander. And how much of it is contained, cultivated, as a now-beloved ethnic personality/type?
Woody Allen still just does whatever he wants!
Kafka was kind of a long time ago, but he was middle class...
Please God, don't let that frisbee land over here.
This also might just be a negative byproduct of the feminist movement, but that's a different story....
And everyone jokes about how Jews and Catholics have GUILT in common. But Catholics are told they're BORN FLAWED.... That's not the case with Jews. (Just ask any Jewish mother.)
!!
OF COURSE you're going to an out-of-state SCHOOL!!

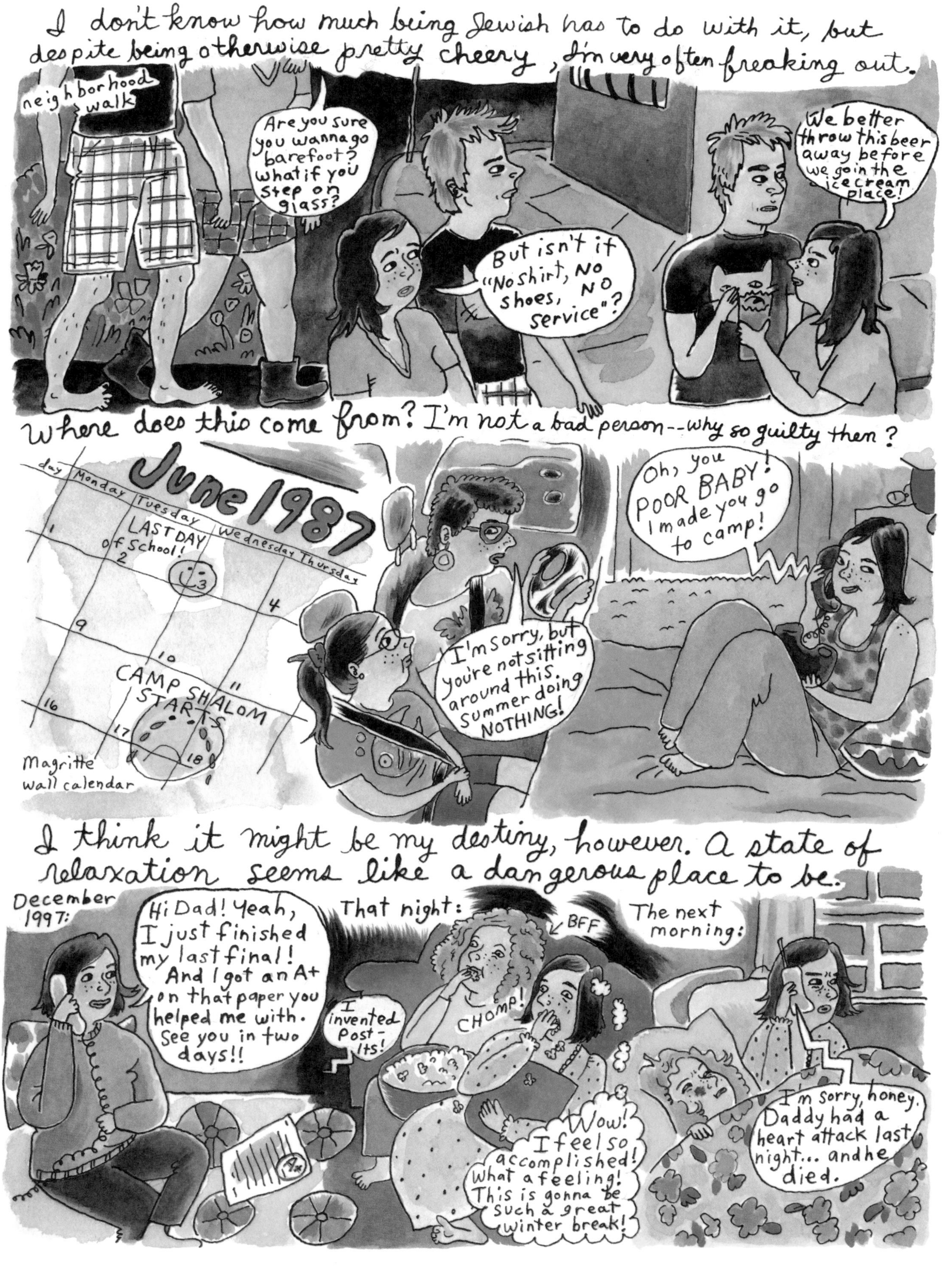
I don't know how much being Jewish has to do with it, but despite being otherwise pretty cheery, I'm very often freaking out.
neighborhood walk
Are you sure you wanna go barefoot? what if you step on glass?
But isn't it "No shirt, NO shoes, NO service"?
We better throw this beer away before we go in the ice cream place!
Where does this come from? I'm not a bad person--why so guilty then?
June 1987
day
Monday
Tuesday
Wednesday
Thursday
1
LAST DAY of School! 2
3
4
9
10
11
CAMP SHALOM STARTS
16
17
18
Magritte wall calendar
I'm sorry, but you're not sitting around this summer doing NOTHING!
Oh, you POOR BABY! I made you go to camp!
I think it might be my destiny, however. A state of relaxation seems like a dangerous place to be.
December 1997:
Hi Dad! Yeah, I just finished my last final! And I got an A+ on that paper you helped me with. See you in two days!!
That night:
BFF
I invented Post-Its!
CHOMP!
Wow! I feel so accomplished! What a feeling! This is gonna be such a great winter break!
The next morning:
I'm sorry, honey. Daddy had a heart attack last night... and he died.

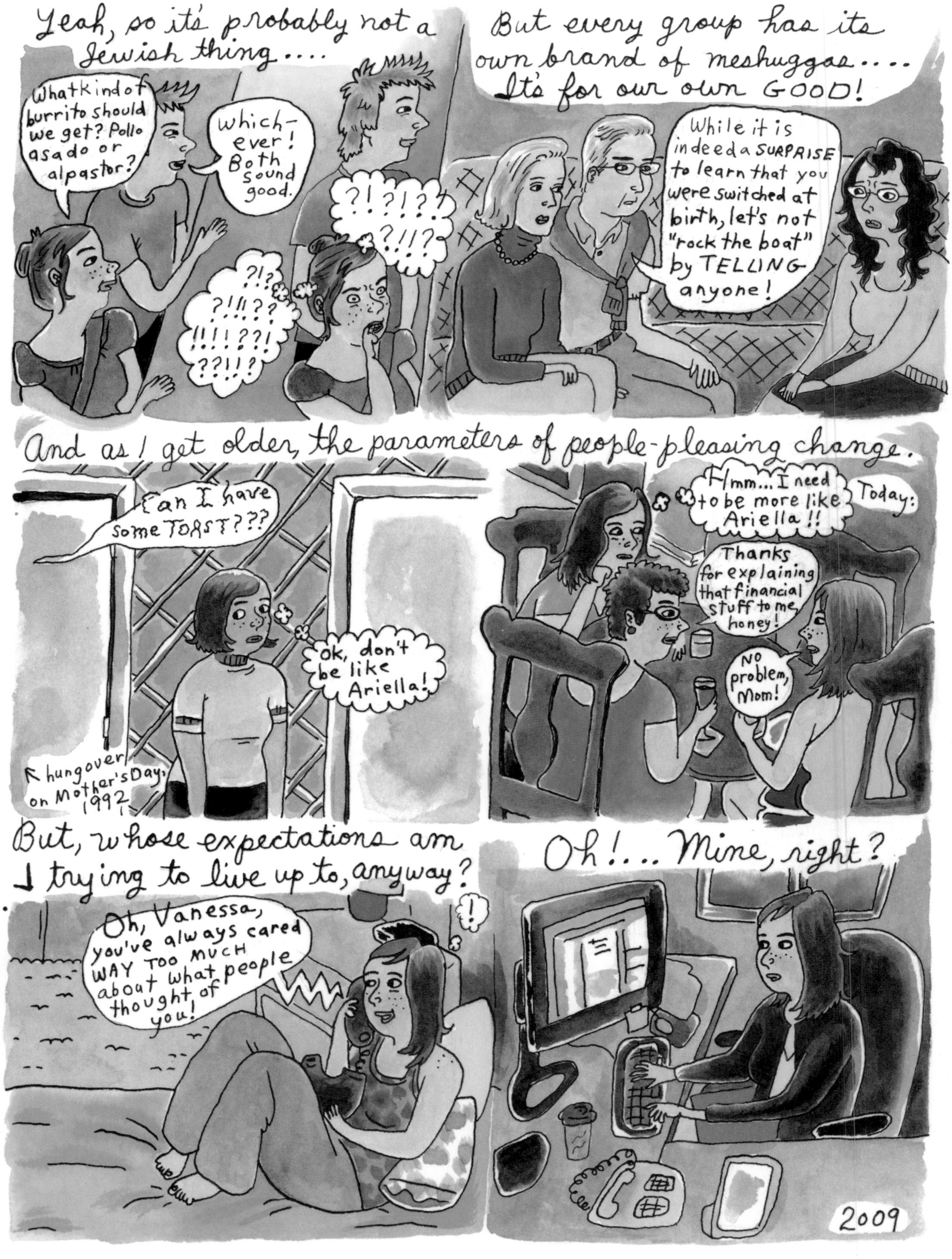
Yeah, so it's probably not a Jewish thing....
What kind of burrito should we get? Pollo asado or al pastor?
Which- ever! Both sound good.
?!?!?
?!!?
?!?
?!!!??
!!!!??!
??!!?
But every group has its own brand of meshuggas.... It's for our own GOOD!
While it is indeed a SURPRISE to learn that you were switched at birth, let's not "rock the boat" by TELLING anyone!
And as I get older, the parameters of people-pleasing change.
Can I have some TOAST???
ok, don't be like Ariella!
hungover on Mother's Day, 1992
Hmm... I need to be more like Ariella!!
Today:
Thanks for explaining that financial stuff to me, honey!
No problem, Mom!
But, whose expectations am I trying to live up to, anyway?
!
Oh, Vanessa, you've always cared WAY TOO MUCH about what people thought of you!
Oh!... Mine, right?
2009

5-11-08

I got some weird coughing bug since I got to W. Palm Bch.

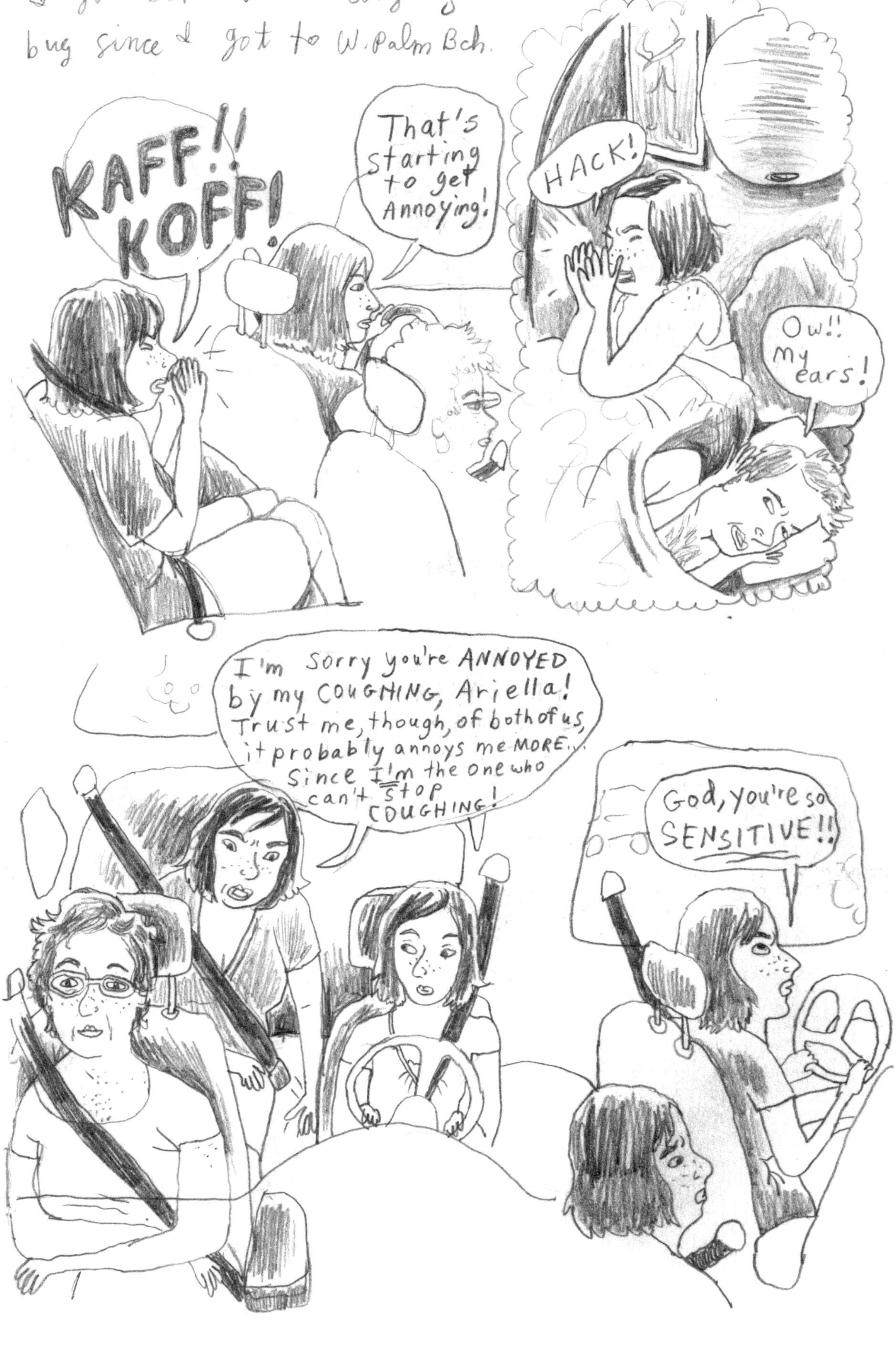
KAFF!! KOFF!
That's starting to get Annoying!
HACK!
Ow!! my ears!
I'm sorry you're ANNOYED by my COUGHING, Ariella! Trust me, though, of both of us, it probably annoys me MORE... Since I'm the one who can't STOP COUGHING!
God, you're so SENSITIVE!!

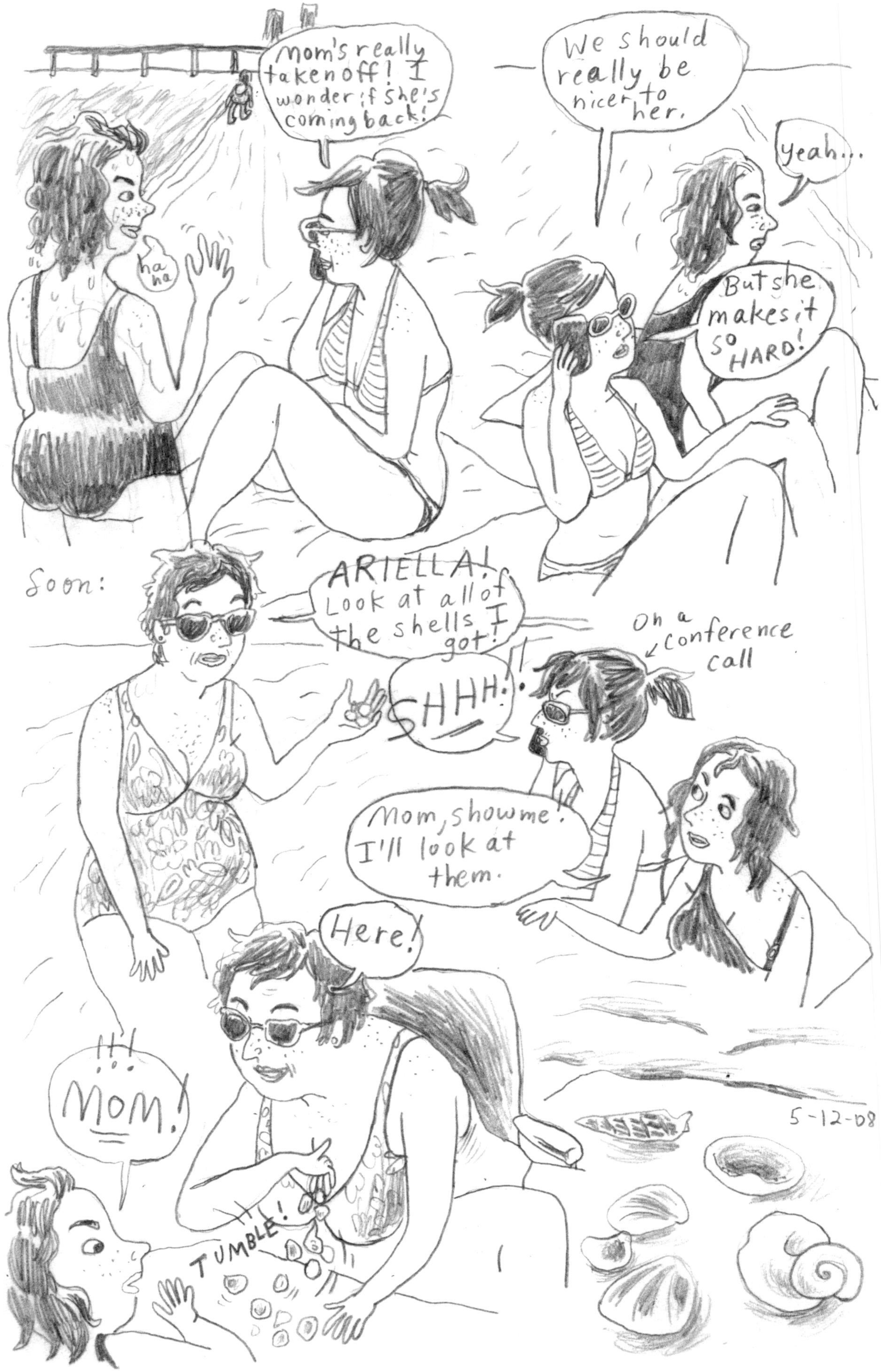
Mom's really takenoff! I wonder if she's coming back!
ha ha
We should really be nicer to her.
yeah...
But she makes it so HARD!
Soon:
ARIELLA! Look at all of the shells I got!
SHHH!!
Oh a conference call
Mom, showme! I'll look at them.
Here!
!!!
MOM!
TUMBLE!
5-12-08

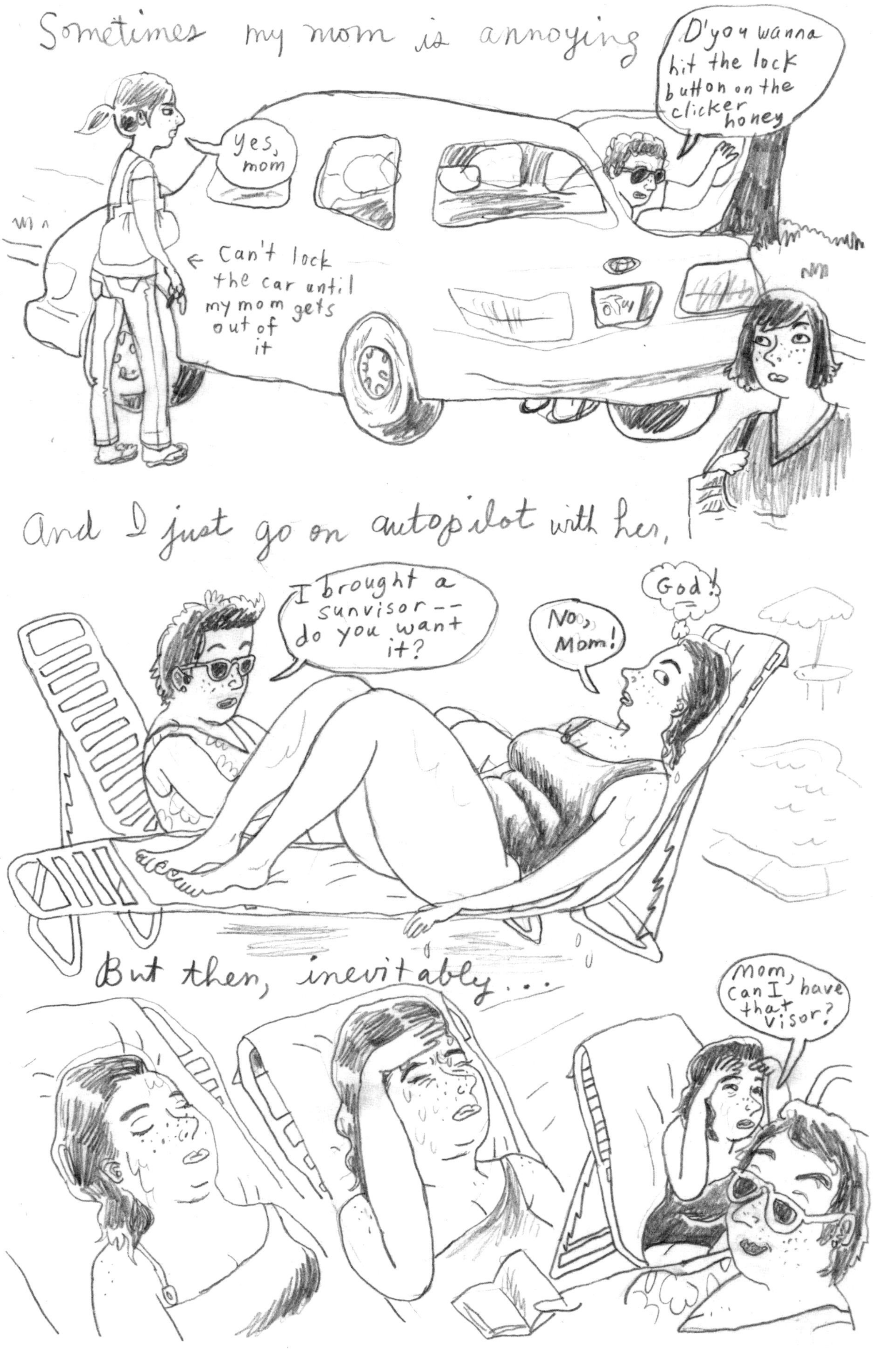
Sometimes my mom is annoying
D'you wanna hit the lock button on the clicker honey
Yes, mom
Can't lock the car until my mom gets out of it
And I just go on autopilot with her,
I brought a sunvisor -- do you want it?
No, Mom!
God!
But then, inevitably...
Mom, can I have that visor?

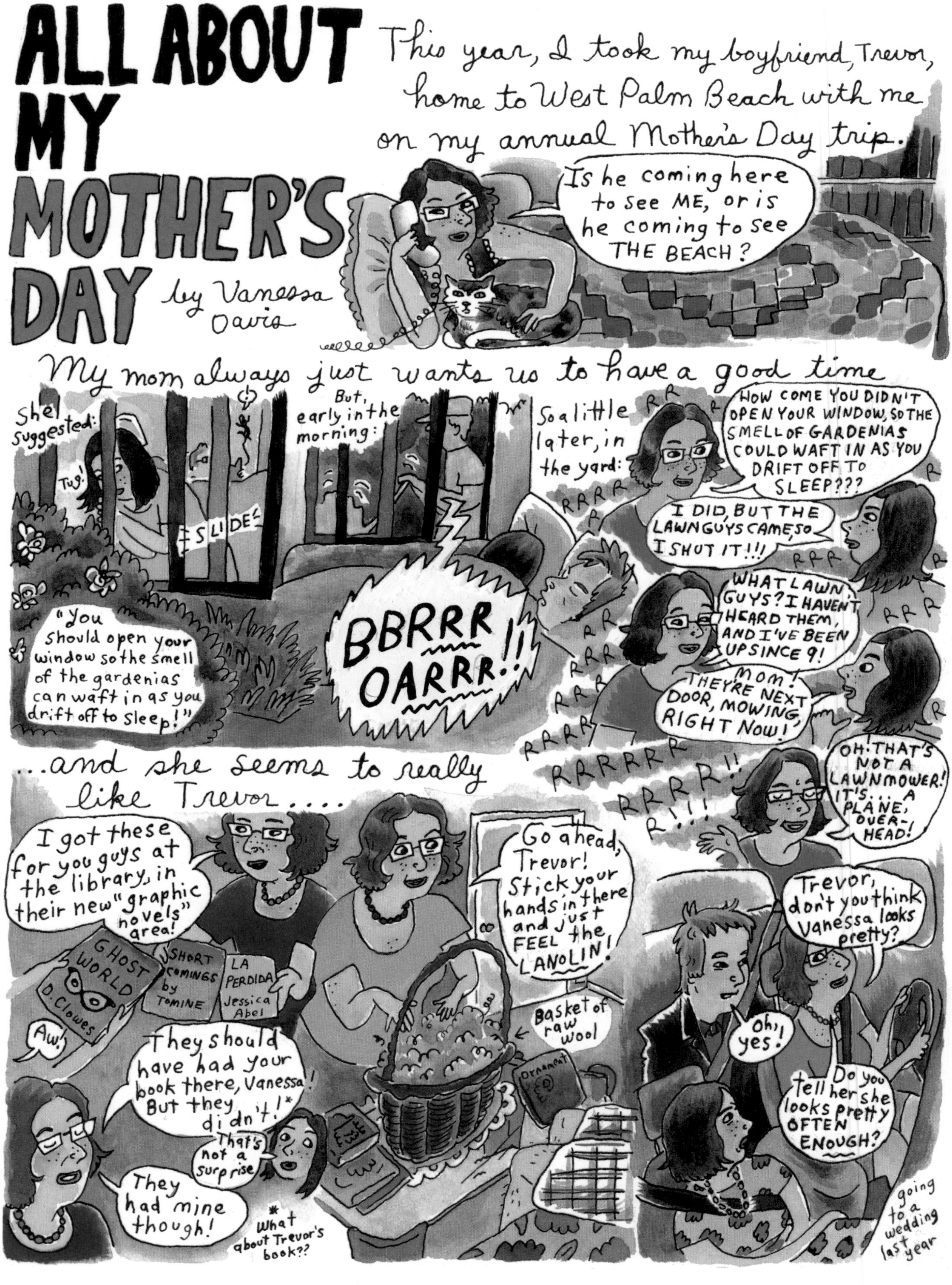
ALL ABOUT MY MOTHER'S DAY
by Vanessa Davis
This year, I took my boyfriend, Trevor, home to West Palm Beach with me on my annual Mother's Day trip.
Is he coming here to see ME, or is he coming to see THE BEACH?
My mom always just wants us to have a good time
She suggested:
"You should open your window so the smell of the gardenias can waft in as you drift off to sleep!"
Tug!
SLIDE
But, early in the morning:
BBRRR OARRR!!
So a little later, in the yard:
HOW COME YOU DIDN'T OPEN YOUR WINDOW, SO THE SMELL OF GARDENIAS COULD WAFT IN AS YOU DRIFT OFF TO SLEEP???
I DID, BUT THE LAWN GUYS CAME, SO I SHUT IT!!!
WHAT LAWN GUYS? I HAVEN'T HEARD THEM, AND I'VE BEEN UP SINCE 9!
MOM! THEY'RE NEXT DOOR, MOWING, RIGHT NOW!
RRRRRR RRRRR!! RRRR R!!!
OH! THAT'S NOT A LAWNMOWER! IT'S... A PLANE, OVERHEAD!
...and she seems to really like Trevor....
I got these for you guys at the library, in their new "graphic novels" area!
GHOST WORLD D. Clowes
SHORT COMINGS by TOMINE
LA PERDIDA Jessica Abel
Aw!
They should have had your book there, Vanessa! But they didn't!*
That's not a surprise
They had mine though!
* What about Trevor's book??
Go ahead, Trevor! Stick your hands in there and just FEEL the LANOLIN!
Basket of raw wool
Ornament
Trevor, don't you think Vanessa looks pretty?
Oh, yes!
Do you tell her she looks pretty OFTEN ENOUGH?
going to a wedding last year

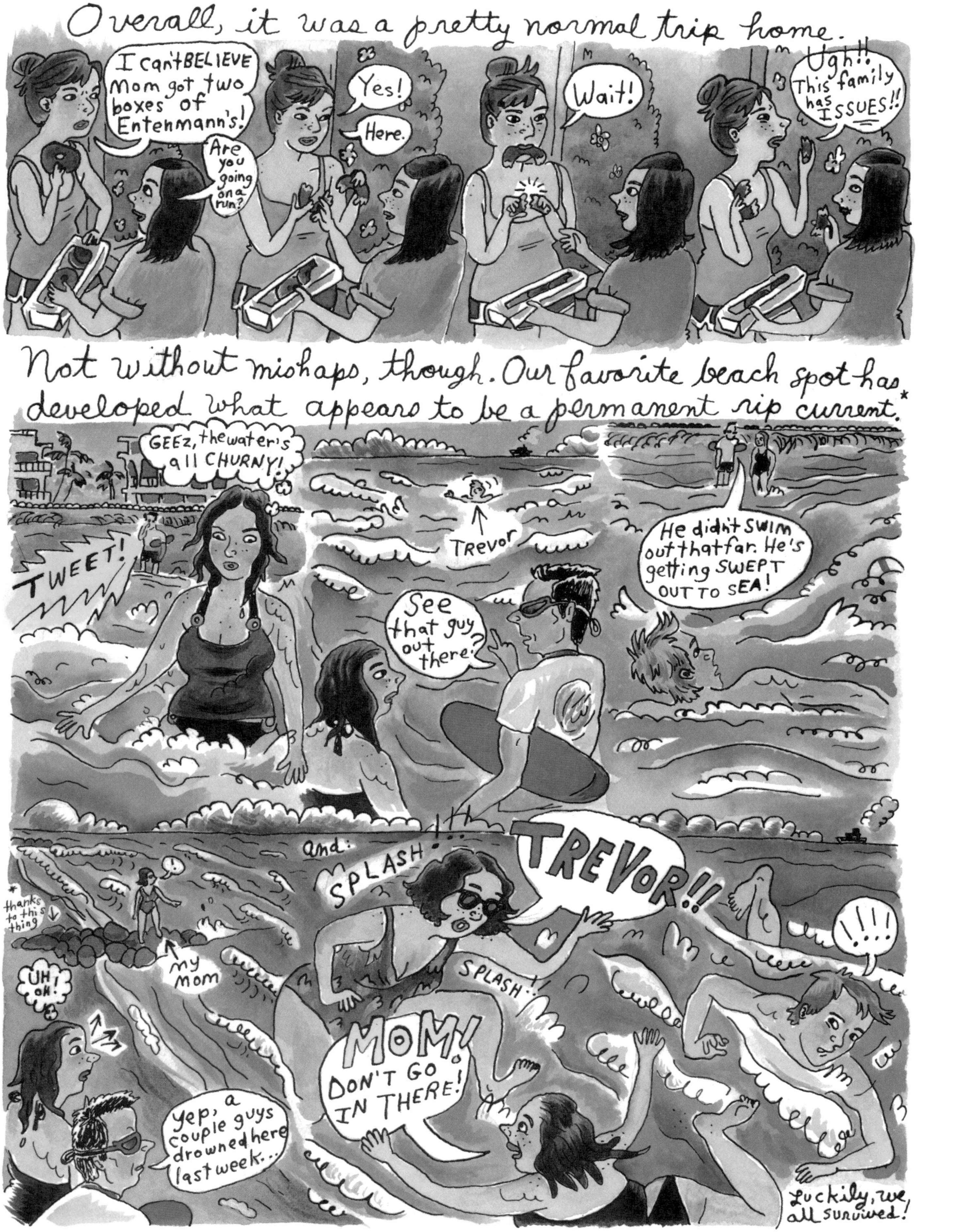

Overall, it was a pretty normal trip home.
I can't BELIEVE Mom got two boxes of Entenmann's!
Are you going on a run?
Yes!
Here.
Wait!
Ugh!! This family has ISSUES!!
Not without mishaps, though. Our favorite beach spot has developed what appears to be a permanent rip current.*
GEEZ, the water's all CHURNY!
TWEET!
TREVOR
See that guy out there?
He didn't SWIM out that far. He's getting SWEPT OUT TO SEA!
and:
SPLASH
TREVOR!!
!
* thanks to this thing
my mom
UH OH!
SPLASH
!!!!
MOM! DON'T GO IN THERE!
Yep, a couple guys drowned here last week...
Luckily, we all survived!

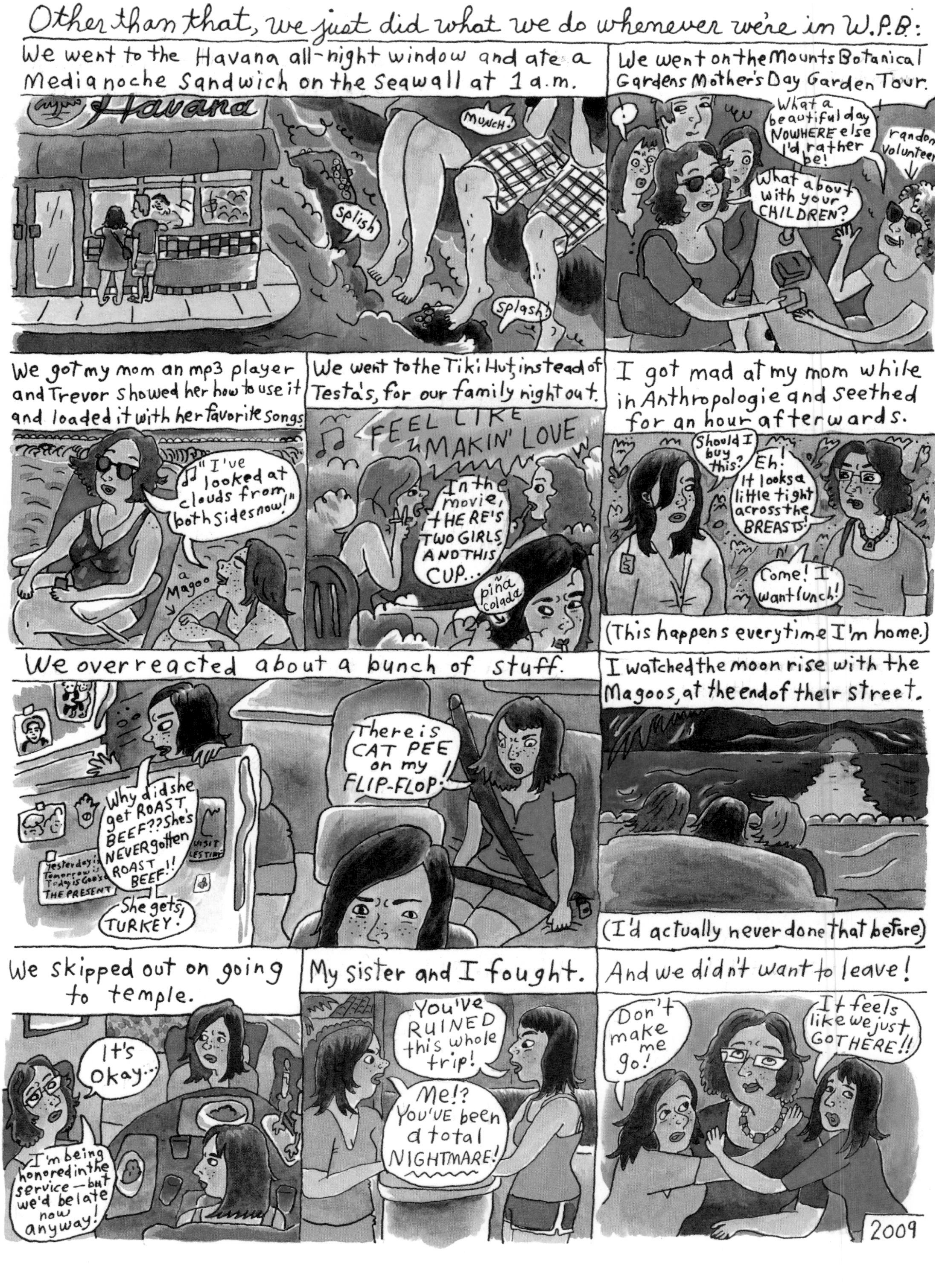

Other than that, we just did what we do whenever we're in W.P.B.:
We went to the Havana all-night window and ate a Medianoche sandwich on the seawall at 1 a.m.
Havana
MUNCH.
splish
splash!
We went on the Mounts Botanical Gardens Mother's Day Garden Tour.
What a beautiful day NOWHERE else I'd rather be!
What about with your CHILDREN?
random volunteer
We got my mom an mp3 player and Trevor showed her how to use it and loaded it with her favorite songs
"I've looked at clouds from both sides now!"
a Magoo
We went to the Tiki Hut, instead of Testa's, for our family night out.
FEEL LIKE MAKIN' LOVE
In the movie, THERE'S TWO GIRLS AND THIS CUP...
piña colada
I got mad at my mom while in Anthropologie and seethed for an hour afterwards.
Should I buy this?
Eh! It looks a little tight across the BREASTS!
Come! I want lunch!
(This happens everytime I'm home.)
We overreacted about a bunch of stuff.
Why did she get ROAST BEEF?? She's NEVER gotten ROAST BEEF!!
She gets TURKEY!
THE PRESENT
There is CAT PEE on my FLIP-FLOP!
I watched the moon rise with the Magoos, at the end of their street.
(I'd actually never done that before)
We skipped out on going to temple.
It's okay...
I'm being honored in the service — but we'd be late now anyway!
My sister and I fought.
You've RUINED this whole trip!
Me!? You've been a total NIGHTMARE!
And we didn't want to leave!
Don't make me go!
It feels like we just GOT HERE!!
2009

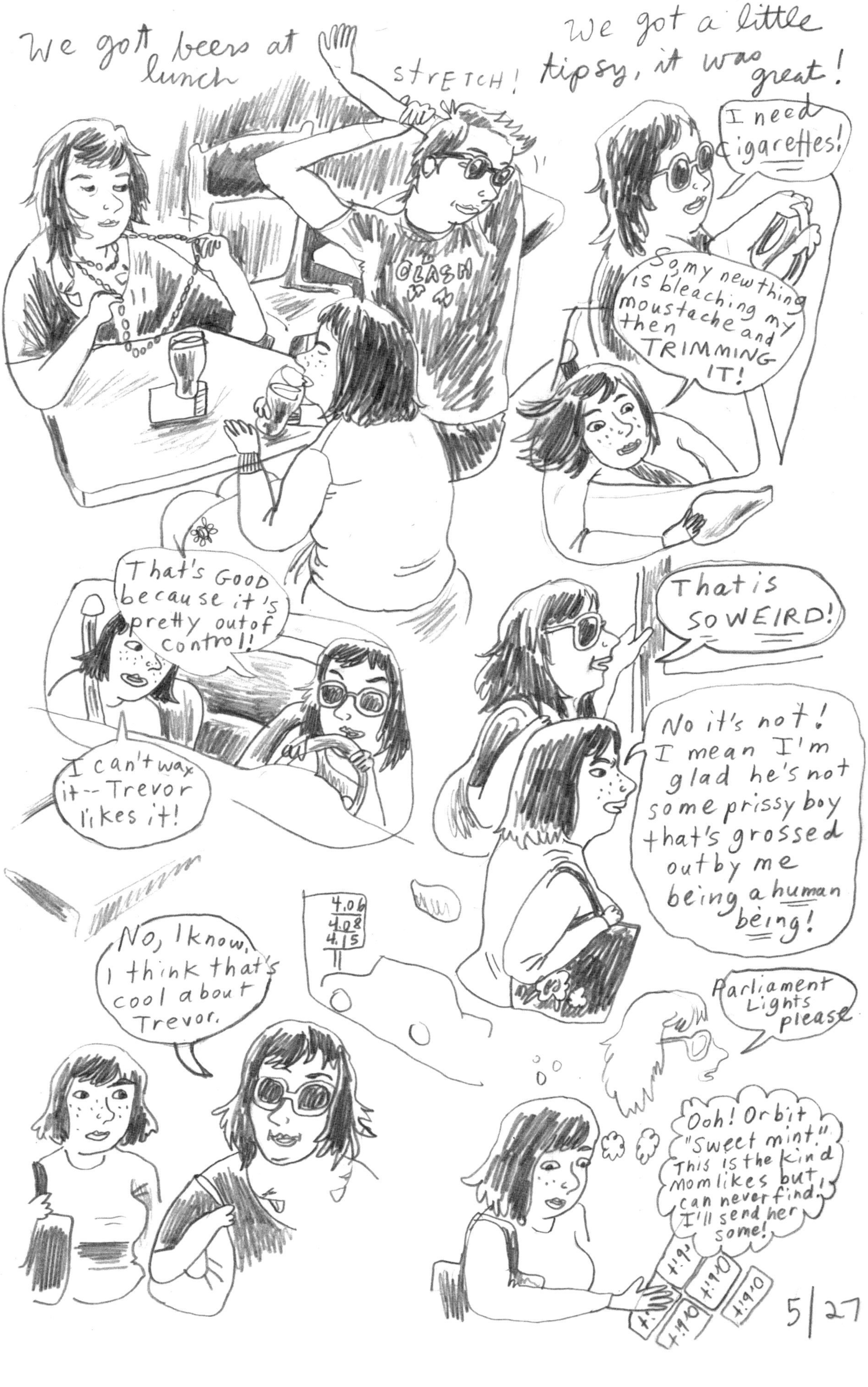
We got beers at lunch
STRETCH!
We got a little tipsy, it was great!
I need cigarettes!
So my new thing is bleaching my moustache and then TRIMMING IT!
That's GOOD because it's pretty out of control!
I can't wax it -- Trevor likes it!
That is SO WEIRD!
No it's not! I mean I'm glad he's not some prissy boy that's grossed out by me being a human being!
No, I know, I think that's cool about Trevor.
Parliament Lights please
Ooh! Orbit "Sweet mint!" This is the kind mom likes but can never find! I'll send her some!
5/27

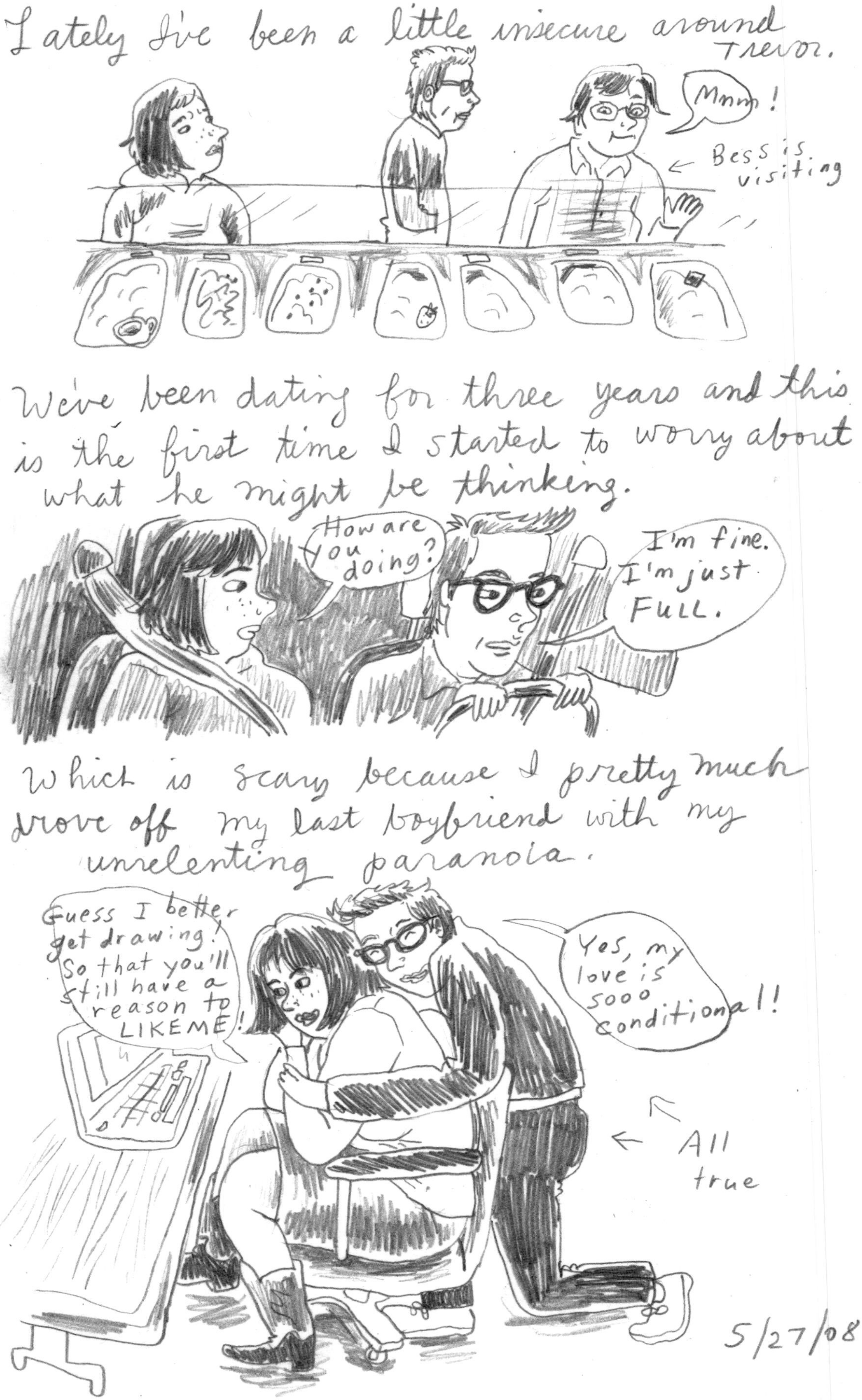
Lately I've been a little insecure around Trevor.
Mmm!
← Bess is visiting
We've been dating for three years and this is the first time I started to worry about what he might be thinking.
How are you doing?
I'm fine. I'm just FULL.
Which is scary because I pretty much drove off my last boyfriend with my unrelenting paranoia.
Guess I better get drawing! So that you'll still have a reason to LIKE ME!
Yes, my love is sooo conditional!
← All true
5/27/08

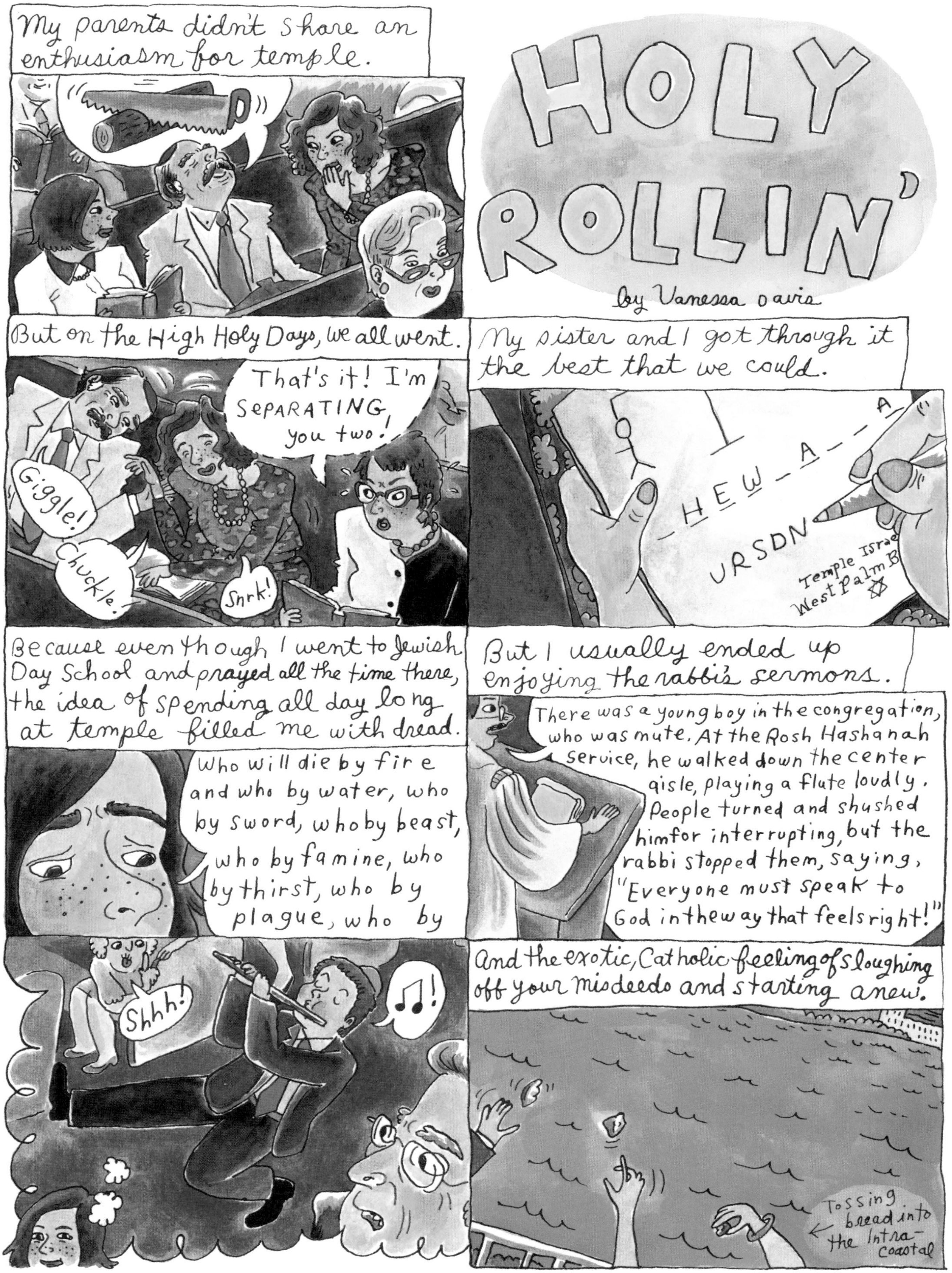

HOLY ROLLIN'
by Vanessa Davis
My parents didn't share an enthusiasm for temple.
But on the High Holy Days, we all went.
That's it! I'm SEPARATING you two!
Giggle!
Chuckle.
Snrk!
My sister and I got through it the best that we could.
_HEW_A_ _ _A
URSDN
Temple Israel
West Palm B
Because even though I went to Jewish Day School and prayed all the time there, the idea of spending all day long at temple filled me with dread.
Who will die by fire and who by water, who by sword, who by beast, who by famine, who by thirst, who by plague, who by
But I usually ended up enjoying the rabbi's sermons.
There was a young boy in the congregation, who was mute. At the Rosh Hashanah service, he walked down the center aisle, playing a flute loudly. People turned and shushed him for interrupting, but the rabbi stopped them, saying, "Everyone must speak to God in the way that feels right!"
Shhh!
♫!
And the exotic, Catholic feeling of sloughing off your misdeeds and starting anew.
Tossing bread into the Intra-coastal

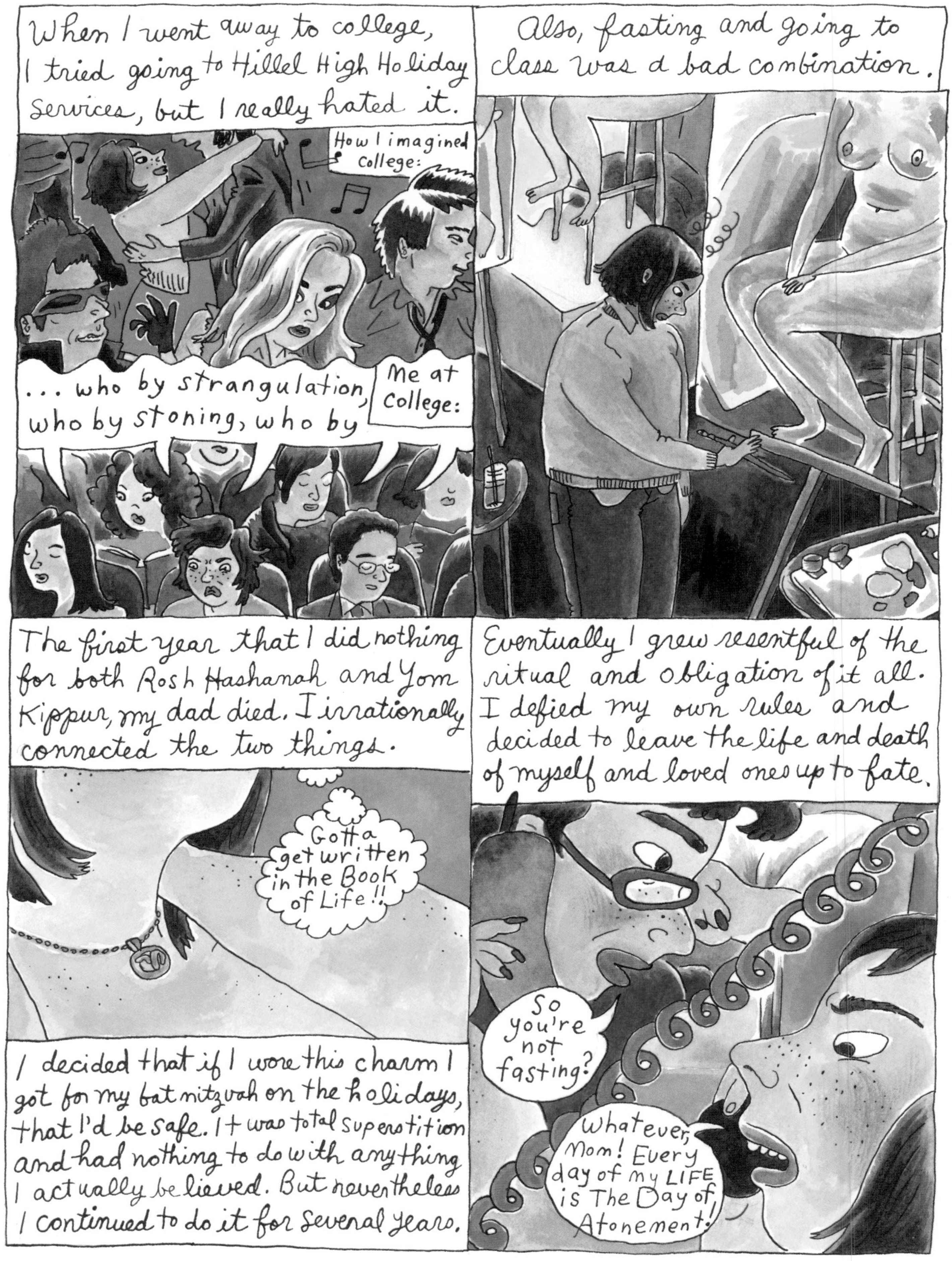
When I went away to college, I tried going to Hillel High Holiday Services, but I really hated it.
How I imagined college:
Me at college:
... who by strangulation, who by stoning, who by
Also, fasting and going to class was a bad combination.
The first year that I did nothing for both Rosh Hashanah and Yom Kippur, my dad died. I irrationally connected the two things.
Gotta get written in the Book of Life!!
I decided that if I wore this charm I got for my bat mitzvah on the holidays, that I'd be safe. It was total superstition and had nothing to do with anything I actually believed. But nevertheless I continued to do it for several years.
Eventually I grew resentful of the ritual and obligation of it all. I defied my own rules and decided to leave the life and death of myself and loved ones up to fate.
So you're not fasting?
Whatever, Mom! Every day of my LIFE is The Day of Atonement!

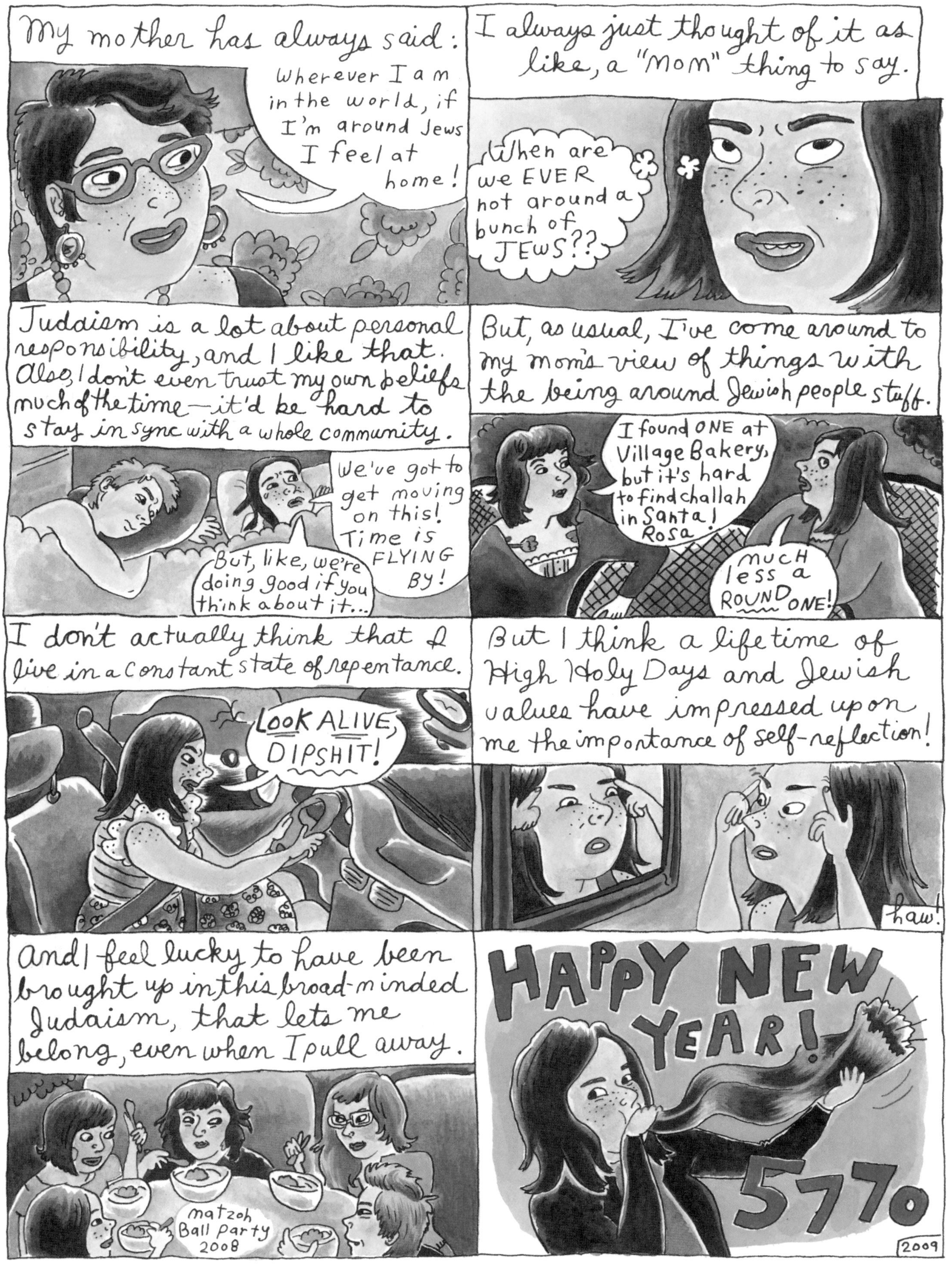

My mother has always said:
Wherever I am in the world, if I'm around Jews I feel at home!
I always just thought of it as like, a "MOM" thing to say.
When are we EVER not around a bunch of JEWS??
Judaism is a lot about personal responsibility, and I like that. Also, I don't even trust my own beliefs much of the time—it'd be hard to stay in sync with a whole community.
We've got to get moving on this! Time is FLYING BY!
But, like, we're doing good if you think about it...
But, as usual, I've come around to my mom's view of things with the being around Jewish people stuff.
I found ONE at Village Bakery, but it's hard to find challah in Santa Rosa!
MUCH less a ROUND ONE!
I don't actually think that I live in a constant state of repentance.
LOOK ALIVE, DIPSHIT!
But I think a lifetime of High Holy Days and Jewish values have impressed upon me the importance of self-reflection!
haw!
And I feel lucky to have been brought up in this broad-minded Judaism, that lets me belong, even when I pull away.
matzoh Ball party 2008
HAPPY NEW YEAR!
5770
2009

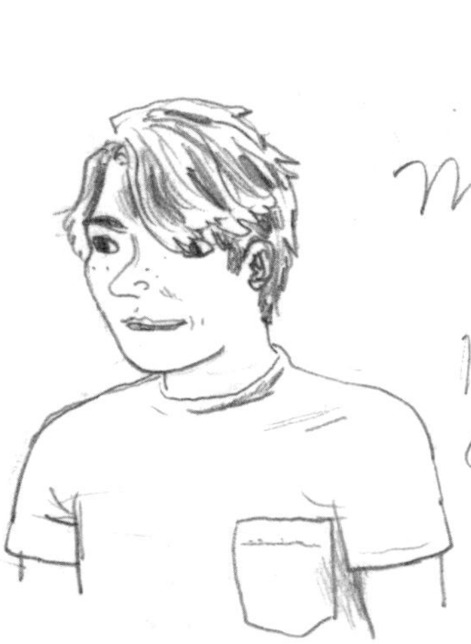

Michael was so cute.
He lived with his grandparents and they made him a country breakfast every morning

S 3
S 1
M 2

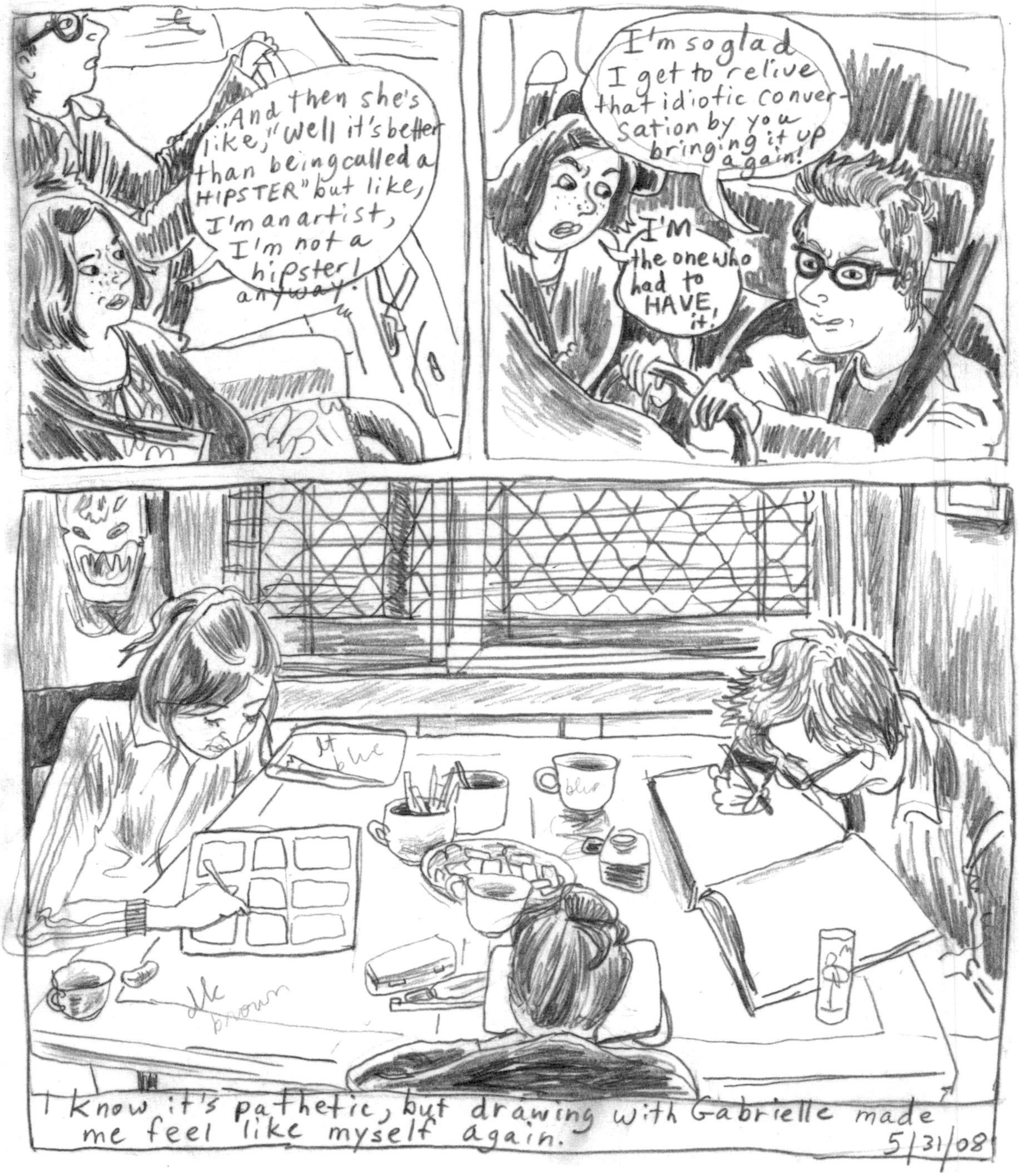

...And then she's like, "Well it's better than being called a HIPSTER" but like, I'm an artist, I'm not a hipster! anyway...
I'm so glad I get to relive that idiotic conversation by you bringing it up again!
I'M the one who had to HAVE it!
I know it's pathetic, but drawing with Gabrielle made me feel like myself again.
5/31/08

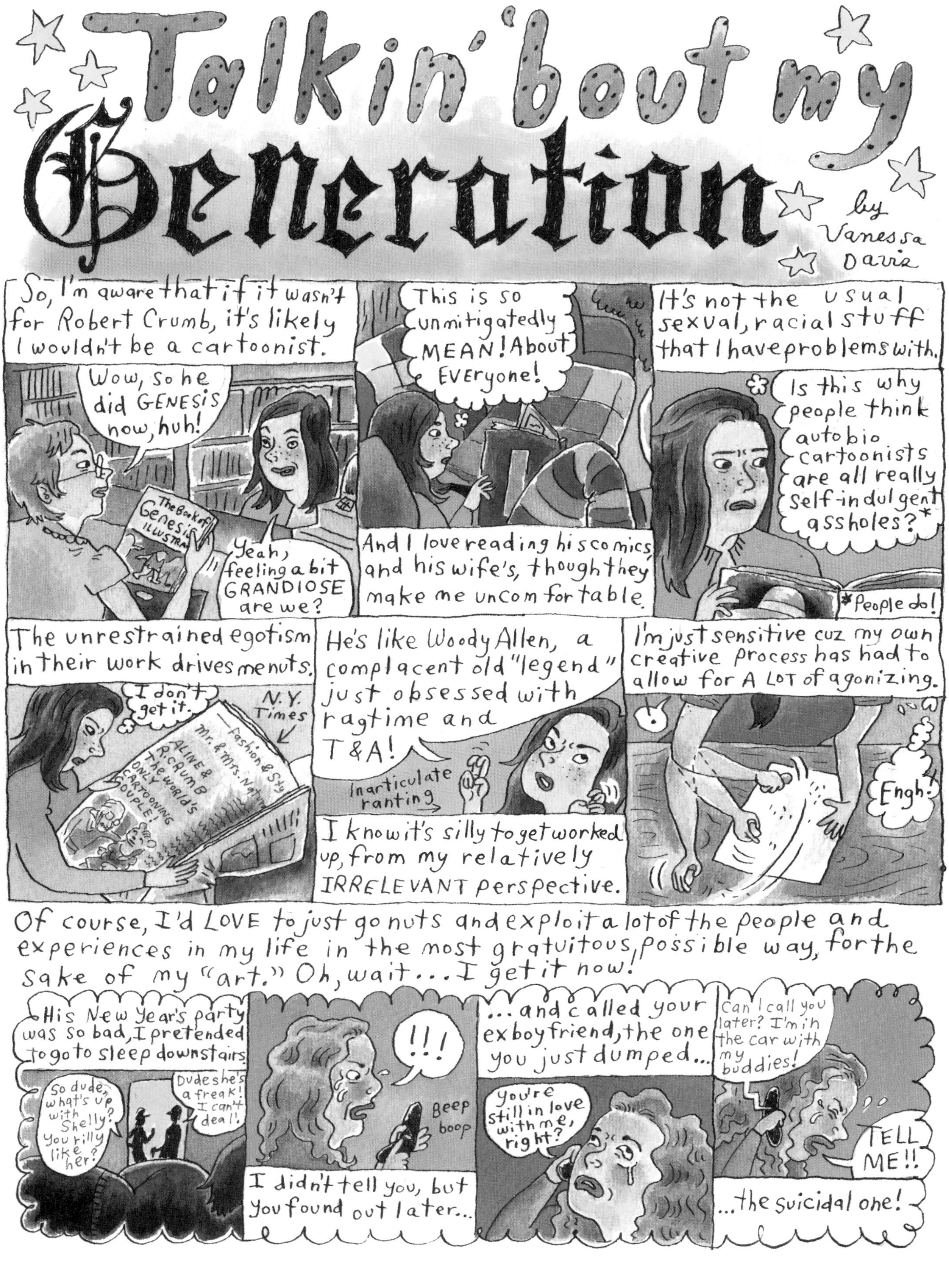
Talkin' 'bout my Generation
by Vanessa Davis
So, I'm aware that if it wasn't for Robert Crumb, it's likely I wouldn't be a cartoonist.
Wow, so he did GENESIS now, huh!
The Book of Genesis ILLUSTRA
Yeah, feeling a bit GRANDIOSE are we?
This is so unmitigatedly MEAN! About EVERyone!
And I love reading his comics, and his wife's, though they make me uncomfortable.
It's not the usual sexual, racial stuff that I have problems with.
Is this why people think autobio cartoonists are all really self-indulgent assholes?*
*People do!
The unrestrained egotism in their work drives me nuts.
I don't get it.
N.Y. Times
Fashion & Sty
Mr. & Mrs. Natur
ALINE & R. CRUMB THE WORLD'S ONLY CARTOONING COUPLE!
He's like Woody Allen, a complacent old "legend" just obsessed with ragtime and T&A!
Inarticulate ranting
I know it's silly to get worked up, from my relatively IRRELEVANT perspective.
I'm just sensitive cuz my own creative process has had to allow for A LOT of agonizing.
Engh!
Of course, I'd LOVE to just go nuts and exploit a lot of the people and experiences in my life in the most gratuitous, possible way, for the sake of my "art." Oh, wait... I get it now!
His New Year's party was so bad, I pretended to go to sleep downstairs
So dude, what's up with Shelly? You rilly like her?
Dude she's a freak! I can't deal.
!!!
Beep boop
I didn't tell you, but you found out later...
...and called your ex boyfriend, the one you just dumped...
You're still in love with me, right?
Can I call you later? I'm in the car with my buddies!
TELL ME!!
...the suicidal one!

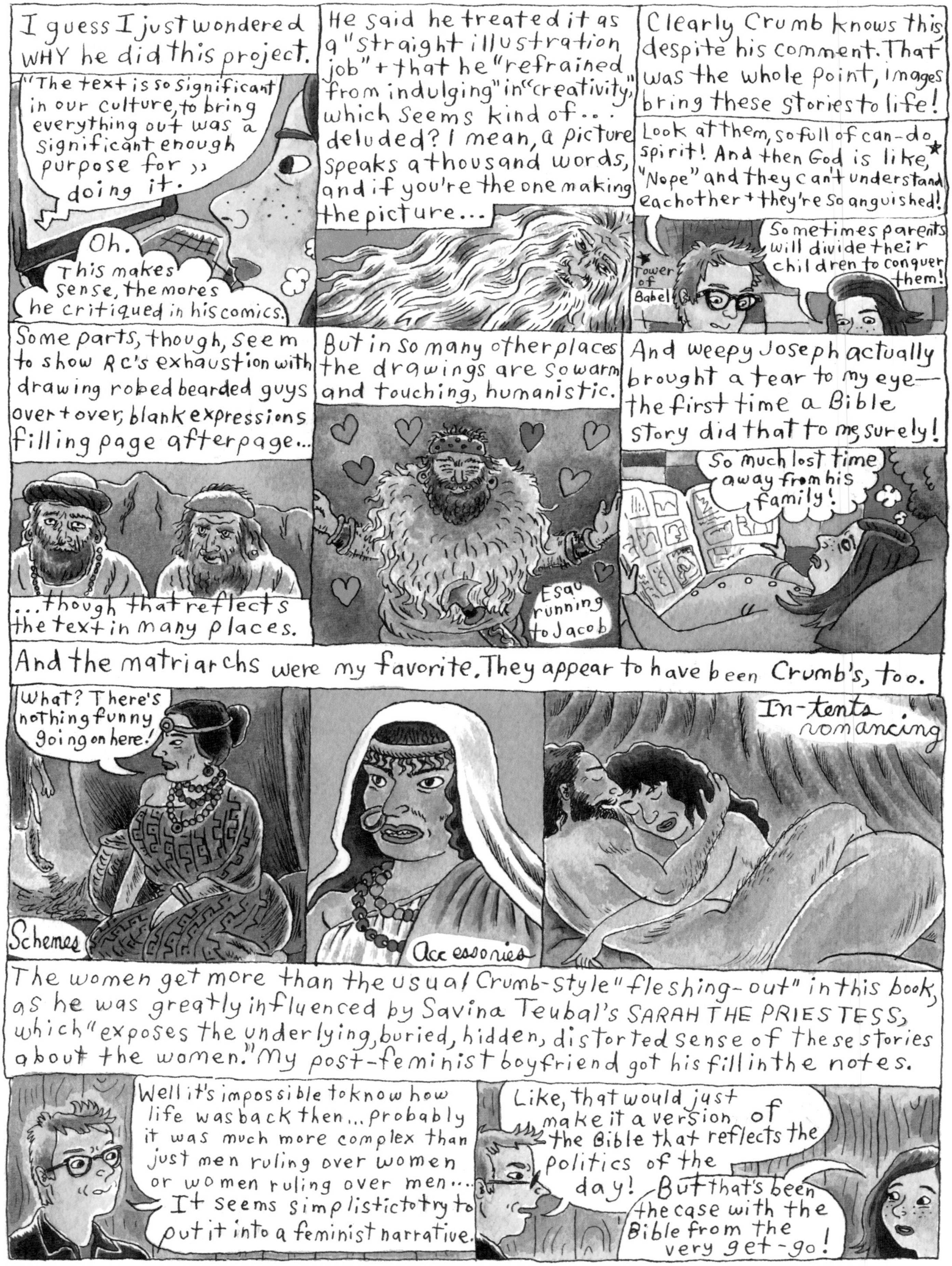
I guess I just wondered WHY he did this project.
"The text is so significant in our culture, to bring everything out was a significant enough purpose for doing it."
Oh. This makes sense, the mores he critiqued in his comics.
He said he treated it as a "straight illustration job" + that he "refrained from indulging" in "creativity," which seems kind of... deluded? I mean, a picture speaks a thousand words, and if you're the one making the picture...
Clearly Crumb knows this, despite his comment. That was the whole point, images bring these stories to life!
Look at them, so full of can-do spirit! And then God is like,* "Nope" and they can't understand each other + they're so anguished!
*Tower of Babel
Sometimes parents will divide their children to conquer them!
Some parts, though, seem to show RC's exhaustion with drawing robed bearded guys over + over, blank expressions filling page after page...
...though that reflects the text in many places.
But in so many other places the drawings are so warm and touching, humanistic.
Esau running to Jacob
And weepy Joseph actually brought a tear to my eye— the first time a Bible story did that to me, surely!
So much lost time away from his family!
And the matriarchs were my favorite. They appear to have been Crumb's, too.
What? There's nothing funny going on here!
Schemes
Accessories
In-tents romancing
The women get more than the usual Crumb-style "fleshing-out" in this book, as he was greatly influenced by Savina Teubal's SARAH THE PRIESTESS, which "exposes the underlying, buried, hidden, distorted sense of these stories about the women." My post-feminist boyfriend got his fill in the notes.
Well it's impossible to know how life was back then... probably it was much more complex than just men ruling over women or women ruling over men.... It seems simplistic to try to put it into a feminist narrative.
Like, that would just make it a version of the Bible that reflects the politics of the day!
But that's been the case with the Bible from the very get-go!

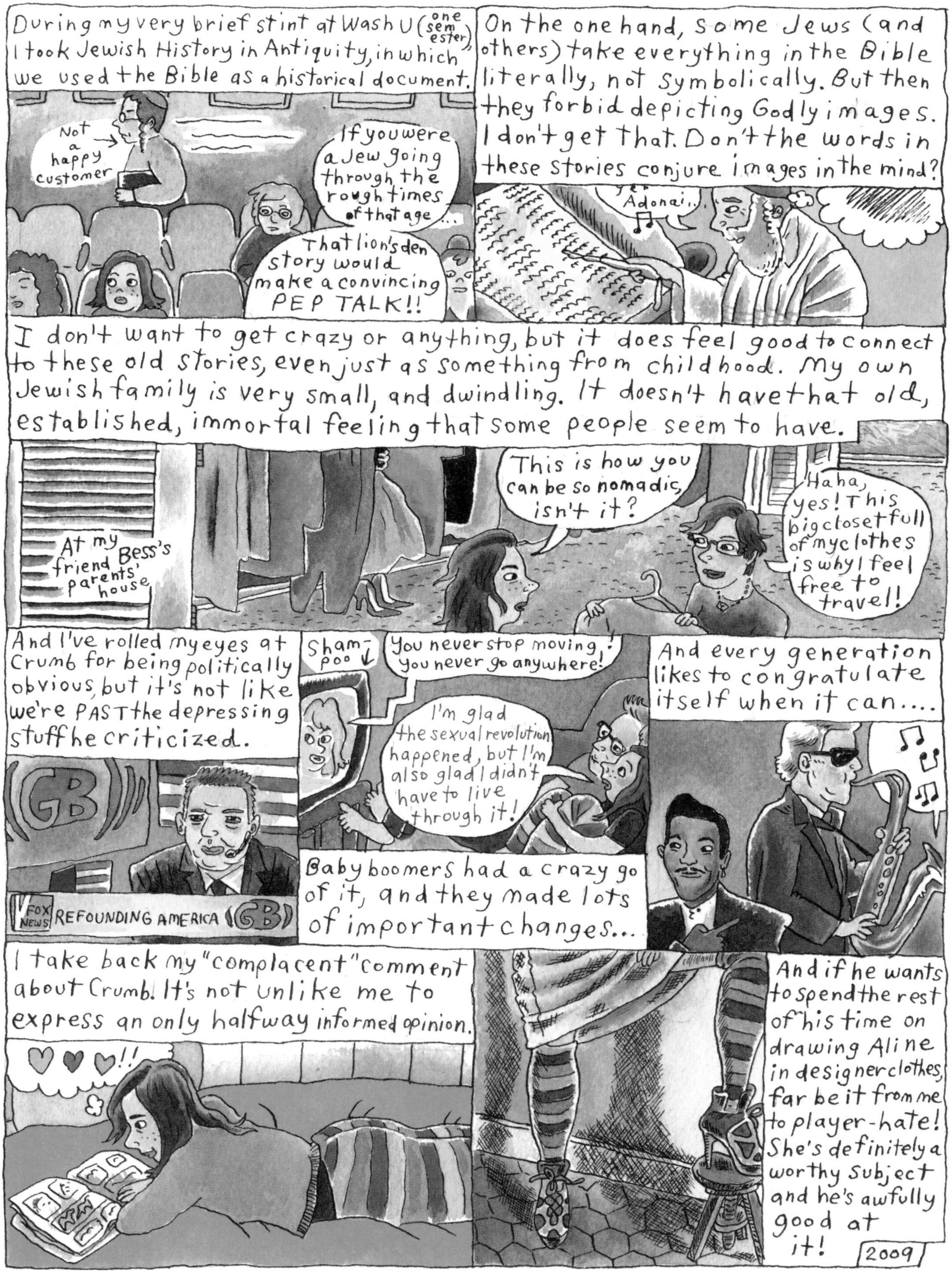

During my very brief stint at Wash U (one semester) I took Jewish History in Antiquity, in which we used the Bible as a historical document.
Not a happy customer
If you were a Jew going through the rough times of that age...
That lion's den story would make a convincing PEP TALK!!
On the one hand, some Jews (and others) take everything in the Bible literally, not symbolically. But then they forbid depicting Godly images. I don't get that. Don't the words in these stories conjure images in the mind?
Adonai..
I don't want to get crazy or anything, but it does feel good to connect to these old stories, even just as something from childhood. My own Jewish family is very small, and dwindling. It doesn't have that old, established, immortal feeling that some people seem to have.
At my friend Bess's parents' house
This is how you can be so nomadic, isn't it?
Haha, yes! This big closet full of my clothes is why I feel free to travel!
And I've rolled my eyes at Crumb for being politically obvious, but it's not like we're PAST the depressing stuff he criticized.
FOX NEWS REFOUNDING AMERICA
Sham-poo
You never stop moving! You never go anywhere!
I'm glad the sexual revolution happened, but I'm also glad I didn't have to live through it!
Baby boomers had a crazy go of it, and they made lots of important changes...
And every generation likes to congratulate itself when it can....
I take back my "complacent" comment about Crumb. It's not unlike me to express an only halfway informed opinion.
And if he wants to spend the rest of his time on drawing Aline in designer clothes, far be it from me to player-hate! She's definitely a worthy subject and he's awfully good at it!
2009

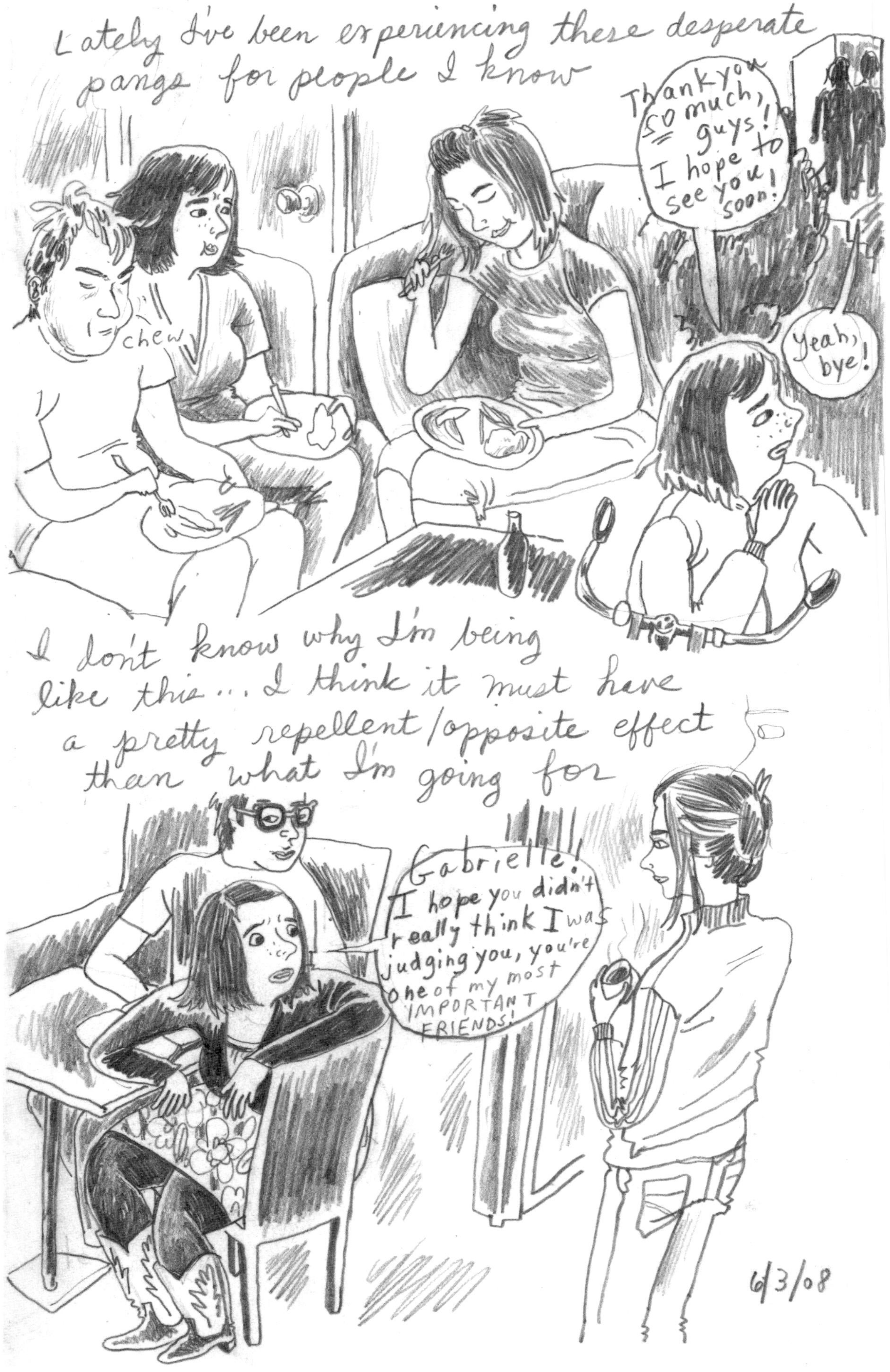
Lately I've been experiencing these desperate pangs for people I know
chew
Thank you so much, guys! I hope to see you soon!
Yeah, bye!
I don't know why I'm being like this... I think it must have a pretty repellent/opposite effect than what I'm going for
Gabrielle! I hope you didn't really think I was judging you, you're one of my most IMPORTANT FRIENDS!
6/3/08

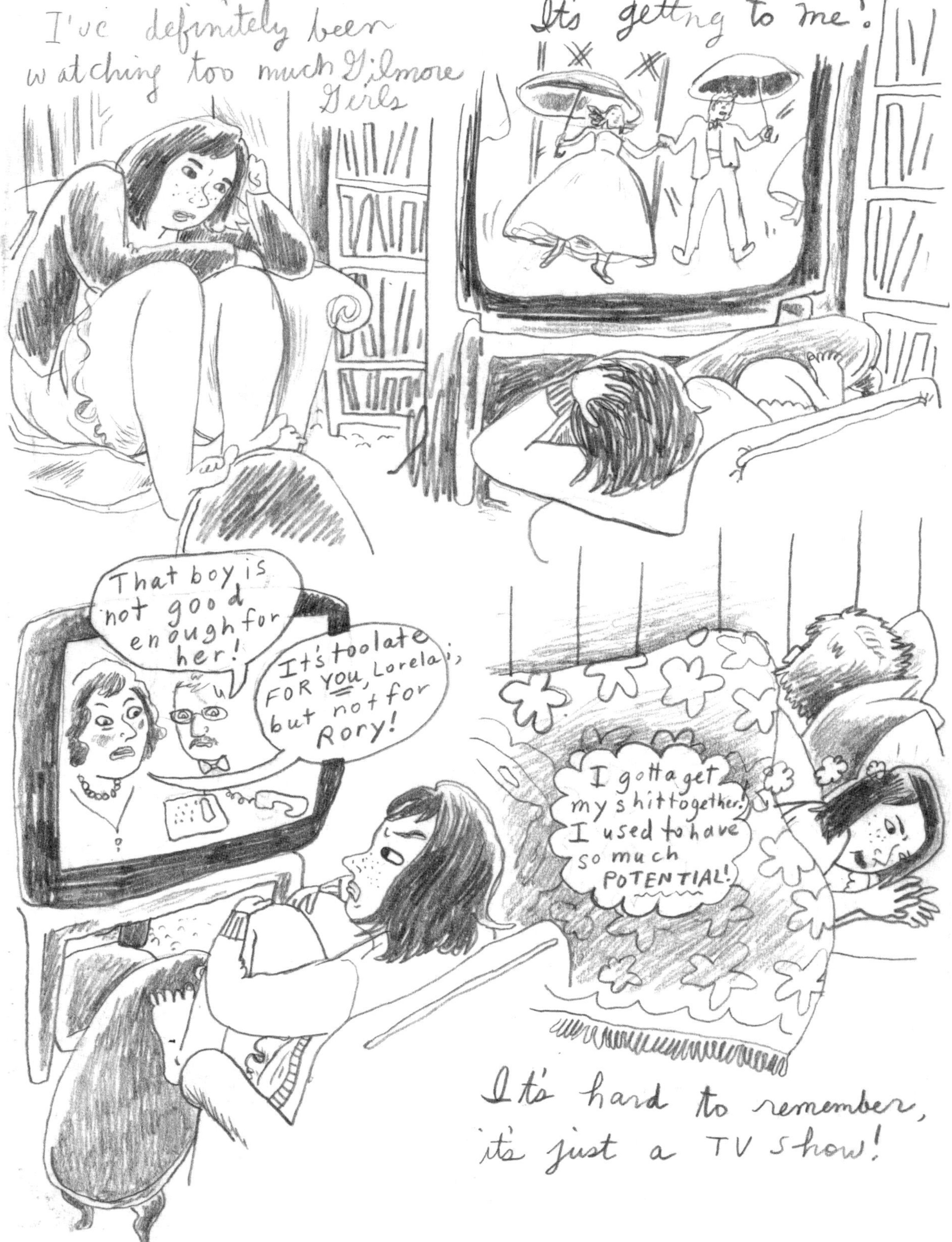
I've definitely been watching too much Gilmore Girls
It's getting to me!
That boy is not good enough for her!
It's too late FOR YOU, Lorelai, but not for Rory!
I gotta get my shit together. I used to have so much POTENTIAL!
It's hard to remember, it's just a TV show!

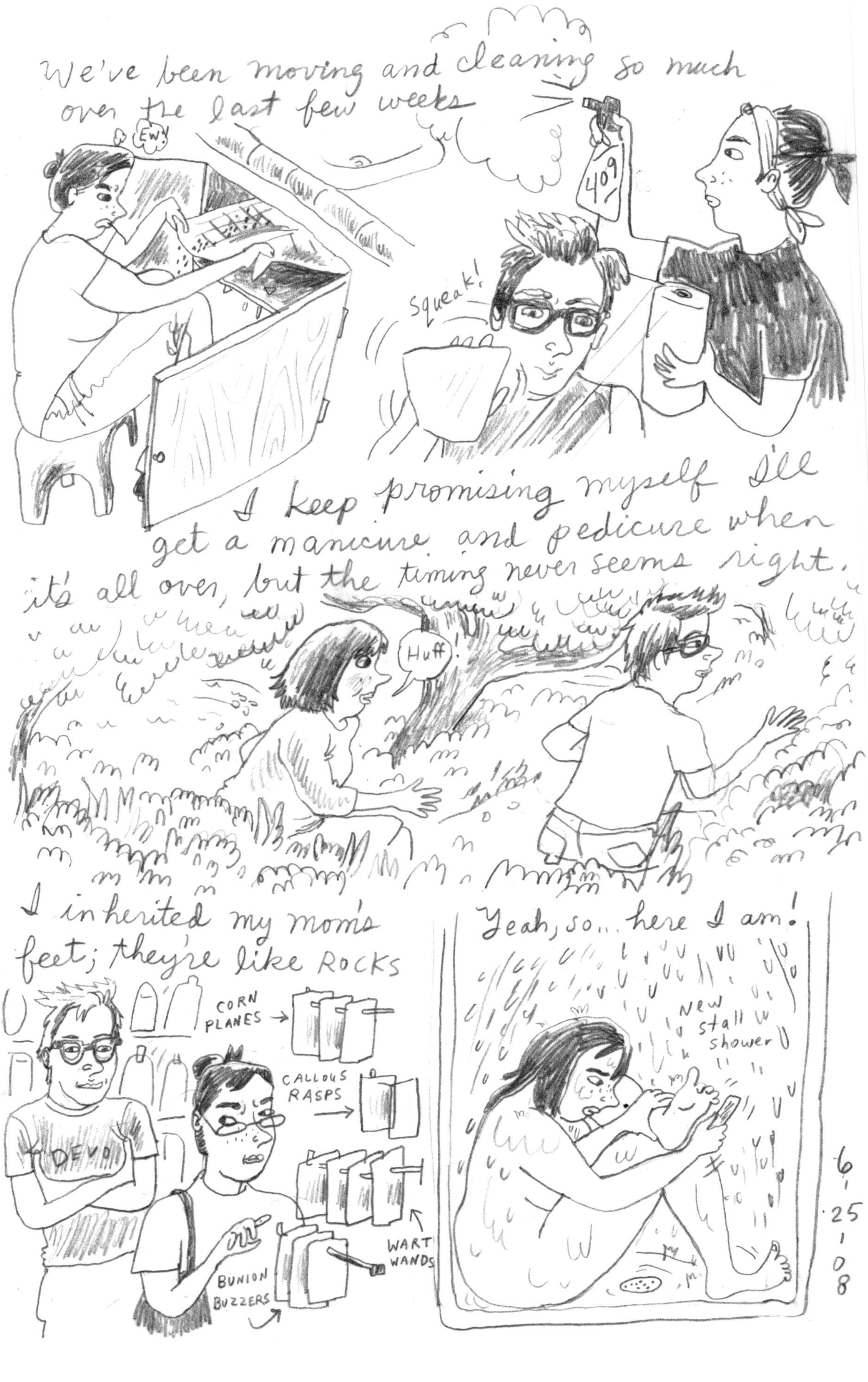
We've been moving and cleaning so much over the last few weeks
EW!
409
Squeak!
I keep promising myself I'll get a manicure and pedicure when it's all over, but the timing never seems right.
Huff!
I inherited my mom's feet; they're like ROCKS
CORN PLANES
CALLOUS RASPS
DEVO
WART WANDS
BUNION BUZZERS
Yeah, so... here I am!
New stall shower
6 · 25 · 08

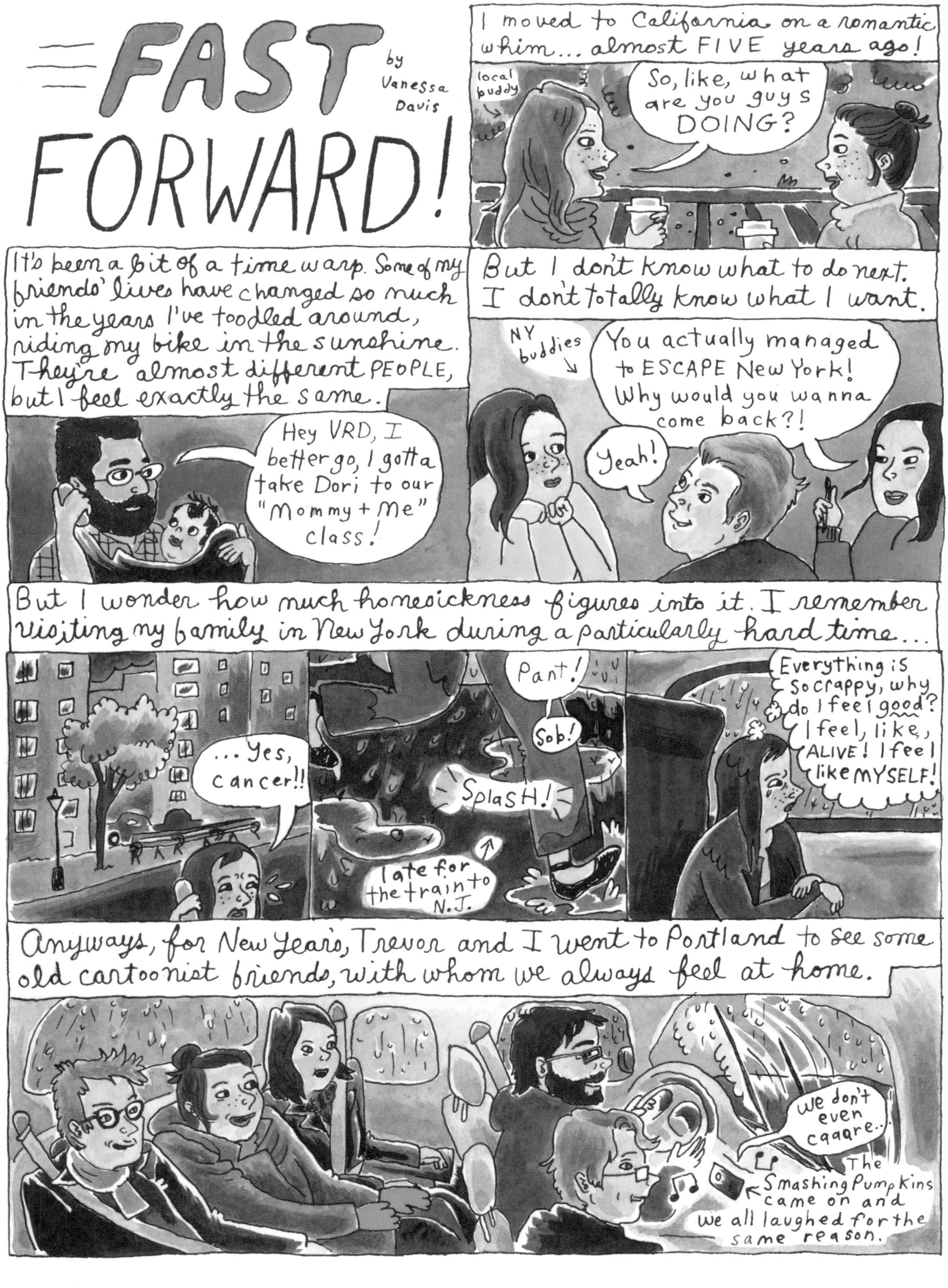
FAST FORWARD!
by Vanessa Davis
I moved to California on a romantic whim... almost FIVE years ago!
local buddy
So, like, what are you guys DOING?
It's been a bit of a time warp. Some of my friends' lives have changed so much in the years I've toodled around, riding my bike in the sunshine. They're almost different PEOPLE, but I feel exactly the same.
Hey VRD, I better go, I gotta take Dori to our "Mommy + Me" class!
But I don't know what to do next. I don't totally know what I want.
NY buddies
You actually managed to ESCAPE New York! Why would you wanna come back?!
Yeah!
But I wonder how much homesickness figures into it. I remember visiting my family in New York during a particularly hard time...
...Yes, cancer!!
Pant!
Sob!
SplasH!
late for the train to N.J.
Everything is so crappy, why do I feel good? I feel, like, ALIVE! I feel like MYSELF!
Anyways, for New Year's, Trevor and I went to Portland to see some old cartoonist friends, with whom we always feel at home.
we don't even caaare...
The Smashing Pumpkins came on and we all laughed for the same reason.

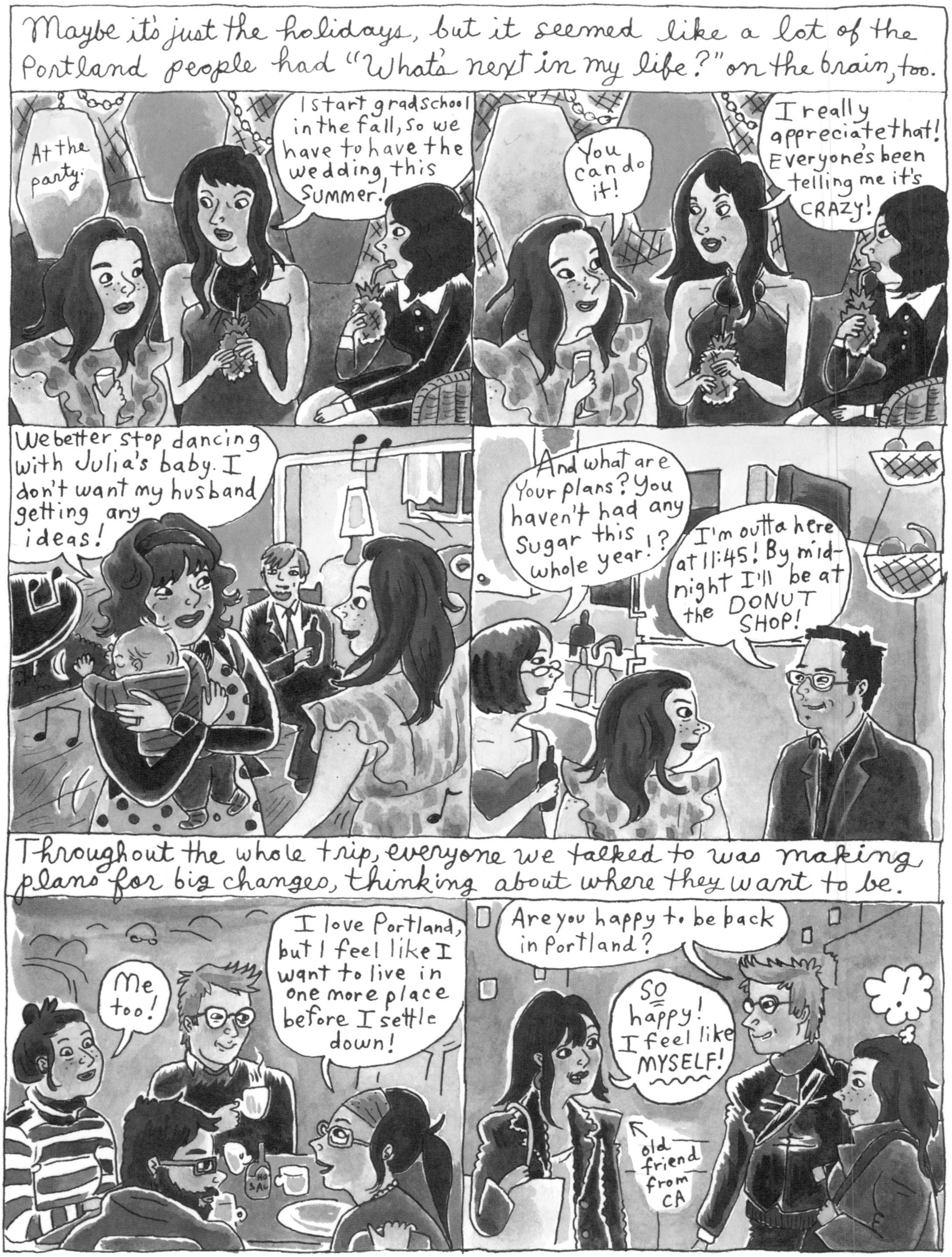
Maybe it's just the holidays, but it seemed like a lot of the Portland people had "What's next in my life?" on the brain, too.
At the party:
I start gradschool in the fall, so we have to have the wedding this summer!
You can do it!
I really appreciate that! Everyone's been telling me it's CRAZY!
We better stop dancing with Julia's baby. I don't want my husband getting any ideas!
And what are your plans? You haven't had any sugar this whole year!?
I'm outta here at 11:45! By midnight I'll be at the DONUT SHOP!
Throughout the whole trip, everyone we talked to was making plans for big changes, thinking about where they want to be.
Me too!
I love Portland, but I feel like I want to live in one more place before I settle down!
Are you happy to be back in Portland?
SO happy! I feel like MYSELF!
!
old friend from CA

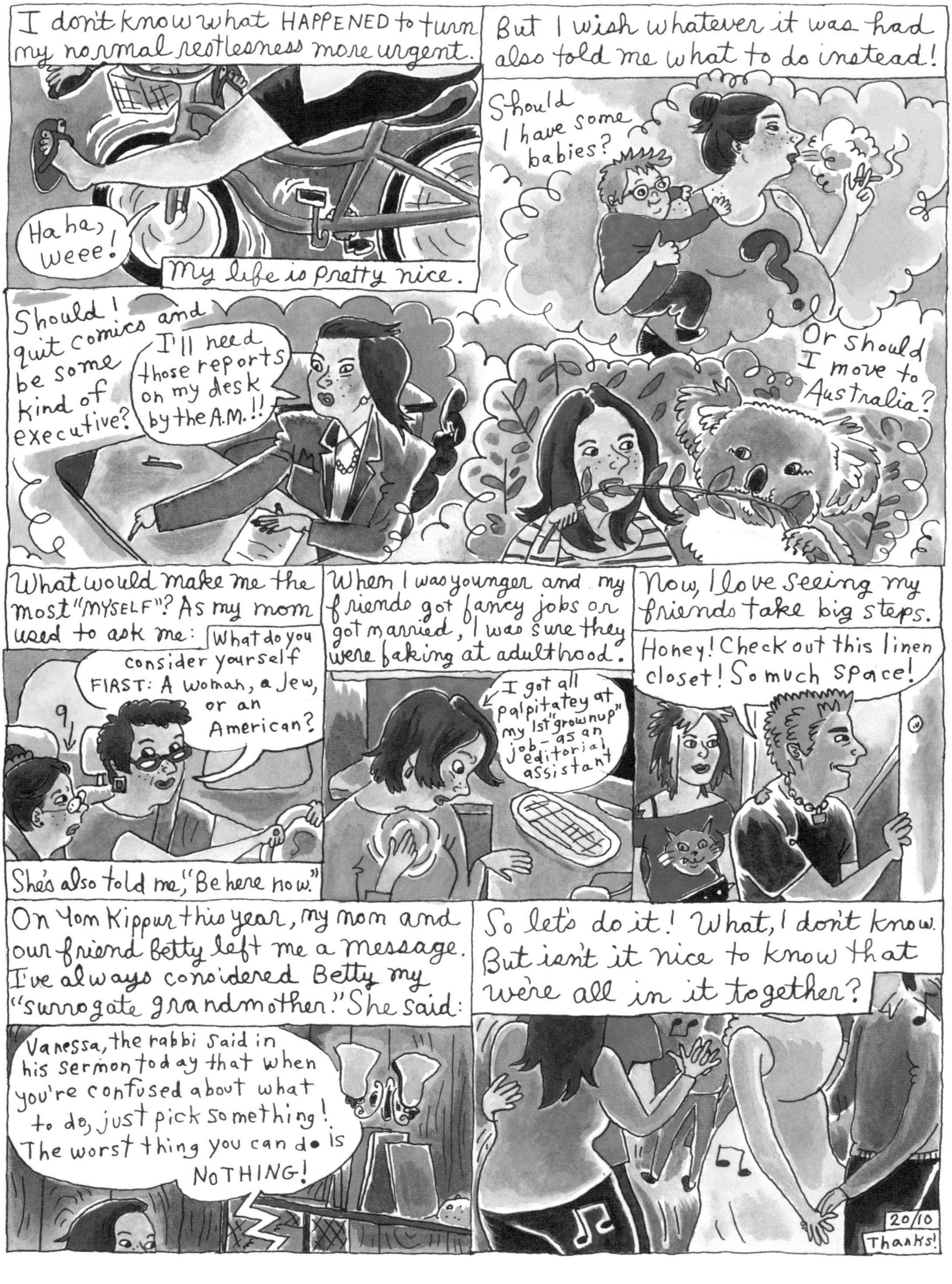
I don't know what HAPPENED to turn my normal restlessness more urgent.
Ha ha, weee!
My life is pretty nice.
But I wish whatever it was had also told me what to do instead!
Should I have some babies?
Should I quit comics and be some kind of executive?
I'll need those reports on my desk by the A.M.!!
Or should I move to Australia?
What would make me the most "MYSELF"? As my mom used to ask me:
What do you consider yourself FIRST: A woman, a Jew, or an American?
9
She's also told me, "Be here now."
When I was younger and my friends got fancy jobs or got married, I was sure they were faking at adulthood.
I got all palpitatey at my 1st "grownup" job - as an editorial assistant
Now, I love seeing my friends take big steps.
Honey! Check out this linen closet! So much space!
On Yom Kippur this year, my mom and our friend Betty left me a message. I've always considered Betty my "surrogate grandmother." She said:
Vanessa, the rabbi said in his sermon today that when you're confused about what to do, just pick something! The worst thing you can do is NOTHING!
So let's do it! What, I don't know. But isn't it nice to know that we're all in it together?
20/10
Thanks!

Any comics in this book not listed here were either just hanging out in my sketchbook or were self-published in Spaniel Rage minis.

- Modern Ritual, Preparation Information, + Make Me a Woman were first in Arthur in '05 + '06.

- Big Fun appeared in Tablet, 8/09.

- Dyspeptic Academic was in Tablet, 2/09.

- B.F.F. was in Stuck in the Middle: Seventeen Comics from an Unpleasant Age, 2007.

- Money Can't Buy Happiness appeared in Tablet, 12/09.

- Wild Ride was in Tablet, 4/09.

- Framed!? was in Tablet, 3/09.

- Sexy Outfit (July 11, 2005) was in The Drama, issue 6.

- September 1, 2005
- September 3, 2005
- September 5, 2005
- September 6, 2005
- September 12, 2005

These were all originally in Kramers Ergot 6.

- Hands Off! (September 3, 2006) was in The Drama, issue 9.

- Night Moves was in Papercutter #4, 2007.

- Crispy Christmas was in Tablet, 12/08.

- Stick in the Mud was in Tablet, 10/09.

- Sandals of Time appeared in The New York Times, 8/13/06.

- Vocation, All I Ever Wanted! was in Tablet, 7/09.

- Stranger in a Strange Land appeared in Tablet, 1/09.

- Jitters was in Tablet, 5/09.

- All About My Mother's Day, Tablet, 6/09.

- Holy Rollin' was in Tablet, 9/09.

- Talkin' 'Bout My Generation appeared in TABLET! 11/09.

- Fast Forward, Tablet, 1/10.

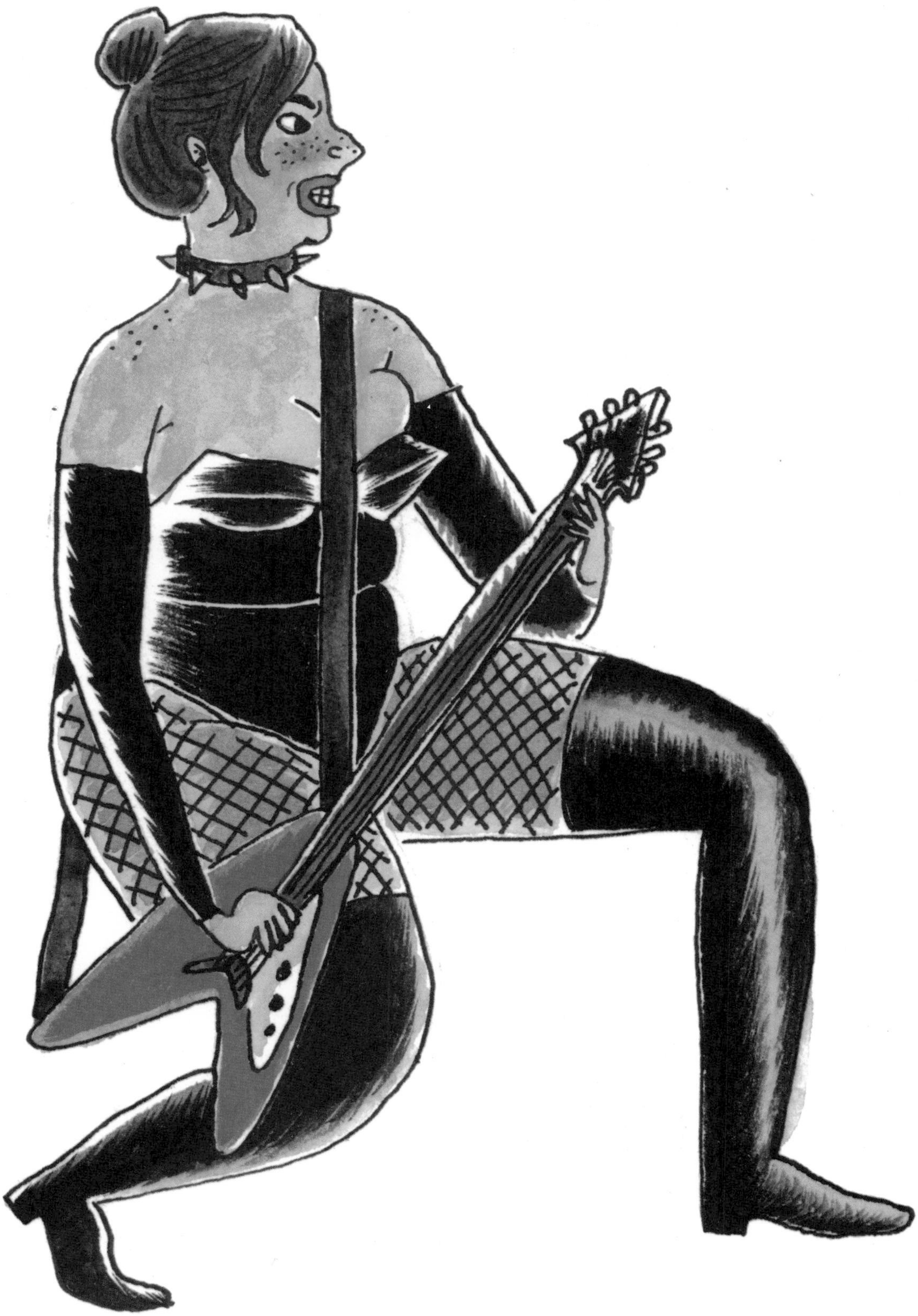

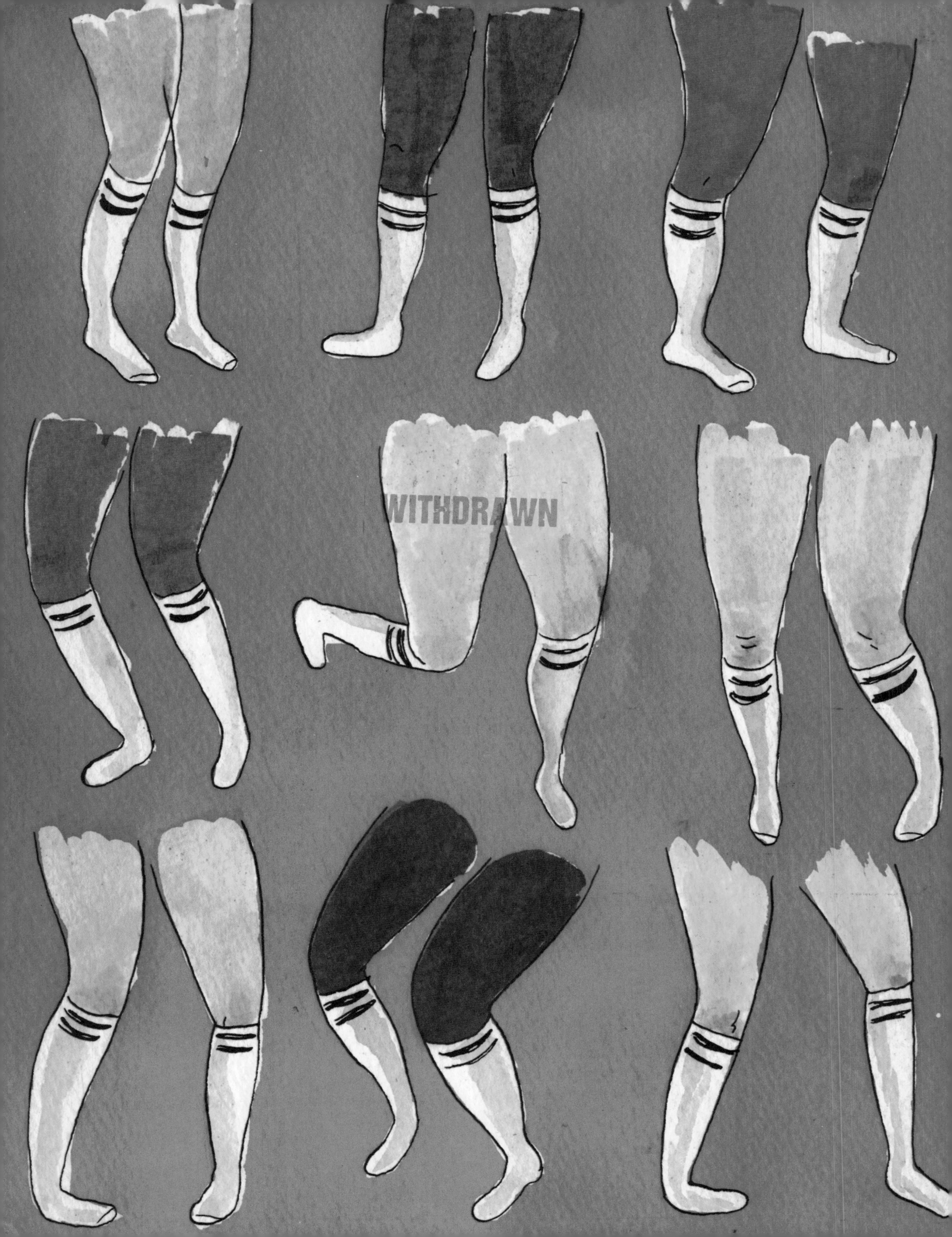